Public Choice and Regulation

Public Choice and Regulation: A View from Inside the Federal Trade Commission

EDITED BY

ROBERT J. MACKAY,

JAMES C. MILLER III,

& BRUCE YANDLE

HOOVER INSTITUTION PRESS

STANFORD UNIVERSITY, STANFORD, CALIFORNIA

The Hoover Institution on War, Revolution and Peace, founded at
Stanford University in 1919 by the late President Herbert Hoover,
is an interdisciplinary research center for advanced study on
domestic and international affairs in the twentieth century. The
views expressed in its publications are entirely those of the
authors and do not necessarily reflect the views of the staff,
officers, or Board of Overseers of the Hoover Institution.

Hoover Press Publication 356

First printing, 1987

Manufactured in the United States of America

91 90 89 88 87   9 8 7 6 5 4 3 2 1

Library of Congress Cataloging in Publication Data
Public choice and regulation.

   Bibliography: p.
   Includes index.
   1. United States.   Federal Trade Commission.
I. Mackay, Robert J.   II. Miller, James Clifford.
III. Yandle, Bruce.   IV. United States.   Federal
Trade Commission.
HD3616.U47P796   1987   353.0082'6   87-3984
ISBN 0-8179-8561-1
ISBN 0-8179-8562-X (pbk.)

Design by P. Kelley Baker

Contents

Contributors

PHYLLIS ALTROGGE is a staff economist with the Federal Trade Commission. She specializes in regulatory analysis with an emphasis on transportation issues. Dr. Altrogge received her Ph.D. in economics from the University of Missouri, Columbia.

RYAN C. AMACHER is Dean of the College of Commerce and Industry and Professor of Economics at Clemson University. Previously, he served as Chairman of the Economics Department at Arizona State University and as a Senior International Economist at the United States Department of Treasury. Dr. Amacher is the author of numerous articles and books, including *Principles of Economics* (3d ed., Cincinnati, Ohio: South-Western, 1986) co-authored with Holley H. Ulbrich. He received his Ph.D. in economics from the University of Virginia.

RONALD S. BOND is Deputy Director for Operations and Consumer Protection at the Bureau of Economics of the Federal Trade Commission. He has taught at the University of Maine, and his research interests include the economics of the professions and the economics of regulation. Among his publications are: *The Effect of Restrictions on Advertising and Commercial Practice in the Professions: The Case of Optometry* (Washington, D.C.: Federal Trade Commission, 1980), and *Sales, Promotion, and Product Differentiation in Two Prescription Drug Markets* (Washington, D.C.: Federal Trade Commission, 1977). Dr. Bond received his Ph.D. in economics from Indiana University.

ROGER L. FAITH is Professor of Economics at Arizona State University. He has been a research associate in the Center for Study of Public Choice at Virginia Polytechnic Institute and State University, and he has served as consultant to the Federal Trade Commission. Dr. Faith's primary research interests are public choice and the economic organization of market and nonmarket institutions. He has authored and coauthored numerous articles in the *American Economic Review*, *Journal of Law and Economics*, *Public Choice*, and other academic journals and volumes. Dr. Faith received his Ph.D. in economics from the University of California at Los Angeles.

RICHARD S. HIGGINS is Deputy Director for Competition and Antitrust in the Bureau of Economics of the Federal Trade Commission. He has also held positions at the University of Georgia, the Consumer Product Safety Commission, and Auburn University. In 1975 he was a Walgreen Fellow at the University of Chicago. Dr. Higgins has published papers in professional journals on the economics of regulation and products liability law. His current research interests include economic analysis of legal procedure. Dr. Higgins received his Ph.D. in economics from the University of Virginia.

WILLIAM E. KOVACIC is Assistant Professor of Law in the George Mason University School of Law. Prior to this he was an attorney with Bryan, Cave, McPheeters, and McRoberts. He also spent four years with the Federal Trade Commission, first with the Bureau of Competition's Planning Office and later as an Attorney Adviser to Commissioner George W. Douglas. Mr. Kovacic also served for one year (1975–1976) as a staff member for the Senate Judiciary Subcommittee on Antitrust and Monopoly and was a law clerk for the Honorable Roszel C. Thomsen, Senior U.S. District Judge for the District of Maryland. His research interests include antitrust, administrative law, and the history of government trade regulation policy. Mr. Kovacic is a graduate of the Columbia University School of Law.

JAMES LANGENFELD is Associate Director for Special Projects in the Bureau of Economics at the Federal Trade Commission. He was most recently an economist with General Motors Corporation. Prior to that assignment, he served as Economic Adviser to Commissioner Terry Calvani of the FTC and as Assistant to the Director of the FTC's Bureau of Competition. He has also served as an economist at the Interstate Commerce Commission and Amtrak. In addition to antitrust, he has written on the automobile industry, cost-benefit analysis, and the rules of evidence. Dr. Langenfeld received his Ph.D. in economics from Washington University, St. Louis.

DONALD R. LEAVENS is Codirector of Billcast, which has developed a computer-based model designed to forecast the likelihood of passage for congressional legislation. He received his Ph.D. in economics from George Mason University.

ROBERT J. MACKAY is Professor of Economics and Associate Director, Graduate Economics Program in Northern Virginia, Virginia Polytechnic Institute and State University. He has taught at the University of California at Berkeley, the University of Maryland, and Tulane University. He has also worked as an economist with the Commodity Futures Trading Commission, the Federal Trade Commission, the Securities and Exchange Commission, and the Board of Governors of the Federal Reserve System. Dr. Mackay has published numerous articles in professional journals on economic theory and public choice. His current research interests include the political economy of regulation, the economics of insurance and information, and public-choice aspects of the executive veto. Dr. Mackay received his Ph.D. in economics from the University of North Carolina at Chapel Hill.

FRED S. MCCHESNEY is Professor of Law in the School of Law at Emory University and Visiting Professor at the University of Chicago Law School. Prior to moving to Emory University, he served as Associate Director for Policy and Evaluation in the Bureau of Consumer Protection at the Federal Trade Commission. His research interests include antitrust, regulation, corporate governance, and property rights. Dr. McChesney received his Ph.D. in economics from the University of Virginia and his J.D. from the University of Miami.

JAMES C. MILLER III is Director of the Office of Management and Budget and served as Chairman of the Federal Trade Commission from October 1981 to September 1985. He has held positions with Georgia State University, the U.S. Department of Transportation, the Brookings Institution, the American Enterprise Institute, Texas A&M University, the Council of Economic Advisers, and the Council on Wage and Price Stability. Dr. Miller is the author of numerous professional articles and is the coauthor or editor of several books. He received his Ph.D. in economics from the University of Virginia.

MARK J. MORAN is Assistant Professor of Banking and Finance at the Weatherhead School of Management, Case Western Reserve University. He received his Ph.D. in economics from Washington University, St. Louis, where he was also a research assistant at the Center for Study of American Business. Dr. Moran's research interests include financial economics and the economics of law and regulation.

ROBERT ROGOWSKY is currently Adviser to the director of the Bureau of Consumer Protection, Federal Trade Commission. He has most recently worked as Executive Assistant to the chairman of the International Trade Commission. Prior to that he was president of a nonprofit economic education institute, Acting Executive Director of the Consumer Product Safety Commission, Economic Adviser to two commissioners at the CPSC, and staff economist in the Bureau of Economics, FTC. Dr. Rogowsky received his Ph.D. in economics from the University of Virginia and has published studies of antitrust and regulation, including *Relevant Markets in Antitrust* (New York: Federal Legal Publications, 1984), edited with Kenneth Elzinga, and *The Political Economy of Regulation* (Washington, D.C.: FTC, 1985), edited with Bruce Yandle.

WILLIAM F. SHUGHART II is Associate Professor of Economics at George Mason University and Research Associate at the Center for Study of Public Choice. Previously, he served as a staff economist with the Federal Trade Commission and as Special Assistant to the Director of the Federal Trade Commission's Bureau of Economics. Dr. Shughart has published numerous articles in professional journals on the economics of antitrust, regulation, and public choice. He received his Ph.D. in economics from Texas A&M University.

ROBERT D. TOLLISON is Director of the Center for Study of Public Choice and Professor of Economics at George Mason University. He served as Director of the Bureau of Economics at the Federal Trade Commission from 1981 to 1983. His research interests include public choice, industrial organization, and the history of economic thought. Dr. Tollison is the author of numerous journal articles and books, including *Mercantilism As a Rent-Seeking Society* (College Station: Texas A&M University Press, 1981) and *Principles of Economics* (Boston: Little, Brown, 1986), both with Robert Ekelund. He received his Ph.D. in economics from the University of Virginia.

GORDON TULLOCK is the Holbert R. Harris University Professor in the Department of Economics and Research Associate in the Center for Study of Public Choice at George Mason University. He is a cofounder of the Public Choice Society and Senior Editor of *Public Choice*. He has written numerous books and articles including *The Calculus of Consent* (Ann Arbor: University of Michigan Press, 1962) with James Buchanan; *Toward a Mathematics of Politics* (Ann Arbor: University of Michigan Press, 1972); *Economics of Income Redistribution* (Norwell, Mass.: Kluwer-Nijhoff, 1983); and *Trials on Trial* (New York: Columbia University Press, 1980). His research interests are in public choice and law and economics. Mr. Tullock received his J.D. from the University of Chicago Law School.

Barry R. Weingast is Senior Research Fellow at the Hoover Institution, Stanford University. He is the author of numerous articles in the areas of regulation, political economy, and legislative policymaking. These include a study of the Securities and Exchange Commission entitled "The Congressional-Bureaucratic System," in *Public Choice*, and "Regulation, Reregulation, and Deregulation," in *Law and Contemporary Studies*. Dr. Weingast received his Ph.D. in economics from the California Institute of Technology.

Bruce Yandle is Alumni Professor of Economics at Clemson University and Adjunct Scholar with the American Enterprise Institute. He served as Executive Director at the Federal Trade Commission from 1982 to 1984. His research interests include regulation and public choice. Dr. Yandle has published numerous articles and books, including *Benefit-Cost Analyses of Social Regulation* (Washington, D.C.: American Enterprise Institute, 1979) with James C. Miller III. He received his Ph.D. in economics from Georgia State University.

Public Choice and Regulation

Introduction

Chapter 1

Public Choice and Regulation: An Overview

ROBERT J. MACKAY,
JAMES C. MILLER III, & BRUCE YANDLE

THE Federal Trade Commission (FTC) is one of the most frequently studied of U.S. regulatory agencies. With its dual mandate of antitrust and consumer protection and its economy-wide focus, the agency has naturally attracted considerable attention among scholars interested in examining the agency's history, evaluating its performance, and suggesting reforms. The sheer volume of this literature might make a skeptical reader wonder what could possibly remain to be said about the FTC. (The lengthy, but by no means exhaustive, bibliography at the end of this volume will give the reader an indication of the extent of this literature.) More directly, it raises the question of what the present volume adds to our already significant store of knowledge about the agency.

Those who have sampled the literature and then read the present collection of studies will see the difference immediately. Until recently, there has been little analysis of the FTC as a political institution—that is, one driven by its internal incentives and its ties to a larger political body that, in turn, responds to its own political and economic pressures. More often than not, past research has viewed the FTC's mandate of antitrust and consumer protection as beyond controversy and has treated the agency as a well-intentioned guardian of consumers and the marketplace. For the most part, critiques of the FTC's performance have focused on particular instances of policy failure and prescribed reforms as correctives that would enable the agency to serve faithfully the public interest. In short, previous discussions of the FTC have been carried out almost exclusively on a normative plane.

By contrast, the studies collected in the present volume take a positive approach to the study of antitrust and consumer protection as practiced by the FTC. They focus on the systematic influence on the agency's behavior of external factors—such as Congress, the executive branch, and interest groups—and internal factors—such as organizational structure and incentives. These studies develop and empirically test theories that attempt to address such questions as why certain groups have benefited from or borne the cost of FTC actions, what form FTC interventions in the economy will take, and what forces determine FTC budgets, enforcement efforts, and program choices.

This collection differs from previous work for yet another reason: fourteen of the sixteen chapters are authored or coauthored by individuals who have experienced the workings of the FTC from the inside. These individuals either have been or currently are associated with the agency; in a number of cases they have served in significant policymaking or advisory positions. In addition, many of these individuals have been or currently are academics who have made significant contributions to the scholarly literature in such related areas as industrial organization, regulation, antitrust, law and economics, and public choice. To our knowledge, this is the first analysis of a federal agency to be conceived, organized, and largely written by authors who have firsthand experience in the innerworkings and politics of that agency.

This volume begins, in Part I, with an examination of the relationship between the FTC and Congress. The issue addressed is the extent to which there is systematic congressional influence on the actions of this nominally independent agency. The first paper, coauthored by Roger Faith, Donald Leavens, and Robert Tollison, argues that a democratic political system based on geographic representation confronts the legislator with strong incentives to represent local interests in the national legislature, even in matters such as antitrust enforcement. In other words, legislators are induced to obtain and exercise political influence as well as to trade votes with fellow legislators so as to advance the interests of their local constituencies, even if this comes at the expense of broader consumer or taxpayer interests.

To test their theory, the authors examine the case-bringing activity of the FTC to see if there is a systematic and statistically significant bias in the disposition of cases in favor of particular firms. The authors find that favorable decisions by the FTC (that is, case dismissals) tend to be nonrandomly concentrated on firms headquartered in the home districts of those members of the House of Representatives who are on committees and subcommittees with budgetary and oversight responsibilities over the FTC. The House appears to have been, in the words of the authors, "a ripe arena for antitrust pork barrel," both in the 1960s and during the heyday of its "reform" in the 1970s. This study provides clear evidence of a systematic effect of congressional influence on the basic actions and decisions of the FTC.

The next paper, coauthored by Barry Weingast and Mark Moran, extends the economic model of interest-group demands for legislation by developing a model of legislative politics in which congressional committees and subcommittees play key roles in determining the supply of regulatory policies. The authors argue that the policy preferences of members of committees with oversight responsibilities play an important, if not primary, role in determining an agency's actions. Accordingly, shifts in these preferences are what cause changes in agency policy.

The authors use this perspective to explain the abrupt reversal in FTC policymaking in 1979 and 1980—the end of nearly a decade of regulatory activism—as resulting from the nearly complete turnover of membership and change of leadership in the FTC's oversight committees in the Senate. In their view, the activist policies of the previous decade simply reflected the activist preferences of the previously dominant, but now displaced, coalition that controlled the committee. The authors also empirically test for any systematic influence of congressional preferences, measured by ADA scores for committee chairmen, committee members, and the entire Senate, on the distribution of cases chosen by the FTC. As in the Faith, Leavens, and Tollison paper, FTC activity, now measured by the distribution of its caseload, is found to be systematically responsive to congressional influence.

The third paper in this section, authored by William Kovacic, provides an extensive historical examination of the FTC's relationship with the congressional oversight committees interested in antitrust enforcement. This study nicely complements the previous paper by providing a detailed legislative and legal history of antitrust policymaking from 1969 to 1976. In addition, this paper traces the major external forces that shaped the FTC's antitrust work throughout its first half century. Kovacic concludes that the FTC, rather than ignoring prevailing congressional sentiment as some suggest, chose antitrust programs that were consistent with and responsive to the clearly articulated policy preferences of its oversight committees in Congress.

The last paper in this section, authored by Bruce Yandle, examines the interactions between Congress, interest groups, and the FTC during the turbulent period 1981 to 1984, when the executive branch, under President Reagan, attempted to bring about major regulatory reform. The agenda for reform included reduction of the agency's budget, application of economic logic to enforcement actions, application of benefit-cost tests throughout the range of agency activities, adoption of a less confrontational approach to compliance, and intervention before other governmental bodies as advocates of competition. According to Yandle, despite some success in reducing the agency's budget, the reform agenda remained only partially implemented by 1984.

Drawing on a theoretical discussion of regulatory equilibrium as a balancing of politically determined demands with bureaucratic supply, Yandle attempts to explain the wrath with which Congress and interest groups reacted to the proposals for scaling back the agency's budget. He relates how Congress limited proposed budget cuts and redirected internal reallocations of efforts and resources by mandating more resources and directly specifying how they were to be spent. No longer able to use budget increases to induce the agency to comply with their wishes, the appropriations committees used legislative language in budget resolutions to impose performance standards specifying precisely both those activities to be provided and those not to be provided by the agency. This episode in the history of the FTC helps to illustrate the bounds imposed by the political process on efforts at regulatory reform.

Taken together, these four papers confirm the suspicions of those who have doubted that independent regulatory agencies such as the FTC are truly independent in formulating and executing regulatory policy.

In Part II, the economic and political determinants of program activities at the FTC are empirically examined. The first paper, coauthored by Ryan Amacher, Richard Higgins, William Shughart II, and Robert Tollison, empirically tests one of the major predictions of the interest-group theory of regulation as refined and developed by Sam Peltzman. According to this theory, regulators seeking to maximize their political support operate according to the marginal principle of "share the gain and share the pain" resulting from favorable or adverse shifts in demand and cost conditions. Over the business cycle, this implies that regulatory activity will shift toward "producer protection" during cyclical contractions and toward "consumer protection" during cyclical expansions.

With particular reference to the FTC, the authors argue that the agency will shift its enforcement efforts under the Robinson-Patman Act in a counter-cyclical fashion. During business downturns, for example, more Robinson-Patman Act cases will be brought, thus limiting the tendency for prices to fall and cushioning producers against further losses. During business expansions, the Robinson-Patman caseload will be reduced, thus mitigating producer gains and transferring wealth, at the margin, to consumers. The authors' empirical work supports this view. They find a countercyclical and statistically significant relationship between FTC enforcement efforts and various measures of general business conditions.

The next paper, coauthored by Richard Higgins, William Shughart II, and Robert Tollison, joins the long-standing debate over whether or not dual enforcement of the antitrust laws by the FTC and the Antitrust Division of the Department of Justice is efficient. The authors provide unique theoretical insight into this issue by developing a model of rivalry between two govern-ment agencies producing essentially the same output in response to the demands of a legislative appropriations committee. Their model predicts that dual enforcement by agencies acting independently of one another leads to greater enforcement activity at a lower unit cost than would obtain with a single enforcement agency. The model also predicts that dual enforcement by agencies acting collusively leads to less enforcement activity at a greater unit cost than would otherwise result.

The historical development of antitrust institutions in the United States approximates the enforcement regimes modeled: 1890 through 1914, which represents an era of single-agency enforcement; 1915 through 1948, which represents an era of independent dual enforcement; and 1949 to 1981, which represents an era of collusive dual enforcement. These changes in enforcement regimes provide a convenient means of testing the theory by examining the impact of regime shifts on enforcement budgets and case-production activity. The authors' empirical results suggest that the 1948 liaison agreement, which initiated the collusive arrangements between the two agencies, caused anti-trust case production per budget dollar to fall by half. Moreover, in budgetary terms, the FTC seems to have gained most from the collusive arrangements.

The third paper in this section, coauthored by Richard Higgins and Fred McChesney, empirically tests several recent extensions of the interest-group theory of regulation that have examined the implications of the diversity of interests that may exist between producers in a given industry. Certain regula-tions may only benefit some producers, with industry rivals and consumers bearing the costs. For example, regulations that raise the cost of marginal firms will increase market price and may increase the economic rents earned by inframarginal firms—that is, those with lower costs and a greater ability to meet or avoid regulatory requirements. According to this view, a significant segment of an industry may actually support the introduction of a regulation or, equivalently, resist its removal, even though the regulation raises the cost to them of operating in the industry.

In applying this theory to the FTC, the authors argue that the agency's ad substantiation doctrine—which requires that advertisers possess a "reasonable basis" for advertising claims *prior* to making such claims—allows the FTC to control output margins in different product markets, thereby creating eco-nomic rents for some advertisers and ad agencies. Viewing advertising regula-tion as a response, at least at the margin, to political demands for wealth redistribution, they argue that large firms will tend to benefit relative to small firms from the excessive levels of substantiation required by the FTC. Not only will large firms tend to be the lower-cost, inframarginal firms, but they will also tend to have substantial brand name capital and thus find it easier to substitute "puffery" for costly factual claims that must be substantiated. The empirical work in this study indicates that the FTC does indeed bring relatively more ad substantiation cases in markets where market share and reputations vary widely—precisely those conditions where demand for regulation will be greatest. The empirical results also indicate that product market leaders and leading ad agencies experienced substantial capital gains with the introduction of the ad substantiation program. These results may suggest why recent proposals to reform advertising regulation have met with opposition by the advertising industry.

The next paper, coauthored by James Langenfeld and Robert Rogowsky, develops and empirically tests a model of efficient antitrust prosecution, focusing on the decision of the enforcement agency either to negotiate a settlement of a merger case or to take the case to litigation. Modeling the agency as if its goal were to maximize consumer welfare, the authors examine the effect of various factors on the agency's decision to settle or litigate; these factors include the magnitude of monopoly losses if no remedy is obtained, the monopoly losses remaining in the event of a negotiated settlement, administrative costs, the probability of successful litigation, and the likely length of litigation.

To test the comparative static predictions of their model, the authors examine a large sample of antitrust cases filed under Section 7 of the Clayton Act by the FTC and the Justice Department from 1968 through 1981. The sample includes horizontal, vertical, and conglomerate mergers terminated by either a consent decree or adjudication. They estimate the changes in the probability of litigation resulting from changes in the independent variables, and they use, in particular, various proxies for the magnitude of monopoly losses. Market shares of the acquiring and acquired firms are found to have a positive and significant impact on the probability of settlement, meaning that settlement is more likely when the gains from litigation would appear to be the highest. Since this finding contradicts the major predictions of the theoretical model of how welfare-maximizing agencies "should" behave, the need for alternative models of enforcement behavior is clearly suggested.

In the next paper, Robert Rogowsky provides a more detailed examination and analysis of antitrust enforcement activity. He begins by summarizing the results of his recent case-by-case analysis of the entire antimerger caseload of the FTC and the Department of Justice from 1968 through 1981. Based on a careful reading of the record, he finds that the antitrust enforcement agencies have consistently generated poor cases, in the sense that the cases lack substantive economic merit. For example, the FTC and Justice Department have frequently—and often aggressively—attacked mergers between firms with small market shares or in industries where the likelihood of competitive injury is slight. They have also challenged acquisitions of obsolete assets. Poor case selection has been compounded by the failure of the agencies to formulate and implement effective remedies when they uncovered mergers that have substantially injured competition.

This paper, then, integrates bureaucratic and political elements of the determinants of agency behavior in an attempt to explain these apparent failures in antitrust enforcement. The author analyzes the internal incentive structure of the bureaucracy—staff attorneys, program managers, and commissioners—and the external political demands by Congress for visible (that is, measurable) output. Drawing on the insights provided by the economics of bureaucracy, this analysis leads to the conclusion that antitrust enforcement efforts will be characterized by the following tendencies: case generation will outweigh proper case selection; proving liability will outweigh the design of effective remedy; and case disposition will be geared to the generation of visible outputs, with consents—no matter how poorly designed or ineffective—counting as successes, and dismissals—no matter how appropriate—counting as failures.

The next paper, coauthored by Phyllis Altrogge and William Shughart II, focuses on consumer-protection enforcement, as opposed to antitrust enforcement, and empirically examines the determinants of civil penalties assessed by the FTC in carrying out its consumer-protection mission. Under its mandate, the FTC can enjoin unlawful activity and seek civil penalties from firms found in violation of its rules and orders. Although instructed by statute to consider certain factors, the agency has substantial discretion in using fines as an enforcement tool. Two hypotheses with regard to the determinants of civil penalties are tested: first, that concentrated interests of large firms will tend to dominate the more diffuse interests of small firms and consumers in the remedy phase of regulatory proceedings; and second, that small business is the FTC's primary constituency.

Based on data derived from 57 civil penalty cases before the FTC between 1979 and 1981, the evidence suggests that civil penalties operate as a regressive tax on law violators, with small firms being fined disproportionately greater amounts than large firms. That is, although civil penalty amounts appear to be influenced by commission judgments concerning culpability and ability to pay, and firms violating previous cease-and-desist orders generally pay higher fines than first offenders, most of the variation in civil penalty amounts is explained by variations in firm size, where size is measured by sales. An increase in firm size, moreover, results in a less than proportional increase in penalty, *ceteris paribus*.

The final paper in this section, coauthored by William Shughart II and Robert Tollison, provides detailed historical data on law-enforcement actions by the FTC involving repeat offenders. The data analyzed covers all FTC complaints reaching the administrative hearing or consent stage between 1914 and early 1982. Recidivism rates are examined over time, by violation involved in the repeat offense, by product sold by the repeat offender, and by the elapsed time between offenses. Representative findings include the observations that repeat offenders were more often charged with unfair or deceptive advertising practices than with traditional antitrust violations and that a large number of recidivist cases involved firms in relatively unconcentrated industries. Overall, matters involving recidivists accounted for nearly one-fourth of agency case output.

Several competing explanations are presented for the extent and pattern of recidivism. These explanations include an absence of effective remedies, the existence of a group of industries whose structural or other economic characteristics are conducive to noncompetitive behavior by incumbent firms, and the presence of law-enforcement institutions and incentives that lower the cost of challenging the practices of firms that have previously been involved in legal proceedings with the agency. Although data limitations prohibit statistical tests that definitively discriminate between these hypotheses, the authors argue that the available evidence is most consistent with the hypothesis that the FTC's institutional structure and incentives make it less costly to challenge the practices of previous offenders than to bring cases against first offenders. This conclusion is consistent with Rogowsky's analysis of antitrust enforcement activity.

Part III contains three papers that examine different aspects of the internal decisionmaking and managerial process at the FTC. The first paper, authored by Bruce Yandle, examines the effect on agency behavior of the method of selecting the chairman and the relative power and responsibility of the chairman. Over its history, the FTC has operated under two quite different administrative regimes. From 1916 to 1949, it operated under a collegial form of management whereby the chairman was chosen annually by a majority vote of the commission. The chairman's authority was effectively limited to presiding at official meetings and acting as public spokesman, since full commission approval was required for making policy and managerial decisions. From 1950 to the present, the agency has operated under a strong chairman form of management, whereby the chairman is appointed by the president and granted authority and responsibility for staffing and managing the agency.

Yandle relates the historical experience of the agency under the two managerial regimes and attempts to test empirically whether or not the change in regimes had a significant impact on agency behavior. In particular, the examines a time series for case output and employment from 1916 to 1975 and finds that average costs (that is, case output per employee) were more variable in the period of weak chairmen, but that changes in output and cost were greater in the latter period, when the party affiliation of the chairman changed with a new appointee. These results are consistent with the author's theoretical discussion and support the view that the institutional structure of decision-making is an important determinant of agency behavior.

The next paper in the section, authored by Robert Mackay, examines the budgetary process at the FTC from a collective-choice perspective. From 1977 until 1983, a unique voting scheme was used by the agency for determining its collective priorities during the annual budgetary process. The FTC's many activities were organized into decision units, with three possible funding levels and plans for action specified for each unit. Each commissioner provided a ranking of decision-unit increments, arrayed the increments in decreasing order of priority, and assigned each a point score. The agency's collective priority ranking was then obtained by summing the scores for each increment over all commissioners and arraying the increments in order of their total score. Each step in the ranking implied a particular budget, with the total cost equal to the cumulative cost of all the included increments. The imposition of an overall funding level by the Office of Management and Budget led to a choice of a recommended budget with a specified mix of activities.

Mackay analyzes the underlying logic and normative properties of this decisionmaking procedure and, in so doing, highlights its advantages and disadvantages. Two perspectives are utilized. First, the procedure is examined under the assumption that all commissioners behave in a sincere fashion, truthfully reporting their preferences on budget priorities. Second, the procedure is examined at a strategically deeper level by considering the incentives for commissioners to vote in a sophisticated fashion and/or to collaborate with other commissioners, trade votes, and adopt joint strategies so as to manipulate the budgetary process and bias outcomes toward their own conception of the "public interest." The analysis raises several difficult questions about the meaning of "priority" and the ability of commissioners to state their preferences for individual programs independent of the overall funding level that is to be imposed. These problems strike at the core rationale for this budgetary procedure. In addition to these difficulties, the system may lead to outcomes that a majority of commissioners would find inferior to other feasible alternatives. Finally, the procedure is shown to create strong incentives for strategic manipulation.

The last paper in this section, coauthored by Ronald Bond and James C. Miller III, continues the analysis of the collegial decisionmaking process at the FTC. Drawing on a unique data set, the authors empirically examine the extent of agreement and disagreement among commissioners on both budgetary priorities and law-enforcement matters from 1977 through 1983. This period, marked by significant changes in policy direction, saw eight individuals serve as commissioners, with four different chairmen appointed by three presidents. To measure the extent of disagreement on budgetary priorities, the authors calculate, for each year, the simple correlation coefficients for the budgetary rankings of all possible pairs of commissioners. Along with other information, they display the average correlation between the rankings of pairs of commissioners, the rankings of the chairmen and other commissioners, and the rankings of commissioners other than the chairman. These correlations are also broken out by appointing president and party affiliation.

The data presented reveals substantially more disagreement in 1977, 1982, and 1983 than during the period 1979 through 1981. The authors note that the first two years of substantial disagreement involved the first year of tenure of a newly appointed chairman under a newly elected president whose political party was different from that of his predecessor. The voting data on law-enforcement actions reveals little disagreement during 1977 and 1978, with still less disagreement during 1979, when the agency came under severe attack by Congress. By 1982 the extent of disagreement had rebounded to double the amount in 1977 and 1978. In 1983 it doubled once again. The extent, timing, and pattern of disagreement reveal quite clearly the substantial differences in priorities between the Reagan appointees and the Carter and Ford appointees.

The volume is concluded with a paper, authored by Gordon Tullock, that provides an overall assessment of our current understanding of the political economy of regulation. He points out the successes and shortcomings of the current literature and offers some thoughts on, and insights into, the economic analysis of bureaucracy.

Part I

Congress and the Federal Trade Commission

Chapter 2

Antitrust Pork Barrel

ROGER L. FAITH,
DONALD R. LEAVENS, & ROBERT D. TOLLISON

RICHARD POSNER, writing in 1969, asserted that the Federal Trade Commission (FTC) was significantly impaired in its task of promoting the public interest by the commission's dependence on Congress. To make this point Posner employed a model of antitrust pork barrel. He emphasized that each member of Congress is obligated to protect and further the provincial interests of the citizens of the jurisdiction that he represents. Specifically, "the welfare of his constituents may depend disproportionately on a few key industries. The promotion of the industries becomes one of his most important duties as a representative of the district." Moreover, because the power to control the FTC is so unevenly distributed among members of Congress, the potential exists for each member of powerful subcommittees to exercise "a great deal of power to advance the interests of businesses located in his district however unimportant the interests may be from a national standpoint." Posner concluded that FTC investigations are seldom in the public interest and are initiated "at the behest of corporations, trade associations, and trade unions whose motivation is at best to shift the costs of their private litigation to the taxpayer and at worst to harass competitors."[1]

This model of FTC behavior builds on a fairly standard characterization of how geographically based representative democracy works in practice. In

Reprinted by permission from *Journal of Law and Economics* 15 (October 1982): 329–42. The views expressed here are those of the authors and do not necessarily reflect those of the Federal Trade Commission, individual commissioners, or other staff.

effect, a geographically based system confronts the legislator with a high payoff from representing local interests in the national legislature by trading votes with other legislators to finance numerous local benefits at the expense of taxpayer-consumers in general and with a correspondingly low payoff from voting in terms of cost-benefit analysis, economic efficiency, or the "national interest." This asymmetry of payoffs to the legislator is partly based on the greater information that voters have about localized benefits as compared with general benefits and partly based on the rational calculation of average taxpayer-consumers that it is not worth their while to try to do anything to stop such transfers of wealth. What is surprising about this model, however, is that it has generated so few efforts at empirical confirmation. The small amount of literature investigating the linkage between representation and local influence—which is the key proposition of the pork-barrel and geography model— shows a mixed bag of results, some supportive of this proposition and some not.[2]

Our purpose in this paper is to contribute to this literature by presenting some empirical evidence on antitrust pork barrel. We examine the case-bringing activity of the FTC to see if there is any bias in the results of this process in favor of firms that operate in the jurisdictions of members of congressional committees that have important budgetary and oversight powers with respect to the FTC. The hypothesis that we expect to be unable to reject is that favorable FTC decisions (that is, dismissals) are nonrandomly concentrated on firms in the jurisdictions of members of key FTC committees.

The data base for this hypothesis-testing exercise covers the case-bringing activity of the FTC from 1961 to June 1979. For the purpose of empirical testing we will split this data into two periods. The first period, 1961–1969, allows us to test Posner's argument on the period of FTC activity that he presumably had in mind when he developed the pork-barrel hypothesis. The second period, 1970–1979, allows us to see if the argument holds up over a period in which it has been claimed that the FTC was subjected to a series of reform measures that greatly improved the commission's record for the promotion of the public interest. This latter view of FTC behavior in the 1970s has been offered in a recent book by Robert Katzmann, who explicitly rejects models of budget maximization and congressional influence as explaining much of recent FTC behavior.[3] Without offering an alternative explanation of outcomes, he chooses to stress instead the role of internal bureaucratic processes, such as the turnover of legal personnel, in explaining the cases that the FTC selects. Although we are interested in FTC case outcomes rather than case selection, it will prove interesting to compare the explanatory power of the private- and public-interest theories with respect to FTC behavior in the 1970s.[4]

EMPIRICAL PROCEDURE

The initial period of study extends from 1961 to 1969. The selection of 1961 as a starting point coincides with the beginning of a congressional session and was dictated by local Virginia Polytechnic Institute data availability. The selection of 1969 as an end point derives from the fact that two highly critical reports on the FTC were published in that year, and reorganization and reform of the FTC were begun in 1970.[5]

According to institutional sources, congressional jurisdiction over the FTC is shared by two Senate committees, one Senate subcommittee, and five House subcommittees: the Senate Committee on Interior and Insular Affairs; the Senate Committee on Commerce, Science, and Transportation; the Senate Subcommittee on Antitrust and Monopoly of the Senate Judiciary Committee; the House Subcommittees on Independent Offices and the Department of Housing and Urban Development, on Agriculture and Related Agencies, and on State, Justice, Commerce, and the Judiciary and Related Agencies (these are all subcommittees of the House Committee on Appropriations); the House Subcommittee on Oversight and Investigations of the House Committee on Interstate and Foreign Commerce; and the House Subcommittee on Monopolies and Commercial Law of the House Judiciary Committee.[6]

The exact jurisdictional relationship of these committees to the FTC is never made clear in institutional sources. Indeed, congressional power over the FTC seems to shift over time, especially among the five House subcommittees. We thus collected data on all of these committees and subcommittees so as to be able to start from a broad definition of congressional influence over the FTC and work toward more narrowly based definitions. The membership of these committees and subcommittees was traced back to 1961 using the *Congressional Quarterly Almanac*.[7] Subsequently, the districts and states represented by the membership were plotted on a map of the United States. It was necessary to use a new map for each session of Congress, since membership changed over the period studied. Moreover, in 1963 and 1973, as a result of the 1960 and 1970 censuses, congressional districts boundaries were changed nationwide. Consequently, three sets of congressional district maps had to be employed, one for the period 1961–1962, one for 1963–1972, and one for 1973–1979.[8]

FTC action against businesses can take place on several levels. Although the FTC is empowered to initiate investigations on its own, by far the majority (80–90 percent) of investigations are begun at the request of the public.[9] The public is permitted to file applications for complaints with the FTC, in which case the staff reviews the applications to determine whether sufficient evidence of a violation exists to warrant further investigation. At this point either the case is closed for lack of evidence or a formal complaint is drawn up.[10] If the case remains open, the business charged is notified by the commission that a formal complaint is about to be served. In effect, the business is given the opportunity to agree to stop whatever action is specified in the complaint. If the business agrees, a consent order to cease and desist is prepared, and, if approved by the commission, the consent order prevents the issuance of a formal complaint. However, if the respondent does not file an answer with the FTC in response to the advance notice or seeks to contest the complaint, a formal complaint is issued. Subsequently, the case is heard by an administrative law judge, and only two outcomes are possible: either the case is dismissed for insufficient evidence of a violation, or a cease-and-desist order is issued. A case to which a respondent has consented can never be dismissed later. Moreover, any business that is issued a cease-and-desist order has the right to appeal to the commission (if the order is issued by an administrative law judge) and (if the commission supports the order) to the Circuit Court of Appeals in the circuit where the firm is located or in the Washington, D.C. circuit.

The outcomes of all contested cases and consent cases are summarized each year in *Federal Trade Commission Decisions*, which reports the nature of the case (consent, cease and desist, or dismissal), the name of the respondent(s), and the respondent(s)'s headquarters address(es).[11] When more than one respondent was named and these respondents were associated with separate businesses, the headquarters address of each separate business was recorded as if separate cases had been involved.[12]

One point should be stressed about this procedure. Assigning firms to congressional districts on the basis of the respondent's headquarters address could be misleading if a division or plant under FTC scrutiny was located in a different district from the firm's headquarters. However, it is consistent with the pork-barrel hypothesis that representatives will seek to wield influence when the profits of one of their constituents (the firm) are in jeopardy because of an FTC action against a division or plant of the firm not located in the district. Indeed, if all pork-barrel activity occurs in the district of the plant, such misassignment of firms to districts serves only to bias our statistical tests against the pork-barrel hypothesis.

After recording all of the relevant FTC data, the respondent addresses were plotted against the maps showing the congressional districts and Senate states of the eight committees and subcommittees.[13] The totals for consents, cease-and-desist orders, and dismissals were tallied individually for the two Senate committees, the Senate subcommittee, each of the five House subcommittees, and the five House subcommittees taken together.

Precisely the same procedure was followed in gathering the data for the 1970–1979 sample period.[14] The data for both periods are summarized in the discussion of our empirical results to follow.

A final caveat about our empirical procedure is in order. Consider the source of cases brought against firms located within a given congressional district. Some of these cases will be initiated by individuals (persons, firms, or organizations) residing outside the district, and some will be initiated by district constituents. In the first case, a dismissal is clearly beneficial to the local firm and the local politician. The pork-barrel hypothesis is straightforward in this case: proportionately more dismissals relative to cases will occur in districts where representatives sit on FTC-relevant committees.[15] In the second case, a dismissal favors the local respondent but harms the local complainant. The representatives must choose to aid one firm or the other, presumably on the basis of greater net gain to themselves. Under these conditions there is no reason to believe that there is any systematic bias by the representatives in favor of dismissal and therefore that there is any systematic bias across districts in the proportion of dismissals to cases brought. The latter point preserves the basis for testing our formulation of the pork-barrel hypothesis, given that some complaints will be brought by district constituents against district constituents.[16]

EMPIRICAL RESULTS: 1961–1969

We test the pork-barrel hypothesis on two sets of data. In Table 2.1 the base is cases brought, which includes all case-bringing activity of the FTC (dismissals, cease-and-desist orders, and consent decrees). In Table 2.2 the base is complaints, which includes only formal actions against firms by the commission (dismissals and cease-and-desist orders). Consent decrees are thus removed from the latter data, and we look for congressional influence on the patterns of formal FTC decisionmaking.

Our category of cases brought is the broadest measure of FTC activity for which data are available. It may also be the most suitable for our tests even if systematic data on the source of complaint applications were available. First, information on which firms are being scrutinized by the FTC is not readily known either to the firms or to their representatives until a complaint is brought. Second, even if the congressmen knew that one of their constituents was the source of the complaint, if the firm did not know, the gain to the representatives from halting any further investigation would be minimized since the benefit to the firm of their activity would be unobservable.

In Tables 2.1 and 2.2 the ratios of dismissals to cases brought and dismissals to complaints are given for the jurisdictions represented by the given committee's membership in column 1 and for the remaining congressional jurisdictions in column 2.[17] According to the null hypothesis, the difference between the proportion of dismissals within and outside the relevant congres-

TABLE 2.1
EMPIRICAL RESULTS FOR CASES BROUGHT: 1961–1969

| Congressional (Sub)Committee | RATIOS OF DISMISSALS TO CASES BROUGHT | | (3) | (4) |
	(1) Within Congressional Areas	(2) Outside Congressional Areas	Z-Statistic	Probability
Senate Committee on Interior and Insular Affairs	17/285 .0596	148/2190 .0678	.52	.400
Senate Committee on Commerce, Science, and Transportation	32/570 .0561	133/1905 .0698	1.14	.748
Senate Subcommittee on Antitrust and Monopoly of the Senate Judiciary Committee	60/638 .0940	105/1837 .0572	3.22	.999
House Subcommittee on Independent Offices and the Department of Housing and Urban Development of the House Appropriations Committee	14/87 .1609	151/2388 .0632	3.59	.999
House Subcommittee on Agriculture and Related Agencies of the House Appropriations Committee	38/461 .0824	127/2014 .0630	1.50	.866
House Subcommittee on State, Justice, Commerce, and the Judiciary and Related Agencies of the House Committee on Appropriations	60/906 .0662	105/1569 .0669	.06	.048
House Subcommittee on Oversight and Investigations of the House Committee on Interstate and Foreign Commerce	4/61 .0656	161/2414 .0667	a	—
House Subcommittee on Monopolies and Commercial Law of the House Judiciary Committee	62/873 .0602	103/1602 .0643	.65	.478
All five House subcommittees	84/1104 .0761	81/1371 .0591	1.69	.909

NOTE: a. Insufficient number of observations. See note 18.

SOURCES: U.S. Federal Trade Commission, *Federal Trade Commission Decisions*, vols. 58–66 (Washington, D.C.: GPO, 1963–1971).

TABLE 2.2

EMPIRICAL RESULTS FOR COMPLAINTS: 1961–1969

| Congressional (Sub)Committee | RATIOS OF DISMISSALS TO COMPLAINTS | | (3) | (4) |
	(1) Within Congressional Areas	(2) Outside Congressional Areas	Z-Statistic	Probability
Senate Committee on Interior and Insular Affairs	17/64 .2656	148/515 .2874	.36	.281
Senate Committee on Commerce, Science, and Transportation	32/140 .2286	133/439 .3030	1.70	.910
Senate Subcommittee on Antitrust and Monopoly of the Senate Judiciary Committee	60/163 .3681	105/416 .2524	2.77	.999
House Subcommittee on Independent Offices and the Department of Housing and Urban Development of the House Appropriations Committee	14/26 .5385	151/553 .2730	2.93	.997
House Subcommittee on Agriculture and Related Agencies of the House Appropriations Committee	38/110 .3454	128/469 .2708	1.56	.881
House Subcommittee on State, Justice, Commerce, and the Judiciary and Related Agencies of the House Committee on Appropriations	60/198 .3030	105/381 .2756	.69	.510
House Subcommittee on Oversight and Investigations of the House Committee on Interstate and Foreign Commerce	4/20 .2000	161/559 .2880	a	—
House Subcommittee on Monopolies and Commercial Law of the House Judiciary Committee	62/176 .3523	103/403 .2556	2.37	.982
All five House subcommittees	84/234 .3590	81/345 .2348	3.25	.999

NOTE: a. Insufficient number of observations. See note 18.
SOURCES: See Table 2.1.

sional jurisdictions should not be significantly different from zero. Column 3 reports the Z-statistic, which tests for a difference in two proportions drawn from binomial distributions of different populations.[18] Column 4 gives the probability of correctly rejecting the null hypothesis.

Institutional sources stress that the Senate committees are relatively passive overseers of the FTC. This conjecture tends to hold for the Committee on Interior and Insular Affairs. However, membership on the Commerce Committee would appear to be related to unfavorable FTC rulings in Table 2.2, while membership on the Subcommittee on Antitrust and Monopoly is significantly related to favorable rulings in both Tables 2.1 and 2.2. This latter result is meaningful, since this subcommittee had a membership in the 1960s that, on average, encompassed only eight states, and we find a highly significant pattern of decisions over this period favoring firms in these states.

For purposes of testing the pork-barrel hypothesis on House data, we present results for individual subcommittees and for all five subcommittees taken together. The pattern of results on individual subcommittees suggests that the Independent Offices Subcommittee wielded substantial power with respect to FTC decisionmaking in the 1960s, both in the broad and narrow definitions of influence. The results also suggest that the Subcommittee on Agriculture and Related Agencies and the Subcommittee on Monopolies and Commercial Law were influential in FTC decisionmaking over this period with respect to favorable rulings for within-district cases. The Subcommittee on State, Justice, Commerce, and the Judiciary and Related Agencies and the Subcommittee on Oversight and Investigations appear to bear no relation to FTC behavior.

The results for all five House subcommittees taken together are reported at the bottom of Tables 2.1 and 2.2. When the broad definition of FTC activity is used, we can reject the null hypothesis at approximately the 10 percent level of confidence. On the more narrowly based definition, where a complaint has been issued, the pork-barrel hypothesis can be accepted at better than the 1 percent level of confidence. The House subcommittees, taken as an observational unit, appear to have been a ripe arena for antitrust pork barrels in the 1960s.

The idea that congressional committee members who have important oversight and budgetary powers with respect to the FTC can deflect commission decisions in favor of firms in their jurisdictions would appear to have useful explanatory power in the 1960s, as it supports the suspicions of Posner and other observers. The question remains for our inquiry whether the much-touted reforms of the commission in the 1970s did anything to mitigate congressional influence in antitrust matters.

EMPIRICAL RESULTS: 1970–1979

As stressed earlier, Katzmann argues that the efforts to reform the FTC to operate more consistently in the public interest have by and large been successful.[19] Katzmann does not mean that there are not biases in commission activities, only that these biases derive from such factors as personnel selection and turnover, not from such forces as congressional influence or FTC aspirations to have a larger budget by currying congressional favor. Our results for commission activity in the 1970s, the period of reform, do not bode well for Katzmann's assessment. These results, using the same format as employed for Tables 2.1 and 2.2, are given in Tables 2.3 and 2.4.

The institutional observation that the Senate committees are passive overseers of FTC activities tends to be borne out in the results for the 1970s. We can observe no statistically reliable relationship over this period between membership on the relevant Senate committees and FTC decisionmaking. This contrasts with the results for the 1960s, in which the Subcommittee on Antitrust and Monopoly in particular appeared to have a significant impact on commission decisions. The Commerce Committee, however, exhibited a dismissal pattern in the 1960s opposed to the pork-barrel hypothesis but reversed itself in the 1970s, particularly with respect to complaints. Still, in the case of the Senate, Katzmann's public-interest argument can perhaps be said to hold. An alternative explanation is that a given firm is an insignificant member of a senator's constituency (the entire state), and the net return from FTC pork barrel is negligible in the Senate.

The House is another matter. The results for all five subcommittees taken as a unit tend to bear out the pork-barrel hypothesis for both definitions of FTC activity. This is probably the strongest counterevidence to the claim that the reforms of the FTC altered the basic underlying relationship of the agency with Congress. If anything, the pork-barrel process became more pronounced and apparent in the data.

Among the individual House subcommittees, the Subcommittee on Independent Offices and the Subcommittee on Monopolies and Commercial Law continued to have an important impact on FTC actions in the 1970s; the latter subcommittee has shown a significantly favorable impact on both cases brought and complaints. Unlike the results for the 1960s, the Subcommittee on State, Justice, Commerce, and the Judiciary and Related Agencies had a strong impact on formal FTC actions, particularly with respect to complaints (see Table 2.4). In an apparent jurisdictional shift, the Subcommittee on Agriculture essentially dropped out of the data in the 1970s. Finally, the

TABLE 2.3
EMPIRICAL RESULTS FOR CASES BROUGHT: 1970–1979

| Congressional (Sub)Committee | RATIOS OF DISMISSALS TO CASES BROUGHT | | (3) | (4) |
	(1) Within Congressional Areas	(2) Outside Congressional Areas	Z-Statistic	Probability
Senate Committee on Interior and Insular Affairs	8/278 .0288	56/1562 .0358	.59	.440
Senate Committee on Commerce, Science, and Transportation	24/558 .0430	40/1282 .0312	1.54	.876
Senate Subcommittee on Antitrust and Monopoly of the Senate Judiciary Committee	7/305 .0230	57/1535 .0358	1.11	.733
House Subcommittee on Independent Offices and the Department of Housing and Urban Development of the House Appropriations Committee	6/72 .0833	58/1768 .0329	2.29	.978
House Subcommittee on Agriculture and Related Agencies of the House Appropriations Committee	0/3	64/1837 .0348	a	—
House Subcommittee on State, Justice, Commerce, and the Judiciary and Related Agencies of the House Committee on Appropriations	19/417 .0436	45/1423 .0316	1.18	.762
House Subcommittee on Oversight and Investigations of the House Committee on Interstate and Foreign Commerce	6/157 .0382	58/1683 .0345	.24	.189
House Subcommittee on Monopolies and Commercial Law of the House Judiciary Committee	18/282 .0682	46/1558 .0295	3.26	.999
All five House subcommittees	29/589 .0492	35/1251 .0280	2.32	.980

NOTE: a. Insufficient number of observations. See note 18.

SOURCES: U.S. Federal Trade Commission, *Federal Trade Commission Decisions*, vols. 67–76 (Washington, D.C.: GPO, 1972–1981).

TABLE 2.4
EMPIRICAL RESULTS FOR COMPLAINTS: 1970–1979

| | RATIOS OF DISMISSALS TO COMPLAINTS | | | |
| | (1) Within Congressional Areas | (2) Outside Congressional Areas | (3) | (4) |
Congressional (Sub)Committee			Z-Statistic	Probability
Senate Committee on Interior and Insular Affairs	8/23 .3478	56/173 .3237	.23	.182
Senate Committee on Commerce, Science, and Transportation	25/64 .3906	39/132 .2954	1.33	.816
Senate Subcommittee on Antitrust and Monopoly of the Senate Judiciary Committee	7/24 .2917	57/172 .3314	.39	.303
House Subcommittee on Independent Offices and the Department of Housing and Urban Development of the House Appropriations Committee	6/6 1.000	58/190 .3052	a	—
House Subcommittee on Agriculture and Related Agencies of the House Appropriations Committee	0/0	64/196 .3776	a	—
House Subcommittee on State, Justice, Commerce, and the Judiciary and Related Agencies of the House Committee on Appropriations	19/38 .5000	45/158 .2848	2.54	.989
House Subcommittee on Oversight and Investigations of the House Committee on Interstate and Foreign Commerce	6/11 .5454	58/185 .3135	1.59	.881
House Subcommittee on Monopolies and Commercial Law of the House Judiciary Committee	18/25 .7200	46/171 .2690	4.49	.999
All five House subcommittees	29/55 .5273	35/141 .2651	3.74	.999

NOTE: a. Insufficient number of observations. See note 18.
SOURCES: See Table 2.3.

Subcommittee on Oversight and Investigations has continued to be unimportant in explaining FTC decisions with respect to complaints.

Overall, the individual subcommittee results suggest that most of the basic results from the 1960s carried over to the 1970s. There were some jurisdictional shifts, to be sure, but most of the important underlying patterns in the data persisted and were strengthened in a statistical sense. The hypothesis of reform in the 1970s simply does not hold up for the House.

One general comparative aspect of the data should be noted. Total cases brought fell from 2,475 in the 1960s to 1,840 in the 1970s. More important, the number of formal actions by the FTC fell from 579 in the 1960s to 196 in the 1970s. It would appear that consents became more important in the 1970s, and moreover, the leverage of four of the House subcommittees over the diminished number of formal commission actions became quite pronounced in that decade. Perhaps the reduction in formal actions is the true result of the FTC reforms.

CONCLUSIONS

Our results lend support to a private-interest theory of FTC behavior over the entire period that we investigated. If anything, the pork-barrel relationship between Congress and the commission became statistically stronger during the reform period of the 1970s. We would claim that those observers who see the FTC as acting in more congruence with the public interest (whatever this may mean) over this period have been misled in their analyses. In contrast to Katzmann, in particular, we would not be so hasty in discarding budget-maximizing or congressional-influence hypotheses about regulatory bureau behavior.[20] The tendencies that we describe are hard to explain with other models.

Also, though our results mask a complicated underlying pattern of pork-barrel activity, representation on certain committees is apparently valuable in antitrust proceedings. In terms of the representation and influence problem, then, we come out on the side of the argument that suggests that representation does matter in determining policy outcomes.

Finally, we should be clear that we do not claim to have a completely specified model of the relationship between Congress and the FTC or of the behavior of the FTC over time. Much work remains to be done on such problems. For example, what are the characteristics of firms (large employers, large campaign contributors?) that benefit from FTC decisionmaking? What is the amount of wealth at stake in a typical FTC case? Does seniority matter among the overseers of the FTC? Our results, however, along with the work of Posner and others, suggest the value of approaching such questions about antitrust decisionmaking with a healthy dose of cynicism about representative democracy, which works in this area much as it does in others.

NOTES

1. Richard Posner, "The Federal Trade Commission," *University of Chicago Law Review* 37 (1969): 47–89. Posner is not the only observer to offer a pork-barrel hypothesis about FTC behavior. Consider the following comments by other students of the commission:

> According to Joseph W. Shea, Secretary of the FTC, any letter the Commission gets from a Congressman's office is specially marked with an expedite sticker. The sticker gives the letter high priority, assuring the Congressman of an answer within five days. No distinction is made between letters—whether from complaining constituents, which Congressmen routinely "buck" over to the FTC, or those from the Congressmen themselves. (Edward F. Cox, Robert C. Fellmeth, and John E. Schultz, *The Nader Report on the Federal Trade Commission* [New York: Richard W. Baron, 1969], p. 134.)

> In September 1969, despite vigorous dissents from his colleagues, Commissioner Elman supported Baum's analysis. He told a Senate group that congressional pressure "corrupts the atmosphere" in which his agency works. He charged that congressmen make private, unrecorded calls on behalf of companies seeking FTC approval of million-dollar mergers. (Susan Wagner, *The Federal Trade Commission* [New York: Praeger, 1971], p. 211.)

2. See Charles R. Plott, "Some Organizational Influences on Urban Renewal Decisions," *American Economic Review* 58 (May 1968): 306–21; George J. Stigler, "The Sizes of Legislatures," *Journal of Legal Studies* 5 (January 1976): 17–34; W. Mark Crain and Robert D. Tollison, "The Influence of Representation on Public Policy," *Journal of Legal Studies* 6 (June 1977): 355–61; James T. Bennett and Eddie R. Mayberry, "Fiscal Tax Burdens and Grant Benefits to States: The Impact of Imperfect Representation," *Public Choice* 34 (1979): 255–69; Kenneth N. Greene and Vincent G. Munley, "The Productivity of Legislators' Tenure: A Case Lacking Evidence," *Journal of Legal Studies* 10 (January 1981): 207–14; and W. Mark Crain and Robert D. Tollison, "Representation and Influence, Again," *Journal of Legal Studies* 10 (January 1981): 215–19.

3. Robert A. Katzmann, *Regulatory Bureaucracy: The Federal Trade Commission and Antitrust Policy* (Cambridge, Mass.: MIT Press, 1980), especially pp. 181–87.

4. In a recently published study, Kenneth Clarkson and Timothy Muris incisively critique the performance of the FTC in the 1970s. Their critique is based on a broad economic analysis of the behavior of the agency and the impact of its policies on consumer welfare. Their resoundingly negative findings are in accord with the type of empirical results that we uncover in this paper. See Kenneth W. Clarkson and Timothy J. Muris, eds., *The Federal Trade Commission Since 1970: Economic Regulation and Bureaucratic Behavior* (Cambridge, Eng.: Cambridge University Press, 1981). In addi-

tion, evidence in support of the congressional influence model with respect to the general policies of the FTC can be found in Chapter 3 of the present volume, "Bureaucratic Discretion or Congressional Control? Regulatory Policymaking by the Federal Trade Commission," by Barry R. Weingast and Mark J. Moran. These authors focus on the entire Senate and the Consumer Affairs Subcommittee of the Senate Commerce Committee to see if the *selection* of cases is biased in favor of the preferences of these two Senate groups. By way of contrast we look at all committees and subcommittees relevant to the FTC and test to see if the *disposition* of cases is biased in favor of firms located in these committee members' districts.

5. See Cox, Fellmeth, and Schulz, *Nader Report,* and American Bar Association, *Report of the American Bar Association Commission to Study the Federal Trade Commission* (Chicago, 1969).

6. Our primary source is Katzmann, *Regulatory Bureaucracy,* especially pp. 141, 143, and 147–50. See also Wagner, *Federal Trade Commission.*

7. *Congressional Quarterly Almanac,* vols. 17–25 (Washington, D.C.: Congressional Quarterly, Inc., 1961–1969).

8. The congressional maps were taken from *Official Congressional Directory, 87th Congress, 1st Session* (Washington, D.C.: Government Printing Office, April 1961); *Official Congressional Directory, 88th Congress, 1st Session* (Washington, D.C.: GPO, April 1963); and *Official Congressional Directory, 93rd Congress, 1st Session* (Washington, D.C.: GPO, April 1973).

9. See Alan Stone, *Economic Regulation and the Public Interest* (Ithaca, N.Y.: Cornell University Press, 1977), pp. 64–65.

10. We are precluded from gaining insight into this initial aspect of FTC case selection because data on the preliminary FTC action is confidential and not available to the public.

11. U.S. Federal Trade Commission, *Federal Trade Commission Decisions,* vols. 58–76 (Washington, D.C.: GPO, 1963–1971).

12. Two additional points are relevant here. First, interlocutory or modified orders were also issued over this period, though infrequently. Since these latter orders cite respondents from earlier complaints or from complaints to follow, they were not included in the study to avoid double counting. Second, if a committee member's district was located in a multidistrict metropolitan area, then companies investigated by the FTC located in adjacent districts were treated as if they were actually located within the member's district. We follow Plott, "Organizational Influences," in this respect, who suggested that representatives of large metropolitan districts share interests in adjacent districts.

13. Our source map was *Rand McNally Road Atlas of the United States* (New York: Rand McNally, 1980).

14. See *Congressional Quarterly Almanac,* vols. 26–35 (Washington, D.C.: Congressional Quarterly, Inc., 1970–1979); and U.S. Federal Trade Commission, *Federal Trade Commission Decisions,* vols. 77–93 (Washington, D.C.: GPO, 1970–1979).

15. Likewise, consider the case where the complainant is a firm in an FTC-relevant district. Assuming the complainant makes the complaint known to that district's representative, logrolling will result in a higher probability of nondismissal of the

complaint, thereby reinforcing the lower ratio of dismissals to cases brought in nonrelevant FTC districts.

16. To the best of our knowledge there are no *systematic* data on the source of FTC complaints that are available to the public. Although it is true that the source of some complaints will become known in the process of discovery, such data are not collected and published by the FTC. Indeed, if the logrolling hypothesis is correct (that is, the public-interest hypothesis is wrong), the FTC has an obvious institutional incentive not to make such data generally available.

17. The totals for all five House subcommittees taken together are less than the sums over the five subcommittees, since some congressmen sit on more than one FTC-related subcommittee. This point carries special force in our data, particularly given our handling of multidistrict metropolitan areas as discussed in note 12.

18. See Paul G. Hoel, *Introduction to Mathematical Statistics* (New York: John Wiley and Sons, 1971), p. 135. Where the Z-statistic is not computed, at least one of the sample populations was not large enough to meet Hoel's criteria for using the normal approximation to a binomial distribution.

19. Katzmann, *Regulatory Bureaucracy*. Again, this view should be contrasted to that recently offered by Clarkson and Muris, *Federal Trade Commission Since 1970.*

20. Ibid. Perhaps Katzmann was led astray by excessive reliance on interviews as a research methodology. Asking people what they do is a notoriously bad way to find out what they are actually doing.

Chapter 3

Bureaucratic Discretion or Congressional Control? Regulatory Policymaking by the Federal Trade Commission

BARRY R. WEINGAST & MARK J. MORAN

THE relationship of the regulatory agencies to the political system of the United States remains an important and controversial issue. The scholarly literature on agency behavior is founded on widely divergent assumptions about agency-legislative relationships and the source of agency decisions. Given this divergence, the lack of systematic empirical tests of opposing views is striking. One body of this literature, which focuses on the bureaucratic components of agency decisions, assumes that agencies are relatively independent of Congress; it argues that to understand policymaking we must understand bureaucratic discretion in operation. Another body of work, however, rests on the opposite assumption, namely, that agencies are controlled by the Congress and that to understand regulatory policymaking we must understand legislative politics. These views clearly differ in their explanation of why agencies make particular policy decisions.

An unfortunate consequence of the diverse and relatively independent academic literature on this topic is the absence of an accurate characterization of the agency-legislative relationships on which major public policy issues hinge. For example, the success of modern regulatory reform efforts—such as sunset legislation and legislative veto—depends on whether the view of regulatory agencies implicit in these reforms aptly characterizes behavior. As

This paper was previously published under the same title in *Journal of Political Economy* 91, no. 5 (1983): 765–800, and has been edited for inclusion here.

Roger Noll emphasizes, much of the regulatory reform debate ignores this lack of consensus on regulatory behavior: "All [regulatory reform] proposals rest upon some theoretical conception of the behavior of government agencies. Yet the proponents of reform rarely justify their proposals by reference to explicit theoretical and empirical observation on bureaucratic behavior."[1] One reason for the lack of discriminating tests is that neither view readily leads to predictions about policy change in a manner that allows these predictions to be contrasted with observed behavior.

In this paper, we develop a model of agency decisionmaking based on the premise that agencies are controlled by the legislature. We argue, therefore, that to understand the genesis of agencies, as well as the stability and change in agency policy, one must understand the underlying legislative politics. With this in mind, we develop a model of legislative choice. The model characterizes the nature of policy equilibrium and, perhaps more important, yields comparative statics results that lead to predictions about policy change. Following the theoretical development of the model, we turn to an empirical application that tests the specific assertions of our model as well as the hypothesis of legislative control. The recent changes that have occurred at the Federal Trade Commission (FTC) and the relation of these changes to Congress provide the setting for our tests. We find substantial evidence for both the hypothesis of legislative control and the predictions of our specific model of Congress.

TWO VIEWS OF AGENCY DECISIONMAKING

The literature on agency policymaking divides into two distinct approaches. The bureaucratic, or traditional, approach argues that agencies are independent of the legislature. The second, or congressional dominance, approach argues that agencies are directly tied to (or operate in alliance with) specific committees within the legislature. In what follows, we summarize the major premises of each and note, on the basis of the usual sort of evidence amassed through case studies, that they are observationally equivalent.[2] That is, they lead to the same observations about the relationship between agencies and Congress during periods of stable policy:

1. The lack of oversight hearings;
2. The infrequency of congressional investigations and policy resolutions;
3. The perfunctory nature of confirmation hearings of agency heads;
4. The lack of ostensible congressional attention to or knowledge about

the ongoing operation and policy consequences of agency choice; and

5. The superficiality of annual appropriations hearings.[3]

According to the traditional approach, these observations represent a failure of Congress to oversee and control the bureaucracy.[4] Several factors contribute to the inability of Congress to control agencies. First, agencies control information from their policy area; second, access to clientele fosters agency-clientele alliances to protect agencies from their nominal overseers in Congress; and third, the high cost of passing new legislation to redirect agency policy limits congressional action in all but the most important cases. The resulting bureaucratic insulation affords bureaucrats a degree of discretion that, in turn, is used to pursue their own private goals rather than the public purposes for which they were originally created. According to Lawrence Dodd and Richard Schott, for example, the federal bureaucracy is "in many respects a prodigal child. Although born of congressional intent, it has taken on a life of its own and has matured to a point where its muscle and brawn can be turned against its creator."[5] Similarly, James Q. Wilson concludes that:

> by and large, the policies of regulatory commissions are not under close scrutiny or careful control of either the White House or Congress. [Moreover,] . . . whoever first wished to see regulation carried on by quasi-independent agencies and commissions has had his boldest dreams come true. The organizations studied for this book operate with substantial autonomy, at least with respect to congressional or executive direction.[6]

While significant differences exist among adherents of this view, these examples illustrate how each hinges on the assumption of agency independence of the legislature. Furthermore, nearly all adherents rely on observations like the five noted above as evidence in support of their approach. Because Congress plays no easily recognizable role in agency relations, traditional analysts conclude that Congress had little influence over agency policy.

The congressional dominance approach begins with the opposite assumption about agencies and Congress.[7] Although in the textbook version of agency control by Congress congressmen publicly debate policy alternatives and then issue directives to agencies, in practice Congress works quite differently. A less visible but nevertheless effective means for congressional control of agencies is through a system of incentives. The five observations on agency-legislative relationships, as we shall see, are consistent with this latter view, but not with the textbook version.

The congressional-dominance approach assumes that congressmen—or, more specifically, particular congressmen on the relevant committees—possess sufficient rewards and sanctions to create an incentive system for agencies. Agency mandate notwithstanding, rewards go to those agencies that pursue policies of interest to the current committee members; agencies that fail to do so are confronted with sanctions. It follows that if the incentive system worked effectively, then agencies would pursue congressional goals even though they received little direct public guidance from their overseers. Congressmen on the relevant committees may appear ignorant of agency proceedings because they gauge the success of programs through their constituents' reactions rather than through detailed study. Public hearings and investigations are resource-intensive activities, so they will hardly be used by congressmen for those policy areas that are operating smoothly (that is, benefiting congressional clientele). Their real purpose is to police those areas functioning poorly. The threat of *ex post* sanctions creates *ex ante* incentives for the bureau to serve a congressional clientele. This view has a striking implication: the more effective the incentive system, the less often we should observe sanctions in the form of congressional attention through hearings and investigations. Put another way, direct and continuous monitoring of inputs rather than of results is an inefficient mechanism by which principals constrain the actions of their agents.

Several factors make up the congressional incentive system. First, in the budgetary process each agency competes with a host of others for budgetary favors. Congressmen pursuing their own electoral goals favor those agencies that provide the best clientele service. Case studies of particular agencies typically focus on an agency in isolation and miss the important effects of this competition that mitigate, in part, the monopoly aspects of agency service.[8] Second, oversight plays an important role in sanctioning errant agencies. This includes new legislation, specific prohibitions on activities, and other means that serve to embarrass agency heads, hurt future career opportunities, and foil pet projects. Finally, and perhaps the most effective means of influence, Congress controls who gets appointed and reappointed.[9] Confirmation hearings may appear perfunctory to traditional analysts (such as Robert Katzmann) because the difficult policy issues are faced at an earlier, less public stage. For instance, while the official confirmation hearings of Interstate Commerce Commission officials lasted an average of seventeen minutes (during the period 1949–1974), a closer investigation revealed that Congress played a crucial role in selecting the nominee in most cases.[10] In sum, the five observations above are consistent with the smooth and effective functioning of a congressional incentive system to control agency decisions.

The point of this brief summary should now be clear: it is possible to explain the lack of direct and continuous congressional action in ongoing agency matters using either the traditional bureaucratic approach or the congressional-control approach. Since both approaches predict little direct agency-legislative interaction, evidence such as the five observations cannot be used to support either view. With this in mind, we turn to the development of a specific model and more appropriate tests.

A Model of Legislative Choice

The modern theory of political allocation parallels the theory of markets. In both cases, agents pursue their own self-interest through interaction with one another. This theory is founded on two principles. The first concerns the mechanisms of political allocation (for example, voting and political representation) and how they differ from market mechanisms.[11] The second is that political decisions supplant market decisions. The approach developed by George Stigler and extended by Sam Peltzman, for example, focuses on a support-maximizing politician (in their case, a political agent who controls regulation). In combination with a framework of interest-group formation, they demonstrate a fundamental bias in the demand for public policy. Because certain groups are more likely to form than others, these groups enjoy a disproportionate share of political benefits.[12]

While this prediction is in considerable accord with the outcomes of regulatory legislation, the approach falls short of complete explanation. The presumption that the interest-group demand for specific legislation is simply translated into political outcomes ignores the political institutions that provide this legislation.[13] If regulation benefits specific constituencies at the expense of others, and if regulatory agencies carry out the bulk of policy administration at the behest of the legislature, then a complete theory of political allocation must have a model of the legislature to complement models of the demand for legislation. Put simply, we need to know how these mechanisms work.

While the Stigler and Peltzman approach helps explain why the Interstate Commerce Commission traditionally benefited the trucking and railroad industries, why the Civil Aeronautics Board benefited airlines, or why professional self-regulation provides benefits to the professions, it does not explain how benefits are simultaneously delivered to so many diverse interest groups. Neither complete chaos nor systematic fighting between groups is the rule. The explanation offered here is that the legislative institutions provide for this. In what follows, we assume that each congressman responds to the interests within his district. Following the argument of Barry Weingast, which builds on the work of Peltzman and Morris Fiorina, each representative chooses actions (such as voting or introducing new legislation) so as to maximize his political support function generated by the interests within his district.[14] In particular, this means he "votes his district."[15]

Because interests are not distributed uniformly across districts, the groups that are important for one legislator's electoral fortunes differ from those that are important for another's. This implies that there are tremendous gains to legislators (and hence to the organized interests they represent) from devising a means of regularizing the provision of benefits to a variety of groups and avoiding intergroup conflict. The mechanism employed for this purpose by the Congress is the committee system. This institutional arrangement—or contract-like agreement among legislators—allocates influence over policymaking in a manner that makes all legislators better off. The system works as follows. First, committees have near-monopoly jurisdiction over a small set of policy issues. This incorporates the power to make proposals that alter the status quo (subject to majority-rule approval by the entire legislature) as well as veto power over the proposals made by others. Thus, committees afford members extraordinary influence over a subset of policies. Second, members are assigned to committees on the basis of self-selection.[16] The advantage to each member is that he gains greater leverage over precisely those issues relevant for his own political support and hence for re-election. Put differently, the committee system enforces the following trade: each legislator gives up some influence over many areas of policy in return for a much greater influence over the one that, for him, counts the most. Thus, we find that representatives from farming districts dominate agriculture committees and oversee the provision of benefits to their farm constituents. Members from urban districts dominate banking, urban, and welfare committees overseeing an array of programs that provide benefits to a host of urban constituents, and members from western states dominate interior and public lands committees that provide benefits to their constituents.[17]

This approach yields two testable implications for policymaking: (1) specific oversight committees should be observed to have more influence than the rest of Congress over a particular agency. (2) The comparative statics result holds if the interests represented on the committee change, then so too should agency policy. For the empirical test of these hypotheses, it is useful to depict this second prediction graphically.

Suppose the legislature is to set policy over a one-dimensional issue space, x. Consider three legislators as pictured in Figure 3.1. The political support functions for each are pictured where x^1, x^2, and x^3 are the policies generating maximum political support for legislators 1, 2, and 3, respectively.[18] As we move away from each representative's maximum support point, alternatives yield lower political support. The support functions induce preferences for legislators. For individual 3, say, policy Y is preferred to policy Z because it yields higher support. Of course, policy x^3 is preferred by 3 to Y (and hence by transitivity to Z).

When faced with a choice between any two alternatives, a legislator votes for the policy that yields higher support. Legislative choice is decided by

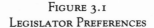

FIGURE 3.1
LEGISLATOR PREFERENCES

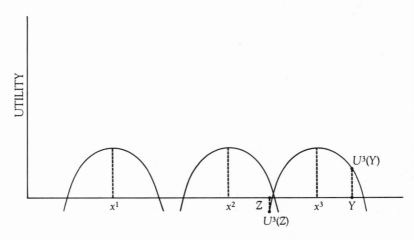

majority rule between alternative policies where the members of the committee have the property right to make proposals for alternatives to the current
status quo. An equilibrium is a point x for which none of the alternatives that
command a majority of votes against x are preferred to x by the committee.[19]

The implications of the model of legislative choice can be illustrated using
Figure 3.2 with reference to a hypothetical legislative choice over the level of
"environmental protection." Low levels of protection are depicted on the left
and high levels on the right. The maximum support points of only three
legislators are depicted, x^L, x^M, and x^H representing preferences for low levels,
the median level, and high levels of environmental protection, respectively.[20]
In our hypothetical example, suppose x^O is the status quo. Does this remain an
equilibrium? The answer depends on which set of voters has the property right
to make proposals, that is, which legislators are on the committee. Suppose
that the low demanders, x^L, dominate the committee. Then x^O is an equilibrium. To see this, note that the majority rule win set, $W(x^O)$, representing
those points that beat the status quo, is the open interval, (x^O, x^*). The set of
points generating greater political support than x^O for the "low demand"
committee consists of all points to the left of x^O, that is, the interval $(0, x^O)$.
Thus, x^O is an equilibrium because none of the points the committee prefers to
x^O commands a majority against x^O.

Comparative Statics

To illustrate the second hypothesis above, consider the effect on policy of
committee turnover.[21] Suppose that the high demanders of x^H take over

FIGURE 3.2
LEGISLATIVE CHOICE OVER ENVIRONMENTAL PROTECTION

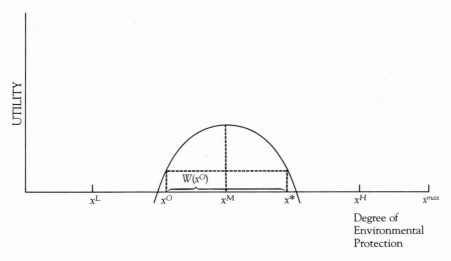

Degree of
Environmental
Protection

control of the committee from the low demanders. Does x^O remain an equilibrium, or is there a new equilibrium? To see what happens, notice that the set of points commanding a majority of votes against the status quo, $W(x^O)$, remains unchanged because the set of legislators is exactly as before. However, policies preferred to x^O by the new committee differ from those preferred by the older committee. The new committee with maximum political support, x^H, prefers all points to the right of x^O, that is, the interval (x^O, x^{max}). Thus, x^O no longer satisfies the equilibrium condition. To find the new equilibrium, observe that the committee treats the win set $W(x^O)$ as a constraint. Since only points within this set command a majority against the status quo, the committee selects the alternative that it prefers over all others, namely, x^*.[22] So the committee proposes and a majority of legislators vote for this point, which becomes the new equilibrium (a simple exercise may verify that the equilibrium conditions hold at this new point).

This example shows how the legislative committee system allocates influence in the legislature and why committee membership is valuable. The power vested by the committee system affects not only the policy chosen but also, through veto power, the ability to insure that future majorities will not overturn this policy. Finally, we derived a major comparative statics result about the nature of policy change that follows from a change in those on the committee with the property right to make proposals.

Implications for Regulatory Policymaking

Several predictions for regulatory agency behavior follow from this model, given the hypothesis of congressional control of agency decisions. First, congressional committees play an important role in determining regulatory policy. Those with the power to control the legislative policy agenda (vested by the committee system) have the power to veto changes proposed by those not on the committee and therefore partially to insulate agency policy from outside influence. Second, if the policy preferences of the committee members remain stable for long periods of time, then *ceteris paribus*, agency policy remains stable. Third, one important determinant of agency policy change is a change in the composition of the oversight committees. Markedly different preferences on the committee lead to major shifts in agency policy. Finally, those agencies not pursuing congressional interests are most likely to bring forth congressional sanctions.

TWO ALTERNATIVE EXPLANATIONS
OF RECENT FTC HISTORY

In the early fall of 1979, Congress publicly lambasted the FTC for a series of its investigations and programs, branding them as examples of regulatory abuse. Policy initiatives begun during the previous decade were publicly criticized. Several FTC investigations were halted outright, and the threat of more stringent sanctions suggested new directions for the FTC. Emphasizing this, the following spring the commission was officially allowed to go "out of business" when funds for its operations were not renewed. This occurred in a specific legal manner that gave the agency only two days to close down operations. It seemed that, by law, the agency had ceased to exist. Although funds were ultimately renewed to continue the FTC's existence, the message was clear: more serious sanctions would follow if the direction and impact of policies were not changed. Responding over the next year and a half, the FTC closed nearly all of its controversial rulemaking investigations and antitrust suits. Congress had demonstrated to the agency that it held the upper hand.

Here is a clear case in which Congress actively intervened, by using public oversight and legislation to question the direction of policy, and attempted to steer the agency along a different course. The issue is, why? How can we account for this unusual congressional action?

Traditional Interpretation

Remarkably, nearly all public and academic explanations fit into the traditional bureaucratic view of agency policymaking.[23] According to the traditional approach, the congressional action in the form of a rare burst of official oversight confirmed, once again, the view of agency discretion. Congress finally caught a runaway, out-of-control bureaucracy. This demonstrated the discretion afforded by the lack of congressional attention: the FTC had operated independently for nearly a decade and, if not stopped by Congress, would have continued along these lines. Nearly the entire collection of ongoing investigations at the FTC received criticism. Examples of the wide range of targets of FTC investigations included advertising aimed at children (the so-called Kid-Vid controversy), the used-car market, the insurance industry, the self-regulating professional organizations such as undertakers, and several of the major antitrust suits such as those against the nation's largest oil companies and largest manufacturers of breakfast cereals.

Evidently it appeared to Congress and the press that the FTC claimed a mandate spanning the entire economy and was prepared to impose its regulatory control without hesitation. Had Congress played a more continuous role in agency decisions, so the argument goes, agency policy initiatives would have taken a different course. Summarizing the September 1979 hearings in which Congress launched its attack on the FTC, the *National Journal* reported that "The FTC roamed far beyond its congressional mandates with a shotgun attempt to regulate all kinds of business activities that should not be the concern of the government." The congressmen participating in this attack on the FTC shared this view. Senator Durkin, for example, described these hearings and sanctions as "shock therapy for bureaucrats."[24] Congressman Levitas announced, "We are seeing the end to government by bureaucratic fiat."[25]

These statements give the flavor of the investigation hearings in 1979 as well as of the appropriation hearings early the next year. The perception that the FTC was inattentive to congressional interests, exercised discretion, and overstepped its mandate seems to support the traditional view of agency-legislative relations. What occurred over the course of late 1979 and early 1980 was simply a case of Congress stepping in to direct policy in an ad hoc manner, "proving" that when congressional action does occur, it has positive effects on policy.

Several recent academic studies of the FTC—by Katzmann in 1980 and by Kenneth Clarkson and Timothy Muris in 1981—are also within this tradition. These scholars analyze FTC behavior throughout the 1970s and conclude that Congress had little to do with FTC decisionmaking. Clarkson, reviewing the legislative constraints on the FTC, articulates many of the important premises of the bureaucratic approach: "The ability of Congress to monitor individual FTC activities effectively is limited. Yet, . . . even with its most effective tools, Congress can redirect resources into or away from specific programs only after detailed analysis at the level beyond the institutional competence of Congress except on an, at most, occasional project. . . Oversight and ad hoc monitoring seldom influence Commission activities."[26] Similarly, Katzmann details the opportunities for congressional evaluation or influence but finds little of either. Rather, congressional attention to policy details is superficial and perfunctory.[27]

An Alternative Explanation: Congressional Choice

Although nearly all the public discussions have fallen into the realm of the first approach, the implications of the legislative model represent a contrasting but equally plausible interpretation. According to the second view, the descriptions in the popular press and the political forums have little to do with FTC policymaking during the 1970s, including the imposition of sanctions in 1979–1980. Rather, all throughout that decade, the commission pursued the interests of the congressional oversight committee.

Many of the commission's major policy initiatives, important cases, and investigations had their inception and design in congressional hearings held prior to FTC action.[28] As Ernest Gellhorn shows, as late as 1977 Congress consistently criticized the FTC for lack of progress on their many investigations—the very investigations that drew so much criticism two years later.[29]

What occurred in the late 1970s was the disappearance of congressional support for an activist FTC. Between 1976 and 1979, the dominant coalition on the relevant congressional committees changed from favoring to opposing an activist FTC. This resulted from the nearly complete turnover of those on and in control of the relevant Senate oversight subcommittee. None of the senior members of the subcommittee responsible for major FTC legislation and direction for the previous decade returned after 1976. Those previously in the minority took control of the subcommittee and began reversing the policies initiated by their predecessors. The 1979 and 1980 hearings were simply the most visible culmination of this process.

The congressional-choice explanation suggests that the FTC initiated controversial policies because it got strong signals to do so from Congress. Far from roaming beyond its congressional mandate as an exercise in bureaucratic discretion, the FTC aggressively implemented its new authority in concert with its congressional sponsors. With the turnover in 1977, however, the FTC lost its congressional support and thus was vulnerable to the subsequent reversals.

As evidence in favor of this view, we have noted that prior to the committee turnover, a small group of dedicated congressmen and senators on the FTC oversight subcommittee spent over a decade developing legislation, holding hearings, and earning a reputation in the area of consumer protection. In addition to sponsoring FTC activism, these senators also played roles in occupational safety, auto safety, and consumer product safety. A detailed analysis of the major FTC initiatives during this period would reveal strong parallels between these programs, the policy positions and legislation sponsored by the relevant senators, and the prescriptions of the consumerists. Because developing these parallels would be an entire topic in itself, we simply note that the parallels reflect an underlying harmony of interest between the relevant congressional subcommittee and the FTC. Senator Magnuson, for example, expressed his views in a book entitled *The Dark Side of the Marketplace*, which does not extoll the virtues of the unregulated market.[30] As another example, one of the first moves after the reorganization in 1969–1970 was the development of the advertising substantiation program. The genesis and practice of this program are rooted in the consumerist view of the manipulative uses of advertising.[31] Similar views underlie other FTC legislation, including the Truth-in-Lending Act, the Truth-in-Packaging Act, the Magnuson-Moss Warranty Act, and many of the controversial rulemakings such as Kid-Vid.

Warren Magnuson and other major senators involved in FTC activities (for example, Frank Moss and Philip Hart) were well known for their support of the consumerist issues from the mid-1960s through the 1970s.[32] Magnuson and Moss in the Senate and John Moss in the House worked for five years to pass the Magnuson-Moss Warranty and FTC Improvements Act. The latter gave the commission its official rulemaking powers, allowing it to promulgate regulations for an entire industry or industrial practice. Could these congressmen have been unaware of the consequences of that delegation? This seems unlikely, since many of the FTC's rulemaking investigations had already begun under a technicality in a court decision.[33] By the time the act finally passed, many of the investigations that would draw criticism in 1979 were well under way. Magnuson, Moss, Hart, and others were trying to foster this process, not hinder it.

Similarly, the major antitrust suit against the petroleum industry began with congressional hearings prior to the "oil crisis" of 1973; the oil crisis markedly increased the political popularity of the case, independent of its economic merits, which led to increased congressional support in 1973–1974. Although the case drew substantial criticism in 1979 from the new subcommittee members, this does not contradict the large role played by the previous subcommittee in launching the case. More generally, the essay by Roger Faith, Donald Leavens, and Robert Tollison (Chapter 2 in this volume) provides additional evidence of congressional influence over antitrust policy. It shows that firms located in districts represented on FTC oversight committees are favored in the commission's antitrust decisions (that is, cases are more likely to be dismissed).

Finally, Michael Pertschuk, the outspoken chairman of the commission during the sanctions, played a major role in the development and passage of nearly all the new legislation entrusted to the FTC in his capacity as Senate Commerce Committee chief of staff and general counsel throughout the 1970s. The appointment of Pertschuk to the head of the commission in 1977 seemed a natural culmination of this phase, not a coincidence.[34] The irony is that, just as he left the congressional domain to manage the FTC, the congressional support for FTC activism began to disappear.

The point of presenting this institutional detail is to illustrate the conclusion of the first section of this essay—namely, that the issue of bureaucratic discretion versus congressional control is not easily resolved by citing this sort of evidence. Because a judicious reading of the facts can support either view, it is difficult to use these details alone as evidence. Rather, we must turn to more systematic investigations, which afford proper discrimination.

EMPIRICAL EVIDENCE

In the empirical portion of this paper, we seek to demonstrate that the legislative-choice model adequately explains the recent behavior of the FTC, namely, that Congress controlled the FTC all along and that the 1979–1980 policy reversals resulted from the change in committee preferences. To establish the plausibility of this explanation and to show that important components of the bureaucratic approach are inconsistent with the evidence, we need to establish (1) that the committee preferences changed in such a way that the comparative statics prediction applies to FTC policy, and (2) that the congressional committees actually influenced FTC choices. In providing evidence for the latter, we establish congressional influence prior to committee change so that a significant change in preferences would have some important bearing on subsequent policy.

Comparative Statics Prediction of Committee Change

The comparative statics result derived from our model states that if preferences of the legislators on the oversight committee change in a particular manner, then so will agency policy. Thus, the first empirical link between our model and the FTC is to show that a market shift in the views of the members of the committee preceded the FTC reversals of 1979–1980.

Figure 3.3 illustrates the precise predictions within this setting. We have depicted the issue dimension over FTC policymaking as one dimensional, with positions in favor of an activist FTC on the right and positions opposed to an activist FTC on the left. This continuum represents the various possible positions of legislators for different levels of FTC regulatory activism. Reducing

FIGURE 3.3
THE COMPARATIVE STATICS RESULT APPLIED TO THE FTC

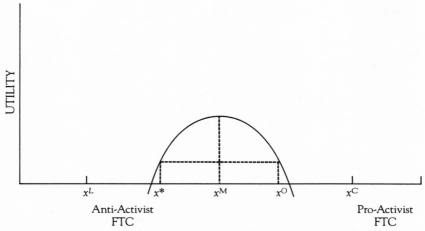

NOTE: $W(x^O)=(x^*,x^O)$. When x^O controls the committee, equilibrium is x^O. When committee control switches to x^L, equilibrium moves to x^*.

complex regulatory issues to a single dimension obviously ignores important distinctions among different types of regulatory policies; however, we make this simplifying assumption for two reasons. First, the main issue throughout the 1970s involved a particular type of activism associated with consumer protection; further, the 1979–1981 controversy was directed against this activism. Second, as we show in the Appendix, the one-dimensional representation holds substantial power for explaining actual congressional voting behavior during this period.

We locate legislator political support functions along this one-dimensional space in Figure 3.3. The status quo of the model represents an activist agency (that is, more activist than the median legislator's maximum support policy). The members on the subcommittee from the mid-1960s through the late 1970s are depicted as preferring an activist FTC. The comparative statics result derived above implies that, if the subcommittee changes from one dominated by pro-activists to anti-activists, then major policy reversals will occur. This is depicted in Figure 3.3 as a move from x^O above the median voter to x^* below the median voter. Because we do not have precise measurements of x^O and x^* relative to the median voter, x^M, our specific prediction takes the form of subcommittee preferences (and hence regulatory policy) moving from above the median (pro-activist) to below the median (anti-activist) prior to the 1979–1981 period of sanctions.

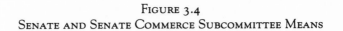

FIGURE 3.4
SENATE AND SENATE COMMERCE SUBCOMMITTEE MEANS

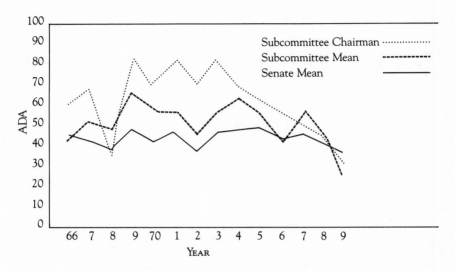

To demonstrate the plausibility of these predictions, we utilize summary statistics about the revealed preferences of those on the FTC oversight subcommittee in the Senate (the Subcommittee on Consumer Affairs of the Committee on Commerce) relative to the entire Senate. Specifically, we use the individual senators' liberal support scores (ADA rating). The higher the score, the greater the support for FTC activism. Using logistic techniques to predict the probability of a pro-activist vote, we can correctly predict 82 percent of individual senator votes solely on the basis of their ADA scores.

The evidence supports our interpretation. The composition of the committee in 1979 differed markedly from the composition prior to 1977. These differences, relative to the entire Senate, are exactly the form necessary for the theory. In Figure 3.4 we have plotted the mean ADA score for the entire Senate, for the Consumer Affairs Subcommittee, and for the subcommittee chairman during the period 1966–1979. Figure 3.5 depicts the standardization scores where the Senate mean is standardized to 50 in each year and the ADA scores are adjusted by the same factor. This standardization reveals qualitative changes more easily. The figures clearly show that the subcommittee mean was greater than the Senate mean throughout the period 1966–1976; the subcommittee variable began falling in 1977, so by 1979 the subcommittee mean fell below the Senate mean. For the period 1966–1977, the average Senate mean was 44 (with a standard deviation of 4.5). The average subcommittee mean for

FIGURE 3.5
STANDARDIZED MEANS

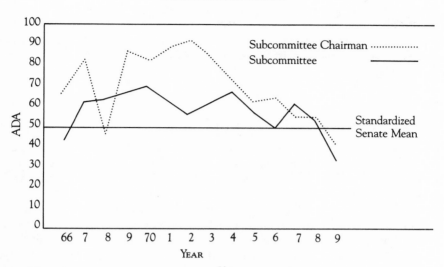

NOTE: Standardized Subcommittee mean$=\dfrac{50}{\text{Senate Mean}}\times$subcommittee mean.

the same period was 55 and is two standard deviations above the average Senate mean. Between 1977 and 1979, the Senate mean fell from 45.5 to 37.5, about one and a half standard deviations, while the subcommittee fell from 57.7 to 26.4, nearly seven times the standard deviation of the full Senate. Figures 3.4 and 3.5 also show that the same pattern occurred for the subcommittee chairman. The average ADA for the chairman was 65 (1966–1977); by 1979 it had fallen to 32.

What was responsible for this dramatic change in subcommittee preferences? It occurred following the nearly complete turnover in the subcommittee in 1977. None of the mainstays of the subcommittee over the previous decade were on the subcommittee. Table 3.1 compares the membership of the subcommittee (along with the number of years of continuous subcommittee service) in 1976 with that in 1977. The table demonstrates that the five senators with the highest seniority (eight years or more), including two of the major consumerist figures in the Senate (Moss and Hart), were no longer on the subcommittee in 1977. None of those with a moderate level of seniority (four to five years) returned, and only two of the five with the lowest level of seniority returned to the committee, where they became the ranking members.[35]

The analysis shows that the condition necessary for the comparative statics result holds. Interpreting ADA scores as an index of preference of FTC activism, committee preferences moved from well above average on this dimension to well below average. Since the latter represented a marked change in committee preferences from pro-activist to anti-activist, it follows from our model that the committee would alter regulatory policy. In these terms, the 1979–1981 changes at the FTC were the result of the new subcommittee members halting the activist commission policies launched by their predecessors rather than an instance of their catching a runaway, uncontrollable bureaucracy.[36]

Testing the Hypothesis of Congressional Influence

In this final empirical section, we test the proposition that the congressional oversight subcommittees and their chairmen dominate the activities undertaken by the FTC. If Congress significantly and regularly influences regulatory agencies, then we should observe its effect on the FTC's operational decisions. Both views discussed above agree that Congress wielded significant influence after 1979, but it remains unsettled whether Congress influenced the FTC before that time. Therefore, we investigate the relationship between Congress and the agency during 1964–1976.

One of the key policy instruments available to the FTC is its choice of cases. By allocating greater resources to particular categories of cases (that is, by emphasizing the enforcement of some statutes over others), the FTC determines its impact on the economy. The commission can emphasize the protection of small businessmen by pursuing Robinson-Patman cases. It can avoid controversy by pursuing trivial cases under the various fur, wool, and textile laws, or it can promote consumerism by pursuing cases under the many new consumer-protection programs such as the advertising substantiation program. In the late 1960s, the innocuous nature of the commission's caseload was a source of substantial criticism,[37] whereas in the late 1970s the agency was maligned because it championed more substantial cases. In sum, the distribution of cases brought before the commissioners constitutes an important FTC policy instrument. To evaluate the congressional influence on agency behavior, therefore, we test for the influence of congressional preferences over the distribution of cases.

Because the set of alternatives open to the commission is categorical, logit analysis is the appropriate empirical tool.[38] Logit analysis can be used to test congressional influence over the FTC caseload by choosing one category of cases as the "benchmark" category and then seeing whether the frequency of opening a case in another category, relative to the benchmark, changes with respect to the independent variables. On the one hand, if the FTC exercises discretion (and is an unresponsive bureaucracy), then we should observe little or no systematic influence of congressional control variables on the case

TABLE 3.1
SUBCOMMITTEE TURNOVER, 1976–1977
(SUBCOMMITTEE ON CONSUMER AFFAIRS
OF THE SENATE COMMERCE COMMITTEE)

Member	NUMBER OF YEARS OF SUBCOMMITTEE SERVICE[a]	
	1976	*1977*
Moss	10[b]	—
Hart	9[c]	—
Pastore	12	—
Hartke	12	—
Inouye	8	—
Beall	5	—
Cannon	4	—
Tunney	4	—
Stevenson	4	—
Weiker	2	—
Buckley	2	—
Baker	2	—
Durkin	2	3
Ford	2	3[b]
Melcher	—	1
Packwood	—	1
Danforth	—	1
Average Years Continuous Service	5.3	1.8

NOTES: a. Data on subcommittee assignments are from the *Congressional Quarterly Almanac* for each year and are verified through assorted publications from hearings during relevant years.

b. Chairman.

c. Vice-chairman.

distribution. On the other hand, if Congress significantly affects the direction of agency policymaking, then the congressional variables should have a statistically significant influence on the odds of bringing different cases. Furthermore, as preferences on the oversight committee change, we should see the relative odds of a given category change.

The structural model for the tests assumes that agency officials make choices to maximize some goal, U, where U is a function of the agency's decisions over its caseload distribution, C, as well as other variables. In the case of the congressional control formulation, other variables include congressional rewards, R, and a shift parameter, $\propto$, that allows the reward structure to

TABLE 3.2

CASES BROUGHT BEFORE THE COMMISSION, 1964–1976

Case Category	Number	Percentage
Robinson-Patman (Clayton Act, Section 2)	228	8.4
Exclusive Dealings (Clayton Act, Section 3)	5	0.2
Mergers (Clayton Act, Section 7)	111	4.1
Interlocking Directors (Clayton Act, Section 8)	21	0.8
Restraint of Trade (FTC Act, Section 5)	139	5.1
Deceptive Practices (FTC Act, Section 5)	984	36.0
Drug and Cosmetic Advertising (FTC Act, Section 12)	53	1.9
Fur, Wool, and Textile (Fur Act, Wool Act, Textile Act)	664	24.3
Flammable Fabrics (Flammable Fabrics Act)	233	8.5
Credit (Truth-in-Lending Act; Fair Credit Reporting Act)	291	10.7
Total	2729	100.0

SOURCE: FTC, *Federal Trade Commission Decisions* (Washington, D.C.: GPO, for years relevant above).

vary as the preferences of the rewarders (that is, the committee members) vary. Thus, $U = U(C, R; \infty)$. The alternative specification is one in which an agency remains independent of Congress. Here, the agency pursues some goals, $U(C)$, which is not directly influenced by Congress. The test between these specifications may be derived from estimations of the first structure. If congressional rewards are important, then rewards and shifts should statistically influence observed choices. Alternatively, if the second specification is correct, then congressional rewards should not be an important determinant of the relative odds of bringing a particular type of case. More important, the year-to-year variations in committee preferences should not affect agency choice.

The data for this test consist of the set of cases considered by the FTC between 1964 and 1976 (see Table 3.2). For our purposes, the case occurs in the year in which it was reviewed by the five commissioners.[39] The categories of case classification in our data set correspond to sections of the major acts enforced by the FTC, and therefore they are quite broad. For example, all mergers under the Clayton Act, section 7, are in one category, as are all deceptive practice cases under the FTC Act, section 5. Because we have data only on the total number of cases per category, we will not observe certain shifts, for example, if the FTC shifts its emphasis from trivial to substantial merger cases, yet the number of cases remains constant.

Although this is a relatively coarse filter, we may nonetheless observe major shifts in emphasis by studying certain changes in this distribution. We thus test our specific hypotheses on a subsample of all cases that are relatively homogeneous and about which we can make specific hypotheses concerning the direction of change. These are those cases falling under the Truth-in-Lending Act or the Fair Credit Reporting Act, which we call credit cases; those falling under the fur, wool, or textile statutes, which we call textile cases; and those falling under Clayton section 2 as amended by the Robinson-Patman Act, which we call Robinson-Patman cases. For the benchmark, we have used cases under Clayton section 7 (mergers), which is the most stable of all categories.[40] These categories represent 47 percent of the 2,729 cases considered by the FTC during this period.

We estimate the probability of a case occurring under one of the three categories, relative to the benchmark, as a function of the following variables: House subcommittee chairman ADA score; House subcommittee ADA mean (subcommittee chairman excluded); House mean ADA (subcommittee excluded); Senate subcommittee chairman ADA; Senate subcommittee mean ADA (chairman excluded); Senate mean ADA (subcommittee excluded); and an FTC budget variable. Notice that by including three separate variables for each body of Congress, we can separate out the influence of the subcommittee and its chairman from the rest of the house. The budget variable is constructed so as to measure the independent influence of the Appropriations Committee.[41]

The coefficients from the estimation describe the effects of the independent variables on the probability of bringing a given type of case relative to the probability of bringing a merger case. Moreover, the availability of credit cases only after 1969 (the statute was not passed until then) can be directly provided for within this framework.[42] The coefficients were estimated using a maximum likelihood function corresponding to our model under the assumptions of logit analysis.[43]

We evaluate the results that follow on three levels. The first concerns statistical significance. If congressional preferences are important, then the ADA scores should be statistically significant. Similarly, if the congressional reward system is an important influence over case distribution, then one of the major tools for this purpose, the budgetary allocation, should show up significantly.[44]

The second evaluation concerns the direction of change. We have hypothesized that higher ADA scores imply greater preferences for FTC activism. Therefore, as ADA scores rise, we expect a greater proportion of cases consistent with this activism and fewer cases of the type that dominated the FTC during the 1950s and early 1960s. The three categories chosen allow us to test these predictions. The Truth-in-Lending Act was hailed as a "consumer bill of rights" upon passage, and cases under this provision became an integral component of the FTC's consumer-protection program. Therefore, higher subcommittee ADA scores should be associated with a greater proportion of credit cases. Second, textile and Robinson-Patman cases were a prominent feature of the commission during the 1950s and early 1960s.[45] We hypothesize that this decline is related to congressional preferences for more activist cases. Therefore, we test whether the proportion of these cases is negatively associated with higher subcommittee ADA scores.

The final level of evaluation concerns the importance of the oversight subcommittees and their chairmen relative to their respective chambers. The legislative choice model predicts that the subcommittee and the subcommittee chairman should have a greater impact on agency decisions than the full chamber. The Senate variables are of particular interest because the activists were primarily in the Senate (that is, Magnuson, Moss, Hart, and the entrepreneurial staff director, Pertschuk) and because the major subcommittee turnover occurred in the Senate. Thus, in what follows, we are interested in both the statistical significance of the variables and whether they have the potential for drastically affecting the distribution of cases when major shifts in preferences are observed, as occurred between 1977 and 1979. Unless we can show that these shifts in preferences result in large changes in caseload distribution, we will have trouble arguing that committee preferences play an important role in agency policymaking.

Results

We report our estimation in Table 3.3. The results provide substantial evidence for the legislative control model as well as for the specific hypothesis about the relative influence of the subcommittees. In all three cases, the Senate variables are highly significant and the House subcommittee variables are important for two of the three categories. Moreover, the budget variable representing the influence of the Appropriations Committee was significant in all three cases. While the Senate is of the opposite sign from the subcommittee for Robinson-Patman and textile cases, the Senate subcommittee variables are of the predicted sign in five out of six cases, as are those House subcommittee variables coefficients that are statistically significant. The model x^2 is also highly significant. Finally, these results are robust across other specifications (not reported).

To determine the relevance of these estimates for FTC behavior, and hence our hypotheses, we calculate in Table 3.4 the partial derivatives of the probability of opening a particular type of case. This allows us to assess the impact of a change in the congressional variables for commission responses. The entries in Table 3.4 show the effect of a one-point change of each of the congressional ADA scores on the probability of opening a particular type of case. Under credit, for example, a one-point increase in the Senate ADA mean increases the probability of opening a credit case by .14.

Using Table 3.4, we can assess the relative impact of the subcommittee

TABLE 3.3

COEFFICIENTS FROM FOUR-CATEGORY LOGIT ANALYSIS

(*t*-VALUES IN PARENTHESES)

$\chi^2(18)=910.00**$

Independent Variable	Credit	Textile	Robinson-Patman
Constant	−27.4**	5.35*	.0643
	(5.14)	(2.38)	(.0233)
Budget residual	−1.67**	−.276*	.386**
	(6.52)	(2.26)	(2.63)
House subcommittee mean ADA	.0362	−.126**	−.146**
	(.507)	(5.43)	(4.88)
House subcommittee chairman ADA	−.0252	−.0314*	−.0823**
	(1.01)	(2.09)	(3.82)
Senate mean ADA	.639**	.190**	.461**
	(4.43)	(3.78)	(6.53)
Senate subcommittee mean ADA	−.258**	−.0556**	−.0520*
	(4.07)	(2.90)	(2.33)
Senate subcommittee chairman ADA	.108*	−.0287**	−.0801**
	(2.19)	(3.02)	(5.22)

NOTES: * indicates significant at the .05 level.

** indicates significant at the .01 level.

versus the rest of the Senate. Consider textile cases. For the three Senate variables, a one-point increase in ADA scores leads to the following changes in probability of a textile case: Senate, .041; the subcommittee, −.012; and the subcommittee chairman, −.006. Although the absolute value of the Senate effect is larger than either the subcommittee or its chairman, this does not reflect its relative influence. To see this, we calculate the effect of a ten-point increase in ADA score of a senator not on the subcommittee (an estimate for a one-point increase in the latter appears on the table in parentheses below the Senate estimate) and for a member on the subcommittee (in parentheses below the subcommittee effect). Using these figures, we see that a ten-point increase in a member not on the committee leads to a .005 increase in probability of opening a textile case. However, a ten-point increase of a member of the subcommittee leads to a .013 decrease; and a ten-point increase in the score of the subcommittee chairman leads to a .06 decrease in probability. Thus, a member of the subcommittee is more than two and a half times as influential as a nonmember, while the subcommittee chairman has twelve times the influence. As Table 3.4 indicates, this pattern holds for each type of case.[46]

Finally, we can use the estimations in Table 3.3 to calculate the implied

TABLE 3.4

PARTIAL DERIVATIVE OF THE PROBABILITY OF A GIVEN CASE TYPE

(CALCULATED AT MEANS OF ALL INDEPENDENT VARIABLES)

Partial Derivative with respect to:	Credit	Textile	Robinson-Patman
House subcommittee ADA mean	.008	−.027	−.023
House subcommittee chairman ADA	−.006	−.007	−.013
Senate ADA mean	.140	.041	.074
[one senator][a]	[.0016]	[.0005]	[.0008]
Senate subcommittee ADA mean	−.057	−.012	−.008
[one subcommittee member][b]	[−.0061]	[−.0013]	[−.0009]
Senate subcommittee chairman ADA	.024	−.006	−.013

NOTES: a. Not on the subcommittee.

     b. Not the chairman.

effect of the change in the independent variables for changes in case proportions. These calculations are reported in Tables 3.5 and 3.6 and demonstrate that the effect of the 1976–1979 changes in the congressional preferences leads to drastic changes in FTC caseload and that these changes are in the predicted direction. Table 3.5 reports the changes from 1976 to 1979 for all congressional variables in Table 3.3. Table 3.6 reports the predicted probabilities of opening each type of case, evaluated at the ADA scores of 1976 and of 1979, and then calculates the predicted changes. Recall that we predicted that falling subcommittee ADA scores would lead to a lower relative frequency of credit cases but higher relative frequency of Robinson-Patman and textile cases. These predictions are borne out by the estimations. Credit falls from .33 to .04, textile increases from .34 to .66, and Robinson-Patman increases from .14 to .28. The predicted change magnitudes are large and are consistent with the hypotheses about congressional influence and ADA scores, FTC activism, and caseload.

Inferences

The evidence provided by our estimations of the relationship of congressional ADA scores and agency budgets to the FTC caseload reveals substantial congressional influence. Our conclusions are: First, the subcommittee variables are generally statistically significant and of the correct sign. Second, the results show that, during the period studied, the Senate was more important than the House (in terms of both the magnitudes of effects and the pattern of statistical significance). Third, the Senate subcommittee and its chairman

TABLE 3.5
CHANGES IN ADA SCORES FROM 1976 TO 1979
(NEGATIVE SIGN INDICATES A DECREASE IN ADA)

Full House	0.25
House subcommittee	−11.31
House subcommittee chairman	4.0
Full Senate	−5.0
Senate subcommittee	−24.75
Senate subcommittee chairman	−28.0

TABLE 3.6
CHANGES IN PREDICTED PROBABILITIES DUE TO 1976–1979 ADA CHANGES

	Credit	Textile	Robinson-Patman
Predicted probabilities, 1976	.33	.34	.14
Predicted probabilities, 1979	.04	.66	.28
Total predicted change	−.29	+.32	+.14

NOTE: Budget residual for 1979 assumed equal to that in 1976.

have a greater impact than the full Senate. Fourth, the implied impact of the changes from 1976 to 1979 in the Senate yields dramatic shifts in relative caseloads. Thus, the 1976–1979 changes in the Senate subcommittee are large enough to result in dramatic shifts in agency decisions. This evidence supports our hypothesis that Congress may influence agency choices without systematic, continuous, and publicly held oversight hearings. The evidence also implies that the FTC is remarkably sensitive to changes in the composition of its oversight subcommittee and in its budget. As a consequence, this evidence is inconsistent with the traditional view of bureaucratic insulation from Congress. Moreover, it provides support for the specific predictions of the legislative choice model concerning the influence of congressional committees.

CONCLUSIONS

The perspective on the Congress provided in this paper cautions against equating the absence of active monitoring with congressional ineffectualness in controlling bureaucratic agencies. Congressional institutions, including interest groups and a variety of *ex post* sanctions, afford considerable influence. These institutions, moreover, allow congressmen to economize on monitoring costs and specialize in other activities more profitable for their own private objectives. This argument parallels that in the literature on the separation of ownership and control in which shareholders need not actively monitor the day-to-day performance of managers because market institutions allow share-holders to remain ignorant.

Two conclusions follow from this perspective. First, because the actions of Congress under this system appear to be precisely the same as those under a system in which Congress has no influence, we cannot conclude that the absence of congressional monitoring is evidence against legislative control. Second, the evidence typical of case studies is therefore also consistent with the congressional control model. As a consequence, tests between these views must take place on other terms. We therefore developed a model of regulatory policymaking under the hypothesis that Congress controls agencies. The model allows comparative statics results from which we derived specific hypotheses about the nature of congressional influence on regulatory change. If observed, these changes could not be explained by the traditional approach. The analysis then turned to the case of the FTC, which seemed suited for the traditional interpretation. A closer inspection, however, revealed significant and important influences by the relevant congressional subcommittees. Furthermore, the form taken by this influence was precisely that predicted by the comparative statics results developed in the theoretical section.

Our specific conclusions derive from studying the FTC prior to the sanctions in 1979 and 1980. Nearly all observers agree that Congress actively intervened in the commission's activity in 1979. The issue is whether the agency followed the interests of Congress over the decade prior to the sanctions. The model of legislative choice outlined above showed that congressional influence before the sanctions was consistent with the sanctions because the members on the subcommittee imposing the sanctions had preferences markedly different from those members who composed the subcommittee during the previous period.

The second series of tests directly addressed our two hypotheses of congressional control. We studied a major commission policy variable: its choice over the distribution of cases across various laws. The results show that FTC activity is remarkably sensitive to changes in the subcommittee composition. In addition, the evidence reveals the greater influence of the relevant oversight subcommittees as compared to the rest of the body. Despite the political rhetoric about a runaway, uncontrollable bureaucracy bringing on the 1979–1980 sanctions, the evidence supports our interpretation that these sanctions reflected the new subcommittee's efforts to reverse the policies of their predecessors.[47]

Several tentative generalizations follow from this study. First, the results suggest that the same may also be true for other agencies: on the surface, little ostensible activity by Congress may mask more subtle but nonetheless strong congressional influence. Lack of regular congressional monitoring may reflect the smoothly working congressional system in which intensive monitoring is unnecessary. Second, the evidence also suggests that congressional institutions play important roles in agency decisions. It is not the entire Congress that seems of most interest but rather the specific committees. No doubt more refined models will yield more specific predictions about policymaking.

APPENDIX
DATA SOURCES

The ADA scores are coded for each senator from 1963 to 1979. The data are taken from assorted issues of ADA World and Annual Voting Record Supplements published by Americans for Democratic Action.

For each year, means, medians, and standard deviations are calculated for the Senate, the Senate Commerce Committee Subcommittee on Consumer Affairs, and the chairman of the subcommittee; the House, the House Committee on Interstate and Foreign Commerce subcommittee overseeing the FTC, and its chairman. The committee and subcommittee assignments are from the Congressional Quarterly Almanac for each year and are verified through assorted publications from hearings during the relevant years.

Data on the annual FTC budget and the total federal budget are from the Budget of the United States Government, Appendix, fiscal years 1964–1977.

Finally, data on the number of cases brought before the commission each year are from FTC Decisions (Washington, D.C.: U.S. Government Printing Office).

The six roll-call votes and sources are:

1965:   Neuberger amendment to the Federal Cigarette Labeling and Advertising Act, providing a one-year prohibition against imposition by the FTC of any requirements that cigarette advertising contain health warnings (rather than the three-year prohibition contained in the bill). Rejected 29–49. Congressional Quarterly Almanac, Senate vote 118, 1965, p. 1050.

1968:   Cotton amendment deleting from the Deceptive Sales Act the FTC's authority to seek temporary restraining orders in deceptive practices cases. Accepted 42–37. Congressional Quarterly Almanac, Senate vote 171, 1968, p. 37-S.

1971:   Hruska amendment to delete Title II of the Magnuson-Moss Warranty and FTC Improvements Act, which expanded the FTC's powers. Rejected 24–57. *Congressional Quarterly Almanac*, Senate vote 265, 1971, p. 45-S.

1974:   Senate vote on the Magnuson-Moss Warranty and FTC Improvements Act. Accepted 70–5. *Congressional Quarterly Almanac*, Senate vote 539, 1974, p. 82-S.

1980a: Amendment allowing a one-house veto of the FTC's rules. Rejected 44–53. *Congressional Quarterly Weekly Report*, Senate vote 35, February 9, 1980, p. 363.

1980b: Amendment to restore the FTC's authority to continue its rulemaking proceedings on children's television. Rejected 30–67. *Congressional Quarterly Weekly Report*, Senate vote 38, February 9, 1980, p. 364.

NOTES

1. Roger G. Noll, "Governmental Regulatory Behavior: A Multidisciplinary Survey," in Roger G. Noll, ed., *Regulatory Policy and the Social Sciences* (Berkeley: University of California Press, 1985), pp. 14–15.

2. Elsewhere, we develop at length the analysis on which this conclusion is based. See Randall L. Calvert and Barry R. Weingast, "Congress, the Bureaucracy, and Regulatory Reform," Mimeographed (St. Louis, Mo.: Center for the Study of American Business, Washington University, 1980), and Randall L. Calvert, Mark J. Moran, and Barry R. Weingast, "Congressional Influence over Policymaking: The Case of the FTC," Mimeographed (St. Louis, Mo.: Washington University, November 1984). See also Noll, "Governmental Regulatory Behavior."

3. In the language of agency theory, the issue concerns the relationship between the principal (Congress) and its agent (the regulatory agency). The traditional approach argues that because little monitoring takes place, considerable shirking occurs—so much so that it is best to ignore the influence of the principal on agent decisions. The congressional dominance view, as discussed below, argues that there exists an *ex post* sanction mechanism that punishes agencies not serving congressional interest and rewards those that do so. To the extent that this system works well, *ex post* consequences provide appropriate *ex ante* incentives, and hence few actual punishments need take place for the threat to be effective. Hence, the "observational equivalence" arises because both views can "explain" the absence of monitoring. Thus, the issue of congressional control of the bureaucracy has many of the same issues present in the debate over separation of ownership and control: little ostensible interest on the part of shareholders is consistent with (1) considerable managerial discretion, and (2) a strong set of incentive mechanisms that obviate the need for direct shareholder monitoring. For an elaboration of this view, see Barry R. Weingast, "The

Congressional-Bureaucratic System: A Principal-Agent Perspective (with Applications to the SEC)," *Public Choice* 44 (1984): 147–91.

4. For further development of this approach, see references in note 2 above. Adherents to this view include James E. Anderson, *Public Policy Making* (New York: Praeger, 1975); Lawrence C. Dodd and Richard L. Schott, *Congress and the Administrative State* (New York: John Wiley and Sons, 1979); James Q. Wilson, "The Rise of the Bureaucratic State," *The Public Interest* 41 (1975): 77–103; James Q. Wilson, ed., *The Politics of Regulation* (New York: Basic Books, 1980); and Francis E. Rourke, *Bureaucracy, Politics, and Public Policy*, 2d ed. (Boston: Little, Brown, 1976), as well as the older public administration theorists such as Herbert Kaufman, "Why Organizations Behave as They Do: An Outline of a Theory," *Administrative Theory* (1961): 37–73. With specific reference to the FTC, see Kenneth W. Clarkson and Timothy J. Muris, "The Federal Trade Commission and Occupational Regulation," in Simon Rottenberg, ed., *Occupational Licensure and Regulation* (Washington, D.C.: American Enterprise Institute, 1981); Kenneth W. Clarkson and Timothy J. Muris, eds., *The Federal Trade Commission Since 1970: Economic Regulation and Bureaucratic Behavior* (Cambridge, Eng.: Cambridge University Press, 1981); Robert A. Katzmann, *Regulatory Bureaucracy: The Federal Trade Commission and Antitrust Policy* (Cambridge, Mass.: MIT Press, 1980); and Robert A. Katzmann, "Federal Trade Commission," in Wilson, *Politics of Regulation*.

5. Dodd and Schott, *Congress*, p. 2.

6. Wilson, *Politics of Regulation*, pp. 388, 391.

7. Adherents to this view fall into various camps. In the economics literature, George Stigler, "The Theory of Economic Regulation," *Bell Journal of Economics and Management Science* 2 (1971): 3–21, and Sam Peltzman, "Toward a More General Theory of Regulation," *Journal of Law and Economics* 19 (August 1976): 211–40, do not distinguish between the agency and the legislature presumably because of the close connection. This assumption is explicitly made by William L. Cary, *Politics and Regulatory Agencies* (New York: McGraw-Hill, 1967); Louis M. Kohlmeier, Jr., *The Regulators* (New York: Harper and Row, 1969); Peter Aranson, "The Uncertain Search for Regulatory Reform," Working Paper no. 79-3 (Law and Economics Center, University of Miami, 1979); Barry R. Weingast, "Regulation, Reregulation, and Deregulation: The Political Foundations of Agency-Clientele Relations," *Law and Contemporary Problems* 44 (1981): 147–77; Richard Barke and William H. Riker, "A Political Theory of Regulation with Some Observations on Railway Abandonments," *Public Choice* 39 (1982): 73–106; and Gary S. Becker, "A Theory of Political Behavior," Working Paper no. 006-1 (Center for the Study of the Economy and the State, University of Chicago, 1982). In addition, a second body of literature in political science largely independent of the bureaucracy literature also assumes direct alliance between agencies and their overseers (and their clientele). Scholars in this "subgovernments" literature include Roger H. Davidson, "Breaking Up Those Cozy Triangles: An Impossible Dream?" in Susan Welch and John G. Peters, eds., *Legislative Reform and Public Policy* (New York: Praeger, 1977); Theodore J. Lowi, *The End of Liberalism*, 2d ed. (New York: W. W. Norton, 1979); and Randall B. Ripley and Grace A. Franklin, *Congress, the Bureaucracy, and Public Policy*, 2d ed. (Homewood, Ill.: Dorsey Press, 1980). See also references in note 2 above.

8. In the budgetary process, the one to two thousand federal agencies face just thirteen subcommittees of the Appropriations Committee. Each subcommittee develops one bill that (as amended) becomes the actual federal budgetary allocation. This contrasts with William A. Niskanen, *Bureaucracy and Representative Government* (Chicago: Aldine-Atherton, 1971), in which he discusses the monopoly bureau. See Noll, "Governmental Regulatory Behavior."

9. Many observers have noted that the congressional constituency regularly exercises veto over nominations. See Cary, *Politics and Regulatory Agencies*; Kohlmeier, *The Regulators*; and Roger Noll, *Reforming Regulation: An Evaluation of the Ash Council Proposals* (Washington, D.C.: Brookings Institution, 1971). Finally, even Katzmann, *Regulatory Bureaucracy*, ch. 9, who argues that the confirmation hearings are perfunctory, reports how the Senate subcommittee virtually dictated appointments in the 1970s.

The last argument has important implications for recent claims that new policy directions are linked to changes in the nature of the types of experts that constitute agency management (see Hugh Heclo, "Issue Networks and the Executive Establishment," in Anthony S. King, ed., *The New American Political System* [Washington, D.C.: American Enterprise Institute, 1978], and Michael Levine, "Revisionism Revised? Airline Deregulation and the Public Interest," *Law and Contemporary Problems* 44 [1981]: 179–95). This observation is again consistent with both views. According to the traditional view, this is evidence of agency discretion since we can associate policy change with different types of managers. From the other standpoint, if Congress controls who gets appointed to agencies, then it controls which experts gain influence and control of agency management. Veto power over appointments implies that the only observable changes in agency management are those preferred by Congress and, thus, new and different managers are the means but not the cause of agency policy change.

10. U.S. Congress, Senate, Committee on Commerce, *Appointments to the Regulatory Agencies: The Federal Communications Commission and the Federal Trade Commission (1949–1974)*, Report prepared by James M. Graham and Victor H. Kramer, 94th Cong., 2d sess., 1976, Committee Print.

11. The approaches falling under this rubric vary considerably. For example, James Buchanan and Gordon Tullock, *The Calculus of Consent* (Ann Arbor: University of Michigan Press, 1962); John Ferejohn, *Pork Barrel Politics* (Stanford, Calif.: Stanford University Press, 1974); and Weingast, "Regulation, Reregulation, and Deregulation," all study voting explicitly; it remains implicit in Stigler, "Theory of Economic Regulation"; Peltzman, "Toward a More General Theory"; and Becker, "Political Behavior."

12. Stigler, "Theory of Economic Regulation"; Peltzman, "Toward a More General Theory." See also Mancur Olson, *The Logic of Collective Action: Public Goods and the Theory of Groups* (Cambridge, Mass.: Harvard University Press, 1965).

13. Kenneth Shepsle, "James Q. Wilson's 'The Politics of Regulation': A Review Essay," *Journal of Political Economy* (1982).

14. Weingast, "Regulation, Reregulation, and Deregulation"; Peltzman, "Toward a More General Theory"; Morris Fiorina, *Representatives, Roll Calls, and Constituencies* (Lexington, Mass: Lexington Books, 1974).

15. See Fiorina, *Representatives*; Richard Fenno, *Home Style* (Boston: Little, Brown, 1978); and especially Sam Peltzman, "Constituent Interest and Congressional Voting," Mimeographed (Chicago: Graduate School of Business, University of Chicago, 1982). Peltzman presents the most systematic empirical evidence for this proposition.

16. Kenneth A. Shepsle, *The Giant Jigsaw Puzzle: Democratic Committee Assignments in the Modern House* (Chicago: University of Chicago Press, 1978).

17. The evidence for this view is contained in Shepsle, *Giant Jigsaw Puzzle*; Richard Fenno, *Congressmen in Committees* (Boston: Little, Brown, 1972); and David R. Mayhew, *Congress: The Electoral Connection* (New Haven, Conn.: Yale University Press, 1974). Shepsle's probit results show that congressmen attain membership on those committees that they value the most. Fenno and Mayhew discuss the relationship between constituency interests and committee assignment.

18. In Peltzman's terms (see "Toward a More General Theory"), these functions are the legislator's political support functions derived from the interests in his district. As discussed in Weingast, "Regulation, Reregulation, and Deregulation," his approach is closely related to Fiorina, *Representatives*. The assumptions made by Peltzman guarantee that the political support functions are "single peaked," that is, with the shape depicted in Figure 3.1.

19. Technically, the conditions for equilibrium are

$P_c(x^o) \cap W(x^o) = \phi$, where

$P_c(x^o)$ is the set of policies preferred by the committee to x^o

and $W(x^o)$ is the set of points that command a majority against x^o.

See Kenneth A. Shepsle and Barry R. Weingast, "Structure Induced Equilibrium and Legislative Choice," *Public Choice* 37 (1981): 503–19, and Weingast, "Regulation, Reregulation, and Deregulation."

20. This analysis can be generalized in two ways: first, in a straightforward manner to any number of legislators; and second, with some modifications, to any number of dimensions.

21. Several different variables may change an equilibrium. See Weingast, "Regulation, Reregulation, and Deregulation," for additional types of comparative statics results that may be derived within this framework.

22. Actually, it is a point imperceptively close to x^*. We have chosen to ignore a technical limit argument here.

23. See, for example, the *National Journal*, October 13, 1979, or the *Wall Street Journal*, October 18, 1979. Most academic scholars also take the traditional view; see Clarkson and Muris, "The Federal Trade Commission" and *The Federal Trade Commission Since 1970*; Katzmann, *Regulatory Bureaucracy* and "Federal Trade Commission"; and Alan Stone, *Economic Regulation and the Public Interest: The Federal Trade Commission in Theory and Practice* (Ithaca, N.Y.: Cornell University Press, 1977). One important exception here is Ernest Gellhorn, "The Wages of Zealotry: The FTC Under Siege," *Regulation* 4 (January–February 1980): 33–40.

24. See James Singer, "The Federal Trade Commission—Business's Government Enemy No. 1," *National Journal*, October 13, 1979, pp. 1676–80.

25. *Wall Street Journal*, October 18, 1979.

26. Clarkson and Muris, *The Federal Trade Commission Since 1970*, p. 34.

27. See Robert A. Katzmann, *Regulatory Bureaucracy*, and Katzmann, "Federal Trade Commission."

28. A systematic review of the Senate hearings during the early 1970s reveals this parallel. Gellhorn, "Wages of Zealotry," also makes this point. Moreover, in William Kovacic's "The Federal Trade Commission and Congressional Oversight of Antitrust Enforcement: A Historical Perspective" (Chapter 4 of this volume), the author details the enormous attention afforded FTC antitrust activity during this period.

29. Gellhorn, "Wages of Zealotry."

30. Warren G. Magnuson and Jean C. Carper, *The Dark Side of the Marketplace: The Plight of the American Consumer* (Englewood Cliffs, N.J.: Prentice-Hall, 1968).

31. See Robert Pitofsky, "Beyond Nader: Consumer Protection and the Regulation of Advertising," *Harvard Law Review* 90 (1977): 661–701, for a report on this program and its relation to consumerism by the man who initiated it. For an economic analysis of this policy, see Ralph Winter, *The Consumer Advocate Versus the Consumer* (Washington, D.C.: American Enterprise Institute, 1972). Winter's paper contains one of the few economic analyses of the consumerist view and its policy implications. Although he focuses on the potential behavior of a Consumer Protection Agency, nearly all the policies he studies became part of the activist FTC during the 1970s.

32. For example, see Mark V. Nadel, *The Politics of Consumer Protection* (Indianapolis, In.: Bobbs, Merrill, 1971), and David E. Price, *The Commerce Committees: A Study of the House and Senate Commerce Committees* (New York: Grossman, 1975).

33. The FTC Improvements Act made these powers more explicit and less uncertain as to their legal basis. They were therefore less vulnerable to court challenges. By 1975 the agency no longer completely favored these changes, in large part because of the increased procedural burden.

34. To quote Gellhorn, "The Wages of Zealotry," p. 33: "The capstone for the consumer movement came three years ago, however—with the election of then Nader-favorite Jimmy Carter to the presidency and the subsequent appointment of consumer activist Michael Pertschuk as FTC chairman. As staff chief of the Senate Commerce Committee (then chaired by consumer champion, Warren G. Magnuson), Pertschuk was a principal architect of many federal consumer laws (including those expanding the FTC's powers) and seemed an ideal choice to lead the Commission into the 1980s."

35. Additional evidence for subcommittee stability and turnover is as follows. The chairman in 1976 had served for ten years (eight years as chairman), while the new chairman in 1977 had served only two previous years. During 1966–1976, the average percentage of members who were also on the subcommittee the previous year was 82 percent, but in 1977 this fell to 33 percent. Finally, the average subcommittee seniority (number of years consecutive service on the subcommittee) increased steadily during 1966–1976 to a high of 5.6 years, but fell to 1.7 years in 1977. Overall, these figures reveal a relatively stable subcommittee prior to 1977 and a massive turnover in 1977, leading to different subcommittee preferences.

36. Looking beyond 1979 to the present, the Senate subcommittee preferences appear to have shifted twice more. This raises some concern about the above interpretation. Notice, however, that during the early period, (1) the committee was stable from 1964 to 1976, and (2) FTC activism did not begin immediately following the first

committee change. The second committee change occurred in 1977, but the new committee took two years to begin implementing its policy reversals. Thus, because of the time lags needed for implementing major policy change (e.g., major cases take several years to investigate), the main impact of two swings in 1980 and 1981 may have been to reinforce commission inaction. Nonetheless, we would expect policy reversals to occur again if the swing toward high ADA scores is sustained over several years.

37. For example, throughout the 1950s and 1960s, the FTC was known for its strict enforcement of the various fur, wool, and textile labeling provisions; its role in antitrust was largely limited to such minor cases as the monopoly in bull semen or the decline in competition among gift shows in the Virgin Islands (see Price, *Commerce Committee*, p. 89). More generally, see the American Bar Association, *Report of the ABA Commission to Study the Federal Trade Commission* (Chicago, 1969) and Edward F. Cox, Robert C. Fellmeth, and John E. Schulz, *The Nader Report on the Federal Trade Commission* (New York: Richard W. Baron, 1969). See also Richard Posner, "The Federal Trade Commission," *University of Chicago Law Review* 37 (1969): 47–89, as well as Posner's dissenting opinion in the *Report of the ABA Commission*.

38. Paul L. Joskow, "The Determination of the Allowed Rate of Return in a Formal Regulatory Hearing," *Bell Journal of Economics and Management Science* 3 (1972): 632–44; Daniel McFadden, "The Revealed Preferences of a Government Bureaucracy: Theory," *Bell Journal of Economics and Management Science* 6 (Autumn 1975): 401–16; and Daniel McFadden, "The Revealed Preferences of a Government Bureaucracy: Empirical Evidence," *Bell Journal of Economics and Management Science* 7 (Spring 1976): 55–72.

39. A case proceeds through many stages within the FTC prior to coming before the five commissioners for review. Thus, a case "occurs" for us only when it reaches this last stage in the process within the commission. This stage was chosen for formal analysis because it is the final disposition of the FTC, because it is not simply a rubber stamp of what occurs in earlier stages, and finally, because the commissioners are likely to be the most sensitive to political pressure. We note, however, that results may be obtained for the critical administrative-law-judge stage that parallel the results reported below for the five commissioners.

40. McFadden has shown that the estimated probability of opening a particular type of case is independent of which case category is chosen as the benchmark. See Daniel McFadden, "Conditional Logit Analysis of Qualitative Choice Behavior," in Paul Zarembka, ed., *Frontiers in Econometrics* (New York: Academic Press, 1974).

41. The actual variable used was the residual from the following regression: FTC budget$_t = a + b$ADA$_t + c$Total Federal Budget$_t + \epsilon$. This equation predicts the FTC's budget as a function of preferences on the subcommittee and the total federal budget. The residuals from this regression should then capture the independent influence on FTC afforded by the Appropriations Committee.

42. McFadden, "Conditional Logit Analysis."

43. Our estimation takes into account the changing case categories—i.e., that credit cases were not feasible prior to 1969. To define the log likelihood function, let the set of cases, T, be indexed by t and the set of case types, K, be 1: mergers; 2: Robinson-Patman; 3: textile; 4: credit. Then define $I(t) = 1$ if $K = \{1, 2, 3\}$ (i.e., if t

occurs before 1970), and $I(t)=2$ if $K=\{1, 2, 3, 4\}$ (i.e., if t occurs after 1969). Then the probability of choosing case type k under $I(i)$ is

$$P_{kt}I(1)=\frac{e^{B_kX}}{1+\sum\limits_{j=2}^{3} e^{B_jX}}; \; P_{kt}I(2)=\frac{e^{B_kX}}{1+\sum\limits_{j=2}^{4} e^{B_jX}}.$$

Finally, the log likelihood function from which the coefficients B_j are estimated is

$$L=\sum\limits_{t|I(t)=1} \sum\limits_{k=2}^{3} R_{tk} \log P_{tk}I(t)+\sum\limits_{t|I(t)=2} \sum\limits_{k=2}^{4} R_{tk} \log P_{tk}I(t),$$

where $R_{tk}=1$ if case t is type k and 0 otherwise (see McFadden 1975, 1976).

44. Political scientists have long claimed that this is a major congressional control device over agencies; see Richard Fenno, *Power of the Purse: Appropriations Politics in Congress* (Boston: Little, Brown, 1966), and Aaron Wildavsky, *The Politics of the Budgetary Process*, 1st ed. (Boston: Little, Brown, 1964). Other scholars observing this process disagree—for example, Katzmann, *Regulatory Bureaucracy*, Clarkson and Muris, "The Federal Trade Commission," and Wilson, *Politics of Regulation*. However, to our knowledge, there exists no systematic test of this hypothesis beyond the sort of evidence that arises in case studies (which we criticized in the first section of this essay).

45. Others have observed a large decline in these two cases during the late 1960s and early 1970s; see *ABA Report* (1969) and Richard Posner, *The Robinson-Patman Act: Federal Regulation of Price Differences* (Washington, D.C.: American Enterprise Institute, 1976). For example, the number of complaints issued under the Robinson-Patman provisions averaged 106 per year from 1960–1964 and fell to 8.3 per year during 1965–1975. The falloff in fur, wool, and textile activity occurred around 1970. During 1964–1969, the commission reviewed an average of 78.5 cases per year, whereas the corresponding figure for 1972–1976 was 18.4 per year. Our statistics go beyond noting simple trends to relating these trends to causal factors.

46. Furthermore, the subcommittee scores are much more variable for the Senate mean. The standard deviation of the Senate subcommittee is twice that of the Senate, while that of the subcommittee chairman is more than four times the Senate score. Therefore, the effects of a one-point ADA change reported in Table 3.4 overstate the effects of the Senate because a one-point change in the latter is a much "bigger" change than a one-point for the subcommittee or its chairman.

47. The evidence provided for this conclusion illustrates a point made by Morris Fiorina in his "Bureaucratic (?) Failures: Causes and Cures" (Mimeographed, Publication no. 43 [St. Louis: Center for the Study of American Business, Washington University, 1981]): "One congressman's bureaucratic failure comes too close to another congressman's bread and butter." See also Fiorina, *Congress: Keystone to the Washington Establishment* (New Haven, Conn.: Yale University Press, 1977).

Chapter 4

The Federal Trade Commission and Congressional Oversight of Antitrust Enforcement: A Historical Perspective

WILLIAM E. KOVACIC

> [The Federal Trade Commission is] a passel of ideologues who are hostile to the business system, to the free enterprise system, and who sit down there and invent theories that justify more meddling and interference in the economy.
>
> David Stockman, Director,
> Office of Management and Budget[1]

IN a striking show of legislative anger, from 1979 through 1982 Congress entertained many proposals to constrict the law-enforcement role of the Federal Trade Commission (FTC). In 1980, after months of intense, widely publicized debate, Congress curtailed the agency's statutory authority, restricted several ongoing programs, and promised continuing, unrelenting scrutiny of the agency's operations.[2]

An important articulated basis for the 1980 legislation was Congress' perception that the commission had contradicted the legislature's policy

This paper first appeared in expanded form as "The Federal Trade Commission and Congressional Oversight of Antitrust Enforcement," *Tulsa Law Journal* 17 (1982): 587–671. The author is deeply grateful to Neil W. Averitt, Donald S. Clark, Kenneth M. Davidson, Kathryn M. Fenton, Albert A. Foer, David P. Frankel, James D. Hurwitz, John B. Kirkwood, Robert H. Lande, Robert J. Mackay, Thomas K. McCraw, Toby J. McIntosh, Ross D. Petty, Michael Pertschuk, and Barry R. Weingast for their useful comments.

preferences in selecting its law-enforcement programs in the 1970s. Representative William Frenzel pungently captured this view in 1979 as Congress debated bills to restrict the agency's activities:

> [T]he FTC is . . . a king-sized cancer on our economy. It has undoubtedly added more unnecessary costs on American consumers who it is charged with protecting, than any other half dozen agencies combined. It is bad enough to be counterproductive and therefore highly inflationary, but the FTC compounds its sins by generally ignoring the intent of the laws, and [by] writing its own laws whenever the whimsey strikes it . . . Ignoring Congress can be a virtue, but the FTC's excessive nose-thumbing at the legislative branch has become legend. In short, the FTC has made itself into virulent political and economic pestilence, insulated from the people and their representatives, and accountable to no influence except its own caprice.[3]

Congress' acute interest in the FTC came roughly a decade after the last comparable congressional assessment of the FTC's performance. In the late 1960s and early 1970s appropriations and oversight committees extensively analyzed the commission's work and recommended a fundamental reorientation of its efforts. They believed that the FTC, in its first half-century, had spent its resources largely on insignificant matters and had fallen unacceptably short of the goals Congress set for it in 1914. The committees generally prescribed a shift to innovative, aggressive enforcement strategies and cautioned that failure to do so would warrant the commission's abolition.

This essay discusses the FTC's response to congressional oversight of its antitrust activities in the 1970s. It begins by reviewing the 1969 *Report of the American Bar Association Commission to Study the Federal Trade Commission* (*ABA Report*), which drew congressional attention to the FTC's antitrust role and deeply influenced Congress' views in the early 1970s about the appropriate course of FTC competition work.[4] From a historical perspective, this paper examines the significance of political institutions and other forces outside the commission for the agency's ability to pursue the bar committee's central antitrust recommendation that the FTC devote its competition resources to economically important problems in complex, unsettled areas of law and economics.

The second half of this paper describes how, from 1969 to 1976, Congress directed the FTC toward more ambitious antitrust initiatives. It shows that strong congressional support for expansive, innovative enforcement endeavors peaked in 1976, after which congressional enthusiasm for some programs markedly declined. Through its analysis of the *ABA Report*, the historical influence of external institutions on FTC competition activities, and the substance of legislative oversight since 1969, the paper demonstrates that the

commission's antitrust programs of the 1970s were consistent with, and responsive to, congressional policy preferences.

THE *ABA REPORT*

On September 26, 1914, Woodrow Wilson concluded the chief antitrust
legislative initiative of his presidency by signing into law the Federal Trade
Commission Act.[5] With its elastic substantive mandate and broad grant of
investigatory powers, the statute embodied high congressional expectations
that the new commission would be a singularly effective tool for maintaining
competition. Three weeks before the bill's enactment, Senator Albert Cummins addressed the Senate in words that expressed the hopes of many of the
legislation's supporters:

> I predict that in the days to come the Federal [T]rade [C]ommission and its
> enforcement of the section with regard to unfair competition . . . will be
> found to be the most efficient protection to the people of the United States
> that Congress has ever given the people by way of a regulation of commerce
> . . . I look forward to its enforcement with a high degree of confidence.[6]

In the commission's first half-century, many commentators and special
committees appraised the agency's antitrust enforcement work. Most concluded that the FTC had accomplished little of what the 63d Congress
envisioned. Virtually every study stimulated attempts at reform, but few were
so influential—and none as significant for the modern commission—as the
ABA Report.

This study was initiated in 1969 at President Richard Nixon's request
months after a Ralph Nader–sponsored critique of the commission had drawn
widespread attention.[7] Severely critical of the agency's antitrust achievements,
the ABA still perceived a uniquely useful antitrust role for the FTC.[8] Anchor-
ing this view was the belief that the FTC had great potential to resolve
economically complex and unsettled competition policy problems.

Findings and Recommendations

The *ABA Report* analyzed the agency as a whole and examined each
operating bureau. This section reviews criticism relevant to antitrust enforcement, beginning with agency-wide functions that significantly affected the
FTC's competition work.

The ABA's overall evaluation of the agency was unfavorable. By any of
several tests, the FTC's performance was "disappointing" and "a failure on many

counts" (p. 35). According to the report, the agency's poor performance stemmed mainly from its failure to establish goals and priorities (p. 77). The FTC was said to have formulated objectives on an ad hoc basis only (p. 12),ʿ with faulty planning yielding "a misallocation of funds and personnel to trivial matters rather than to matters of pressing public concern" (p. 1). Even where the FTC had set priorities systematically, it ineffectively communicated these objectives to its staff (p. 13).

To cure these flaws, the ABA recommended that the FTC promptly "embark on a program to establish goals, priorities, and effective planning controls" (pp. 3, 77). An attractive approach would be an "immediate expansion and reinvigoration" of the FTC's existing planning apparatus, which would review long-range goals, measure anticipated returns from enforcement initiatives against their cost, and prepare "an agenda of projects that ought to be undertaken by each bureau and division . . . and indicate priorities with respect to each" (pp. 78, 80). By relying less on the "mailbag" and other "passive" case-selection tools, the project agenda would help correct the agency's "unfortunate tendency to involve itself in investigations and projects of marginal importance" (p. 80). To give this process practical effect, the planning office would write enforcement guidelines for the FTC's staff (p. 79).

A second basic defect, according to the report, was the commission's inability to manage its work "in an efficient and expeditious manner" (p. 1). The FTC's haphazard system for monitoring the progress of cases and investigations severely hampered attempts to bring enforcement efforts to a timely conclusion (pp. 15, 81). Moreover, the agency's procedures suffered from a "crippling delay," which the ABA found to be "about as serious . . . as at any time in the agency's history" (p. 34).

To reduce delay, the ABA *Report* proposed that the FTC systematically supervise the progress of cases and investigations (p. 81), review its procedural rules "to modernize and maximize the efficiency of the Commission's operations" (p. 84), and delegate more authority to its staff (pp. 3, 81–83). Beyond reducing delay, delegation would diminish the potential conflict the ABA perceived to exist when commissioners judged matters that had required their approval for commencement (pp. 82–83).

A third important source of ineffectiveness reportedly lay in the FTC's enforcement tactics. From enforcement statistics, the ABA discerned that "the FTC has resorted less frequently to formal proceedings, and has increased its reliance upon an 'informal' or 'voluntary compliance' approach to bring about industry-wide compliance" (pp. 8–9).[10] De-emphasis of formal enforcement had "gone too far," damaging the agency's enforcement credibility, and "voluntary compliance" was suspect without effective programs to ensure compliance (pp. 25–26). Accordingly, the ABA recommended greater use of compulsory enforcement proceedings and expanded efforts to check compliance with existing orders (p. 79).

Focusing on antitrust issues, the ABA called the FTC's performance in this area "less than satisfactory" and attributed its disappointing record largely to the agency's failure "to take advantage of the unique strengths conferred upon it by Congress...in 1914" (pp. 64–65).[11] With its investigatory powers, institutional expertise, jurisdictional flexibility, and equitable remedies, the FTC appeared ideally suited to address the mixed economic and legal issues that dominate antitrust.

Since 1914, however, the agency had seldom realized this potential. Merger enforcement aside, the ABA found few FTC accomplishments on the frontiers of antitrust law:

> If the measure of the quality of FTC performance in the antitrust area is whether the agency has broken new ground and made new law by resort to its unique administrative resources, it seems clear that the record is largely one of missed opportunity. However, the FTC did lead the way in implementation and interpretation of Section 7 of the Clayton Act. Moreover, that program has been carried out not simply by the institution of formal proceedings, but by the publication of economic reports and the promulgation of guides, *i.e.*, by use of the full panoply of administrative resources available to the FTC. (p. 65)

Expecting that the agency could repeat its merger enforcement "success" in other areas, the ABA recommended that the FTC retain its antitrust authority: "However well the federal judiciary may now be thought to be functioning in this area, there is an important role for the administrative process in solving difficult and complex antitrust questions" (p. 64). Because the FTC might apply the "full panoply" of its resources to break new ground and make new law in many "difficult and complex" areas, the ABA endorsed continued FTC antitrust responsibility (pp. 2, 65). This view is evident in the ABA's suggested future division of labor between the Department of Justice and the FTC:

> [T]he FTC should take no action in situations in which the conduct at issue, if challenged by the Department of Justice, would be likely to be challenged in a criminal proceeding. Cases of *per se* illegality, such as price-fixing, market allocation, and boycotts designed to enforce price-fixing cartels should thus be left to the Department of Justice...On the other hand, where issues of anticompetitive effects turn essentially on complicated economic analysis, and where decided cases have not yet succeeded in fashioning a clear line

marking the boundary between legal and illegal conduct, such matters should generally be assigned to the FTC. (p. 66)[12]

The ABA also proposed three specific changes in the FTC's antitrust programs. First, vertical restraints constituted one "complicated and economically significant" area in which the FTC had "foregone opportunities to participate in the constructive development of law that might contribute to the attainment of antitrust objectives" (p. 68). Second, the ABA said the FTC should expand its merger enforcement efforts (p. 69). Finally, the agency should "initiate a study and appraisal of the compatibility of the Robinson-Patman Act and its current interpretations to the attainment of antitrust objectives" and, during this appraisal, enforce the act only in "instances in which injury to competition is clear" (pp. 67–68).

The success of the ABA's recommended program depended on the quality of the FTC's leadership and staff, both of which the ABA found deficient (pp. 1, 34). The ABA acknowledged, however, that whether and how far the FTC would press its renewal were questions that only Congress and the president could answer:

[I]f the FTC is to fulfill the role we believe it can play, it must have the continuous vigorous support of the President and Congress. The first important manifestation of that support should be the appointment of a Commission Chairman with executive ability, knowledge of the tasks Congress has entrusted to the agency, and sufficient strength and independence to resist pressures from Congress, the Executive Branch, or the business community that tend to cripple effective performance by the FTC. (p. 35)

If Congress, the president, and the agency's own leaders did not pursue a comprehensive reform program, the ABA flatly favored the FTC's abolition:

In conclusion, this Commission believes it should be the last of the long series of committees and groups which have earnestly insisted that drastic changes were essential to recreate the FTC in its intended image. The case for change is plain. What is required is that the changes now be made, and in depth. Further temporizing is indefensible. Notwithstanding the great potential of the FTC in the field of antitrust and consumer protection, if change does not occur, there will be no substantial purpose to be served by its continued existence; the essential work to be done must then be carried on by other government institutions. (p. 3)

As this passage shows, the ABA was struck by the apparent similarity of its findings to earlier evaluations of the FTC.[13] The ABA's review of previous critiques suggested steadfast FTC resistance to needed change (p. 9).[14] At first glance, experience with the critical historical commentary indicated the futility of still another report that recited the same basic flaws and yet, like most of its predecessors, said the FTC should retain its antitrust authority. The crucial question was why the FTC had not heeded previous reform proposals. To be convincing, the ABA had to show why its recommendations might take hold where other critiques had apparently failed.[15]

The ABA suggested two reasons for the earlier commentaries' minimal effect. One was the tepid quality of previous FTC reform efforts. With exceptions, the ABA perceived a near contentment with unobtrusive law enforcement, interrupted by rare attempts to test the full potential of the FTC's charter (p. 10). Recognizing that some reform goals, such as effective planning, were intrinsically elusive, the ABA did not claim to have exhausted all possible explanations, short of outright neglect, for the agency's seeming disinclination to pursue significant antitrust matters (p. 15).[16] Nevertheless, the ABA concluded that the FTC, to an inexcusable degree, had merely shrugged off previous reform proposals. Lest its own views be ignored, the ABA said the appropriate alternative to serious reform was abolition.

Though doubting the commission's fortitude, the ABA indicated that frail institutional will was not the only reason for the scant discernable impact of earlier studies. The ABA intimated that forces outside the agency had deadened the FTC's reform impulses. This is why its report called for the appointment of a strong and independent chairman. The ABA made surprisingly little mention of the environment surrounding the FTC in 1969, but it necessarily seems to have assumed the willingness of actors outside the agency, particularly the president and Congress, to support the agency's rejuvenation.

External Influences on FTC Antitrust Performance

The FTC's history certifies that the attitudes and behavior of institutions outside the agency were indeed important to the ABA's reform proposals. The agency's relationships with the president, Congress, the judiciary, and the business community had all influenced the scope and quality of its antitrust endeavors. Drawing on major events in the agency's history, the balance of this section addresses several important events and trends that help explain the ABA's implicit view in 1969 that external circumstances favored the agency's antitrust transformation.

The Stature of Competition Policy.   Since 1914 the content of FTC antitrust enforcement has depended fundamentally on how dearly the country has valued competition over rival systems for organizing the nation's economy.[17] The antitrust laws embody, among other things, a social preference for the primacy of market forces and limited government supervision of the economy.[18] These measures, however, are neither the sole nor final expressions of national policy toward economic organization. For much of this century, they have coexisted with many other statutes and policies that either stress a greater government role in guiding economic activity or exempt various industries from the competition rules applying to business generally. As political scientist Pendleton Herring observed in 1936, the country's refusal to give competition policy a more certain endorsement hindered the FTC's antitrust work: "An agreed-upon policy concerning government regulation of industry has not yet been developed with the clarity or objectivity essential in establishing a basis for the free exercise of discretion by an independent commission. Vacillations as to fundamental policy have disrupted the career of the Federal Trade Commission."[19]

The question of competition's proper role in governing economic activity dates back to the FTC's very creation. The problem of monopoly occupied a prominent place in the presidential election campaign of 1912.[20] All three candidates—Taft, Wilson, and Theodore Roosevelt—addressed the issue, but attention focused mainly on Wilson's and Roosevelt's antitrust enforcement views.[21] Wilson proposed supplementing the Sherman Act with legislation banning the specific, illicit devices that enabled firms to achieve market power: "Our purpose is the restoration of freedom. We propose to prevent private monopoly by law, to see to it that the methods by which monopolies have been built up are legally made impossible."[22]

Roosevelt, the Progressive Party candidate, took a different tack. Viewing substantial industrial concentration as inevitable, he recommended that the federal government guide the great accumulations of private economic power toward public ends.[23] Roosevelt envisioned a federal commission with authority to regulate the issuance of securities; compel publication of company accounts; investigate any business activity; control hours, wages, and other conditions of labor; and set maximum prices for goods produced by monopolists who had attained their positions by honest means.[24]

Wilson denounced Roosevelt's industrial commission as an "avowed partnership between the government and the trusts" in which business interests would dictate national policy,[25] but his spirited objections placed him further away from Roosevelt than their views actually warranted.[26] To most observers in 1912, however, their ideas mirrored a deep ideological division among progressives over the correct approach to economic organization. Historian George Mowry defined the difference in these terms: "The one school cherished the competitive system with its individual values and feared the powerful state; the other welcomed concentrated power whether in industry or politics, looked to a paternalistic state staffed by an educated elite for leadership, and depreciated individualism."[27]

After defeating Roosevelt and Taft to gain the presidency, Wilson, in his original antitrust package, asked Congress to augment the Sherman Act with a roster of specific illegal practices and to create a new trade commission with advisory and investigatory powers—a concept that, at least in organizational form, resembled the Rooseveltian agency he had earlier derided. On the advice of Louis Brandeis and George Rublee, Wilson gradually came to support a commission with adjudicatory authority to apply a broad standard proscribing unfair competitive practices.[28]

At Wilson's urging, Congress put the expanded trade commission proposal atop its antitrust agenda. The legislators soon directly addressed the commission's role: should it promote competition policy or exercise public-utility regulation functions, including ratemaking? Congress firmly endorsed the former in passing the FTC Act.[29] The new agency's founders believed it would remove impediments to competition, but would not plan or coordinate the affairs of business. The commission's establishment, however, did not dismay disciples of Roosevelt who preferred pervasive business-government cooperation and central planning. For them the new agency might have other uses as well. Because the statute's terms were so broad, the FTC could supply a flexible instrument for joining government and business in a cooperative venture to direct the economy.[30]

The struggle between the competition and cooperation models most strongly affected the FTC's role from World War I through the late 1930s.[31] Central planning and cooperation made their first major inroads into U.S. economic policy during World War I.[32] The war mobilization virtually suspended antitrust enforcement and reoriented the FTC mainly toward information-gathering. Through the War Industries Board, the federal government exercised sweeping power over the country's economic activities by controlling priorities, allocation, and pricing.[33]

The mobilization provided the country's first major experiment in comprehensive economic planning and created a new class of leaders in government, business, and academia who felt government-business cooperation should be pursued in peacetime.[34] Following several unsuccessful efforts at the war's end to obtain a continuing formal relaxation of antitrust enforcement, these individuals focused their energies on the development of systems for industry self-regulation and business-government cooperation.[35] The principal patron of this "associationalist" movement was Herbert Hoover, who, as secretary of commerce and as president, encouraged the formation of trade associations and professional societies.[36] Hoover urged these groups to prepare codes of ethical business behavior, collect and disseminate data on production and inventories, and promote "product simplification" by reducing the number of sizes and types of goods.[37]

The FTC's activities in the 1920s strongly reflected the influence of associationalism.[38] The most important manifestation was the development of the trade-practice conference.[39] The commission initiated the conferences by inviting all firms in an industry to meet with a commissioner and members of the agency's staff to discuss practices within the trade. When a consensus of the conference participants opposed some business tactic, the conferees drafted resolutions banning the suspect practice. If the FTC approved the conferees' views, it classified the proposals as either "Group I" or "Group II" rules. The commission treated violations of Group I rules as prima facie violations of the FTC Act and sought cease-and-desist orders to halt them. For Group II rules, the FTC based its decision to prosecute on the circumstances of each claimed infraction.

From several meetings per year in the early 1920s, the trade conference became the agency's dominant enforcement approach by the decade's end.[40] Many commentators found the device a constructive means to understand business and promote commercial ethics without litigation.[41] For some, the FTC's reliance on the conferences displayed a healthy inclination to replace competition-preserving enforcement with associationalist policies.[42] For competition policy advocates, the conferences' effect hinged mainly on whether the FTC, in endorsing certain rules, was sanctioning collusion. By the late 1920s, however, the extreme retreat from formal litigation had diminished the commission's enforcement credibility.[43] Toward the end of that decade, the commission was routinely approving codes that effectively sanctioned price-fixing and other horizontal trade restraints.[44] Some codes so alarmed the Justice Department that in 1930 it called for the FTC to rescind provisions that seemed to violate Section 1 of the Sherman Act. The commission re-evaluated the codes and eventually deleted the suspect provisions.[45]

The war mobilization and the associationalism experiments of the 1920s gave the central planners important, limited tests of their theories. The economic collapse of 1929, however, provided a dramatic opportunity to sweep the competition model aside, perhaps permanently. This movement reached its peak in Franklin Roosevelt's first administration, which drew mainly on the country's war mobilization and associationalism experiences to stimulate recovery.[46]

The country embarked on an unprecedented program of peacetime economic planning in 1933 with the National Industrial Recovery Act (NIRA), the cornerstone of recovery efforts until 1935. The statute created the National Recovery Administration (NRA), which obtained codes of fair practice from each industry. Under the NRA's often casual review, businesses prepared and implemented codes covering, among other things, pricing and output.[47] By delegating power over price and production to industry trade groups, "the NRA created a series of private economic governments . . . The large corporations which dominated the code authorities used their powers to stifle competition, cut back production, and reap profits from price-raising rather than business expansion."[48]

Following a brief surge of enthusiasm accompanying its creation, the NRA swiftly fell into disfavor. Internal conflict among the cooperation advocates undercut NRA attempts to form and execute a coherent policy.[49] At the same time, supporters of antitrust enforcement relentlessly assailed the agency as a conduit for cartelization.[50] By the time the Supreme Court struck down the NIRA in 1935, the NRA was collapsing under its own weight. Until its official demise, however, the NIRA significantly affected the FTC's competition work. FTC and Justice Department antitrust enforcement virtually halted.[51] By the mid-1930s, said one observer, the FTC's chief function had become "preventing false and misleading advertising in reference to hair restorers [and] anti-fat remedies . . . a somewhat inglorious end to a noble experiment."[52]

The restoration of antitrust as an important national policy began in the late 1930s. In his second term, Roosevelt gave greater credence to the thinking of Felix Frankfurter, Benjamin Cohen, and Thomas Corcoran, who embraced the Brandeisian preference for active antitrust enforcement.[53] His appointment, in 1938, of Thurman Arnold as assistant attorney general triggered an unparalleled period of activity in the Antitrust Division. In five years, Arnold brought almost as many antitrust suits as the Justice Department had in the previous fifty.[54] The FTC also shared in this rejuvenation and began its most serious litigation initiative to that time—a comprehensive assault on basepoint pricing (discussed below in more detail).

The 1938 antitrust revival was a turning point for U.S. competition policy. The World War II mobilization blunted many antitrust cases launched before 1942, but the competition model would not again face a challenger as formidable as the early New Deal cooperation and planning programs. Competition policy emerged from the Great Depression with a degree of social support that made possible the comparatively stable, substantial government antitrust work of the postwar era.[55] While not all peacetime economic policy since 1938 has conformed to the competition model, competition policy has enjoyed comparatively broader support since 1938 than it did in the century's first decades. Thus, a recommendation in 1969 that the FTC strengthen its antitrust programs arguably had greater practical significance than one made 40 years earlier.

The Federal Judiciary.   A second important external factor shaping FTC antitrust enforcement has been judicial review.[56] The judiciary's influence on the commission's choice of competition programs emerged vividly in the courts' interpretation of the FTC's authority from 1914 to 1934. In creating an administrative agency to enforce the antitrust laws, Congress sought to ensure greater fidelity to its own competition policy goals.[57] This choice stemmed mainly from the Supreme Court's Standard Oil and American Tobacco decisions in 1911.[58] The court's adoption of the "rule of reason" standard showed that the Sherman Act's effectiveness depended greatly on how judges interpreted its general provisions.[59] Although some congressmen found the rule of reason standard substantively deficient, Congress' main concern in passing the FTC Act was the process through which the antitrust laws would be interpreted.[60]

Under Congress' plan, the judiciary was to determine whether the FTC's conclusions about the propriety of various business practices had evidentiary support. Courts were not to probe the wisdom of the commission's choice among policy alternatives where the agency's preference had sufficient evidentiary support. By this design, Congress intended the commission to account primarily to it, not the courts, for its policy decisions. Senator Cummins described how the proposed FTC statute would distribute authority among the agency, the judiciary, and the legislature:

> I would rather take my chance with a commission at all times under the power of Congress, at all times under the eye of the people, for the attention of the people is concentrated to a far greater degree upon the commission which is organized to assist in the regulation of commerce or to administer the law regulating commerce than it has upon the abstract propositions, even though they be full of importance, argued in the comparative seclusion of our courts.
>
> If we find that the people are betrayed either through dishonesty or through mistaken opinion, the commission is always subordinate to Congress . . . Congress can always destroy the commission; it can repeal the law which creates it.[61]

In adopting a relatively narrow standard of judicial review, Congress also sought to supply the institutional means with which to enhance the stature of the FTC's work. In Section 5 of the FTC Act, Congress had given the commission interpretational and adjudicatory responsibilities traditionally reserved for courts.[62] Congress expected the FTC's main tool for overcoming judicial opposition to this intrusion would be its competition policy expertise. This expertise would have essentially three sources: the commission's repeated exposure to antitrust problems; its authority to employ specialists of various backgrounds; and its extraordinary investigative and reporting powers.[63]

Congressional expectations received a serious blow in 1920 in the first commission case to come before the Supreme Court, Federal Trade Commission v. Gratz (253 U.S. 421). The court decided the case on a procedural issue, but proceeded to limit the act's ban on "unfair method[s] of competition":

The words "unfair method of competition" are not defined by the statute and their exact meaning is in dispute. It is for the courts, not the commission, ultimately to determine as matter of law what they include. They are clearly inapplicable to practices never heretofore regarded as opposed to good morals because characterized by deception, bad faith, fraud, or oppression, or as against public policy because of their dangerous tendency unduly to hinder competition or create monopoly. The act was certainly not intended to fetter free and fair competition as commonly understood and practiced by honorable opponents in trade. (pp. 427–28)

As applied by the courts in the 1920s, the Gratz decision virtually barred the commission's development of antitrust principles not already established by judicial interpretation. Although its bare terms were potentially generous in their implication that the commission could cover areas "heretofore regarded as opposed to good morals . . . or as against public policy because of their dangerous tendency unduly to hinder competition or create monopoly" (p. 427), Gratz deflected the FTC away from the pathbreaking initiatives that were a major reason for the agency's creation.[64]

The Supreme Court imposed a second damaging limitation on the FTC's powers in 1927 in Federal Trade Commission v. Eastman Kodak Co. (274 U.S. 619). One year before the Kodak suit, the court had ruled Section 7 of the Clayton Act inapplicable to asset acquisitions.[65] The commission sued Kodak under Section 5 to require the film company to divest three recently acquired processing plants. The court ruled that the FTC lacked divestiture power under Section 5.[66] By removing an essential remedy, the Kodak case prevented the commission from plugging the Clayton Act's assets loophole and, more generally, from having an important role in the areas of monopolization and attempted monopolization.[67]

Early court decisions also interpreted the FTC's investigative and reporting powers narrowly.[68] One set of cases barred investigations on the grounds that the FTC had sought data on manufacturing and production—activities the courts in this era often treated as exclusively "intrastate" commerce and thus beyond the FTC's jurisdiction.[69] A second, more important line of rulings prohibited the FTC from gathering information unrelated to alleged antitrust violations.[70]

Two principal theories explain the generally unsympathetic treatment the courts gave the commission in its first two decades. One is that the FTC failed to explain its decisions in full, narrative opinions and left the courts little basis for upholding the agency's judgment.[71] The agency's cryptic opinions and other infirmities in its operations, however, were probably not the dominant cause of its failures on appeal. The more likely decisive factor was the judiciary's distaste for economic regulation by legislative or administrative decree.[72]

Attempts to classify judicial attitudes for a given era risk oversimplification, but it is reasonable to say that the judiciary viewed economic regulation more tolerantly after the 1930s and afforded administrative tribunals greater latitude.[73]

Whatever their exact origin, the Supreme Court's interpretations of the commission's substantive, remedial, and investigative authority seriously retarded the agency's development of a distinctive antitrust enforcement role.[74] The judicially imposed restrictions forced the commission "to concentrate its energies within the narrow confines of the field of action set by the courts, and to refrain from a more experimental and venturesome exercise of its powers."[75] In antitrust, the FTC was left to work in terrain already largely explored by the Justice Department.[76]

Since the 1920s, the courts have either reversed or substantially modified the limitations imposed by Gratz, Kodak, and other early restricting interpretations of the agency's powers.[77] By 1969 the agency had obtained Supreme Court rulings construing its authority in a manner more consistent with congressional expectations in 1914. The court's affirmation in the mid-1960s of FTC authority to order divestiture under Section 5, and its endorsement of an expansive view of "unfair methods of competition," were particularly significant.[78] This trend gave reason to expect that the ABA recommendations would receive consideration in a judicial environment more favorable to ambitious FTC antitrust ventures than existed only a decade before.

The President.   More sympathetic courts by themselves would not have guaranteed that the early FTC would have used its authority effectively. Much depended on the agency's leadership. The president and Congress share responsibility for selecting commissioners, but the president has historically been the dominant force in choosing the FTC's leadership.[79] White House attitudes toward antitrust have deeply affected the course of FTC competition programs. The commission's first twenty years illustrate the importance of presidential antitrust preferences to FTC enforcement policy.

As a candidate and in the first two years of his presidency, Woodrow Wilson depicted himself as a foe of monopoly and special privilege. Soon after he signed the FTC Act, however, Wilson's position toward business and antitrust turned to the right. Consequently, Wilson's first appointments to the commission "gave dominance to men who had an anxious regard for the traditional concerns of business and finance."[80] To chair the new agency, he selected John Davies, a lawyer who had directed the Bureau of Corporations. Wilson also chose George Rublee, an attorney and Wilson adviser, and three men with business backgrounds, Edward Hurley, William Harris, and Will Parry.[81]

The first commission soon divided sharply over the direction it should take. Rublee and Harris favored antitrust litigation, while Hurley, Davies, and Parry preferred programs limited to advising businessmen of the legality of various anticipated acts.[82] The rift nearly paralyzed the agency. Seeking to establish a cordial relationship with the business community, the FTC did not issue its first complaint until February 1916, eleven months after it had officially opened its doors.[83]

Upon Rublee's departure and Hurley's elevation to chairman in 1916, the agency grew increasingly conservative. Hurley "devoted his talents to making the Commission useful to businessmen and to preaching the doctrine of cooperation between government and business . . . [U]nder his leadership, the Commission practically abandoned its role as watchdog of business practices."[84] Although many of the FTC Act's original supporters thought that giving guidance to business was worthwhile,[85] the degree to which Hurley stressed the FTC's purely advisory functions chagrined many who believed the agency's effectiveness as a promoter of competition policy rested heavily on the prosecution of antitrust suits.[86]

Wilson's appointments to the commission in his second term aligned the agency more closely with the preferences of congressmen who expected the FTC to be an effective antitrust enforcer. This shift, however, only partly compensated for the policies that guided the agency from 1915 to 1917. The first commission's inability to pursue a substantial antitrust enforcement program made the FTC appear ill-suited to perform its assigned competition policy role.[87]

The 1920 election of Warren Harding as president augured the beginning of an unparalleled period of government solicitude for business interests.[88] During the terms of Harding and his immediate successors, Calvin Coolidge and Herbert Hoover, two lines of thought molded presidential antitrust policies. The first was the associational view of business-government cooperation born in the World War I mobilization. Most closely identified with Hoover, associationalism promoted greater industry "self-regulation" under government guidance. A second, distinct strand of thought saw government's proper role as serving business interests as businessmen defined them. Harding embraced this ideal, but Coolidge became its foremost champion and "deliberately converted his administration into a 'businessman's government.'"[89]

Harding and Coolidge initially considered limiting the federal regulatory agencies, including the FTC, by modifying their statutory charters. Though no longer in control of Congress, progressives in both houses had sufficient strength to make this seem a Pyrrhic route.[90] Consequently, Harding and Coolidge turned to devices more directly under presidential control, including the appointment power.[91] Early in the 1920s, the FTC was led by the last Wilson appointees, who began several major initiatives, including the agency's controversial meatpacking industry study in 1919. With William Humphrey's appointment to the FTC in 1925, however, Coolidge achieved a working majority of commissioners who shared his views on the correct relation of government to business.[92]

As commissioner, Humphrey publicly denigrated the policies the agency had followed from the end of World War I until his appointment and declared his intention to "help business help itself."[93] Under Humphrey's influence, the commission imbued its enforcement programs with the values of Coolidge and the associationalists. One important step was increased use of trade-practice conferences, as discussed above.

Humphrey's influence also emerged in new procedures adopted soon after his appointment.[94] Among the most important were: (1) a declaration that the agency would settle all cases informally "except when the public interest demands otherwise"; and (2) a commitment that the FTC would neither announce the issuance of complaints "until after final determination of the case," nor make public matters settled informally before a complaint was filed.[95] In Humphrey's tenure, the rules reduced the number of compulsory enforcement proceedings and kept many formal complaints and consent agreements out of the public eye.[96]

For congressmen who supported active FTC antitrust enforcement in the 1920s, the appointment and confirmation of commissioners with disdain for the statute's original aims was a searing disappointment.[97] Some found Humphrey so disturbing that they called for the agency's abolition.[98] Humphrey's tenure, however, had graphically demonstrated how appointments could set the tone and content of commission policies. To many commentators, the FTC's ineffectiveness in its first two decades was caused by the successful efforts of the president and, on occasion, of Congress to restrain the agency's pursuit of the competition policy goals of the 1914 statute.[99] The commission's experience in this era firmly supported the ABA's conclusion in 1969 that the FTC's antitrust revitalization required the willingness of the White House to appoint, and of the Senate to confirm, commissioners who preferred a forceful antitrust role.

Congress.   A fourth major external factor affecting the FTC's competition programs has been Congress.[100] Through oversight, appropriations, and efforts to amend the agency's charter, Congress has significantly influenced the commission's choice and execution of antitrust matters. As a general rule, the FTC has successfully pursued few economically significant initiatives that lacked legislative approval. Fulfilling the active antitrust role Congress envisioned in 1914 has always run the risk of provoking business to seek legislative relief from the agency's actions. The FTC Act and its legislative history defined the nominal boundaries of commission authority, but each new Congress determines how far the agency may go in exercising its powers.[101]

The political risk inherent in translating the broad mandate of 1914 into specific enforcement initiatives is evident in two past FTC competition projects, each the most ambitious and visible commission initiative of its time: the meatpacking industry report of 1919, and the Cement Institute base-point pricing case of the 1940s. The meatpacking report controversy involved the agency's investigation and reporting powers.[102] In 1917 President Wilson requested the FTC to investigate the food industry as part of a wartime price study. Despite vigorous lobbying by meatpacking firms to avoid the food inquiry, the commission comprehensively examined the packing business.[103] The investigation yielded a six-volume report presenting evidence of collusion among the nation's five largest packers and exclusionary tactics to thwart new competitors.[104] The commission recommended that the packers be forced to relinquish control of stockyards and limit their activities in unrelated product lines.

The study stimulated impassioned debate in Congress.[105] After months of hearings and discussion, Congress passed the Packers and Stockyards Act of 1921, which gave the Agriculture Department exclusive jurisdiction over the operation and practices of meatpackers, stockyards, and livestock commission houses.[106] Congress' vesting of authority over the packers in the Agriculture Department had an immediate, demoralizing effect on the FTC.[107] For the longer term, however, the meatpacking incident prompted Congress to keep the agency's economic work on a shorter appropriations leash.[108] This reduced the number of economic investigations ordered by Congress,[109] and left the FTC to initiate an increasing proportion of its own economic studies.[110]

Decreasing congressional involvement in the initiation of the FTC's economic work had important political implications. Historically, the least politically vulnerable FTC investigations and studies had been those begun at Congress' request.[111] Studies begun at the president's request or by the commission itself more often provoked congressional efforts to limit the agency's authority.[112]

A second area in which Congress has significantly affected the commission's choice of competition programs is litigation. An outstanding example is Congress' effort in the early 1950s to overturn the result in *Federal Trade Commission v. Cement Institute*.[113] During the antitrust revival of the late 1930s, the commission made base-point pricing its principal antitrust litigation priority.[114] The main product of this program was *In re Cement Institute*, in which the agency ordered the members of the cement producers' national trade association to abandon a multiple base-point pricing system.[115] The Seventh Circuit Court of Appeals reversed the commission, but the Supreme Court reinstated the agency's order.[116]

The Supreme Court's ruling triggered instant demands from cement industry officials that Congress declare base-point pricing legal.[117] Congress considered several bills designed to overturn the Cement Institute decision and closely questioned the commission about future enforcement plans.[118] The climax came in June 1950 when Congress passed the O'Mahoney Freight Absorption Act, which effectively overturned Cement Institute. With the FTC's urging, President Truman vetoed the bill, and later efforts to revive the measure died.[119]

Although the O'Mahoney proposal failed, its narrow defeat exposed the precariousness of FTC lawsuits involving substantial economic stakes but lacking either the active support or, at a minimum, the tolerant acquiescence of Congress. Clair Wilcox, the economist and business historian, summarized the lessons of the Cement Institute controversy for future economically significant FTC antitrust initiatives:

> An administrative agency . . . is peculiarly vulnerable to political attack. If inert, lenient, and ineffective, its placid existence may be undisturbed. But if vigorous in the performance of its duties, it will be headed for trouble. Its powers may be curtailed, its appropriation slashed, its administrators refused confirmation, its personnel subject to persecution, its very existence jeopardized . . . If the Federal Trade Commission comes to grief, it will not be because it has been too lax, but because it has been too tough. If it values survival, an agency thus attacked is likely to draw in its horns.[120]

Implications for FTC Competition Programs

Lassitude, as Wilcox suggested, may be the surest path to long-run survival for administrative agencies with politically sensitive law-enforcement duties. In 1969, however, the pervasive perception of FTC "inertness, leniency, and ineffectiveness" greatly threatened its well-being.[121] The ABA proposed that the FTC satisfy three broad criteria in choosing competition initiatives: Focus on projects with genuine economic significance, concentrate on matters involving unsettled legal doctrine and requiring complicated economic analysis, and resort more to compulsory enforcement proceedings.[122]

A central feature of the ABA criteria was their tendency, if closely followed, to have the FTC draw increasingly from the risk-laden end of the spectrum of all possible antitrust programs and enforcement methods. Each guideline advanced a change—from "trivial" to economically important programs, from per se offenses to complex, unsettled areas of law and economics, and from voluntary to compulsory enforcement—that would replace a safer approach with a riskier one.[123] To succeed in a comparatively higher risk role, the commission needed to pursue the ABA's suggested internal reforms. The agency's own substantive skill and political acumen would be important in determining whether the agency developed meritorious programs and executed them without provoking serious collateral political attack.[124] However, the success of the ABA's proposals also depended as much on the attitudes of Congress, the president, the judiciary, and the nation at large as it did on the FTC's skill in pursuing them.[125]

In recommending that the FTC retain its antitrust powers, the ABA presumably perceived that institutions outside the agency were amenable to the risk-taking its guidelines implicitly required. The ABA appeared to believe that the president and Congress would play the most important roles in determining the form and content of FTC antitrust work. Executive branch preferences would emerge through the selection of commissioners, particularly the agency's chairman.[126] Whether Congress wanted the FTC to assume the ABA's suggested antitrust role would become apparent through the demands Congress placed on nominees to the commission; the competition program that oversight and appropriations committees urged the FTC to pursue; the breadth and durability of congressional backing for specific initiatives to implement Congress' broad preferences; and appropriations.[127] The actual response of Congress and the commission to the 1969 *ABA Report* is the subject of the next section.

The Federal Trade Commission's Competition Programs: 1969–1980

From the date of its release, the *ABA Report* became a congressionally accepted standard for measuring the commission's antitrust performance.[128] Oversight and appropriations committees believed that the study had, in general, diagnosed the agency's ills correctly and presented a sensible reform blueprint. Congress agreed that the FTC had used its antitrust powers timidly and unimaginatively, and it insisted that future programs deal forthrightly with difficult, economically important antitrust problems. Congress also perceived a longstanding indifference by the FTC to weaknesses the ABA had emphasized. Underscoring their demands for improvement, congressional leaders reiterated the ABA view that reform was essential to the agency's continued existence.[129] Though perhaps overstated, such admonitions made clear that Congress would no longer tolerate plodding, insignificant antitrust enforcement.

This section analyzes in two parts the development of the FTC's competition programs since the *ABA Report*. The first covers the period from 1969 through the second session of the 94th Congress in 1976. The second covers the period from 1977 through 1980. Each section discusses the general antitrust role Congress wanted the agency to perform, as well as specific ways in which it preferred the FTC to use its competition resources, and each reviews the commission's response to this guidance.

1969–1976

Congressional Guidance.   The oversight and appropriations committees frequently articulated the general tone and character of antitrust enforcement they expected from the FTC leadership.[130] They demanded a fundamental redirection of the agency's competition programs. Indeed, the hearings of this period abound with pointed instructions that FTC antitrust programs stress boldness, experimentation, and a willingness to tackle major sources of consumer injury.

The redirection process began in earnest in November 1969 during hearings to confirm Caspar Weinberger as the agency's new chairman. Warren Magnuson, chairman of the Senate Commerce Committee, told the nominee that the commission was "very important" to the Commerce Committee and that Weinberger should begin "expanding the existing Trade Commission programs in order to perform the job well."[131] Miles Kirkpatrick, Weinberger's successor, received similar encouragement upon his first appearance before the Senate Appropriations Committee in 1971. Subcommittee chairman Gale McGee told Kirkpatrick that his committee wanted the commission to act aggressively and take risks in applying its competition powers:

> For a long time many of us have felt . . . that the FTC . . . seemed to be either sitting on its position rather than moving with the changing times or in many instances actually retreating from what its original intent had been . . . I think you would find a much friendlier Congress up here than some of your [budget] requests might suggest . . . that a great part of the Commission's duty is to strike blows in behalf of the consumer . . . Too often it has been either shy or bashful . . . That is why we were having a rather closer look at your requests just in the hopes of encouraging you, if anything, to make mistakes, but I think the mistakes you are to make ought to be mistakes in doing and trying rather than playing safe in not doing. I believe that is the most serious mistake of all . . . you are not faulted for making mistakes. You may be for making it twice in a row, for not learning properly, but we would rather you make a mistake innovating, trying something new, rather than playing so cautiously that you never make a mistake.[132]

When Lewis Engman appeared before the Senate Commerce Committee as chairman-designate in 1973, the committee's members likewise exhorted him to follow the path traveled by Weinberger and Kirkpatrick during the preceding three years.[133] During the hearings, Senator Norris Cotton complained that the FTC "has had a need for some kind of injection to pep it up so it would fulfill its mission." Senator Ted Stevens told Engman that he expected bold action: "I am really hopeful . . . that you will become a real zealot in terms of consumer affairs and some of these big business people will complain to us that you are going too far. That would be the day, as far as I am concerned."[134] On these and other occasions, the oversight committees left the commission's leaders with little doubt about the basic direction the FTC should pursue.[135]

Beyond fixing the broad objectives and tone they wanted FTC antitrust work to achieve, congressional committees actively suggested specific uses for the commission's competition resources. As a first general step, Congress urged the FTC to establish an effective system for choosing priorities. Various committees emphasized the need for a planning mechanism that filtered out "trivial" matters and focused the FTC's resources on major antitrust problems. In the committees' view, the commission should also translate the fruits of improved planning into guidelines by which FTC attorneys and economists could organize their work.[136]

As it promoted the creation of a strong institutional planning base, Congress singled out many specific competition problems and industry sectors for FTC scrutiny. They told the agency to use a substantial part of its antitrust resources to study industrial concentration and the influence of market structure on economic performance—subjects that Congress regarded as among the country's most urgent competition problems.[137]

Congress was especially concerned about mergers, particularly conglomerate acquisitions contributing to aggregate industrial concentration.[138] Interest in this phenomenon took two forms. First, Congress encouraged the FTC to refine its techniques for measuring the performance of diversified firms and their constituent parts. For example, in 1973 Congress facilitated FTC adoption of a line-of-business reporting program through measures approved as part of the Trans-Alaska Pipeline Authorization Act.[139] Second, Congress enacted legislation increasing the FTC's ability to identify and halt anticompetitive mergers. The 1973 Pipeline Act authorized the FTC to move in federal court to enjoin existing or impending antitrust violations, notably, illegal mergers. In 1976 Congress amended the Clayton Act to require firms to notify the FTC and the Justice Department before making certain acquisitions; the statute also established a mandatory waiting period for firms attempting certain acquisitions and tender offers.

A second generic competition problem in which Congress took an active interest was Robinson-Patman Act enforcement. Several committees called on the commission to explain a perceived neglect of the statute. Discussions of Robinson-Patman enforcement demonstrated that, while Congress agreed with the ABA's proposal that the FTC expand its antitrust efforts in other areas, it wanted the agency to maintain other programs Congress had traditionally supported.

In the course of identifying generic competition problems the commission should address, Congress also earmarked specific industries and economic sectors it believed merited antitrust inquiry. Congress initially regarded the food industry as its preferred FTC competition priority and instructed the agency to give special emphasis to concentration in the industry's manufacturing and retailing sectors. With the sudden tightening of fuel supplies in the early 1970s, however, energy soon displaced the food industry atop Congress' list.

By 1972 the commission had received numerous congressional requests to study various aspects of the energy industry, and soon virtually every committee with responsibility for antitrust or energy policy indicated that energy should be the FTC's chief antitrust priority. In a characteristic exchange during hearings on the FTC's budget in April 1973, Representative Mark Andrews conveyed to Chairman Engman the perceived need for immediate commission intervention:

> In the last six months in this country we have come smack up against an energy crisis. We have specific knowledge that small independent refineries in mid-America are unable to get crude oil because the majors are cutting them off. . . Here right under your nose is something where obviously you haven't been doing your job or you would have it resolved. . . I might ask the question where were you then and what are you doing now to force the majors, out of a sense of Christian justice if not economic survival for mid-America, to allow these small independent refineries to get a supply of crude so they can serve their customers. . . As far as I can see, the Federal Trade Commission has been sitting fat, dumb, and happy doing nothing about it.[140]

In short order many committees directed the commission to investigate fuel shortages and urged it to protect independent refiners and marketers from a loss of petroleum supplies. Committee members closely questioned commission officials about features of major oil company structure and behavior that might warrant formal FTC intervention.[141] Still other committees, without specifically requesting FTC action, expressed serious concern about the viability of the petroleum industry's independent sector.[142]

In July 1973 the commission issued a complaint charging the country's eight largest petroleum companies with maintaining a noncompetitive market structure in the Atlantic and Gulf Coast states.[143] The complaint, however, did not diminish congressional interest in having the commission continue to monitor and address industry developments.[144] Through legislation Congress substantially expanded the commission's competition advocacy responsibilities, including requirements that the FTC analyze the effects of the mandatory petroleum allocation program adopted pursuant to the Emergency Petroleum Allocation Act of 1973.[145]

Although food and energy were Congress' most important competition priorities in the early 1970s, they were not the only industries arousing antitrust interest. Various committees earmarked several other areas as particularly deserving of FTC competition analysis. Most frequently mentioned were steel, automobiles, and medical care.[146]

As the materials above suggest, Congress in the early and mid-1970s often indicated that, while reports and studies were a useful part of the FTC's work, the commission should rely more heavily on compulsory enforcement procedures such as litigation. Congress was also concerned that the FTC paid insufficient attention to ensuring compliance with existing orders. Consequently, the committees encouraged the commission to bolster its compliance efforts, and in 1973 Congress doubled the maximum civil penalty for each violation of a commission order to $10,000. To increase flexibility in prosecution, Congress also gave the FTC power to bring civil penalty actions in federal court where the Justice Department declined to do so.[147]

Exhortations about the appropriate style and content of FTC antitrust programs had little chance of stimulating a major revitalization. An especially telling test of congressional commitment was appropriations.[148] When asked in 1969 by Senator Charles Mathias what FTC renewal would require, Chairman Dixon responded, "[S]ee to it that the agency has the money and the manpower."[149] In the 1970s, Congress took this advice. The agency's total budget rose from $20.9 million in fiscal year 1970 to over $70 million in fiscal year 1980.[150]

The question then arose of how to measure the FTC's effectiveness in using the increased funds. Two different and somewhat conflicting standards emerged from the oversight hearings. On the one hand, the committees largely agreed with the ABA view that the FTC should not inflate its enforcement statistics through trivial endeavors. This guidance implied that the commission should raise the overall significance and quality of its caseload, even though the number of matters on its docket might fall below or not exceed pre-1970 levels.[151] On the other hand, Congress sometimes attached great importance to FTC case and investigation statistics. Acknowledging that numbers alone were sometimes a suspect criterion, the committees intimated that greater appropriations ought to yield a larger absolute number of cases and investigations.[152]

Chairman Kirkpatrick and his successors sought, with difficulty, to convince the committees that the statistics did not reflect reduced FTC antitrust enforcement, but stemmed instead from basic changes in the types of cases the FTC was pursuing.[153] The commission explained that its more stringent preliminary screening procedures also tended to reduce the number of matters certified as formal investigations.[154] Nonetheless, FTC officials and Congress were unable to resolve what relative values the qualitative and quantitative criteria should receive in evaluating the FTC's caseload. The uneasy consensus among the oversight bodies seemed to be that the numbers were neither controlling nor insignificant.

Commission Response.   During the late 1960s and early 1970s, congressional and public ferment about the FTC's antitrust role triggered extensive change within that commission.[155] Agency officials took seriously Congress' view that the agency should upgrade its antitrust programs substantially.[156] The commission understood that the expected product of this overhaul would be innovative, vigorous antitrust enforcement that addressed vital competition issues.

Internal FTC reform efforts had several dimensions. In line with congressional preferences, the first priority was to build an effective system for choosing enforcement targets. The foundation for this effort was the creation of planning and evaluation offices.[157] The commission also attempted to integrate its Bureau of Economics more closely into the antitrust program selection process. To aid in choosing future enforcement ventures, the Bureau of Economics and the new planning and evaluation offices began devoting more resources to assessing the effects of proposed and completed commission cases.[158]

An important result of the agency's new emphasis on central planning was greater use of the budget process to set priorities. In 1975 the FTC adopted its first program-based budget, which allocated resources according to the types of violations or industry sectors to be examined.[159] At the same time, commissioners began formally reviewing resource commitments and expenditures twice annually in meetings with bureau directors and staff.[160] The budget review sessions were part of a broader agency effort to translate the product of its planning systems into guidelines for agency staff.[161]

As it developed new planning tools, the FTC sought to improve the information sources it used to choose economic sectors and industry behavior for antitrust analysis. During his chairmanship, Caspar Weinberger said the commission wanted to enhance its "ability to monitor more precisely price and profit trends within the array of industries in which it has regulatory responsibility and to collect more detailed data on corporations."[162] In 1971 FTC chairman Kirkpatrick reported to the Senate Appropriations Committee that the commission had transformed Weinberger's suggestions into a line-of-business data collection project.[163] Majorities in both chambers supported the line-of-business initiative and approved the appropriations needed to conduct it.[164]

Applying its new planning methods, the commission earmarked several industries for careful antitrust inquiry. A major selection criterion was the industry's importance to day-to-day consumer purchases. The FTC established the food, energy, and health care industries as its highest competition priorities. The decision to build comprehensive programs for these industries also reflected the commission's view that industry-wide analysis was the best means for identifying and addressing the underlying causes of poor performance.[165]

To address competition problems in these and other economic sectors, the commission used several enforcement strategies. The most visible approach was litigation.[166] In the first half of the 1970s, the agency initiated a number of significant suits, some involving new applications of Section 5.[167] Most prominent were the FTC's monopolization and attempted monopolization cases involving breakfast cereals, petroleum, and office copiers.[168] These monopolization suits presented the FTC with special opportunities and difficulties. Even with congressional support for commission efforts to deal with market structure and firm behavior in concentrated industries, the agency feared proceeding at a pace that outstripped its resources and its progress in instituting planning, personnel, and management reforms.[169]

A second, major litigation priority was mergers.[170] The agency assigned substantial resources to conglomerate mergers with possible horizontal consequences,[171] and continued its scrutiny of more traditional horizontal and vertical acquisitions.[172] A third important category of cases dealt with vertical and horizontal restraints.[173] The commission challenged vertical territorial restrictions in the soft-drink bottling industry and opposed resale price maintenance and distribution restraints in several consumer goods industries.[174] The commission's major horizontal restraints cases addressed delivered pricing in the plywood industry, shopping-center leases limiting the entry of discounters, and limitations on advertising, pricing of services, and entry in the health-care industry.[175] The FTC brought substantially fewer Robinson-Patman cases than it had in the 1960s[176] and focused more attention on industry-wide investigations, including substantial inquiries in the transportation and health-care fields.[177]

Coupled with these litigation programs was increased emphasis on monitoring compliance with orders obtained from previous lawsuits.[178] The FTC enlarged its compliance program and initiated several important civil penalty actions, many of which applied new powers Congress gave the agency in 1973.[179]

The second principal element of the commission's competition policy work was the preparation of reports. The main subjects of its published studies were mergers and acquisitions, energy, and food.[180] An increasing number of these reports responded to legislation directing the FTC to analyze the competitive consequences of newly established regulatory programs or to examine specific industries. Drawing on expertise acquired in performing these studies and developing cases, the commission also expanded its competition advocacy efforts before other agencies and branches of government.[181]

As it upgraded the quality of its case and investigation workload, the FTC also attempted to increase its institutional ability to execute the new competition initiatives successfully. This process of reform had several elements. The most fundamental was improving the quality of the agency's staff. Congress gave Chairman Weinberger broad latitude to make personnel changes and actively followed his progress in doing so. The recruitment and retention of capable attorneys and economists remained a high priority of Weinberger's successors.[182]

The second major reform was a reorganization in 1970 that gave the FTC the basic form it retains today. The move consolidated the existing Bureaus of Textiles and Furs, Industry Guidance, Deceptive Practices, and Restraint of Trade into two principal operating bureaus—Competition and Consumer Protection—and substantially reduced the levels of review through which staff work had to pass before reaching the commission.[183] The agency also began developing a comprehensive, computer-based information management system for monitoring the status of its competition programs.[184]

Another endeavor was establishing new internal procedures for screening cases, setting deadlines, reviewing the progress of competition matters, and correcting delays. The commission expanded its existing ground-level evaluation tools and created new devices (such as the preliminary investigation) to establish, at an early stage, a sufficient basis for deciding whether matters warranted further expenditure of FTC funds. The improved operating procedures and information management system were designed to reduce delay and to support planning activities.[185]

Despite the FTC's organization and management reforms, Congress in late 1975 and early 1976 began questioning the commission's ability to bring its largest litigation efforts to a timely end. Attention focused on the cereal and petroleum monopolization suits, filed in April 1972 and July 1973, respectively (the Xerox suit ended in a consent decree in 1975). Early in these proceedings commission officials informed Congress that cases such as In re Exxon would be time-consuming and expensive.[186] Some congressional supporters of the commission's actions regarded protracted litigation as unacceptable. Fearing that the FTC proceedings would bring relief too late, Congress in 1975 and 1976 seriously considered several proposals to vertically restructure the petroleum industry.[187] At no time, however, did congressional sponsors of divestiture legislation suggest that the FTC end its Exxon case.

1977–1980

By the fall of 1976, the FTC had attained perhaps its greatest level of congressional respect. Congress seemed generally pleased with the commission's renewed antitrust enforcement approach. Objective measures of legislative feeling certainly supported such a conclusion. Since 1969 both the agency's total budget and competition expenditures had more than doubled, and Congress had significantly expanded its statutory authority. Less tangible, but still important signs of congressional opinion pointed in the same direction. In a report on federal regulatory bodies issued in October 1976, the Subcommittee on Oversight and Investigations of the House Committee on Interstate and Foreign Commerce praised the FTC's competition work and said the FTC had become "one of the more effective regulatory agencies."[188] There was little question that Congress endorsed the course that the FTC's competition programs had taken.

Although the commission's antitrust work had enjoyed solid congressional backing through 1976, the durability of this support was much less certain. Major segments of the business community viewed the content and tone of the agency's new antitrust and consumer-protection programs with alarm, and spoke increasingly of seeking substantial, legislatively mandated retrenchment of the agency's litigation, rulemaking, and information-gathering efforts.[189] When the 95th Congress convened in January 1977, the legislature's membership had changed significantly. Gone were Philip Hart, Vance Hartke, Mike Mansfield, Gale McGee, Frank Moss, John Pastore, and John Tunney,[190] senators who had strongly advocated the commission's antitrust revitalization and had mustered congressional support for the agency's ambitious programs and the enlargement of its budget and statutory powers.[191]

As programs begun in the early and mid-1970s came to fruition in the late 1970s, the commission would be unable to rely on the support of many key individuals who had championed its initiatives. Instead, it would have to justify its competition projects before a Congress with significantly less stake in defending or maintaining FTC work begun through 1976 and a stronger inclination to review new proposals more critically. It was a Congress more likely to listen sympathetically to claims that the agency had erred in its choice and execution of competition programs.[192]

Congressional Guidance.   From 1977 through 1980 the oversight and appropriations process did not constitute a complete departure from earlier legislative scrutiny of the agency's competition programs. Congress continued developing themes spoken at the decade's beginning.

Like their predecessors in the early 1970s, the committees encouraged the commission to refine its system for selecting enforcement priorities.[193] Both chambers placed greater emphasis on cost-benefit studies for choosing future cases and investigations. In an area related to planning and case selection, Congress sustained its support for the agency's line-of-business program. The oversight committees expressed concern about the delays caused by lawsuits challenging the program and considered (but did not enact) legislation to expedite the data collection. The appropriations committees continued to fund the program, but also urged the commission to reduce its reporting requirements.

Congressional interest in planning and priorities was part of a broader concern with the FTC's ability to manage its programs capably. As in the first half of the decade, the committees pressed the commission to monitor its use of resources closely and expedite ongoing matters.[194] The committees also questioned the FTC's care in using compulsory process to elicit information.[195]

Beyond analyzing the commission's planning and management systems, Congress specified several competition problems and industries the FTC should scrutinize. Though less forcefully than it once had, Congress still regarded economic concentration as meriting serious antitrust attention. During antitrust oversight hearings in 1977, Senator Paul Laxalt commented: "To me, the undue concentration of economic power in this country is troublesome. I think that undue concentration constitutes as big a threat to the individual liberties of Americans as anything that I can perceive."[196] Similarly, in March 1980 Representative Neal Smith of the House Appropriations Committee advocated a continuing concern with concentrated industries during hearings on the FTC's 1980 budget request:

> I happen to be one who thinks that you ought to be spending a lot of time on some major problems, such as oligopolies which have a direct impact and effect upon inflation in this country. This is especially true in food processing and some areas where imports do not keep a cap on domestic prices or have an impact as they do in some areas of manufacturing.[197]

Merger enforcement remained an area of concern that Congress believed deserved a high FTC priority. In 1979 the Senate Appropriations Committee asked the commission what action it had taken "in response to the current conglomerate merger wave."[198] Later that year, Senator Kennedy introduced legislation limiting large conglomerate acquisitions and prohibiting certain mergers involving the nation's sixteen largest oil companies.[199] As it considered these proposals, the Senate Judiciary Committee also encouraged the FTC to use its statutory power to block anticompetitive acquisitions.[200]

In enumerating specific economic sectors, Congress reaffirmed its interest in stimulating competition in energy, food, medical care, and transportation. Congress occasionally singled out other areas of economic activity for FTC attention, including concentration in the ownership of the news media. Of all industries, Congress most stressed energy. The appropriations committees directed the FTC to expedite the energy industry studies that had been funded by special congressional appropriations in the early 1970s. Congress also substantially expanded the commission's competition advocacy responsibilities under several new energy statutes, including the Petroleum Marketing Practices Act of 1978 and the Outer Continental Shelf Lands Act Amendments of 1978. The food industry also remained a high antitrust priority for Congress; the committees suggested that the commission pay more attention to food retailing and the beef processing industry.[201]

Congress gave close, and often critical, scrutiny to three other major FTC competition initiatives during this period: the automobile investigation, the Formica trademark cancellation suit, and cases affecting the professions. The House and Senate appropriations committees were especially apprehensive about the automobile inquiry's purpose and scope. They were concerned that the commission had slighted the role of foreign automobile makers and had imposed excessive document demands on U.S. firms.[202]

The committees also expressed reservations over the agency's effort to cancel the Formica trademark and asked whether the case foreshadowed efforts to cancel other well-known trademarks.[203] Early in 1979, several bills were introduced in the House to bar the FTC from exercising its powers to cancel trademarks on the ground that the marks had become common, descriptive names.[204]

The third troublesome FTC initiative was the agency's competition work involving the professions, particularly lawyers and physicians.[205] Several committees questioned the commission about its interest in professional associations.[206] Although the appropriations and oversight panels did not explicitly oppose the program or suggest its modification, the tone of their inquiries conveyed discomfort with these initiatives.

Commission Response. Oversight and appropriations hearings from 1977 to 1980 revealed a perceptible change in congressional attitudes toward the FTC's competition programs. Until late 1979, this adjustment was relatively quiet. Congress continued endorsing many initiatives it had promoted earlier in the decade, including the FTC's line-of-business, energy, and food programs. Moreover, it had sustained the pattern of budget increases set in the early 1970s, raising the commission's total appropriation from about $47 million in 1976 to nearly $70 million in 1980. Mixed with these threads of continuity, however, were important differences in tone and emphasis. Before 1976, Congress encouraged the FTC to test the boundaries of its authority. After 1976, the legislature was less amenable to further expansion and considerably more disposed to scrutinize ambitious FTC antitrust ventures already underway.

In its antitrust activities from 1977 to 1980, the commission was responsive to these changes in congressional attitude. This was particularly evident in the agency's attempt to strengthen its priority selection processes. This effort proceeded along four lines. First, the Bureau of Competition in 1977 created two new planning offices, one to examine broad economic factors—such as technological change—which influence the competitive process, and a second to develop legal and economic analyses for selecting new cases and investigations and to evaluate the effects of completed FTC antitrust cases.

Second, the agency improved its methods for periodically examining the FTC's workload and evaluating proposals for new projects. In 1977 the commission commenced a series of policy review sessions to review individual agency programs and explore future strategies. Subjects for these sessions included the automobile industry, compliance, mergers, health services, media ownership, and industry-wide enforcement. The commission also expanded its budget review process, which was a planning mechanism the agency adopted early in the decade.

Third, the agency sought to more fully integrate its economists into the selection of competition programs and the generation of cases and investigations. Agency-wide task forces of lawyers and economists were created to examine existing areas of antitrust concern and assess possible new areas of inquiry.[207]

The final major planning reform was the enlargement and improved use of the agency's information sources. The commission published its first analysis of data obtained through its line-of-business program,[208] and it extensively used information received through its premerger notification program under the Hart-Scott-Rodino Act of 1976. As it employed these new data sources in planning and evaluating enforcement programs, the agency made its internal data sources more accessible to staff.

Consistent with the interests of the oversight and appropriations committees, the commission placed greater emphasis on managing its competition work effectively. The FTC finished installing the management information system begun in the early 1970s and exerted more stringent early review of case and investigation proposals.[209] The planning and priority selection reforms outlined above were one step toward identifying genuinely meritorious projects. Another was to expand the use of the Bureau of Competition's Evaluation Office and Evaluation Committee in examining complaint and investigation recommendations.[210]

The commission also analyzed its existing information-gathering programs, investigations, and lawsuits more rigorously. In 1979 the FTC substantially reduced the number of stock and asset acquisitions that must be reported under the agency's premerger notification program.[211] The following year the commission narrowed its automobile industry investigation and its Exxon monopolization suit—steps that Congress had urged the agency to consider.[212]

In selecting subjects for competition study, the commission emphasized industries providing consumer goods and services.[213] The FTC devoted over half its antitrust resources to the energy, food, health-care, and transportation industries. The agency used a variety of approaches to raise competition concerns about these and other industries. The most salient initiatives begun from 1977 to 1980 were commission lawsuits, including significant antitrust cases dealing with monopolization and attempted monopolization, mergers, horizontal restraints, and vertical restraints.[214] The commission issued complaints or decisions in cases involving important, complex legal and economic issues such as strategic entry deterence, predation, dominant firm behavior generally, market signaling, and the Colgate doctrine.[215] Other important litigation programs included greater use of injunctions to halt potentially anticompetitive mergers and the development of new remedial devices such as restitution.[216]

These litigation projects constituted but one of several commission approaches for developing competition policy. Programs to stimulate research, analysis, and discussion of important antitrust issues were also an important strategy. From 1977 to 1980, for example, the commission sponsored conferences on, among other subjects, health-care competition, media concentration, social consequences of firm size and market structure, and predation. In this period the FTC's attorneys and economists performed research that yielded numerous working papers, protocols, and articles dealing with significant competition policy issues. The commission also funded research by distinguished academicians on industrial organization subjects as a supplement to studies performed within the Bureaus of Competition and Economics.[217]

Another important field was competition advocacy. The commission expanded the intervention role it had begun earlier in the decade and participated extensively in proceedings before other government agencies. In addition, it studied rulemaking as a competition enforcement approach.[218] The FTC considered but declined to issue rules that would govern certain conglomerate mergers, bar physician organizations from controlling Blue Shield and other open-panel medical prepayment plans, or prohibit the ownership of crude oil and petroleum products pipelines by major integrated oil companies.[219]

Proposed Limitations. In 1979 and 1980 congressional dissatisfaction with some FTC competition and consumer protection programs swelled into a forceful movement to curtail specific projects and to redefine the agency's underlying authority.[220] The intensity and breadth of this drive have been equaled only twice before in the agency's history: in the meatpacking report and Cement Institute confrontations discussed earlier. Divisions within Congress over the extent of restrictions to be imposed were so severe that the commission's funding lapsed on two occasions, forcing the agency to close its doors for the first time.[221] The commission had gone without an authorization bill for fiscal years 1978, 1979, and 1980; this was a portent of the discontent that surfaced graphically in congressional consideration of the FTC Improvements Act of 1980.

Most of the act's provisions dealt with the consumer-protection programs, but it also affected several FTC competition matters. It prohibited the FTC from petitioning the commissioner of patents for cancellation of a registered trademark on the ground that the trademark had become the common, descriptive name for an article or substance.[222] The act barred the commission from conducting any study or investigation of agricultural marketing orders or prosecuting agricultural cooperatives for conduct exempt from the antitrust laws by the Capper-Volstead Act.[223] The measure also banned investigations relating to the business of insurance unless such studies were authorized by a vote of either the House or Senate commerce committees.[224]

The only other specific antitrust restriction to gain Congress' approval in this period was the Softdrink Interband Competition Act of 1980, which exempted softdrink bottlers' exclusive territorial franchises from antitrust challenge so long as there is competition in the area from other softdrink brands. The act culminated long efforts by the bottlers to gain relief from the FTC's suit challenging the industry's exclusive geographic territories.[225]

In addition to restrictions it enacted, Congress considered other sweeping measures to limit the agency's competition work. The House Appropriations Subcommittee nearly banned further funding for the commission's automobile industry investigation and Exxon monopolization suit; Senator Orrin Hatch introduced a bill to require the FTC to bring its antitrust cases in the federal district courts, eliminating the agency's adjudicatory function in the competition field; and during consideration of the Senate version of the FTC's authorization bill, Senator James McClure offered an amendment prohibiting FTC scrutiny of state-regulated professions.[226] Finally, Senator Howard Heflin proposed eliminating the commission's power to order divestiture or other forms of structural relief in nonmerger cases.[227]

The policy views behind these measures were present in Congress in the early 1970s but were held by a relatively small minority of the congressional membership and were virtually absent from the leadership ranks of the committee structures, the House, and the Senate. Thus, although one could identify legislators in the early 1970s who wanted little to do with the FTC's chosen reform path, the actual and proposed restrictions of the congressional backlash in 1980 signified a basic change in the antitrust role Congress had urged upon the FTC for most of the decade.[228]

CONCLUSION

In 1914 Congress gave the FTC expansive competition authority, in large measure because the legislature expected to play an active role in ensuring that the agency faithfully pursue the enabling statute's goals. Rigorous congressional review of the FTC's competition programs fits squarely within the system of careful legislative oversight Senator Cummins envisioned 70 years ago. Indeed, it should startle no one that Congress would closely appraise the commission's antitrust initiatives or evaluate its competition policy role. From this paper's examination of the FTC's experience in the 1970s and the forces that have shaped the agency's evolution since 1914 emerge several considerations relevant to congressional debate over the commission's future.

The first consideration concerns the proper basis for altering the FTC's statutory charter. Although the desirability of scrupulous congressional oversight is beyond dispute,[229] the grounds on which some members of Congress have proposed to restrict the FTC's antitrust powers are questionable. Congress can legitimately probe many aspects of the agency's competition performance and ask searching questions about both the substantive merits of the commission's antitrust programs and the skill with which the FTC has carried them out, but there is no principled basis for curtailing the agency's antitrust authority on the premise that the commission has contradicted congressional guidance.[230] The FTC's choice of competition programs and enforcement strategies during the 1970s was consistent with the legislature's articulated preferences. Any new limiting legislation that grounds itself on the commission's supposed past infidelity to Congress' will builds on an illusion.[231]

An issue closely related to the consistency of FTC programs with congressional guidance is whether Congress in fact exerts meaningful influence over the commission's choice of enforcement programs.[232] Many of the proposed limits on the commission's authority have stemmed from the assumption that Congress exercises only minimal control over the FTC's activities. A major implication of the analysis in this paper is that the substantial congruency of congressional antitrust preferences and FTC antitrust programs in the 1970s was not mere coincidence. Rather, the 1970s was a period of powerful legislative influence in the commission's competition activities. From 1969 to 1976, in particular, Congress used virtually every tool at its disposal to move the FTC toward far-reaching applications of its antitrust powers. With great force and effect, Congress stressed that the commission's well-being depended on its development of ambitious, aggressive enforcement programs. Moreover, the history of congressional oversight since 1914 indicates that the FTC would not have pursued such a course had Congress not urged it to do so. To depict the 1970s as a time when Congress functioned as an inattentive, ineffective overseer, leaving the FTC to account only to itself, stands the situation on its head.[233]

In addition to questioning some proposed bases for limiting the commission's authority, this paper also suggests several factors that deserve serious consideration during congressional debate about the commission's future. One important factor in weighing the merits of the agency's antitrust performance would be to review what Congress expected of the agency throughout the 1970s. Since the FTC's creation in 1914, Congress and the nation generally have expected different things of the commission at different times. Any evaluation of the FTC's antitrust record in the 1970s that ignores the rules to which the commission was expected to conform at that time can hardly serve as a reliable guide for prescribing the agency's future activities or rewriting its statute. A complete and accurate assessment must necessarily acknowledge changes in the views of congressmen and commentators about what constitutes good performance.[234]

Thoughtful review of the FTC's history would shed light on the commission's record in at least one other important respect. By almost any yardstick, the 1970s differed markedly from any in the FTC's past. Immense strain was placed on the commission by the expansion (by way of judicial interpretation and statute) of the agency's substantive, remedial, and investigatory powers; by major, sustained budget increases; and by the sudden, substantive reorientation of its competition and consumer-protection agendas. These developments required it to simultaneously develop new planning and management systems and to initiate programs that fulfilled the more ambitious role Congress expected it to perform. The late 1970s produced a gradual consolidation of the agency's expanded resources, authority, and management and planning reforms. Outward signs of this trend include stronger emphasis on planning, research, and preliminary screening in choosing and shaping competition programs; closer attention to program management and the refinement of information systems on which such management greatly depends; and greater sensitivity to theoretical and practical concerns affecting the economically sensible application of competition policy. The legislative activity of 1980 obscured these significant developments.

Finally, a broad historical review would offer a useful perspective on what substantive functions the FTC should serve in the antitrust field. Congress in 1914 perceived a serious need for an administrative body that could adjust the boundaries of antitrust law incrementally to conform with modern learning in law and economics. As it prescribes the FTC's antitrust role for the 1980s, Congress might profitably consider whether its predecessors' conception of the agency in 1914 suits its needs today. This issue, not an imagined refusal of the commission to heed legislative guidance, arguably lies at the heart of the matter.

NOTES

1. *Chicago Tribune*, February 23, 1981, p. A1. Stockman's remark followed an Office of Management and Budget proposal—soon withdrawn—to cease funding for the

FTC's Bureau of Competition, the agency's antitrust enforcement division. See U.S. Congress, House, Committee on Government Operations, *Impact of OMB-Proposed Budget Cuts for the Federal Trade Commission. Hearings Before a Subcommittee of the House Committee on Government Operations*, 97th Cong., 1st sess., 1981.

2. Federal Trade Commission Improvements Act of 1980, *Statutes at Large*, vol. 94, ch. 374 (1980), codified as amended in scattered sections of *U.S. Code*, vol. 15. Since 1980, Congress has exercised close and often critical review of FTC law-enforcement initiatives affecting physicians, attorneys, and other professionals whose activities are regulated by state governments. In 1984, following the FTC's issuance of an antitrust complaint challenging certain municipal taxicab regulations, Congress approved an appropriations measure prohibiting the commission from using its fiscal year 1985 funds to prosecute antitrust cases against cities. This limitation was soon lifted. See *Washington Post*, December 2, 1982, p. A2; *National Journal*, March 27, 1982, p. 535; and *CCH Trade Regulation Reports*, September 4, 1984, p. 7, and October 31, 1984, p. 4.

3. *Congressional Record*, 96th Cong., 1st sess., November 14, 1979, vol. 125: 32, 465–66. During debate over the 1980 FTC Improvements Act, Senator Cannon, one of the principal Senate sponsors of the act, emphasized that the FTC had ignored congressional policy guidance: "The real reason that we have proposed this legislation for the FTC is because the Commission appeared to be fully prepared to push its statutory authority to the very brink and beyond . . . Good judgment and wisdom had been replaced with an arrogance that seemed unparalleled among independent regulatory agencies" (*Congressional Record*, 96th Cong., 2d sess., May 21, 1980, vol. 126: 11,917.

4. American Bar Association, *Report of the American Bar Association Commission to Study the Federal Trade Commission* (Chicago, 1969). Hereafter this is cited as the *ABA Report*, and the ABA commission is referred to simply as the ABA.

5. Federal Trade Commission Act, *Statutes at Large*, vol. 38, ch. 311, 317 (1914), *U.S. Code*, vol. 15, secs. 41–58 (1976). In 1914 Wilson regarded the FTC Act as the centerpiece of his antitrust program. On the evolution of Wilson's antitrust thinking as it affected the FTC's formation, see Arthur S. Link, *Wilson: The New Freedom* (Princeton, N.J.: Princeton University Press, 1956), pp. 417–44, and Arthur S. Link, *Woodrow Wilson and the Progressive Era, 1910–1917* (New York: Harper and Row, 1954; Harper Torchbook, 1963), pp. 66–74.

6. *Congressional Record*, 63d Cong., 2d sess., September 5, 1914, vol. 51: 14,770. On Cummins' central role in the passage of the FTC Act, see Neil W. Averitt, "The Meaning of 'Unfair Methods of Competition' in Section 5 of the Federal Trade Commission Act," *Boston College Law Review* 21 (January 1980): 231–38.

7. Edward F. Cox, Robert C. Fellmeth, and John E. Schulz, *The Nader Report on the Federal Trade Commission* (New York: Richard W. Baron, 1969); *ABA Report*, p. 88.

8. The ABA panel's chairman, Miles Kirkpatrick, later chaired the FTC from 1970 to 1973. Robert Pitofsky, the panel's counsel and principal author of the *ABA Report*, headed the agency's Bureau of Consumer Protection in the early 1970s and served as a commissioner from 1978 to 1981. Of all its members, only Richard Posner opposed the panel's recommendations. *ABA Report*, pp. 92–119.

9. An exception to this criticism was the FTC's merger program, which the ABA praised. *ABA Report*, p. 13 n.33.

10. The informal devices included industry guides, advisory opinions, and assurances of voluntary compliance.

11. The ABA identified the "unique strengths" as (1) broad investigatory powers; (2) centralization in one agency of commissioners, administrative law judges, attorneys, and economists who could develop special antitrust policy competence; (3) the ability to decide questions without necessarily relying on case-by-case precedent; and (4) the power to issue antitrust studies to the president, Congress, and the public.

12. If established, per se violations were the sole concern of antitrust policy, the ABA might have suggested a different course.

13. The ABA cited eight previous studies of the FTC: U.S. Bureau of the Budget, *Federal Trade Commission Study 4 (No. CF-60-124)* (1960); Commission on Organization of the Executive Branch of the Government (Hoover Commission), *Task Force Report on Regulatory Commissions (Appendix N)* (Washington, D.C., 1949); Thomas C. Blaisdell, *The Federal Trade Commission: An Experiment in the Control of Business* (New York: Columbia University Press, 1932); Gerard C. Henderson, *The Federal Trade Commission: A Study in Administrative Law and Procedure* (New Haven, Conn.: Yale University Press, 1924); Louis M. Kohlmeier, Jr., *The Regulators* (New York: Harper and Row, 1969); Carl A. Auerbach, "The Federal Trade Commission: Internal Organization and Procedure," *Minnesota Law Review* 48 (1964): 383–522; U.S. Congress, Senate, Committee on the Judiciary, *Report on Regulatory Agencies to the President-Elect*, Report prepared by James M. Landis, 86th Cong., 2d sess., 1960; Cox, Fellmeth, and Schulz, *Nader Report*.

14. Although they possess important similarities, the earlier critiques lacked the uniform point of view assumed in the ABA's analysis. The ABA ignored significant disagreements or variations in emphasis in the critiques' discussions of the nature and causes of the agency's weaknesses, the appropriate standards for measuring performance, and the correct path for reform. In doing so, the ABA imparted a misleading simplicity to the problems and policy choices facing the FTC throughout its history. For a review of the literature assessing the work of the FTC and other regulatory agencies, see Thomas K. McCraw, "Regulation in America: A Review Article," *Business History Review* 49 (Summer 1975): 162–83.

15. Most earlier evaluations of the FTC and antitrust enforcement had either recommended that the commission continue to exercise antitrust authority or made proposals that assumed the FTC would retain its antitrust jurisdiction. Kovacic, "Congressional Oversight," pp. 600–601 n.61.

16. See also Robert A. Katzmann, *Regulatory Bureaucracy: The Federal Trade Commission and Antitrust Policy* (Cambridge, Mass.: MIT Press, 1980), pp. 76–85, 180–89. He observes that the opening of some small, easily prosecuted cases may be important to recruiting and retaining a capable litigation staff.

17. For an illuminating historical review of antitrust enforcement as a function of changing social attitudes toward competition and the market system, see Richard Hofstadter, *The Paranoid Style in American Politics and Other Essays* (New York: Alfred A. Knopf, 1966), pp. 188–237. See also Morton Keller, "The Pluralist State: American

Economic Regulation in Comparative Perspective, 1900–1930," in Thomas K. Mc-
Craw, ed., *Regulation in Perspective* (Cambridge, Mass.: Harvard University Press, 1981),
pp. 56–94.

18. For an excellent recent discussion of the legislative and popular aims that guided
Congress in passing the nation's antitrust laws, see Robert H. Lande, "Wealth Transfers
as the Original and Primary Concern of Antitrust: The Efficiency Interpretation
Challenged," *Hastings Law Journal* 34 (September 1982): 65–151.

19. E. Pendleton Herring, *Public Administration and the Public Interest* (New York:
McGraw-Hill, 1936), p. 110. For an impressively similar view spoken twenty years later,
see Marver H. Bernstein, *Regulating Business by Independent Commission* (Princeton,
N.J.: Princeton University Press, 1955), p. 222.

20. Henderson, *Federal Trade Commission*, pp. 16–19, 22–24; Richard Hofstadter,
The Age of Reform (New York: Alfred A. Knopf, 1966), pp. 246–50; Link, *Progressive
Era*, pp. 18–21.

21. Hofstadter, *Age of Reform*, pp. 247–49; Link, *Progressive Era*, pp. 18–21.

22. Woodrow Wilson, *The New Freedom* (New York: Doubleday, Page, 1913), p. 222.
The architect of Wilson's position on antitrust during the campaign was Louis D.
Brandeis. Link, *Progressive Era*, pp. 20–21.

23. Two major works of progressive thought helped move Roosevelt to this position:
Herbert Croly, *The Promise of American Life* (New York: Macmillan, 1909), and Charles
R. Van Hise, *Concentration and Control: A Solution of the Trust Problem in the United
States* (New York: Macmillan, 1912). Croly attacked the historical perception that
equated a Hamiltonian policy of intervention with aristocracy and special privilege—
an attitude that inhibited the creation of national policies to achieve Jeffersonian, or
democratic, ends. To Croly, the country needed a "new nationalism" in which the
federal government would work actively to change economic and social conditions.
Van Hise saw economic concentration as predetermined by the evolution of modern
business, but believed administrative control of the products of this evolutionary trend
was essential. On Croly's significance to Roosevelt's thought, see Eric F. Goldman,
Rendezvous with Destiny (New York: Alfred A. Knopf, 1952), pp. 204–7. On Van Hise's
importance, see Arthur M. Schlesinger, Jr., *The Crisis of the Old Order, 1919–1933*
(Boston: Houghton Mifflin, 1957), p. 22.

24. Roosevelt described the main elements of his program in "The Trusts, the People,
and the Square Deal," *Outlook*, November 18, 1911, pp. 649–56. See also John M.
Blum, *The Republican Roosevelt*, 2d ed. (Cambridge, Mass.: Harvard University Press,
1977), pp. 116–23.

25. Wilson, *New Freedom*, p. 202. "If the government is to tell big business men how
to run their business," Wilson asked, "then don't you see that big business men have to
get closer to the government even than they are now? Don't you see that they must
capture the government, in order not to be restrained too much by it?" (pp. 201–2).

26. Hofstadter, *Age of Reform*, pp. 247–48. Wilson feared size wrought by consolidation or illicit practices, but he disclaimed any desire to disturb firms that achieved
dominance through "fair competition" alone. Wilson appeared to assume that those
who pursued monopoly profit by exclusively benign means were doomed to Sisyphean
frustration. Nonetheless, he seemed willing to let such ambition have its day. Wilson,

New Freedom, pp. 163–91. His implicit faith that purely innocent behavior could virtually never yield a monopoly was probably the major respect in which his views differed from Roosevelt's.

It is wrong to attribute to Roosevelt in 1912 the total contempt for the Sherman Act that possessed some progressives who scorned the statute as a foolish bar to beneficial national planning. See, for example, Croly, *Promise of American Life*, p. 274; Walter Lippman, *Drift and Mastery* (New York: Mitchell, Kennerly, 1914). Roosevelt in 1913 saw a continuing usefulness for the Sherman Act as a means for dissolving firms that had acquired monopoly power through sharp practices. By the end of the decade, however, he had turned against the measure whose application had once stamped him as a "trustbuster." See Theodore Roosevelt, *The Foes of Our Own Household* (New York: George H. Doran, 1917), pp. 121–26.

27. George E. Mowry, *The Era of Theodore Roosevelt* (New York: Harper and Row, 1958; Harper Torchbook, 1962), p. 57.

28. Link, *New Freedom*, pp. 436–42.

29. The Senate Interstate Commerce Committee explicitly defined the issue of the proposed commission's role as a choice between comprehensive regulation that "contemplates even the regulation of prices" and limited intervention as "a necessary adjunct to the preservation of competition." U.S. Congress, Senate, Committee on Interstate Commerce, *S. Rep. No. 597*, 63d Cong., 2d sess., 1914, p. 10. See also Blaisdell, *Federal Trade Commission*, p. 2.

30. Douglas W. Jaenicke, "Herbert Croly, Progressive Ideology, and the FTC Act," *Political Science Quarterly* 93 (Fall 1978): 471–93.

31. Richard Hofstadter has called this period the "era of neglect" for antitrust enforcement. Hofstadter, *Paranoid Style*, p. 193.

32. Robert D. Cuff, *The War Industries Board: Business-Government Relations During World War I* (Baltimore, Md.: Johns Hopkins University Press, 1973); Robert F. Himmelberg, "The War Industries Board and the Antitrust Question in November 1918," *Journal of American History* 52 (June 1965): 59–74.

33. William E. Leuchtenburg, *The Perils of Prosperity, 1914–32* (Chicago: University of Chicago Press, 1958), pp. 40–41; Schlesinger, *Crisis of the Old Order*, pp. 37–38; Bernard M. Baruch, *American Industry in the War* (New York: Prentice-Hall, 1941).

34. William E. Leuchtenburg, "The Impact of the War on the American Political Economy," in Arthur S. Link, ed., *The Impact of World War I* (New York: Harper and Row, 1969), pp. 58–63; Goldman, *Rendezvous with Destiny*, pp. 237–38; Baruch, *American Industry*, pp. 104–7. Baruch, who headed the War Industries Board, said the mobilization had enabled businessmen to enjoy "the tremendous advantages, both to themselves and to the general public, of combination, of cooperation and common action, with their natural competitors" (p. 105).

35. For an analysis of the failed movements during and after World War I to revise the antitrust laws, see Cuff, *War Industries Board*, and Himmelberg, "Antitrust Question in November 1918." For a discussion of postwar efforts by business and government to promote industry self-regulation and cooperation between the private and public sectors, see Robert F. Himmelberg, *The Origins of the NRA: Business, Government, and the Trade Association Issue, 1921–1933* (New York: Fordham University Press, 1976).

36. Arthur R. Burns, *The Decline of Competition* (New York: McGraw-Hill, 1936), pp. 69–75; Ellis W. Hawley, "Herbert Hoover, the Commerce Secretariat, and the Vision of an 'Associative State,' 1921–1928," *Journal of American History* 61 (June 1974): 116–40.

37. Burns, *Decline of Competition*, pp. 68–69; Hawley, "Herbert Hoover," pp. 117–18.

38. U.S. Federal Trade Commission, *Annual Report* (Washington, D.C., 1928), p. 5; Thomas C. Cochran and William Miller, *The Age of Enterprise* (New York: Macmillan, 1942; Harper Torchbook, 1961), pp. 345–56.

39. Sumner S. Kittelle and Elmer Mostow, "A Review of the Trade Practice Conferences of the Federal Trade Commission," *George Washington Law Review* 8 (January–February 1940): 427–51; U.S. Federal Trade Commission, *Trade Practice Submittals 1919 to 1923* (Washington, D.C., 1923).

40. Blaisdell, *Federal Trade Commission*, pp. 93–98. Blaisdell calculated that between 1919 and 1929 there were 83 trade-practice conferences, and 60 of these were held between July 1927 and November 1929.

41. See, for example, Henderson, *Federal Trade Commission*, pp. 82, 244.

42. In 1930, one former commission official said the FTC's trade practice conferences marked the "beginning of systematic cooperative effort between various progressive industries and the government," which would ultimately enable business to carry out its affairs "on sound economic principles of cooperative effort as distinguished from destructive competition." Harry C. McCarty, "Trade Practice Conferences," *Corporate Practice Review* 2 (June 1930): 29.

43. Blaisdell, *Federal Trade Commission*, pp. 93–98; Herring, *Public Administration*, pp. 129–31. Use of the conferences peaked in the winter of 1929–1930, when 57 were convened.

44. Schlesinger, *Crisis of the Old Order*, p. 65; John D. Clark, *The Federal Trust Policy* (Baltimore, Md.: Johns Hopkins University Press, 1931), pp. 231–32; Kittelle and Mostow, "Trade Practice Conferences," pp. 436–38.

45. Himmelberg, *Origins*, pp. 93–98; Ellis W. Hawley, *The New Deal and the Problem of Monopoly* (Princeton, N.J.: Princeton University Press, 1966), p. 39; Herring, *Public Administration*, pp. 131–32.

46. Leuchtenburg, *Perils of Prosperity*, pp. 41–42.

47. Arthur M. Schlesinger, Jr., *The Coming of the New Deal* (Boston: Houghton Mifflin, 1958), pp. 119–35. Several industrialists, including Gerard Swope of General Electric, Walter Teagle of Standard Oil of New Jersey, and Myron Taylor of U.S. Steel, had previously urged the government to adjust production to demand. Schlesinger, *Crisis of the Old Order*, pp. 181–82. The NRA appears to have modeled its industry code program after the FTC's trade-practice conference procedure. Burns, *Decline of Competition*, p. 403.

48. William E. Leuchtenburg, *Franklin D. Roosevelt and the New Deal, 1932–1940* New York: Harper and Row, 1963), p. 69.

49. The NIRA's passage masked formidable tensions among cooperation advocates in business and government who differed over the exact form such cooperation should take. Hawley, *Problem of Monopoly*, pp. 135–42.

50. Schlesinger, *Coming of the New Deal*, pp. 100–101, 130–35, 167–69.

51. U.S. Congress, House, Select Committee on Small Business, *Staff Report on Statistics on Federal Antitrust Activities*, 84th Cong., 1st sess., 1956, pp. 3–4.

52. Herring, *Public Administration*, p. 115 (quoting Abram Myers, a commissioner from 1926 to 1929). Myers's remark understated the commission's work as a competition advocate in the early 1930s, particularly its efforts to draw attention to the cartelizing effects of several NRA codes. See Hawley, *Problem of Monopoly*, pp. 94–95, 108–9, 117.

53. Leuchtenburg, *Franklin D. Roosevelt*, pp. 148–49, 154–56, 163.

54. House Select Committee on Small Business, *Statistics on Federal Antitrust Activities*, p. 3. Ironically, in 1937 Arnold had argued that antitrust was a charade that enabled the country to express harmlessly its indignation at the discomforting but ultimately necessary process of industrial concentration. Thurman W. Arnold, *The Folklore of Capitalism* (New Haven, Conn.: Yale University Press, 1937), pp. 96, 207–29.

55. Hofstadter, *Paranoid Style*, p. 233.

56. See, for example, Blaisdell, *Federal Trade Commission*, pp. 259–86, and Carl McFarland, *Judicial Control of the Federal Trade Commission and the Interstate Commerce Commission, 1920–1930* (Cambridge, Mass.: Harvard University Press, 1933).

57. In this discussion of the institutional aims that moved Congress to create the FTC, the author is indebted to Robert Lande and Neil Averitt.

58. Standard Oil Company of New Jersey v. United States, 221 U.S. 1 (1911) and United States v. American Tobacco Company, 221 U.S. 106 (1911).

59. Henderson, *Federal Trade Commission*, p. 15; James M. Landis, *The Administrative Process* (New Haven, Conn.: Yale University Press, 1938), pp. 32–34.

60. Averitt, "Unfair Methods of Competition," pp. 233–34.

61. *Congressional Record*, 63d Cong., 2d sess., July 31, 1914, vol. 51: 13,047–48.

62. Experience with the Interstate Commerce Commission had shown that federal judges generally begrudged bestowing traditionally judicial functions on an administrative body. McFarland, *Judicial Control*, pp. 102–24.

63. Kovacic, "Congressional Oversight," pp. 612–13.

64. Blaisdell, *Federal Trade Commission*, p. 21. During the legislative debates in 1914, Senator Newlands predicted that Section 5 "will have such an elastic character that it will meet every new condition and every new practice that may be invented with a view to gradually bringing about monopoly through unfair competition." *Congressional Record*, 63d Cong., 2d sess., July 13, 1914, vol. 51: 12,024.

65. Federal Trade Commission v. Western Meat Co., 272 U.S. 554 (1926). As enacted in the original Clayton Act, Section 7 barred consolidations achieved by stock purchases. Businesses quickly realized that they could escape the statute's reach simply by buying the target firm's assets. Henderson, *Federal Trade Commission*, pp. 40, 321.

66. Federal Trade Commission v. Eastman Kodak Co., 274 U.S. 619 (1927), at pp. 623, 625.

67. U.S. Federal Trade Commission, *Annual Report* (Washington, D.C., 1927), p. 67. Without divestiture authority, the commission's ability to deal effectively with firms that had achieved near or actual monopoly power was severely diminished. Alan Stone, *Economic Regulation and the Public Interest: The Federal Trade Commission in Theory and Practice* (Ithaca, N.Y.: Cornell University Press, 1977), pp. 121–22.

68. Blaisdell, *Federal Trade Commission*, pp. 172, 258–62, 271–73; Burns, *Decline of Competition*, p. vi.

69. See, for example, Claire Furnace Co. v. Federal Trade Commission, 285 F. 936, 942 (D.C. Cir. 1923). See also Blaisdell, *Federal Trade Commission*, pp. 266–70, and Milton Handler, "The Constitutionality of Investigations by the Federal Trade Commission," *Columbia Law Review* 28 (June 1928): 714–20.

70. See, for example, Federal Trade Commission v. American Tobacco Co., 264 U.S. 298 (1924). See also Brunson MacChesney and Walter D. Murphy, "Investigatory and Enforcement Powers of the Federal Trade Commission," *George Washington Law Review* 8 (January–February 1940): 588, and Myron L. Watkins, "An Appraisal of the Work of the Federal Trade Commission," *Columbia Law Review* 32 (February 1932): 278–80.

71. Henderson was the main proponent of this view. Henderson, *Federal Trade Commission*, pp. 117, 163, 334.

72. Landis, *Administrative Process*, p. 150; Blaisdell, *Federal Trade Commission*, pp. 289–90; McFarland, *Judicial Control*, pp. 92–99; Milton Handler, "Unfair Competition and the Federal Trade Commission," *George Washington Law Review* 8 (January–February 1940): 401–2.

73. Robert G. McCloskey, *The American Supreme Court* (Chicago: University of Chicago Press, 1960), pp. 136–79; Arnold M. Paul, *Conservative Crisis and the Rule of Law* (Ithaca, N.Y.: Cornell University Press, 1960); Benjamin R. Twiss, *Lawyers and the Constitution* (Princeton, N.J.: Princeton University Press, 1942).

74. These early rulings greatly diminished the FTC's standing as a law-enforcement agency and injured its efforts to attract competent personnel. In 1936 Arthur Burns observed, "An administrative body hampered as the Federal Trade Commission has been by the judiciary cannot attract able men." Burns, *Decline of Competition*, p. 574.

75. Handler, "Unfair Competition," p. 402.

76. The power to proscribe large asset acquisitions under Section 5 conceivably would have afforded the FTC at least the opportunity to become the nation's principal body for the formation and application of merger antitrust policy.

77. See, for example, Federal Trade Commission v. Sperry and Hutchinson Co., 405 U.S. 233, 241–43 (1972); Federal Trade Commission v. Dean Foods Co., 384 U.S. 597, 606 n4 (1966) (dictum) (rejecting Kodak); United States v. Morton Salt Co., 338 U.S. 632, 641–42 (1950). See also Neil W. Averitt, "Structural Remedies in Competition Cases Under the Federal Trade Commission Act," *Ohio State Law Journal* 40 (1979): 788–94.

78. Federal Trade Commission v. Brown Shoe Co., 384 U.S. 316 (1966); FTC v. Dean Foods Co., 384 U.S. 597 (1966).

79. U.S. Congress, Senate, Committee on Commerce, *Appointments to the Regulatory Agencies: The Federal Communications Commission and the Federal Trade Commission (1949–1974)*, Report prepared by James M. Graham and Victor H. Kramer, 94th Cong., 2d sess., 1976, Committee Print.

80. John M. Blum, *Woodrow Wilson and the Politics of Morality* (Boston: Little, Brown, 1956), pp. 79–80.

81. Until 1950 the FTC chairmanship rotated annually among the commissioners.

Since 1950 the president has designated the chairmen for all independent regulatory agencies. In 1950 James Mead became the first presidentially designated FTC chairman; his tenure ended in 1955. Senate Committee on Commerce, *Appointments to the Regulatory Agencies*, p. 10. The tendency for lawyers to occupy all of the commissioner posts is a relatively recent phenomenon. In 1981 James C. Miller III, an economist, became the first nonlawyer to serve as a commissioner since James Mead.

82. E. Pendleton Herring, "The Federal Trade Commissioners," *George Washington Law Review* 8 (January–February 1940); 344–45.

83. Henderson, *Federal Trade Commission*, p. 87; George S. Rublee, "The Original Plan and Early History of the Federal Trade Commission," *Proceedings of the Academy of Political Science* 11 (January 1926): 671.

84. Link, *Progressive Era*, p. 75. Hurley explained his enforcement approach to the National Industrial Conference Board in July 1916:

> I do not know anything about the law, and that applies to the Clayton Act and to the Federal Trade Commission Act. In my position on the Federal Trade Commission I am there as a businessman . . . when I was offered the place, I told the President that all I knew was business, . . . and that I would apply the force that I might have in the interest of business . . . I think that the businessmen of the country will bear me out when I say that I try to work wholly in the interest of business.

Gabriel Kolko, *The Triumph of Conservatism: A Reinterpretation of American History, 1900–1916* (New York: The Free Press, 1963), pp. 274–75.

85. Robert H. Wiebe, *Businessmen and Reform: A Study of the Progressive Movement* (Cambridge, Mass.: Harvard University Press, 1962), pp. 138–41.

86. Louis Brandeis later referred to Wilson's early appointments to the commission as "a stupid administration." Link, *Progressive Era*, p. 74. In the fall of 1916, Wilson told a grain dealer's trade association, "It is hard to describe the functions of that Commission; all I can say is that it has transformed the Government of the United States from being an antagonist of business into being a friend of business." Herring, *Public Administration*, p. 112.

87. Herring, "The Federal Trade Commissioners," pp. 345–49; Link, *Progressive Era*, p. 75.

88. Blaisdell, *Federal Trade Commission*, p. 75; Herring, *Public Administration*, pp. 125–38; John D. Hicks, *Republican Ascendency, 1921–1933* (New York: Harper and Row, 1960; Harper Torchbook, 1963), pp. 64–66. Arthur Link cautions that the Harding administration's regulatory policies constituted a change in degree from Wilson's views rather than an abrupt break. Arthur S. Link, "What Happened to the Progressive Movement in the 1920s?" *American Historical Review* 64 (July 1959): 848–49. For an overview of government antitrust policy in the 1920s, see Himmelberg, *Origins*.

89. Leuchtenburg, *Perils of Prosperity*, p. 96; Schlesinger, *Crisis of the Old Order*, p. 57; Goldman, *Rendezvous with Destiny*, pp. 220–47.

90. Leuchtenburg, *Perils of Prosperity*, p. 97.

91. Hicks, *Republican Ascendency*, p. 64–66.

92. G. Cullom Davis, "The Transformation of the Federal Trade Commission, 1914–1929," *Mississippi Valley Historical Review* 49 (December 1962): 437–55.

93. Herring, *Public Administration*, p. 125. In a 1931 speech Humphrey said the FTC's "old policy of litigation" had made the agency "an instrument of oppression and disturbance and injury instead of a help to business" (p. 125). Of Humphrey's remarks Herring wrote in 1936, "It is not that these declarations are particularly cogent or marked by profundity of thought; it is rather that they reflect in bald and obvious form the prevailing views of the conservative leaders in his party and in business at the time" (pp. 125–26).

94. Blaisdell, *Federal Trade Commission*, pp. 82–86.

95. U.S. Federal Trade Commission, *Annual Report* (Washington, D.C., 1925), p. 11. The latter rule applied even to cases involving fraud and misrepresentation. Herring, *Public Administration*, p. 129.

96. Blaisdell, *Federal Trade Commission*, p. 85; Herring, *Public Administration*, p. 129. FTC commissioners John Nugent and Huston Thompson attacked the publicity limitations on the grounds that they deprived the agency of an important means of deterring anticompetitive behavior. Davis, "Transformation," pp. 448–49.

97. Reflecting on Humphrey's first year in office, Senator George Norris lamented, "It seems to me that if the commission is . . . to continue to perform the work that the law designed it to perform, its personnel must be of men who believe in that kind of a law." *Congressional Record*, 69th Cong., 1st sess., March 20, 1926, vol. 67: 5962.

98. Senator William King sponsored a bill to achieve this end, saying the FTC was "not only a useless appendage, but . . . a real menace." Senator Tom Connally said the agency had become "a city of refuge to which the guilty may flee, a sanctuary for those who violate and defy the laws of the United States." Davis, "Transformation," pp. 453–54.

99. See, for example, Blaisdell, *Federal Trade Commission*, pp. 289–90.

100. This paper has already touched on congressional influence over FTC antitrust activities. Significant examples include passage of the NIRA in 1933 and Humphrey's confirmation as FTC chairman in 1925.

101. See, for example, Herring, *Public Administration*, pp. 115–16. Congress, as Daniel Baum has described it, continually restates and defines the FTC's mandate: "The question no longer is . . . what the agency acting independently has the power to do under statute, but rather . . . how far the agency can go without incurring the wrath of Congress." Daniel J. Baum, "Antitrust Functions of the Federal Trade Commission: Area Discrimination and Product Differentiation," *Federal Bar Journal* 24 (Fall 1964): 600.

102. Congress expected the commission to use its information-gathering authority to advise Congress and the president on antitrust matters and to collect data whose publication alone might correct market imperfections. The House report on the FTC Act, for example, anticipated that publication of business profits would attract entry into lucrative markets and depress prices. U.S. Congress, House, Committee on Interstate and Foreign Commerce, *H.R. Rep. No. 533*, 63d Cong., 2d sess., 1914, pp. 3–4. Access to business records would also improve the empirical basis for the commis-

sion's selection of antitrust priorities and specific enforcement programs. Blaisdell, *Federal Trade Commission*, pp. 113–14.

103. Herring, *Public Administration*, p. 118; Blaisdell, *Federal Trade Commission*, pp. 188–91.

104. U.S. Federal Trade Commission, *Food Investigation: Report of the Federal Trade Commission on the Meatpacking Industry. Summary and Part I (Extent and Growth of the Five Packers in Meat and Other Industries)* (Washington, D.C., 1919). The report was submitted to President Wilson in summary form in 1918 and given to Congress in its entirety in 1919. Herring, *Public Administration*, p. 118.

105. Reaction to the report provided "a concrete illustration of the political and administrative problems involved in attempting to regulate a powerful industry . . . The sweeping character of this investigation and the bold changes suggested caused a political backlash almost fatal to the Commission." Herring, *Public Administration*, pp. 118–19. Senator Thomas Watson, a leading advocate of the packers' position, called for an investigation of the commission employees who made the study. Watson said the FTC's Chicago headquarters were "centers of sedition and anarchy . . . a nesting place for socialists, a spawning ground for sovietism." *Congressional Record*, 66th Cong., 1st sess., October 20, 1919, vol. 58: 7169. The commission investigated and exonerated the employees in question, but dismissed them nonetheless, a move widely seen as an effort to placate Watson. Blaisdell, *Federal Trade Commission*, pp. 78–79; Herring, *Public Administration*, p. 119.

106. "The packers were desirous of getting from under the jurisdiction of the Federal Trade Commission. They seemed to feel that they would receive more sympathetic treatment from the officials in the Department of Agriculture." Herring, *Public Administration*, p. 120. See also Davis, "Transformation," p. 441, and Landis, *Administrative Process*, pp. 112–13.

107. Davis, "Transformation," p. 441.

108. Formal congressional efforts to retrench the FTC's economic work began in the middle and late 1920s with proposals to cease or sharply limit funds for the agency's economic division. Robert E. Cushman, *The Independent Regulatory Commissions* (New York: Oxford University Press, 1941), p. 220. Spearheading this effort was Representative Wood, chairman of the House Appropriations Subcommittee for Independent Offices, who said the FTC's chief economist, Francis Walker, did little but "promulgate a lot of wild-eyed theories and idealism." Herring, *Public Administration*, p. 128. In 1933 Congress barred the FTC from beginning new investigations pursuant to legislative resolutions unless the requests were in the form of concurrent resolutions. W. H. S. Stevens, "The Federal Trade Commission's Contribution to Industrial and Economic Analysis: The Work of the Economic Division," *George Washington Law Review* 8 (January–February 1940): 549–53.

109. A. Everette MacIntyre and Joachim J. Volhard, "The Federal Trade Commission," *Boston College Industrial and Commercial Law Review* 11 (May 1970): 755–56. Through 1933, Congress or the president had originated most of the FTC's general studies. U.S. Federal Trade Commission, *Annual Report* (Washington, D.C., 1939), pp. 203–24.

110. Stevens, "Economic Division," p. 553. In 1970 MacIntyre and Volhard esti-

mated that before 1933 some 43 investigations had been initiated by a resolution of the Senate and five by the House. Only three were requested between 1933 and 1938, and none were sought from 1938 to 1970. MacIntyre and Volhard, "Federal Trade Commission," p. 755.

111. The FTC's study of electric and gas utility holding companies, which followed a Senate resolution, is a noteworthy example. See U.S. Federal Trade Commission, *Summary Report on Holding and Operating Companies of Electric and Gas Utilities,* 74th Cong., 2d sess. (1935), S. Doc. no. 92, pt. 73-A: 59–76.

112. The meatpacking study was performed at President Wilson's request. Two other examples illustrate this trend. In 1952 President Truman asked the FTC for a comprehensive study of consumer expenditures. Congress barred the agency from spending any funds on such a study. Similarly, in 1963 the FTC's Bureau of Economics proposed a study of the nation's 1,000 largest firms, but Congress banned any expenditure of the agency's funds on that venture. Stanley E. Boyle, "Economic Reports and the Federal Trade Commission: 50 Years' Experience," *Federal Bar Journal* 24 (Fall 1964): 501.

113. Federal Trade Commission v. Cement Institute, 333 U.S. 683 (1948). See Corwin Edwards, *The Price Discrimination Law* (Washington, D.C.: Brookings Institution, 1959), pp. 400–438, and Earl Latham, *The Group Basis of Politics* (Ithaca, N.Y.: Cornell University Press, 1952).

114. U.S. Congress, House, Staff of the Subcommittee on Monopoly of the House Committee on Small Business, *Report on United States Versus Economic Concentration and Monopoly,* 79th Cong., 2d sess., 1946, p. 27, Committee Print.

115. In re Cement Institute, 37 F.T.C. 87 (1943). The FTC had filed the complaint in 1937.

116. Aetna Portland Cement Co. v. Federal Trade Commission, 157 F.2d 533 (7th Cir. 1946); FTC v. Cement Institute, 333 U.S. 683 (1948). For the court majority in the latter decision, Justice Black wrote, "We are persuaded that the Commission's long and close examination of the questions it here decided has provided it with precisely the experience that fits it for performance of its statutory duty" (p. 720). More than mechanical deference to administrative expertise, this comment ackowledged that the commission had built the Cement Institute lawsuit upon extensive economic and legal analysis—following the model Congress had envisioned in 1914.

117. Earl Latham, "The Politics of Basing Point Legislation," *Law and Contemporary Problems* 15 (Spring 1950): 273–77. Joining ranks with the cement industry were the country's steelmakers, which were also losing an FTC basing-point suit. See Triangle Conduit and Cable Co. v. Federal Trade Commission, 168 F.2d 175 (7th Cir. 1948), aff'd by an equally divided Court sub nom. Clayton Mark and Co. v. FTC, 336 U.S. 956 (1949).

118. The proposed legislation is discussed in Latham, *Group Basis of Politics,* pp. 54–208. See also Baum, "Antitrust Functions," p. 597, which states that "the hearings . . . were used to achieve two hurried ends: (1) the exertion of pressure to force the Commission to back down, and not enforce the rulings of the Court, and (2) the enactment of legislation which would soften existing antitrust laws."

119. Edwards, *Price Discrimination Law,* pp. 430–32.

120. Clair Wilcox, *Public Policies Toward Business* (Chicago: Richard D. Irwin, 1955), pp. 259–60. Baum has observed:

> The storm following the Cement [Institute] case left destruction and a message. . . . The will of Congress cannot be ignored; statutory power must, at times, be exercised in a political context. The question is not always what the Commission can in theory do, but, rather what it can in reality accomplish. This calls for the agency to be aware of the mood of Congress, and, more precisely the measure of opposition to proposed policy decisions.

Baum, "Antitrust Functions," p. 606. See also John M. Blair, "Planning for Competition," *Columbia Law Review* 64 (March 1964): 525.

121. Cox, Fellmeth, and Schulz, *Nader Report*. The Nader study mainly discussed the FTC's consumer-protection activities, but its criticisms often applied to the entire agency; devoting "its dwindling energies to the prosecution of the most trivial cases," the FTC was said to be "engaged in active and continuing collusion with business interests—particularly big-business interests" (pp. 45, 121).

122. *ABA Report*, pp. 37, 68.

123. The risk comes in two principal forms. First, the commission is likely to win fewer cases as it brings more lawsuits affecting large economic stakes and dealing with complex, unsettled areas of law and economics. Effective litigation strategy dictates that respondents will contest economically significant suits vigorously and will urge judicial officers to shun "novel" economic or legal theories and avoid departures from existing doctrine. Second, enforcement programs affecting substantial economic interests run a greater risk of spurring affected firms to seek intervention by Congress or the executive branch on their behalf, particularly where the FTC rests its actions on "novel" or "unproven" theories. As Cushman notes, "The authority to investigate . . . mammoth business concerns . . . is a power loaded with political dynamite. It is bound to arouse the bitter antagonism of those being investigated and to set in motion powerful political pressures." Cushman, *Independent Regulatory Commissions*, p. 219.

124. Political adroitness can be as important to the success of an administrative agency's programs as technical proficiency. See Francis E. Rourke, *Bureaucratic Power in National Politics*, 2d ed. (Boston: Little, Brown, 1972), p. 2. Rourke states that "each agency must constantly create a climate of acceptance for its activities and negotiate alliances with powerful legislative and community groups to sustain its position. It must, in short, master the art of politics as well as the science of administration."

125. Richard Posner's dissent to the *ABA Report* argued that the career interests of FTC commissioners alone made it extremely unlikely that the agency would begin or sustain politically risky programs. *ABA Report*, pp. 116–17.

126. This paper does not analyze the appointment of commissioners by the president in the decade following the *ABA Report*. As a group, these appointments placed the agency's leadership in the hands of individuals who shared many of the ABA's views and were committed to revitalizing the agency. Senate Committee on Commerce, *Appointments to the Regulatory Agencies*, pp. 333–56, 369–70. President Nixon's appointment of Miles Kirkpatrick, who headed the ABA panel, to chair the FTC in 1970 is an outstanding example of this trend.

In addition to the appointments process, the executive branch can influence the FTC's activities through the budget process. On at least two occasions, the Office of Management and Budget (OMB) has tried to shape FTC antitrust work through the president's annual budget request. In 1937 the Bureau of the Budget, the OMB's predecessor, sought unsuccessfully to eliminate the FTC's economic division by refusing to ask funds for its operation. See U.S. Congress, House, Committee on Appropriations, *Independent Offices Appropriation Bill for 1937. Hearings Before the Subcommittee of the House Committee on Appropriations*, 74th Cong., 2d sess., 1936, pp. 218–60. More recently, in 1981, the OMB asked Congress to cease funding the FTC's Bureau of Competition. See House Committee on Government Operations, *Impact of OMB-Proposed Budget Cuts.*

127. The FTC's success would require legislative support for antitrust enforcement generally and for the agency's specific antitrust programs. The purposes that inspire congressmen to create regulatory structures may differ from those motivating legislators' reactions to specific enforcement initiatives. See David R. Mayhew, *Congress: The Electoral Connection* (New Haven, Conn.: Yale University Press, 1974), pp. 134–35, who states: "Regulatory statutes are the by-products of congressional position taking at times of public dissatisfaction . . . What happens in enforcement is largely a result of congressional credit claiming activities on behalf of the regulated; there is every reason to believe that the regulatory agencies do what Congress wants them to do."

128. Kovacic, "Congressional Oversight," p. 630 n.216.

129. Senator Edward Kennedy, then chairman of the Senate Judiciary Subcommittee on Administrative Practice and Procedures, underscored this point during an FTC oversight hearing on the day the *ABA Report* was released:

> The subcommittee hopes . . . to see to it that the proposals we have received do not merely become grist for the mill of future students of the FTC . . . Surely, 45 years after Henderson's landmark work on the FTC, first exposing many of the same problems we see today, the time has come either to do something about them, or, . . . to consider abolishing the agency and starting it from the ground again.

U.S. Congress, Senate, Committee on the Judiciary, *Federal Trade Commission Procedures. Hearings Before the Subcommittee on Administrative Practice and Procedures of the Senate Committee on the Judiciary*, 91st Cong., 1st sess., 1969, pt. 1: 110.

Two major recent discussions of the FTC's relations with Congress in the 1960s and 1970s have demonstrated the existence of strong congressional sentiment favoring vigorous government antitrust and consumer-protection initiatives at least as early as the mid-1960s. See Michael Pertschuk, *Revolt Against Regulation: The Rise and Pause of the Consumer Movement* (Berkeley: University of California Press, 1982), and Barry R. Weingast and Mark J. Moran, "Bureaucratic Discretion or Congressional Control? Regulatory Policymaking by the Federal Trade Commission" (Chapter 3 of this volume). The chief functions of the *ABA Report* and the *Nader Report* seem to have been to (1) sharply increase public and congressional attention to the FTC and its performance, and (2) catalyze powerful pre-existing congressional reform impulses by supplying a concrete program for renewing the institution.

130. As mentioned above, several scholars have concluded that, since the FTC's founding, the Senate has reviewed most commission appointments cursorily. See Senate Committee on Commerce, *Appointments to the Regulatory Agencies* (cited in this note as *Appointments*), p. 400, and Katzmann, *Regulatory Bureaucracy*, pp. 140–42. This view accurately describes Senate participation in the appointments process for much of the FTC's history, but not for the 1970s. The Senate Commerce Committee and its staff actively screened potential commission appointees before their appointments and used confirmation hearings to elicit pledges that the nominees would execute the agency's responsibilities aggressively. *Appointments*, pp. 333–51, 370–71. The driving forces on the Senate Commerce Committee were Senator Warren Magnuson, the committee chairman, and Senators Frank Moss and Philip Hart, who were chairman and vice chairman, respectively, of the Subcommittee for Consumers. All shared an abiding interest in the FTC's revitalization and used the committee's power to achieve that end. Pertschuk, *Revolt Against Regulation*, pp. 15, 20–28; Weingast and Moran, "Regulatory Policymaking." The Commerce Committee staff (whose chief counsel was Michael Pertschuk) and other staff members at the disposal of these senators were instrumental in seeing that nominees were suitable to the committee leadership. *Appointments*, pp. 350–51. The joint efforts of the senators and their staffs ensured the selection of appointees—particularly nominees for the chairmanship—who shared the committee's enforcement goals and the abandonment of potential nominees who did not. Katzmann, *Regulatory Bureaucracy*, pp. 143–45. Indeed, the prevailing sentiment in the oversight committees in the early and mid-1970s was expressed by Senator Moss in 1973 during hearings on Lewis Engman's nomination to become the commission chairman. Moss told Engman, "We consider it one of our solemn duties to protect the Commission from economic and political forces which would deflect it from its regulatory zeal." U.S. Congress, Senate, Committee on Commerce, *Nomination of Lewis A. Engman, to Be a Commissioner of the Federal Trade Commission. Hearings Before the Senate Committee on Commerce*, 93d Cong., 1st sess., 1973, p. 5.

131. U.S. Congress, Senate, Committee on Commerce, *Nomination of Caspar W. Weinberger to Be Chairman of the Federal Trade Commission. Hearings Before the Senate Committee on Commerce*, 91st Cong., 1st sess., 1970, p. 5. The appropriations committees of the House and Senate conveyed the same message to Weinberger in his first appearances before them. For example, Senator John Pastore said to Chairman Weinberger: "There is a new ball game down there now . . . I think you ought to tighten it up . . . We keep passing these laws in Congress and there is no need to pass them unless you are going to enforce them." U.S. Congress, Senate, Committee on Appropriations, *Independent Offices and Department of Housing and Urban Development Appropriations for Fiscal Year 1971. Hearings Before a Subcommittee of the Senate Committee on Appropriations*, 91st Cong., 2d sess., 1970, p. 494.

132. U.S. Congress, Senate, Committee on Appropriations, *Agriculture—Environmental and Consumer Protection Appropriations for Fiscal Year 1972. Hearings Before a Subcommittee of the Senate Committee on Appropriations*, 92d Cong., 1st sess., 1971, p. 2673. The following year, Senator McGee noted approvingly that Kirkpatrick had "responded to the criticism . . . by both Mr. Nader and the American Bar Association

by moving aggressively against some of the major industries in the United States...If you step on toes you are going to catch flak for it, but I hope we will be able to push this even more aggressively by backing you more completely with the kind of help that I think you require...Stay with it, and flex your muscles, clench your fists, sharpen your claws, and go to it." U.S. Congress, Senate, Committee on Appropriations, *Agriculture—Environmental and Consumer Protection Appropriations for Fiscal Year 1973. Hearings Before a Subcommittee of the Senate Committee on Appropriations.* 92d Cong., 2d sess., 1972, pp. 1483, 1490, 1507.

133. For example, Senator Moss welcomed Engman to his confirmation hearings by telling him that, under Weinberger and Kirkpatrick, "the Commission has taken on new life...reaching out with innovative programs to restore competition." Moss explained further:

> Under their direction, the Commission has not shied away from tangling with giants of American commerce. That is as it should be. The Commission has stretched its powers to provide a credible countervailing public force to the enormous economic and political power of huge corporate conglomerates which today dominate American enterprise. That is as it should be. This Committee has stood in solid support of the Commission's efforts.

Senate Committee on Commerce, *Nomination of Engman*, pp. 4–5. See also Kovacic, "Congressional Oversight," p. 633 n.222.

134. Senate Committee on Commerce, *Nomination of Engman*, pp. 25, 31.

135. The committees routinely emphasized the importance of taking congressional views seriously. See Kovacic, "Congressional Oversight," p. 634 n.225

136. Ibid., pp. 634 nn.226, 227; 635 n.228.

137. See, for example, U.S. Congress, Senate, Committee on the Judiciary, *S.2387 and Related Bills. Hearings Before the Subcommittee on Antitrust and Monopoly of the Senate Committee on the Judiciary*, 94th Cong., 1st sess., 1975, pt. 1: 47–48. During those hearings, Senator Robert Packwood said: "When we in Congress see this inevitable result of the concentration of power,...the stifling of competition...[t]he answer is to require the breaking up and divestiture of the giant business conglomerates into smaller parts so that the competitive system may flourish and grow again." See also Kovacic, "Congressional Oversight," p. 635 n.229.

138. As the source of the following discussion on congressional concern, refer to Kovacic, "Congressional Oversight," pp. 635 nn.230, 231; 636 nn. 235, 236, 237; 637 nn.238, 239; 637–38 n.243.

139. The amendments authorized the FTC to issue certain questionnaires without first obtaining clearance from the OMB, as previously required. In 1972 and 1973 the FTC had sought OMB approval for its line-of-business questionnaires but was turned down each time. The 1973 legislation transferred this approval authority to the General Accounting Office, a body more favorably disposed to the FTC proposal.

140. U.S. Congress, House, Committee on Appropriations, *Agriculture—Environmental and Consumer Protection Appropriations for 1974. Hearings Before the Subcommittee on Agriculture—Environmental and Consumer Protection of the House Committee on Appropriations*, 93d Cong., 1st sess., 1973, pt. 6: 101. Lest Engman take

his views lightly, Andrews added: "If [farmers] can't get gasoline to put in their crops . . . you are likely to have a lot of them down here standing with pitchforks at your door some day. I might be tempted to join them" (p. 103).

141. Kovacic, "Congressional Oversight," pp. 638 n.245, 638–39 n.246.

142. Ibid., p. 639 n.247.

143. In re Exxon Corp., [1973–1976 Transfer Binder] Trade Reg. Rep. (CCH) ¶20,388 at 20,269 (No. 8934, July 17, 1973). One respondent to the Exxon suit later sought unsuccessfully to have the complaint dismissed on the grounds that the FTC lacked "reason to believe" that the FTC Act had been violated and instead had issued the complaint mainly in response to congressional pressure. See Federal Trade Commission v. Standard Oil Company of California, 449 U.S. 232 (1980). In 1976, during hearings by the House Subcommittee on Oversight and Investigations, FTC Bureau of Competition director Owen Johnson and Representative James Collins had discussed the origins of the Exxon complaint:

> Mr. Johnson: . . . I suppose that, in 1973, with the advent of the energy crisis, there was a lot of public pressure brought to bear on the Commission over the conduct of [the FTC's pending petroleum industry] investigation.
>
> Representative Collins: Most of that pressure came out of Congress who, in its wisdom, decided the oil industry was a target that should receive consideration. I think most of the encouragement you have received has been from Congress.

U.S. Congress, House, Committee on Interstate and Foreign Commerce, *Regulatory Reform, Volume IV. Hearings Before the Subcommittee on Oversight and Investigations of the House Committee on Interstate and Foreign Commerce*, 94th Cong., 2d sess., 1976, pp. 615–16.

144. The committees and individual congressmen expressed strong interest in FTC and other government actions that might protect the competitive position of independent refiners and marketers. See Kovacic, "Congressional Oversight," p. 639 n.249.

145. A major congressional aim in ordering the FTC study was to measure the allocation system's impact on the petroleum industry's independent sector. Ibid., p. 639 n.250.

146. Ibid., p. 640 nn.253, 254, 255.

147. Ibid., pp. 640 nn.256, 257, 258; 641 n.260. The increase in civil penalties was accomplished through provisions contained in the Trans-Alaska Pipeline Authorization Act of 1973 and the Magnuson-Moss Warranty and FTC Improvements Act. The Magnuson-Moss bill also expanded the FTC's jurisdiction under Section 5 to matters "in or affecting commerce," included "persons and partnerships" as entities subject to the agency's investigatory powers, and gave the commission authority to seek Supreme Court review of its rulings where the solicitor general declined to do so.

148. Throughout its history, the commission had received only modest financial support. Beginning with $200,000 in 1915, the FTC's budget grew by miniscule increments through the next five decades. Its total outlays reached nearly $2 million in 1935, $3.5 million in 1949, $4.3 million in 1952, $5.5 million in 1957, $10.3 million in 1962, and nearly $17 million in 1969, the year of the *ABA Report*. Through fiscal

year 1969, Congress had appropriated a total of approximately $230 million for the FTC, roughly $100 million of which had gone to support antitrust enforcement. This slow rate of growth took place at a time when Congress was adding substantially to the agency's antitrust and consumer-protection responsibilities. See Kovacic, "Congressional Oversight," p. 641 n.261.

149. Senate Committee on the Judiciary, *FTC Procedures*, p. 24. See also Kovacic, "Congressional Oversight," p. 641 n.262.

150. Kovacic, "Congressional Oversight," p. 641 n.263.

151. From 1965 to 1979, the total number of FTC antitrust complaints ranged from 25 in 1965 to 37 in 1976 and again in 1979. The chief departures from this pattern occurred in 1966, when the agency issued 95 complaints, including 73 Robinson-Patman actions) and in 1978, when it filed a low of 12.

152. Katzmann, *Regulatory Bureaucracy*, p. 146; Kovacic, "Congressional Oversight," p. 642 nn.265, 266.

153. Kirkpatrick told the committees that the reduction had stemmed from commission efforts to "put greater emphasis on industry structure, and on seriously anticompetitive behavior." He added that FTC "efforts to get effective relief in these more complicated cases will mean that fewer cases will be settled." U.S. Congress, House, Committee on Appropriations, *Agriculture—Environmental and Consumer Protection Appropriations for 1973. Hearings Before a Subcommittee of the House Committee on Appropriations*, 92d Cong., 2d sess., 1972, p. 426.

154. Kovacic, "Congressional Oversight," p. 642 n.268.

155. Ibid., p. 643 n.269.

156. See, for example, U.S. Congress, House, Committee on Interstate and Foreign Commerce, *Federal Trade Commission Practices and Procedures. Hearings Before the Special Subcommittee on Investigations of the House Committee on Interstate and Foreign Commerce*, 93d Cong., 2d sess., 1974, pp. 219–20. In these hearings, former Bureau of Competition director Alan Ward said: "Before I came to the Commission [in the early 1970s], the enforcement stance of the Commission was beginning to change. It had already begun to respond to the report of the ABA Commission, which urged a concentration 'on difficult and complex problems,' with which the FTC was uniquely equipped to deal."

157. Kovacic, "Congressional Oversight," p. 643 nn.271, 272. In 1972 the Bureau of Competition created an Evaluation Office to screen proposals for new investigations and to monitor the progress of ongoing projects.

158. Ibid., p. 644 nn.273, 274. The economists' principal planning role was to identify economic sectors worthy of careful antitrust scrutiny.

159. Ibid., p. 644 n.275; Katzmann, *Regulatory Bureaucracy*, pp. 122–25.

160. Kovacic, "Congressional Oversight," p. 644 n.276.

161. An early step in this direction stemmed from Caspar Weinberger's desire to "probe the frontiers" of the agency's statutes to devise new strategies for addressing competition and consumer-protection problems. He told the agency's staff that the "Commission is receptive to novel and imaginative provisions in orders seeking to remedy alleged unlawful practices." U.S. Congress, Senate, Committee on Commerce, *Nomination of Miles W. Kirkpatrick to Be Chairman of the Federal Trade Commis-*

sion. Hearings Before the Senate Committee on Commerce, 91st Cong., 2d sess., 1970, pp. 133–36. Chairmen Kirkpatrick and Engman built upon this technique by developing guidelines and policy protocols to signal changes in priorities and enforcement strategies.

162. Ibid., p. 138.

163. Senate Committee on Appropriations, *Fiscal Year 1972,* p. 2643.

164. Kovacic, "Congressional Oversight," p. 645 n.280. Not until 1978, however, after prolonged litigation with firms subject to the program's reporting requirements, did the FTC begin to collect the bulk of the data it had sought to obtain. See In re FTC Line-of-Business Report Litigation, 1978-2 Trade Cas. (CCH) ¶62,152 (D.C. Cir.), cert. denied sub nom. American Air Filter Co. v. FTC, 439 U.S. 958 (1978). In 1984 the FTC voted to disband the program.

165. Kovacic, "Congressional Oversight," p. 645 nn.281, 284, 285, 286. Although it received less emphasis, the transportation industry constituted a fourth prominent area of concern.

166. The commission's litigation efforts corresponded with a major de-emphasis on voluntary, nonbinding proceedings. See, for example, Senate Committee on Appropriations, *Fiscal Year 1972,* p. 2684.

167. One rough measure of the importance of the FTC's work is the size of respondent firms in its suits. Data on FTC antitrust cases suggest that the absolute size of firms sued from 1970 to 1979 substantially exceeded the size of firms prosecuted by the FTC in the 1960s. "FTC Data Indicates Bureau of Competition, Not Antitrust Division, Sights Bigger Targets," *BNA Antitrust and Trade Regulation Reports,* July 3, 1980, p. A7.

168. See In re Kellogg Co., [1970–1973 Transfer Binder] Trade Reg. Rep. (CCH) ¶19,898 (No. 8883, April 26, 1972), complaint dismissed, 3 Trade Reg. Rep. (CCH) ¶21,864 (September 10, 1981), appeal denied, 3 Trade Reg. Rep. (CCH) ¶21,899 (January 15, 1982); In re Exxon Corp., [1973–1976 Transfer Binder] Trade Reg. Rep. (CCH) ¶20,388 (No. 8934, July 17, 1973), complaint dismissed, 3 Trade Reg. Rep. (CCH) ¶21,866 (September 16, 1981); In re Xerox Corp., 86 F.T.C. 364 (1975) (consent order). Explaining the enforcement approach that ultimately gave rise to these initiatives, Chairman Kirkpatrick told the Antitrust Law Section of the New York State Bar Association in the early 1970s that, "We are moving into high gear in the task of preserving and promoting competition throughout the American economy, and . . . we fully intend to be in the vanguard of exploration of the new frontiers of antitrust law." "Federal Trade Commission: '43 Grad Transforms Agency into a 'Growling Watchdog,'" *University of Pennsylvania Law Alumni Journal* (Fall 1971): 9.

169. As late as the fall of 1974, some committees were criticizing the commission for being insufficiently vigorous in attacking perceived monopolies, notwithstanding the pendency of the Kellogg, Exxon, and Xerox cases. See Kovacic, "Congressional Oversight," pp. 646–47 n.297, 647 n.298.

170. Ibid., p. 647 n.299.

171. See, for example, In re Kennecott Copper Corp., 78 F.T.C. 744 (1971), aff'd, 467 F.2d 67 (10th Cir. 1972), cert. denied, 416 U.S. 909 (1974). Chairman Weinberger in 1970 gave the House Judiciary Committee the following rationale for the FTC's concern with conglomerate firms and transactions:

If the probability of anticompetitive performance resulting from conglomerate-induced concentration is a proper subject of concern, and I believe it is, then our focus should be broadened to cover concentration in its entirety. We should consider the extent to which concentration is the result of anticompetitive behavior or structural change induced by mergers. In the allocation of the Commission's limited resources I would also assign high priority to the development of coherent policy on such matters as undue concentration, product differentiation, advertising (which we know creates a barrier to entry by new companies), oligopoly pricing, and power buying.

U.S. Congress, House, Committee on the Judiciary, *Investigation of Conglomerate Corporations. Hearings Before the Antitrust Subcommittee of the House Committee on the Judiciary*, 91st Cong., 2d sess., 1970, pt. 7: 250.

172. See, for example, In re Georgia-Pacific Corp., 81 F.T.C. 984 (1972) (consent decree resulting in the creation of Louisiana-Pacific as a new lumber products firm).

173. Kovacic, "Congressional Oversight," p. 647 n.302.

174. See, for example, In re Coca-Cola Co., 91 F.T.C. 517 (1978) (complaint issued July 15, 1971), remanded, 642 F.2d 1387 (D.C. Cir.), complaint dismissed, 3 Trade Reg. Rep. (CCH) ¶21,845 (July 28, 1981); and In re Levi Strauss Co., 92 F.T.C. 171 (1978) (consent decree; complaint issued on May 5, 1976).

175. See In re Boise Cascade Co., 91 F.T.C. 1 (1978) (complaint issued April 18, 1974), enforcement denied, 637 F.2d 573 (9th Cir. 1980); In re Tyson's Corner Regional Shopping Center, 85 F.T.C. 970 (1975); and In re American Medical Association, 94 F.T.C. 701 (1979) (complaint issued December 19, 1975), aff'd in part, modified in part, 638 F.2d 443 (2d Cir. 1980), aff'd by an equally divided Court, 455 U.S. 676 (1982).

176. Except in 1966, the commission brought roughly ten Robinson-Patman cases per year from 1965 to 1969. In 1966 the FTC issued 73 Robinson-Patman complaints, most being consent cases involving small clothing manufacturers. In the early 1970s the average number of Robinson-Patman suits fell to four per year, and they dropped to two per year in the late 1970s.

177. On February 26, 1976, the commission authorized an investigation of physician control of Blue Shield plans. On August 2, 1976, it authorized an investigation to study the concentration, structure, and performance of the domestic automobile industry.

178. Kovacic, "Congressional Oversight," p. 648 nn.312, 313.

179. For an example of a major civil penalty action, see United States v. Beatrice Foods Co., 351 F. Supp. 969 (D.Minn. 1972). For a case applying the new powers, see Federal Trade Commission v. Consolidated Foods Corp., 396 F. Supp. 1353 (S.D.N.Y. 1975).

180. Kovacic, "Congressional Oversight," pp. 648–49.

181. Ibid., p. 649 n.321.

182. Ibid., p. 649, 649 n.326; Katzmann, *Regulatory Bureaucracy*, pp. 117–18, 127–29.

183. Katzmann, *Regulatory Bureaucracy*, pp. 113–15, 118–25, 127–29; Kovacic, "Congressional Oversight," p. 650.

184. Kovacic, "Congressional Oversight," p. 650 n.329.

185. Ibid., p. 650 nn.330, 331, 332.

186. Ibid., p. 651 n.337.

187. On October 8, 1975, the Senate defeated by a vote of 45 to 54 a vertical divestiture measure offered as an amendment to a pending natural gas bill. Two weeks later a modified version of the vertical divestiture proposal was reintroduced as an amendment to the same bill and was defeated by a vote of 40 to 49. *Congressional Record*, 94th Cong., 1st sess., October 8 and 22, 1975, vol. 121: 32,289–96, 33,593–616. On June 15, 1976, the Senate Judiciary Committee approved and reported to the full Senate a bill requiring the vertical divestiture of the nation's eighteen largest petroleum firms. U.S. Congress, Senate, Committee on the Judiciary, S. *Rep. No. 1005*, 94th Cong., 2d sess., 1976, pt. 1. This bill did not reach the Senate floor.

Senator Packwood, who cosponsored a vertical divestiture bill in the 94th Congress, argued that new legislation afforded a speedier, less costly alternative to continued pursuit of the Exxon litigation. Legislative intervention, he argued, would correct an important deficiency in the antitrust laws: "The present antitrust laws . . . even if rigidly enforced, will not achieve what is necessary in this country: a breakup of the concentrations of power in the major industries in this country, oil and otherwise, so that we might return to the numerous, small- and medium-size competitive industries that made this country grow, and continue to be needed to keep this country great." Senate Committee on the Judiciary, *S.2387 and Related Bills*, p. 50.

188. U.S. Congress, House, Committee on Interstate and Foreign Commerce, Subcommittee on Oversight and Investigations, *Report on Federal Regulation and Regulatory Reform*, 94th Cong., 2d sess., 1976, p. 57. Noting that the FTC had previously been criticized for "excessive concentration upon matters of small consequence," this House report applauded the agency's efforts "to consider some major antitrust and consumer protection problems" (p. 57). The report singled out the cereal and petroleum monopolization suits, the challenge to the American Medical Association's restrictions on advertising by physicians, and the automobile industry investigation as examples of a desirable trend in this direction. In 1977 the Senate Governmental Affairs Committee also praised the FTC's antitrust revitalization and cited the agency's antitrust activities since 1969 as a basis for recommending the maintenance of FTC antitrust jurisdiction. U.S. Congress, Senate, Committee on Governmental Affairs, *Study on Federal Regulation: Regulatory Organization*, 95th Cong., 1st sess., 1977, vol. V: 246–54.

One business periodical said, "With its turnabout to activism, the [FTC] has clearly won the approval of Congress." See "The Escalating Struggle Between the FTC and Business—Executives Openly Challenge the Actions and Policies of the Newly Activist Agency," *Business Week*, December 13, 1976, p. 53. Some observers also believed it likely that the agency's status in Congress would improve with the appointment in 1977 of Michael Pertschuk, an influential Senate staff member, to chair the agency. See "Caught in a Cross Fire of Praise at the FTC," *New York Times*, March 20, 1977, sec. 3, p. 3.

189. See, for example, "Escalating Struggle," *Business Week*, p. 52.

190. Senators Hart, Mansfield, and Pastore retired and did not seek re-election in 1976; Senators Hartke, McGee, Moss, and Tunney were defeated in the general election. The departure of these senators marked the start of erosion in the ranks of congressmen who had urged the FTC to occupy ever larger territory in the antitrust and

consumer-protection fields. This process continued in 1978 with the deaths of Lee Metcalf and Hubert Humphrey, the retirement of James Abourezk, and the election defeat of Dick Clark, Floyd Haskell, and Thomas McIntyre.

191. As a group, these senators held a disproportionate number of important positions in the Senate hierarchy and occupied pivotal seats on committees with oversight and appropriations responsibility for the FTC. See Weingast and Moran, "Regulatory Policymaking."

192. Through a review of voting records, Weingast and Moran have documented a major shift in congressional preferences for FTC policy. "Between 1976 and 1979," they write, "the dominant coalition on the relevant congressional committees changed from favoring to opposing an activist FTC." Ibid.

193. Kovacic, "Congressional Oversight," pp. 654 nn.346, 347, 348, 349; 655 n.350.

194. The Exxon and Kellogg monopolization suits most often provided the point of departure for discussions about the agency's management performance. The committees also raised the possibility of narrowing the issues in the Exxon case. Ibid., p. 655 n.351.

195. Ibid., p. 655 n.352.

196. U.S. Congress, Senate, Committee on the Judiciary, *Oversight of Antitrust Enforcement. Hearings Before the Subcommittee on Antitrust and Monopoly of the Senate Committee on the Judiciary*, 95th Cong., 1st sess., 1977, p. 5. See also the remarks of subcommittee chairman Kennedy on pp. 2–3.

197. U.S. Congress, House, Committee on Appropriations, *Departments of State, Justice, and Commerce, the Judiciary, and Related Agencies Appropriations for 1981. Hearings Before the Subcommittee of the Departments of State, Justice, and Commerce, the Judiciary, and Related Agencies of the House Committee on Appropriations*, 96th Cong., 2d sess., 1980, p. 143. See also Senate Committee on Governmental Affairs, *Study on Federal Regulation*, p. 246.

198. U.S. Congress, Senate, Committee on Appropriations, *Departments of State, Justice, and Commerce, the Judiciary, and Related Agencies Appropriations for Fiscal Year 1980. Hearings Before a Subcommittee of the Senate Committee on Appropriations*, 96th Cong., 1st sess., 1979, pt. 2: 2145. See also Kovacic, "Congressional Oversight," p. 656 n.355.

199. Kovacic, "Congressional Oversight," p. 656. Legislation similar to that proposed by Senator Kennedy received the support of President Carter.

200. Ibid., p. 656 n.358.

201. Ibid., pp. 656 nn.359, 360; 657 n.365.

202. Ibid., p. 657 nn.368, 369.

203. Federal Trade Commission v. Formica Corp., 5 Trade Reg. Rep. (CCH) ¶50,372 (1978). See also Kovacic, "Congressional Oversight," p. 657.

204. Kovacic, "Congressional Oversight," p. 658 n.373.

205. In his economic message to Congress on October 8, 1974, President Ford had said his administration would "zero in on more effective enforcement of laws against price-fixing and bid-rigging. For instance, noncompetitive professional fee schedules and real estate settlement fees must be eliminated." *Congressional Record*, 93d Cong., 2d sess., October 8, 1974, vol. 120: 34,422.

206. Kovacic, "Congressional Oversight," p. 658 n.375.

207. Ibid., p. 660, 660 n.382.

208. Ibid., p. 660 n.385.

209. The management information system afforded FTC commissioners and other supervisors the agency's first effective means for obtaining reliable, timely information about the status of ongoing investigations and cases, as well as the disposition and content of closed matters.

210. This type of preliminary analysis, coupled with efforts to evaluate and learn from the agency's previous lawsuits, helped the Bureau of Competition to sharpen the focus of contemplated investigations and complaints.

211. U.S. Federal Trade Commission, *Annual Report* (Washington, D.C., 1979), p. 13.

212. Kovacic, "Congressional Oversight," p. 661 nn.391, 392.

213. Ibid., p. 661 n.394.

214. See, for example, In re Sunkist Growers, Inc., [1976–1979 Transfer Binder] Trade Reg. Rep. (CCH) ¶21,315 (No. 9100, May 31, 1977), consent order issued, 3 Trade Reg. Rep. (CCH) ¶21,793 (May 5, 1981); In re E.I. DePont de Nemours and Co., 96 F.T.C. 653 (1980); In re Exxon Corp., 3 Trade Reg. Rep. (CCH) ¶21,599 (No. 9130, August 1, 1979); In re Indiana Dental Association, 93 F.T.C. 392 (1979) (consent order); and In re Russell Stover Candies, Inc., 3 Trade Reg. Rep. (CCH) ¶21,719 (No. 9140, July 1, 1980), enforcement denied, 718 F.2d 256 (8th Cir. 1983).

215. See, for example, In re Reuben H. Donnelley Corp., 95 F.T.C. 1 (1980), enforcement denied sub nom. Official Airline Guides v. FTC, 630 F.2d 920 (2d Cir. 1980), cert. denied, 450 U.S. 917 (1981); In re Ethyl Corp., [1976–1979 Transfer Binder] Trade Reg. Rep. (CCH) ¶21,579 (No. 9128, May 30, 1979), enforcement denied sub nom. E.I. DuPont de Nemours and Co. v. FTC, 729 F.2d 128 (2d Cir. 1984); and In re Russell Stover Candies, Inc., 718 F.2d 256 (8th Cir. 1983). See also Kovacic, "Congressional Oversight," p. 662 n.403.

216. Kovacic, "Congressional Oversight," p. 662 nn.408, 409; In re Binney and Smith, Inc., 96 F.T.C. 625 (1980).

217. Kovacic, "Congressional Oversight," pp. 663–64, 664 n.425. From 1977 to 1980 the commission published many studies, including reports on selected industries and issues earmarked by Congress for special attention.

218. Ibid., pp. 664 n.426, 665 n.427.

219. FTC consideration of a rule governing petroleum pipelines began with a petition from Senator Kennedy. Ibid., p. 665 n.428.

220. For illuminating contemporaneous assessments of the reasons behind congressional moves to limit the FTC's authority in 1979 and 1980, see "Debate: The Federal Trade Commission Under Attack: Should the Commission's Role Be Changed?," *Antitrust Law Journal* 49 (1982): 1481–97; Ernest Gellhorn, "The Wages of Zealotry: The FTC Under Siege," *Regulation* 4 (January–February 1980): 33–40; Robert A. Katzmann, "Capitol Hill's Current Attack Against the FTC," *Wall Street Journal*, May 7, 1980, p. 26; Pertschuk, *Revolt Against Regulation*.

221. The FTC formally ceased operations for two days (May 1 and June 2) in 1980. See *Washington Post*, May 1, 1980, p. B1, and *New York Times*, May 2, 1980, p. D1. Some

congressmen applauded the funding lapse. Calling it a "renegade agency," Representative John Ashbrook said the FTC "has consistently violated its mandate by the Congress and has tried time and time again to rise above the law in the name of some self-determined policy directive... If we defeat the FTC funding resolution we will have sent a message to the FTC that we do not approve of their cavalier attitude toward the law and this Congress." *Congressional Record*, 96th Cong., 2d sess., March 26, 1980, vol. 126: 1536 (daily edition).

222. This provision effectively ended the commission's Lanham Act proceeding to cancel the Formica trademark, and it represented the first time in the agency's history that Congress had prohibited the FTC from continuing an ongoing adjudicatory proceeding.

223. The statute allowed the agency to complete its ongoing monopolization suit against the Sunkist growers. See In re Sunkist Growers, Inc.

224. In another measure affecting the FTC's competition investigations, the act required all compulsory process to be signed by a commissioner acting pursuant to a commission resolution.

225. FTC Improvements Act, *Statutes at Large* 94, 939 (1980), *U.S. Code*, vol. 15, secs. 3501–3 (1980). Since 1972 Congress had considered many bills similar to the 1980 softdrink bottlers statute. Kovacic, "Congressional Oversight," p. 666 n.439.

226. *Washington Post*, September 14, 1979, p. A11; Kovacic, "Congressional Oversight," p. 666 nn.441, 442. If approved, McClure's measure would have ended the agency's antitrust proceedings dealing with the legal and medical professions. The proposal failed by two votes to gain Senate approval.

227. U.S. Congress, Senate, Committee on Commerce, Science, and Transportation, *Federal Trade Commission—Divestiture. Hearings Before the Subcommittee for Consumers of the Senate Committee on Commerce, Science, and Transportation*, 96th Cong., 1st sess., 1979, pp. 1–5, 97–110. Perhaps more than any other proposed antitrust limitation to receive attention in 1979 and 1980, the Heflin measure abruptly departed from the substance and tone of congressional guidance to the commission in the 1970s.

228. Since passage of the 1980 act, the FTC has abandoned many of the specific competition initiatives—including its cereal and petroleum monopolization suits—that drew congressional rebuke in 1979 and 1980.

229. "It is not enough for a legislature to enact policies... into law; it must check to see how those policies are being executed, whether they are accomplishing the desired results, and, if not, what corrective action the legislature may appropriately prescribe." Joseph P. Harris, *Congressional Control of Administration* (Washington, D.C.: Brookings Institution, 1964; Anchor Books, 1965), p. 1.

230. This paper has focused on congressional guidance concerning the FTC's antitrust activities, but its conclusions are largely applicable to congressional oversight of commission consumer-protection programs, as well. Many initiatives subjected to intense congressional criticism in recent years received strong legislative support in the early and mid-1970s. The FTC's efforts to regulate advertising directed toward children are an outstanding example. Several oversight and appropriations committees directed the FTC to give this program a high priority and to emphasize binding enforcement

strategies, rather than voluntary, cooperative programs with industry. Kovacic, "Congressional Oversight," p. 668 n.447.

231. "Despite the political rhetoric about a runaway, uncontrollable bureaucracy bringing on the 1979–80 sanctions, . . . these sanctions reflected the new subcommittee's efforts to reverse the policies of their predecessors." Weingast and Moran, "Regulatory Policymaking."

232. There is an active debate among commentators over the extent to which Congress controls the activities of the FTC and other regulatory agencies. One view contends that independent regulatory bodies generally operate without significant constraint by the legislature. See, for example, Kenneth W. Clarkson and Timothy J. Muris, eds., *The Federal Trade Commission Since 1970: Economic Regulation and Bureaucratic Behavior* (Cambridge, Eng.: Cambridge University Press, 1981), pp. 18–34; James Q. Wilson, ed., *The Politics of Regulation* (New York: Basic Books, 1980), p. 391; and Lawrence C. Dodd and Richard L. Schott, *Congress and the Administrative State* (New York: John Wiley and Sons, 1979), p. 2. The opposing view holds that regulatory agency actions are the products of congressional guidance. Under this model, Congress decisively affects agency behavior through its use of a variety of incentive systems. See, for example, William L. Cary, *Politics and Regulatory Agencies* (New York: McGraw-Hill, 1967), pp. 57–59; Mayhew, *Electoral Connection*, pp. 134–35; and Weingast and Moran, "Regulatory Policymaking," pp. 792–93.

233. The argument that the FTC operated in the 1970s without effective external constraint assumes that institutions other than Congress also declined to restrain the agency. In assessing the role of the federal judiciary in this period, for example, some commentators have concluded that the federal courts gave uncritical review to FTC cases that rested on disputed or expansive applications of the agency's authority. See Clarkson and Muris, *Federal Trade Commission Since 1970*, pp. 35–49. Some decisions of this period, such as the Supreme Court's opinion in FTC v. Sperry and Hutchinson Co., unquestionably read the FTC's substantive powers broadly. But an arguably truer measure of the closeness of judicial scrutiny in the 1970s and afterward (and its effect on the FTC) is the manner in which the courts reviewed the products of specific FTC attempts to apply nominally generous definitions of its authority. Decisions on the merits of FTC antitrust complaints by the federal courts (and by the commission itself) from the mid-1970s to the present reveal no apparent inclination to give the FTC free rein in its choice and prosecution of antitrust theories. See In re Russell Stover Candies, Inc.; In re Reuben H. Donnelley Corp.; and In re Ethyl Corp.

234. As Thomas McCraw has observed, "Individual regulatory experiments and episodes must be judged against a standard true to the particular historical moment." Thomas K. McCraw, *Prophets of Regulation* (Cambridge, Mass.: Belknap, 1984), p. 308.

Chapter 5

Regulatory Reform in the Realm of the Rent Seekers

BRUCE YANDLE

WOULD-BE reformers of regulation are generally aware of special interests, rent seekers, and linkages to them that have been forged between committed politicians and the bureaucracy that delivers on political commitments.[1] Even so, some may feel that sudden and dramatic shifts in regulation can and will occur. That is, there are differing expectations associated with regulatory reform in the realm of the rent seekers.

This paper examines elements of a reform phenomenon that occurred at the Federal Trade Commission (FTC) during the period 1981–1984.[2] The experience described suggests that reform can occur, but that it will be limited by important public and private interest groups.[3] The paper provides some background on institutional characteristics that relate to the process of reform, presents a theoretical framework for examining the allocation of resources to and within the FTC, and then focuses specifically on the budget process to describe how interactions with Congress affected the reforms attempted at the agency. The paper finally draws no normative conclusions, but instead describes a process of change that is illuminated by the theory of rent-seeking behavior.

The author would like to express his appreciation to participants in the Public Choice Seminar at George Mason University for their comments on an earlier version of this paper. The views expressed here are those of the author and do not necessarily reflect those of the Federal Trade Commission or of individual commissioners.

FTC CHARACTERISTICS

The FTC can be thought of as a bureau suspended between two larger bureaus: the executive and legislative branches of government. As a politicized administrative unit of a democracy, the FTC has certain organizational characteristics:

1. The majority of the staff is composed of career employees and managers;

2. The agency receives an annual dollar and workyear budget;

3. The leadership of the agency is a five-person commission, whose members, nominated by the president, have seven-year staggered terms of office;

4. A chairman with strong management capabilities is selected from the commission by the president; and

5. The chairman selects and names top managers for the major offices and operating units of the commission.

The law-enforcement activities of the commission are conducted under a collection of specific and broad statutes that allow for considerable discretion in selecting cases and taking final actions. The FTC is monitored closely by congressional committees, which have far-reaching and diverse interests in the agency's actions, budget, and expenditures.[4] The agency's budget and activities are also monitored by the Office of Management and Budget (OMB).

Because of its diverse production activities, we can think of the FTC as a multiproduct bureau. In some cases its exclusive statutory responsibilities make it a federal monopolist—for example, its enforcement of advertising statutes. Its antitrust responsibilities are shared with another federal bureau, the Justice Department, in a cartelized duopoly arrangement.[5] In any case, the commission is able to choose from a broad array of activities when defining characteristics and activity levels for product mix, and it can then choose specific law-enforcement actions it will take from among candidates generated by investigation activities.

While being a monopolist or duopolist in the enforcement of certain federal statutes, many, if not all, FTC actions have close supply substitutes in the larger economy. For example, state and local governments offer similar law-enforcement products in the consumer-protection area. Furthermore, individuals can bring private antitrust and tort actions to accomplish the same ends as an FTC complaint.[6] However, jurisdictional rigidities in the law-enforcement market (perhaps partly because of the existence of the FTC) arguably provide efficiency reasons for a federal law-enforcement bureau in some cases. Economies of scale in the production of other actions might also argue for federal law enforcement. As with accepted theoretical models of a bureau, the FTC's costs of its various outputs are not easily defined and recognized by its monitor, but the broad contours of its costs are readily observable.[7]

Given that the FTC, which does not charge directly for its legal services, is in competition with private attorneys, who do charge, it is clear that demanders will shift their business to the FTC. If not for bureaucratic reasons, the agency may expand output beyond the socially efficient margin. That is, unless rationed somehow or adjusted for any public-goods content of activities, output will tend to expand to the point where marginal private benefits to litigants and complainants are almost zero. It is also conceivable that the FTC engages in all-or-nothing trades with Congress when negotiating for its budget.[8]

In a broad sense then, we might initially visualize the FTC as a multi-product bureau of a larger government that is in equilibrium in its political economy and has output expanded beyond the social margins. When political interests are included, however, we might expect the regulator-legislator equilibrium to be precisely at the appropriate margins, from the standpoint of the larger bureaus that monitor and fund the agency.[9]

A THEORETICAL MODEL

We can consider a theoretical model of regulator behavior at the level of a bureau, where regulations are produced, by stating a preference function for the decisionmakers and by noting the relative prices they face when choosing some mix of efficiency (or cost effectiveness) characteristics versus redistribution characteristics (rent) in a regulation or mix of regulatory products.[10] For the analysis, assume the regulator's utility function is: $U_r = U_r(X_e, X_r)$, where X_e is the efficiency gain characteristic of a regulation and X_r is a welfare-reducing gain in rent for a particular group affected by the regulation. The regulator's budget, M_r, is itself a function of X_e and X_r, so that U_r is indirectly a function of M_r. We initially characterize the regulator as obtaining positive utility from both characteristics; that is, their partial derivatives are positive. In other words, as the regulatory agency produces regulation at some positive rate, the regulator bundles together combinations of private and public benefits, which are labeled X_r and X_e.

The regulator faces a budgeted transformation function with respect to the characteristics that embodies the production costs and therefore the preferences of staff who may produce the mix of characteristics. The production function is: $f(X_e, X_r, x_i) = 0$, where the implicit function contains the internal bureau outputs, X_i, which are used in the production of a given regulation, and inputs, x_i, which are constrained by M_r. Changes in the characteristics of the staff will obviously change the relative cost of producing efficiency versus redistribution characteristics. That is, the private incentives of staff for producing regulation characterized by relatively more or less of the two characteristics are embodied in the wages they receive, or the managerial costs incurred when altering the mix of characteristics. Staff characteristics are assumed to be fixed in the short-run analysis.

The larger legislative body that regulates the regulators is an indirect party to the output decision. In other words, the ultimate mix of regulation characteristics is an input for the production of political support by the legislature, which has ultimate control over the regulation-producing bureau. The political support production function employed by the legislature uses the characteristics, X_e and X_r, which are transformed or packaged by the legislature and used to obtain political revenues. Since special-interest groups are more likely to support regulations that produce rents for them and guard those rents, we will assume the legislature demands a rent-rich final product from the regulatory agency.

For a given regulation, the legislature's demand is the marginal revenue product of X_r. The marginal cost of producing the legislature's preferred characteristic is determined by the regulator's preference function and budget constraint. Once the regulator is in private equilibrium, having selected the optimal mix of characteristics, he will adjust, if given marginal inducements that offset his net loss in utility. The final equilibrium level of the produced characteristic will be determined by the intersection of the legislature's marginal revenue product curve and the regulator's marginal cost curve.

Demand and Supply of Regulation Characteristics

A demand-supply analysis can be visualized by considering a standard preference function for the regulator and a linear transformation locus he faces. A bureau equilibrium is obtained at Y^* units of redistribution characteristics and an associated level of efficiency characteristics. This level of redistribution is observed by the legislature. At output level Y^*, there are potential gains from trade for the regulator and legislature. In other words, the legislature will attempt to buy more of the preferred characteristic from the regulator, since the marginal value of redistribution characteristics exceeds the additional cost incurred when the legislature entices the regulator to move from his privately determined allocation.

Given the disequilibrium as between the regulator and the legislature, adjustment will occur, with the legislature providing additional funds or in some other way, altering the budget constraint of the regulator to obtain relatively more redistribution from regulation. The adjustment process leads ultimately to a higher equilibrium level of redistribution characteristics.

An alternative view of the problem can be considered where the regulator obtains positive utility from efficiency characteristics and negative marginal utility from redistribution. While the regulator might be described as a committed reregulator, he still assigns positive marginal value to budgeted dollars, since he desires to produce revised regulations.

In this deregulation model, the regulator chooses zero redistribution characteristics. The legislator who receives the external effect is again prompted to bargain for more redistribution. However, bargaining at the margin is much more costly for the legislature, since the marginal cost incurred by the regulator is now much higher than before. In this case, the legislature will either provide larger budgets or resort to destructive tactics, such as attempting to undermine the authority of the regulator, perhaps making it illegal for him to engage in the efficiency-enhancing activities that he desires. Alternatively, the legislature may bring strong pressures to bear on the regulator, forcing his removal from office, while hoping to replace him with a more compatible regulator.

In a final and distinct case, the regulator, who is a committed deregulator, faces a fixed-proportion function, so that he cannot obtain efficiency characteristics alone. To obtain efficiency, he must obtain rent-generating characteristics as well. Given the negative utility, total and marginal, associated with redistribution effects, the regulator chooses to seek smaller budgets, always reducing the output of regulation so as to reduce the loss in utility associated with the redistribution characteristic that inevitably accompanies all regulation from the bureau.

In this case, the regulator will request smaller budgets from the legislature and will seek to alter the production relationship so as to find a way to substitute efficiency characteristics for redistribution characteristics in the longer-run production period. In other words, he will engage in the costly process of rebuilding the production relationship while minimizing the level of production in the short run.

If the legislature continues to demand redistribution, the resulting output from the bureau will have relevant external effects. There are no potential gains from trade, however. That is, there is no supply curve of the desired characteristic. Furthermore, the requests for lower budgets make the potential loss in revenues for the legislature even more costly. As a result of the combination of no bargaining and the large potential loss, the legislature will be prompted to undertake drastic action to alter the regulator's behavior. A shutdown of the particular agency and creation of another is one alternative that might be chosen. The more destructive the strategy of the legislature, the greater the importance of having strong support from constituents, since the resulting confrontation with the regulator is likely to be highly visible. Because of the costly nature of such efforts to revise regulator behavior, it is important that some broad public-interest benefit be associated with the effort.

In all cases described, the legislature responds to the economic pressures (demand) of interest groups who operate in the political process. As constructed, the regulator-legislature model predicts an increase in redistribution characteristics, so long as their marginal product to the legislature is positive. Of course, the regulator's preferences can be revised, with substitution in favor of efficiency characteristics, as can the demand of the legislature. That revision is empirically meaningful when there are special-interest groups whose demand results in relatively more efficiency. Such groups do form, of course, when their private interests are negatively affected by other special-interest regulation. For example, the soybean growers association and steel fabricators have effectively lobbied to stop or modify the implementation of protective quotas and tariffs sought by other special interests. One can argue that the result was efficiency enhancing.

The discussion of the regulator-legislator model has emphasized solutions with transfers of resources as the inducement for preferred production. The use of command and control has been the exception. In other words, economic incentives have been used for internalizing an externality, instead of using performance- and technology-based standards.

If economic incentives are used to resolve this standard externality case, enforceable contracts must be derived and regulator performance must be bonded.[11] In the typical situation, the regulator might make an agreement with key members of the legislature, accept the resource increase, and deliver the desired goods. Output characteristics can be observed when they are produced.

If the production period is long, as is often the case with complex regulation, the legislature will predictably use a combination of performance standards and economic incentives. Bonding particular regulators by placing the good name of the individual in jeopardy may not be workable, given the potential for turnover during the long production period. As a consequence, laws will be written describing rather precisely the characteristics to be produced. Budgets can be altered to fund the desired production. To assure that budget dollars are not siphoned away from the desired product's production, command and control regulation can be devised that dictates the exact amount to be spent on other activities.

In the extreme case, that of the fully committed deregulator, technology-based standards can be applied by the legislature. The legislature can require precise combinations of human capital—requiring, for example, a particular ratio of economists to lawyers or specifying personnel to be devoted to the production of distribution activities. In addition, the legislature may specify output targets to be achieved in a given period. Put differently, the regulatory agency can be put on a short leash.

The challenge faced by the legislature in this theoretical analysis involves a complex agent-principal problem. The legislature views the regulator as an agent but, due to the political process used in naming regulators, lacks complete sanctions to control the agent's behavior. At the same time, the regulated view the legislature as their agent and have even fewer sanctions available to use in controlling the legislature's behavior. In both cases, that of the regulated and the legislature, long lags prevail after the contract period. Bonuses in the form of campaign contributions and budget adjustments can be used to adjust behavior of the respective agents. The derived demand for the regulator's product is, of course, crucial to the legislature's production of publicly approved output. Once equilibrium is obtained, adjustments that may be inspired by temporary forces are resisted.

The External Negotiations

The theoretical discussion thus far indicates that the budget process will reveal efforts by Congress to adjust bureau production when an ideal mix of output characteristics is not presented. In the actual budget process, however, Congress receives an OMB-approved FTC budget plan with price tags attached to numerous programs and activities, not just for one program. The agency plan, developed initially by staff managers and then discussed, altered and approved by the commission, reflects the preferences of FTC staff and commissioners. However, the FTC chairman's preferences tend to dominate the agency budget plan because of his power to fill key staff positions at the agency. After examining the budget, Congress considers its priorities—both public and private interests—and adjusts the FTC plan accordingly. Since resources allocated by Congress to the FTC come at the expense of private and social rents that may be produced by other government activities, we can safely assume that considerable care is exercised in making each allocation.[12]

The allocation process undertaken by Congress can be thought of as involving an array of demand curves for FTC products. The curves are derived on the basis of efficiency and redistribution characteristics, and some points on the curves are assumed to be observed clearly by Congress, while others are not so clearly recognized. The underlying FTC-production function can be viewed as completely flexible in producing a wide variety of products, which are themselves distinguishable.

Some of the demand for FTC products represents social benefits of the public-interest variety derived from FTC actions, which might be termed the purest form of demand for FTC services. There is no strategic behavior reflected in this demand. It is efficiency based. There are public goods elements in these services provided by the agency, along with strictly private goods.

For example, one such demand curve could represent the values assigned to various levels of antitrust law enforcement, when the central issue involves collusion. An individual buyer might call attention to the case and receive direct benefits from an enforcement action.[13] Other buyers might free ride on the activity, not even incurring the minor cost of attracting the attention of the FTC. Alternatively, the locus could represent values associated with increased levels of antifraud enforcement. Again, numerous parties can gain from the national elimination of one interstate fraud operator.

A component of strategic demand felt by Congress could be added to the previously described antitrust demand curve. Here we find another form of special-interest demand. The special-interest benefits described could accrue to particular firms when antitrust enforcement is applied to a merger, where the result of the merger brings an efficiency gain in production. Competitors might wish to stop the merger.

An example relating to fraud could be found in high pressure selling, where gullible buyers are parted from their money. Again, competitors might wish to reduce opportunities for entry in their industry through stringent use of antifraud enforcement and could therefore support FTC action.

There is also a distinctly different demand component: congressional demands for political support and revenues, that is, the marginal revenue product curve. The desired actions here could include those just mentioned, along with a demand for multifirm antitrust investigations and antifraud rulemakings, activities that might benefit some consumers and also cause political action groups to more effectively organize the market demand for *stopping* the FTC activity.

Consideration of these various demands sheds some light on the problem encountered at the congressional level when efforts are made to reduce the budget and to reform FTC activities. First, the rent-seeking components of demand represent well-entrenched and well-organized forces. Efforts to scale back on cases denying services to these demanders will bring an outcry. An agency request to scale back the budget predictably raises the wrath of Congress and other external rent seekers. Internal rent seekers join the battle and may engage in strategic behavior to weaken the agency's demand for less. Congress can obviously counteract efforts to reduce budgets by mandating more resources and by specifying how the budget will be spent.

In effect, the easiest budget cuts are those associated with activities that provide social benefits across large, diverse groups of citizens. However, the turbulence caused by efforts to eliminate rent-seeking activities can also stir up trouble in that market for agency services. These demanders can be led to believe that the agency intends to scale back on services they value. In any case, the resulting competition for fewer resources and the risk of losing benefits provide an incentive for scattered consumers to become better organized and to push for larger budgets.

Internal Allocations

Funds allocated to the FTC through the congressional budget process, based on the plan submitted by the agency, are subject to internal reallocation. The discretion of staff and the commission enter the process again. In other words, the allocation process is dynamic; the contract between Congress and the agency formed by the appropriations process must be monitored to ensure that it is maintained.

Within the agency, law enforcement and other activities can each be portrayed with some accuracy as budgeted funds are allocated to various programs. When decomposed (vertically), there are two marginal benefit components for each activity, of which one captures purely private-interest demand. This is the demand that generally stimulates FTC action. There is also a social demand for the same activity, the marginal benefits to all other than the special interests previously accounted for. To illustrate, consider Robinson-Patman antitrust cases. There is private benefit that accrues when cartel agreements are enforced by the FTC through Robinson-Patman actions. However, if graphed in a standard two-quadrant diagram, recalling the vertical summation involved when considering the aggregated marginal-benefit locus, the social marginal-benefit locus would be located in the negative quadrant throughout, since Robinson-Patman actions reduce price competition. If the two marginal-benefit curves were summed vertically, the resulting locus could also be in the negative quadrant. Alterations in the relative magnitudes of the two benefit functions can be contemplated to suit one's convictions, but the principal point here is that there are negative and positive benefits associated with the activity.

Next, consider advertising substantiation activity. There is arguably a range of positive social benefits from this activity. Consumers are willing to pay for products whose claims have been substantiated by independent laboratories. There is value attached to *some* levels of the implied service. There are also positive benefits to private interests, who may deter competitors by means of ad substantiation. Special-interest demand is part of the market for this FTC product.

Intervention activities before the International Trade Commission, where the FTC argues the merits of competition, are another case to consider. Here the marginal social benefits are positive; the marginal private benefits are negative. Simply put, the competition that may result when the FTC argues successfully against petitions for tariffs and quotas is harmful to firms that might be protected by those devices.

Finally, consider economic analysis at the agency, where the marginal-benefit locus is described as being positive throughout. Arguably, there can be rent-seeking activities associated with this activity. For example, the agency can be directed to undertake an industry study and thereby signal to the industry that rules or regulations may follow. Such an interpretation of a study will trigger a reaction and cause the industry to respond favorably to congressional interests.

In the process of managing the agency, there is a large stochastic element in cases that come to the attention of the agency, which result in allocations of resources to staff. For example, merger filings occur spontaneously, and alleged violations of law are randomly called to the attention of agency staff. There is also a deterministic element of case generation activity that is under the control of the commission and commission managers. At any given moment, resources can be allocated to a range of activities illustrated, given the preferences of managers, commissioners, and the external pressures on the commission.

If the demand conditions discussed were known *ex ante*, and if a rent-extinguishing regulator were unconstrained externally in managing resources, total resources available to the agency would be allocated so as to equate marginal social benefits across the four activities. As constructed, the marginal benefit schedule for Robinson-Patman cases, for example, would preclude activity in that area, since the summed private and social marginal-benefit curves are negative. Depending on the amount of resources allocated, activities would occur in each of the other three areas.

If, however, activities are already underway in the four functional areas described, even with negative social benefits, reductions of resources will elicit sharp reactions from the affected special interests. Again, the highly organized private parties will make their concerns known to the agency and to Congress, so that reactions will occur.

A reconsideration of the activities discussed identifies where, in the face of resource reductions, rent-seeking wrath is most expected—namely, when private party benefits are a factor in demand. Alternatively, we can see where expansions of activity carry the greatest rent-seeking opportunity cost. Accordingly, economic reports have little value. International Trade Commission filings have negative value. Advertising related actions have some value, and Robinson-Patman cases have greatest value, all in rent-seeking or rent-extinguishing terms.

While pondering these simple analytics, we might also consider the importance to Congress of being assured that its directives are taken seriously, recognizing that the agency can adjust the composition of output, even after

Congress has approved an agency plan. How does Congress know when its desired plan is being undertaken? Reports and frequent testimony provide some information; however, suits and other legal actions provide superior information. No amount of protestation about efficiency, cost cutting, and informal action seems to substitute for bringing highly visible suits.

Early in its history, the commission learned that publicity was an effective device to be used in achieving its mission. At first, the commission took a low profile approach, penalizing offenders but not subjecting them to front-page news coverage. Arguably, law enforcement is enhanced when people learn what happens to law violators. Clearly, the good faith of the commission is communicated to oversight committees when news is released with great fanfare.

Assessing Regulatory Reform

Based on the foregoing discussion, we can now assess the situation encountered by the recent reform efforts at the FTC. The reform program emphasized:[14]

1. Applying economic logic to antitrust and consumer protection law-enforcement actions;
2. Applying a benefit-cost test to eliminate activities that predictably generate more harm than good;
3. Reducing the level of resources committed to the agency, while increasing the level of benefits obtained from each action;
4. Substituting informal, nonconfrontational activities for suits and adversarial proceedings in gaining compliance with statutes;
5. Intervening before other regulatory bodies as advocates for competition and efficiency; and
6. Improving the management of the agency through the application of greater control at the top of the agency.

The emphasis on assessing economic benefits and costs results in rent seekers being highlighted and further increases the level of analysis, for which there is no special-interest component of demand. Budget reductions endanger entrenched special interests in and out of the agency. Informal approaches to law enforcement raise congressional monitoring costs. Intervention activities provide no interest-group benefits, divert resources from activities that might support special interests, and further emphasize economics. Finally, improved management—a noncontroversial issue, perhaps, on the administrative side of the agency—reduces the influence of staff in the agency in determining investigation priorities and, therefore, can be rent extinguishing in some areas. All of these effects ultimately generated congressional concern about the real intentions of the regulator-decisionmaker.

Messages from the Monitors

The first Reagan appointees to the FTC arrived at the agency in early October 1981. On October 28 the newly appointed chairman of the commission testified before the House Appropriations Committee in support of a budget reduction for fiscal year 1982.[15] The agency's first 1982 budget request for $69.4 million had been increased by the House to $71.9 million. With the arrival of the new chairman, the agency subsequently requested $61.0 million, following the administration's effort to reduce all government expenditures by 12 percent.

The messages communicated from the committee members to the chairman were mildly cautious regarding the proposed cuts. A few questions were asked of the FTC chairman about his commitment to the mission of the agency and his belief that the mission could be accomplished with a smaller budget. Other questions probed into the planned reduction for antitrust and consumer-protection activities. There were also exchanges about the commission-approved plans to reduce the number of regional offices from ten to six, although the precise offices for closing had not yet been identified. An exchange between House Appropriations Committee chairman Neal Smith and FTC chairman James Miller contained a theme that would be repeated many times over in the next few years:

Mr. Neal Smith: Let me ask two or three more questions about exactly what would happen under this budget. Would you discontinue existing Robinson-Patman cases or investigations?

Mr. James Miller: Sir. Robinson-Patman cases are a substantial problem at the Commission. Analyses of prior Robinson-Patman cases have led to the conclusion they have not generally helped small business. In fact, they have created quite the reverse impact. We will not discontinue Robinson-Patman. We will look very carefully at them. There may be cases of anticompetitive behavior which would be best addressed through Robinson-Patman cases.

Mr. Smith: Am I to interpret that you would or would not then open any new cases?

Mr. Miller: We would open new cases if the appropriate type of case was presented to us, yes.[16]

Miller then commented on the merits of competition and efficiency and his plan to continue to apply the principles in his new work. Smith expressed agreement and indicated that he expected those principles to be applied in both horizontal and vertical antitrust matters.

Following a year's activity at the agency, deeper concerns about the agency's future fortunes were communicated in direct terms by members of the two appropriations committees in 1982 during hearings on the fiscal year 1983 budget. The commission had again proposed cuts for each of its three major missions, as shown in Table 5.1. After a long and intense colloquy with the FTC chairman regarding plans to pare the budget and to close certain specified regional offices, as well as regarding agency reviews of proposed mergers, Senator Lowell Weiker, who was already bothered about the plan to close the FTC office in his region, said:

> I have stood on the Senate floor and withstood some attacks from colleagues of mine. There are more of them now that honestly feel neither the administration nor you are committed to the legal mandate of your Commission. That is the problem, and your statements, your public statements, certainly give aid and comfort to that perception. These closings give aid and comfort to that perception.
>
> The budget gives aid and comfort to that. I suppose what I am saying, if I am beating out there, [is that] I have a strange feeling right now the Congress is not prepared to go ahead and put the FTC out of business, or if we are going to do so, let's go ahead and repeal the authorizing legislation and put you out of business. Fair enough? But we are not going to do it by way of the back door.[17]

TABLE 5.1
FTC FISCAL 1983 BUDGET
(DOLLARS IN THOUSANDS)

Mission	FISCAL 1982		FISCAL 1983		CHANGES	
	Workyears	Amount	Workyears	Amount	Workyears	Amount
Maintaining competition	665	$31,520	615	$28,689	−50	$−2,831
Consumer protection	649	30,866	596	27,742	−53	−3,124
Economic activities	141	6,388	99	4,407	−42	−1,981
Total	1,455	$68,774	1,310	$60,838	−145	$−7,936

SOURCE: Division of Budget and Finance, Federal Trade Commission.

In hearings before a subcommittee of the House Appropriations Committee, again following intense questioning about the commission's plan to reduce sharply the budget and to close regional offices, as well as other matters relating to law enforcement, Representative Joseph Early from Boston, the location of an office then slated to be closed, said:

> Mr. Chairman, the OMB book on Budgets and Themes indicates that the FTC's budget would continue to be reduced to a 45.42 million dollar budget for the FTC in 1987. Now with inflation, that amount would fund the Commission at less than half of the fiscal year 1981 level. Do you support that kind of plan? What I am saying is, do you want to abolish the FTC?[18]

Later in the same hearing, the topic of Robinson-Patman cases was discussed and concern was expressed over the level of enforcement of that law. Neal Smith pursued the point, noted that neither the FTC nor the Justice Department seemed enthusiastic about bringing Robinson-Patman investigations, and asked for data on the number of investigations opened by the commission. The data reflected the shift in emphasis brought by the commission and highlighted the concerns of the first subcommittee chairman. Investigations had fallen from a six-year high of 38 in 1980 to two in 1982.[19] Heated discussions also emerged on the topic of resale price maintenance (RPM).[20] In hearings before House appropriations and oversight committees, attention was focused on the agency's lack of action against firms that sought to set and enforce resale prices. Investigations by the agency in the area of distribution restraints, which includes RPM matters, had fallen from a six-year high of 76 in 1980 to six in 1982.[21]

Long discussions developed on RPM in hearings before the agency's reauthorization hearings in March 1983, when Representative James Florio asked for clarification of the chairman's views regarding the procompetitive effects of allowing firms to set resale prices for their dealers.[22] Florio expressed deep concern about the agency's apparent decision to make new law, even in the face of Supreme Court rulings on RPM. He went so far as to suggest that the commission was once again becoming a "rogue agency," going off on its own to establish novel economic theories about matters well established in case law.

FTC chairman Miller responded at length to the questions, pointing out that the commission had a number of RPM cases under investigation, but that in his opinion the agency should not vote out complaints when the result was harmful to consumers and to competition. After Miller stated his desire to apply a rule of reason, a kind of benefit-cost analysis, to matters relating to vertical agreements between producers and retailers, Florio was still not persuaded. He said: "If the Commission, under an economic theory, decided that in certain instances price fixing was a good thing for the preservation of quality in the marketplace, I think it would be preposterous for the Commission to define, under the public interest, as an exception to the fact, that price fixing is something that can be appropriate."[23]

Finally, in 1983 during the budget hearings for the agency's fiscal year 1984 budget, Neal Smith referred to concerns about Robinson-Patman and RPM enforcement and explained his committee's strategy in dealing with the agency's efforts to reduce its budget:

> My objective is that you be as efficient and effective as you can be; you are the only game in town. We are giving $43 million to the Department of Justice, and, so help me, half of the money is being used to work against what we are supposed to be doing. It really concerns a lot of Members of Congress, mergers, acquisitions, the need to look into all of these things, and you seem to be the only game in town. *That is the reason this Subcommittee has been consistently putting in more money than has been requested, and trying to make you as efficient and effective as possible.*[24] (Emphasis added)

The Budget As Evidence

The resistance of Congress to the proposed reductions and reallocations of FTC resources is reflected graphically when the commission's OMB-approved budget requests are compared with the appropriations finally determined by Congress. Table 5.2 contains the relevant data. As shown, the fiscal year 1981 Carter budget was the last request to be reduced by Congress. After that, sharp reductions were proposed by the administration for 1982, 1983, and 1984 and were supported by the FTC chairman. Those reductions were countered by Congress with appropriations larger than those requested by the administration.

A controversy included in the figures, mentioned earlier, relates to commission efforts to reduce the number of regional offices and the resources committed to those operations. The agency requested funding for six offices, instead of the existing ten, in 1983 and again in 1984. Finally, the effort to reduce the number of offices was ended when Congress, with specific appropriations language, directed the agency to keep ten offices, allowing a reduction in resources committed to them. That correction came in the fiscal year 1984 budget process.[25]

In any case, regulatory reform brought reductions in workyears committed to the agency from the 1981 appropriation of 1,698 to the 1984 level of 1,231. Reform efforts were extended into decisionmaking by staff regarding the opening of investigations, the kinds and frequency of formal actions recommended to the commission, and the acceleration of the agency's appearances as competition advocate before other regulatory bodies.

TABLE 5.2
FTC APPROPRIATION HISTORY,
FISCAL YEARS 1981–1985
(NOMINAL VALUES IN THOUSANDS OF DOLLARS)

	1981	1982	1983	1984	1985
FTC request	$71,000[a]	$61,123[b]	$60,838	$59,457[d]	$66,481
(workyears)	(1,720)	(1,400)	(1,310)	(1,199)	(1,234)
Congressional appropriation	$70,774	$68,774	$66,871[c]	$63,500	—
(workyears)	(1,698)	(1,455)	(1,360)	(1,231)	—
Public law	P.L. 96-536	P.L. 97-161	P.L. 97-377	P.L. 98-166	—
Percent gain					
(dollars)	−.3	+12.1	+10.0	+6.8	—
(workyears)	−1.3	+3.9	+3.8	+2.7	—

NOTES: a. President Carter's original request was $72,558, which OMB reduced by $1,558. The new administration rescinded $226 (P.L. 97-12) of 1981 funds.

b. The original Carter budget requested $77,971 and 1,750 workyears. In March 1981, President Reagan adjusted this request downward to $69,458 and 1,579 workyears. In October 1981, a second reduction of $8,335 was proposed. This would have reduced the FTC's request to $61,123 and assumed major reductions in regional offices.

c. Congress appropriated additional funds to keep ten regional offices open.

d. The original fiscal 1984 request assumed only six regional offices. Appropriated budget maintained ten regional offices.

Although not intended as a positive summary of the success of regulatory reform at the FTC, a statement by Commissioner Michael Pertschuk, former chairman of the agency during the Carter administration, provided documentation of the effects of internal reallocations that had occurred at the commission. Referring to antitrust activities, Pertschuk stated: "There is no escaping the fact that antitrust enforcement has been drastically reduced since Chairman Miller came to the FTC." He then provided data for the record, reported here in Table 5.3. He summarized: "Total enforcement actions have dropped 40 percent from the level before the Chairman took office. Only in the category of order modification—weakening existing order provisions—is the current administration threatening to set a new record."[26]

Focusing next on the commission's record in consumer-protection activities, Pertschuk provided additional data, reported in Table 5.4. As indicated, the frequency of consent orders was down, while injunctions and civil penalty actions were at historic averages or higher. The Pertschuk statement finally focused on merger reviews conducted by the agency and described the likelihood of a merger challenge. Second requests, an indication that the agency was taking a closer look at a merger application, had fallen sharply since 1979, even though the number of merger filings had risen sharply.

TABLE 5.3
FTC ANTITRUST ACTIONS

FTC Action	FISCAL YEAR						
	1977	*1978*	*1979*	*1980*	*1981*	*1982*	*1983*
Administrative complaints	9	6	11	13	7	2	1
Part II consent orders	15	6	26	21	16	5	9
Part III consent orders	4	3	8	3	4	1	4
Litigated commission orders	6	8	10	4	10	7	8
Civil penalty actions filed	2	2	3	1	3	1	1
Civil penalty judgments	1	0	2	2	2	4	2
Preliminary injunctions filed	5	2	4	0	2	3	0
Total enforcement actions	42	27	64	44	44	23	25
Order modifications	1	3	0	2	6	15	17

Special Legislative Language

Although aggregate budget values and internal adjustments tell some of the story about negotiations between a regulator and a legislature, there is still more to be reported. As suggested earlier, rent seekers obviously resist costly reform and Congress must attempt to enforce agreements made with special interests that affect agency operations. Accordingly, the agency's appropriations, after being increased for the years discussed, also contained special language on certain agency activities. That is, the appropriations committees inserted legislative language in the budget resolution.

Ideally, the FTC's authorization committees would periodically review and amend the agency's statutes, taking into account any special circumstance they wished to consider and setting the institutional framework for a three- or four-year period. The appropriations committees would then concern themselves solely with funding levels and programs designed to carry out the authorized activities. In this ideal setting, special interests have a major opportunity every three or four years to obtain legislative language.

The FTC's last authorization legislation was written in 1980.[27] After that, all controversies fell on the shoulders of the appropriations committees, which then dealt continually with the special interests and their political pressures. A failed attempt in 1983 by the Senate to formulate an authorization bill for the agency gives insight to restrictions that were then in vogue. Senate Bill S.1714 (July 25, 1983) contained special language that protected the rights of states to regulate quality of service and entry requirements for professional groups.

TABLE 5.4
FTC CONSUMER-PROTECTION ACTIONS

	FISCAL YEAR						
FTC Action	1977	1978	1979	1980	1981	1982	1983
Administrative complaints	8	8	2	3	5	1	6
Part II consent orders	45	20	34	21	17	15	12
Part III consent orders	12	12	13	5	5	0	4
Litigated commission orders	5	11	3	6	7	0	3
Civil penalty actions filed	14	19	17	26	27	13	21
Injunctions filed	0	4	2	3	1	3	10
Total enforcement actions	84	74	71	64	62	32	56
Order modifications	2	2	5	7	10	7	14

Agricultural cooperatives were again given exemption from FTC investigations and actions, as were savings and loans and federal credit unions. While the rent-seeking aspect is not clear cut, trademarks continued to be protected from FTC cancellation efforts, and language was included to limit the definition of what is considered unfair and deceptive acts or practices, the basic foundation of FTC law. The proposed limiting language included a "reasonable consumer" rule. However, after a controversial period during which the medical profession went all out to block authorization that might maintain FTC jurisdiction over their business activities, the authorization effort ended without passage of a bill.

The agency's 1982 appropriation (P.L. 97-92) filled the special-language vacuum. It instructed the commission to maintain its regional operation, to review its plans concerning them, and to keep Congress informed of final decisions on any actions that might alter regional offices. The appropriation also spoke to the issue of a pending rule on the care labeling of textile products and urged the agency to restudy the need for such a rule.[28] The 1984 appropriation (P.L. 98-166) went on to deny the use of any funds for the purpose of overturning or altering a per se interpretation of antitrust laws regarding RPM.

CONCLUSION

The 1981–1984 reform efforts at the FTC, and the resulting encounters as revealed through the appropriations process and related hearings, were filled with controversy, as might be expected. Major thrusts to bring quick change were often parried by Congress, although changes were accomplished in the reduction and allocation of budgeted resources to the agency. As described in the theoretical treatment of agency activities, there was immediate and sharp reaction to budget cuts when it appeared those cuts would reduce activities valued by Congress. In some cases, the agency was accused of attempting to close itself down. In other cases, the new leadership was charged with attempting to make novel economic interpretations of basic laws.

The internal reallocation of resources at the commission that brought increased attention to activities of state-regulated groups, such as the professions, provided a high incentive for those groups to organize politically and to counter the FTC's newly focused antitrust efforts. Other groups, such as retailers, were bothered by price competition and so organized a new effort to increase the level of enforcement of the Robinson-Patman Act. Somewhat paradoxically, the same retailers, in some cases, expressed grave concern about the agency's new approach to the enforcement of RPM, which allowed such agreements when they were deemed to be procompetitive. Retailers wanted discounting when it was beneficial to them; they did not want discounting when it hurt their sales.

The revised approach taken in the review of merger filings called on the new learning in antitrust that sharply reduced the importance attached to domestic concentration ratios and brought a reduction in complaints issued against new mergers.[29] Existing firms in the affected industries, perhaps fearful of new lower-cost competitors, brought pressure to bear on Congress, pressure that was quickly related to the agency. The increased review of old consent orders that had placed restrictions on the behavior of firms provided opportunities to unleash competitive forces in numerous markets. At the same time, the consent modifications were interpreted by some competitors as damaging to their industries and the stable relationships formed partly by the FTC's enforcement of old orders.

Throughout the period described there was clearly an interaction of public and private interests as the agency was being trimmed and redirected. Although the story related here has been cast in terms of rent-seeking resistance to agency reform, it is clear that no particular evidence has been offered that unambiguously supports that assertion. To accept the notion that rent seeking made a difference, one must accept the theoretical interpretation of FTC activities offered at the beginning of this paper—for example, it must be agreed that Robinson-Patman cases are on balance more costly than beneficial to society. If those interpretations are accepted, the result is a plausible story about regulatory reform in the realm of the rent seekers.

NOTES

1. For a review of the political economy involved, see Roger G. Noll and Bruce M. Owen, eds., *The Political Economy of Deregulation* (Washington, D.C.: American

Enterprise Institute, 1983). Also, for theoretical treatment of the subject of rent seeking, see James M. Buchanan, Robert D. Tollison, and Gordon Tullock, eds., *Toward a Theory of the Rent-Seeking Society* (College Station: Texas A&M Press, 1980).

2. This period followed the election of Ronald Reagan to the presidency. Regulatory reform was a major plank in the election platform. James C. Miller III, executive director of the Reagan administration's Regulatory Reform Task Force, was appointed chairman of the FTC in October 1981.

3. It is difficult to disentangle special interests from public interests when contemplating the effects of FTC actions—or, for that matter, of governmental actions in general. See Gordon Tullock, "A (Partial) Rehabilitation of the Public Interest Theory," *Public Choice* 42 (1984): 89–99.

4. For a discussion and analysis of the FTC that focuses on these points, see Kenneth W. Clarkson and Timothy J. Muris, eds., *The Federal Trade Commission Since 1970: Economic Regulation and Bureaucratic Behavior* (Cambridge, Eng.: Cambridge University Press, 1981). See also Barry R. Weingast and Mark J. Moran, "The Myth of Runaway Bureaucracy—The Case of the FTC," *Regulation* 6 (May–June 1982): 31–36.

5. For more on this point, see Richard S. Higgins, William F. Shughart II, and Robert D. Tollison, "Dual Enforcement of the Antitrust Laws" (Chapter 7 in this volume).

6. For a recent illustration of a private action involving truthful advertising, see *Wall Street Journal*, August 23, 1984, p. 54. The suit involves advertising statements regarding the relative sugar content in competing cocoa mixes.

7. See William A. Niskanen, "Bureaucrats and Politics," *Journal of Law and Economics* 18 (December 1975): 617–43, and Barry R. Weingast, "The Congressional-Bureaucratic System: A Principal-Agent Perspective," *Public Choice* 44 (1984): 147–91.

8. See Niskanen, "Bureaucrats and Politics."

9. There are also special-interest pressures within the FTC, and it is difficult to assess completely the net effect of these economic agents, since some actions are either offsetting or arguably efficiency enhancing. Due to longer-term career goals, attorneys and economists prefer particular kinds of cases. Indeed, lawyers prefer cases and economists prefer studies. Commissioners also have longer-term career objectives that may be supported by bringing highly visible controversial suits and by developing industry-wide rules. Perhaps the demand for controversy and visibility partly explains the occurrence of leaks of confidential material from the FTC and other government agencies. As Gene Talmadge once said: "Bad publicity is preferred to no publicity at all."

10. This section is based on Bruce Yandle, "Models of Political Economy of Regulation," Paper presented at the Southern Natural Resources Committee meeting, Charleston, S.C., September 1984.

11. The standard externality model is presented in James M. Buchanan and William C. Stubblebine, "Externality," *Economica* 29 (1962): 371–84.

12. In 1980 the FTC was operating on an emergency 45-day funding resolution, having been shut down by Congress because of a series of controversial actions. Each time the agency was funded, another agency's budget was tapped. The debate over the

transfers and their relative values is illuminating. See *Congressional Record*, 96th Cong., 2d sess., March 26, 1980, vol. 126: 2206.

13. Of course, it can be argued that treble damage antitrust awards distort the demand for antitrust service. See Kenneth G. Elzinga and William Breit, *The Antitrust Penalties* (New Haven, Conn.: Yale University Press, 1976). An even more critical concern about antitrust actions is discussed by Dominick T. Armentano in *Antitrust and Monopoly: Anatomy of a Policy Failure* (New York: John Wiley and Sons, 1982). See also Robert H. Bork, *The Antitrust Paradox* (New York: Basic Books, 1978).

14. The text of the alleged FTC transition team report was printed in the *Congressional Record*, 97th Cong., 1st sess., September 21, 1981, vol. 127: 101162–69, and the summary section of the same report was published under the title, "Conclusions and Recommendations from Federal Trade Commission Transition Team Report Submitted to President Reagan," *BNA Antitrust and Trade Regulation Reports*, November 29, 1981, sec. G. (Members of the presidential transition team will neither confirm nor deny the accuracy of the published version of the report, since all such reports were intended to remain confidential.) The conclusions and recommendations of the team given in these sources parallel the points mentioned in the above text. Specific recommendations include: reducing the budget by 30 percent; gaining a statutory definition of the term "unfairness" as contained in Section 5 of the FTC Act; emphasizing horizontal collusion cases; totally de-emphasizing Robinson-Patman cases; cautiously reviewing shared monopoly, vertical, and horizontal merger cases with an eye toward reducing emphasis of measures of concentration; focusing on the cartelization effects of occupational regulation; terminating consumer-protection cases based on novel social theories; and accelerating the agency's participation in intervening as a competition advocate before other regulatory bodies. Throughout the recommendations, emphasis was placed on using economic analysis in all commission decisionmaking.

15. U.S. Congress, House, Committee on Appropriations, *Hearings Before a Subcommittee of the House Committee on Appropriations*, 97th Cong., 1st sess., 1981, p. 695. The earlier Carter budget called for $74.3 million in 1981, $77.9 million in 1982, $80.0 million in 1983, and increases to $85.2 million in 1986. See U.S. Office of Management and Budget, *Additional Details on Budget Savings* (Washington, D.C., April 1981), p. 352.

16. House Committee on Appropriations, *Hearings* (1981), p. 768.

17. U.S. Congress, Senate, Committee on Appropriations, *Departments of State, Justice, and Commerce, the Judiciary, and Related Agencies Appropriations for 1983. Hearings Before a Subcommittee of the Senate Committee on Appropriations*, 97th Cong., 2d sess., 1982, p. 887.

18. U.S. Congress, House, Committee on Appropriations, *Hearings Before the Subcommittee on the Departments of State, Justice, and Commerce, the Judiciary, and Related Agencies of the House Committee on Appropriations*, 97th Cong., 2d sess., 1982, p. 242.

19. Ibid., p. 245.

20. A roundtable discussion on resale price maintenance is found in "'Round and 'Round on RPM," *Regulation* (January–February 1984): 19–32.

21. House Committee on Appropriations, *Hearings* (1981), p. 245.

22. U.S. Congress, House, Committee on Energy and Commerce, *Federal Trade Commission Reauthorization, 1983. Hearings Before the Subcommittee on Commerce, Transportation, and Tourism of the House Committee on Energy and Commerce*, 98th Cong., 1st sess., March 8 and 11, 1983, pp. 73–77.

23. Ibid., p. 75.

24. U.S. Congress, House, Committee on Appropriations, *Hearings Before a Subcommittee on the House Committee on Appropriations*, 98th Cong., 1st sess., 1983, p. 155.

25. The increase in the dollar budget for 1985 reflects primarily increased rent for federal buildings, a charge that is set administratively, and other input price increases.

26. U.S. Congress, House, Committee on Government Operations, *Oversight of Federal Trade Commission Law Enforcement: Fiscal Years 1982 and 1983. Hearings Before the Commerce, Consumer, and Monetary Affairs Subcommittee of the House Committee on Government Operations*, 98th Cong., 1st sess., November 9, 1983, pp. 298–325.

27. The Federal Trade Commission Improvement Act of 1980 (P.L. 96-825) provides several examples of special language. Included in the act were restrictions on investigations of the business of insurance; directions to reduce the burden of small businesses in complying with data requests for FTC-published quarterly financial reports; denial of authority to promulgate any rule in the agency's children's advertising proceeding; denial of authority to initiate any rulemaking having to do with advertising; denial of authority to cancel trademarks on the basis of the mark having become generic in use; and denial of authority to investigate or prosecute agricultural cooperatives. Prior to the 1980 act, the commission had operated without authorization since 1977, mainly because of its controversial rulemaking activities. See *Congressional Record*, 96th Cong., 1st sess., September 20, 1979, vol. 125: 8230.

28. After passage of the Magnuson-Moss Act of 1975, in which Congress reinforced the power of the FTC to enact industry-wide rules, the agency undertook twenty rulemakings. Four of those were withdrawn by the commission; nine, with about two million pages of related record, were in process at the commission in 1981. Each rulemaking proceeding set in motion powerful incentives for industries to organize politically and provided opportunities for rent-seeking behavior. The care labeling rule was one such proceeding. See Timothy J. Muris, "Rules Without Reason: The Case of the FTC," *Regulation* 5 (September–October 1982): 20–26, and Bruce Yandle, "Care Labeling: Does Any One Care?" *Review of Industrial Management and Textile Science* 20 (Spring 1981): 21–28.

29. See Harvey J. Goldschmid, H. Michael Mann, and J. Fred Weston, eds., *Industrial Concentration: The New Learning* (Boston: Little, Brown, 1974).

Part II

Empirical Studies of
the Determinants of
Program Activities at the
Federal Trade Commission

Chapter 6

The Behavior of Regulatory Activity Over the Business Cycle: An Empirical Test

RYAN C. AMACHER, RICHARD S. HIGGINS,

WILLIAM F. SHUGHART II,

& ROBERT D. TOLLISON

GEORGE STIGLER was the first to recognize that, because "the political process automatically admits powerful outsiders to the industry's councils," regulation does not maximize industry revenue.[1] In extending Stigler's theory, Sam Peltzman derived some testable implications about the behavior of regulatory activity over the business cycle.[2] Specifically, Peltzman developed the empirical proposition that "regulation will tend to be more heavily weighted toward 'producer protection' in depressions and toward 'consumer protection' in expansions."[3] This hypothesis represents a formalization of a venerable argument, which contends that firms have increased incentives to collude—or will seek legislation or other forms of government intervention—during economic downturns in order to prevent the "cutthroat" competition normally motivated by the existence of excess productive capacity.[4]

In this paper we provide a straightforward test of Peltzman's hypothesis employing data on Federal Trade Commission (FTC) enforcement activities under the Clayton Act. In particular, we find a negative and statistically significant *ceteris paribus* relationship between cases alleging violations of Section 2 of the Clayton Act following its amendment in 1936 by the Robinson-Patman Act and several alternative measures of general business conditions. Since Robinson-Patman enforcement is generally condemned as

Reprinted by permission from *Economic Inquiry* (January 1985): 7–20. The views expressed here are those of the authors and do not necessarily reflect those of the Federal Trade Commission, individual commissioners, or other staff.

anticonsumer by the economics profession, this result supports Peltzman's prediction that regulatory activity limiting price decreases rises when aggregate demands fall.[5]

The paper is organized as follows. The first section contains a brief review of Peltzman's theory and describes the model's basis for predicting the cyclical behavior of regulation. The empirical test is presented in the second section, which is followed by concluding remarks.

REGULATION AND ECONOMIC ACTIVITY

Peltzman's model posits a vote-maximizing regulator who faces a trade-off when setting a regulated price between the gains conferred on producers and the costs imposed on consumers. Specifically, the regulator seeks to maximize his political majority subject to the constraint that higher prices generate greater producer support but antagonize consumers, and vice versa. Given this trade-off, the theory implies that neither group achieves all that it wants from regulation in the sense that the price consistent with political equilibrium is neither the monopoly-profit-maximizing price nor the competitive price.

According to Peltzman, changes in aggregate demand displace the political equilibrium by altering "the total surplus . . . over which the regulator might have control and, *pari passu*, the political payoff for its redistribution." As in the standard consumer choice model, a parametric shift generates a substitution effect and what Peltzman terms a "political wealth" effect, which lead to a new equilibrium. Because the regulator operates on two margins, however, he "will, in general, not force the entire adjustment onto one group."[6] This tendency is reinforced by diminishing political returns to changes in the regulated price.

Suppose that aggregate demand falls, decreasing the total surplus available for redistribution. Producer profits decline, but if the political wealth effect is important, it will attenuate the regulator's incentive to reduce price by as much as it would fall in an unregulated setting—that is, Peltzman's regulator will call on consumers to "buffer some of the producer losses."[7] Similarly, regulatory agencies will cushion consumers against producer gains when aggregate demand rises because increased wealth increases the political payoff from redistribution. Thus, the regulated price will not be increased by as much as it would rise in an unregulated setting.[8]

In summary, Peltzman's model of regulation leads to the prediction that regulatory agencies will buffer producer losses during contractions and attenuate producer gains during expansions. That is, regulatory activity that lowers consumer welfare will tend to be countercyclical, intensifying when demand declines and abating as demand increases. (Jack Hirschleifer characterizes this aspect of Peltzman's hypothesis as "share the gain, share the pain.")[9]

In the next section we provide a test of this hypothesis using the incidence of Robinson-Patman Act cases as a measure of welfare-reducing regulation. Several economic hypotheses about the effects of the Robinson-Patman Act have been suggested; none of them has been verified empirically. According to these hypotheses, Robinson-Patman cases benefit independent retailers relative to chain stores, lower the cost of collusion, and protect small firms relative to larger firms with some degree of market power.[10] Under the first hypothesis, the demand for Robinson-Patman regulation is unlikely to have a significant cyclical component; this is not so in the other two cases. First, the conventional wisdom holds that cartel cheating increases when demand declines relative to normal demand; thus, the demand for Robinson-Patman cases, which reduce chiseling, increases. Second, during phases of the business cycle when demand is strong, there is pressure on price to rise above normal, and price-takers do not encounter price cuts that lower their profits. Thus, the demand for Robinson-Patman cases is low. In contrast, in a downturn there is pressure on price and profits to fall below normal. Price-takers gain at the expense of larger firms having some degree of market power if price cutting is restricted. Thus, the demand for Robinson-Patman enforcement activity is increased.

Depending on the elasticity of the FTC supply response, consumer welfare is reduced in a cyclical downturn, since increased Robinson-Patman activity mitigates the redistribution of income away from cartels (hypothesis 2) and away from fringe firms (hypothesis 3) that would occur during a contraction in an unregulated market. In the guise of protecting small business, Robinson-Patman enforcement therefore operates as welfare-reducing regulation in a manner akin to the more traditional price-entry regulation considered by Stigler and Peltzman.

EMPIRICAL RESULTS

In this section we present empirical evidence that lends support to Peltzman's hypothesis concerning the behavior of regulation over the business cycle. Specifically, we find the number of complaints charging violations of the Robinson-Patman Act to vary inversely with the general level of economic activity. This result suggests that regulation stresses producer protection during contractions and consumer protection during expansions.

The Model

The empirical results are derived from estimates of the following regression equation:

$$CASES = b_o + b_1 RGNP + b_2 U + b_3 FAIL + b_4 EXCAP + b_5 BUDGET + b_6 TREND + b_7 TREND^2 + e,$$

where

CASES = the annual number of antitrust cases;
RGNP = real gross national product;
U = unemployment rate of the civilian labor force;
FAIL = business failure rate per 10,000 firms;
EXCAP = excess capacity rate;
BUDGET = real annual FTC appropriations;
TREND = a linear time trend; and
e = the regression error term.

The dependent variable, CASES, represents the output of the FTC. The commission has sole responsibility for enforcing the FTC Act of 1914, which states that "unfair methods of competition in commerce and unfair or deceptive acts or practices in commerce are hereby declared illegal." The FTC may also bring cases under the Sherman Act (1890) and Clayton Act (1914), although its authority with respect to the former was not declared until 1948.[11]

To provide a test of Peltzman's hypothesis about producer-protection regulation, we estimated the regression model using cases brought under the Robinson-Patman Act as the dependent variable. Although Section 2 of the original Clayton Act prohibited price discrimination, Section 2 had little impact prior to its amendment in 1936 by Robinson-Patman, which followed "all sorts of demands for government assistance to businessmen" during the early 1930s.[12]

In separate regressions we used FTC cases net of Clayton Act Section 2 matters as the dependent variable. These cases represent allegations of more traditional antitrust violations, such as monopolization or collusion, which may be associated with consumer-protection concerns and matters nominally linked with proconsumer regulation, including advertising and product defect cases. Prior to enactment of Robinson-Patman in 1936, the commission issued on average slightly less than ten Section 2 price-discrimination complaints annually. Thus, total and net FTC cases do not differ substantially in the pre-Robinson-Patman era.

RGNP, U, FAIL, and EXCAP are alternative measures of general business conditions. The hypothesis of countercyclical producer-protection regulation is supported if the coefficient on RGNP is negative in the Robinson-Patman regression. Positive coefficients on the other three variables will also refute the null hypothesis that Robinson-Patman activity is neutral.

BUDGET represents yearly input expenditures by the enforcement agency and is expected to be unrelated or mildly positively related to Robinson-Patman activities. Finally, TREND allows for secular growth (or contraction) in caseloads arising from factors exogenous to the regulation-business condition relation; the coefficient on TREND is indeterminant a priori. Squaring the time trend allows for nonlinear growth.

The Data

Observations for all but one of the right-hand-side variables were available for the period 1915 through 1981.[13] Because the excess capacity series was not reported prior to 1948, the results displayed below contain separate estimates for the 1948–1981 subperiod. The Robinson-Patman results cover 1937–1981, and net FTC cases cover 1915–1981.

Cases were assigned to years on the basis of dates on which the FTC complaint was issued. Although we expected law-enforcement activities to lag behind the various measures of economic conditions, lags of up to four years were highly correlated with contemporaneous values of the independent variables. No lag structure was therefore introduced into the final estimates. In running the regressions, the observations on all variables except the time trend were first transformed logarithmically, and then generalized least squares was employed to correct for the serial correlation apparent in ordinary least squares estimates.

The Results

The results shown in Table 6.1 offer strong support for Peltzman's prediction. Robinson-Patman cases are negatively related to real gross national product (GNP), though not at a standard level of significance. Each 1 percent decline in real GNP results in a 2.5 percent increase in complaints charging price discrimination violations. Moreover, Robinson-Patman cases are increased by higher unemployment rates, by greater business failure rates, and by increases in excess capacity. The coefficients on these three explanatory variables are significantly different from zero at the 5 or 10 percent levels.

Although our test of Peltzman's hypothesis focuses on cyclical behavior of the Robinson-Patman series, we also include counterpart estimates for the series of FTC cases net of Clayton Act Section 2 matters. The behavior of this series does not provide evidence for or against Peltzman's hypothesis because we are not confident about the welfare effects of these activities. If we could be relatively sure that the non-Robinson-Patman cases constituted welfare-enhancing activities, then procyclical behavior of such enforcement efforts would be consistent with the Peltzman hypothesis, but we cannot be so certain.

In fact, the results in Table 6.2 indicate that FTC cases net of Clayton Act

TABLE 6.1
REGRESSION RESULTS
(DEPENDENT VARIABLE: LOG OF ROBINSON-PATMAN CASES)

	1937–1981			1948–1981
Intercept	5.9417	−5.0909	−5.2361	2.4748
LNRGNP	−2.4648			
	(−1.33)			
LNU		0.6749		
		(2.08)**		
LNFAIL			0.4649	
			(1.80)*	
LEXCAP				1.5840
				(2.64)**
LNBUD	1.2633	0.7200	0.7403	0.3588
	(1.33)	(0.74)	(0.74)	(0.25)
TREND	0.2191	0.1728	0.1086	0.1627
	(2.54)**	(3.51)***	(2.45)**	(1.48)
TREND²	−0.0054	−0.0057	−0.0044	−0.0080
	(−3.72)***	(−4.14)***	(−2.89)***	(−4.26)***
$\hat{\rho}$	0.1379	0.1016	0.0922	0.0898
D-W	2.02	2.01	2.01	1.97
R²	0.515	0.561	0.554	0.655

NOTES: t-values are in parentheses; $\hat{\rho}$ is the estimated autocorrelation coefficient; and D-W is the Durbin-Watson statistic. Asterisks denote significance at the 1 percent (***), 5 percent (**), and 10 percent (*) levels.

SOURCES: FTC cases and appropriations were obtained from the Office of the Secretary, Federal Trade Commission. Macroeconomic data were obtained from *Economic Report of the President of the United States* (Washington, D.C.: GPO, 1982), and U.S. Department of Commerce, Bureau of the Census, *Historical Statistics of the United States, Colonial Times to 1970*, 2 vols. (Washington, D.C.: GPO, 1975).

Section 2 matters are procyclical with respect to real GNP and unemployment, but countercyclical with respect to excess capacity rates.[14] Non-Robinson-Patman enforcement appears to be unrelated to business failure rates, and passage of the Robinson-Patman Act had a negative but insignificant effect on FTC activity net of price-discrimination enforcement.

The positive sign on excess capacity contradicts the GNP and unemployment findings. There is some reason to believe, however, that this result might be driven by institutional changes during the 1970s and 1980s, which led to a major shift in the commission's workload toward industry-wide rulemaking and away from traditional cases.[15] By omitting rulemaking activity, we would tend to underestimate the output of FTC regulation, with the effects boding larger during the 1948–1981 subperiod than in the regressions utilizing the longer 1915–1981 series.

TABLE 6.2
REGRESSION RESULTS
(DEPENDENT VARIABLE: LOG OF NET FTC CASES)

	1915–1981			1948–1981
Intercept	−20.6606	−10.3368	−10.4342	6.5415
LNRGNP	1.7569			
	(1.94)*			
LNU		−0.2867		
		(−2.10)**		
LNFAIL			−0.0941	
			(−0.51)	
LEXCAP				0.5760
				(2.14)**
LNBUD	1.8311	1.7389	1.7647	−0.2166
	(4.98)***	(4.78)***	(4.70)***	(−0.33)
RPDUM	−0.5138	−0.4974	−0.4065	
	(−1.08)	(−1.05)	(−0.84)	
TREND	0.0696	0.1189	0.1007	0.2455
	(1.53)	(2.88)***	(2.51)**	(4.86)***
TREND^2	−0.0027	−0.0025	−0.0023	−0.0070
	(−5.25)***	(−5.02)***	(−4.83)***	(−8.10)***
$\hat{\rho}$	0.6316	0.6447	0.5875	0.1258
D-W	1.60	1.56	1.44	1.66
R^2	0.436	0.440	0.409	0.712

NOTES: The net of FTC cases is the net of Clayton Act Section 2 matters. t-values are in parentheses; $\hat{\rho}$ is the estimated autocorrelation coefficient; and D-W is the Durbin-Watson statistic. Asterisks denote significance at the 1 percent (***), 5 percent (**), and 10 percent (*) levels.

Although the generally procyclical behavior of the non-Robinson-Patman series provides additional support for Peltzman's hypothesis if this series represents procompetitive law enforcement, we prefer a more skeptical interpretation of the results in Table 6.2[16] In particular, if Robinson-Patman cases are the primary activity of the FTC, mitigating the losses that small firms or cartels would incur absent the Robinson-Patman Act, and if the set of non-Robinson-Patman matters is a mixed bag of alternatively pro- and anticonsumer regulation, then the procyclical character of the non-Robinson-Patman series may merely reflect an effective budget constraint.[17] As Robinson-Patman enforcement—and the small subcategory of non-Robinson-Patman cases that systematically serve the same end as Robinson-Patman matters—abate, in an upswing the other activities of the FTC take up the slack. According to this view, non-Robinson-Patman cases represent residual activities that necessarily move procyclically, since the Robinson-Patman series behaves countercyclically.

Overall, the empirical results lend strong support to Peltzman's hypothesis concerning the behavior of regulatory activity over the business cycle. Welfare-reducing regulation, represented by complaints charging violations of the Robinson-Patman Act, is countercyclical with respect to four macroeconomic variables: real GNP, unemployment, business failure, and excess capacity rates.

Concluding Remarks

In this paper we reported evidence favoring Peltzman's hypothesis about the weight attached over the business cycle to different types of regulation. Our findings suggest that in business contractions the FTC moves to cushion producer losses by increasing the number of complaints issued under the Robinson-Patman Act, which serves to limit the tendency for prices to fall. This result can be rationalized under the view that the FTC is in the business of transferring wealth from consumers either to protect small business or to shore up cartels.[18]

In contrast, during business expansions the commission reduces its Robin-son-Patman enforcement efforts. If the FTC's non-Robinson-Patman activities are welfare enhancing, such a change in case mix serves to mitigate producer gains, transferring wealth to consumers at the margin. In any case, our results imply that the business cycle is important in explaining the level and pattern of regulatory activity.

Notes

1. George J. Stigler, "The Theory of Economic Regulation," Bell Journal of Economics and Management Science 2 (Spring 1971): 7.

2. Sam Peltzman, "Toward a More General Theory of Regulation," Journal of Law and Economics 19 (August 1976): 211–40.

3. Ibid., p. 227.

4. The hypothesis that private attempts at cartelization will be more prevalent during recessions has an extensive literature. Examples are Peter Asch and J. J. Seneca, "Is Collusion Profitable?" Review of Economics and Statistics 58 (February 1976): 1–12; Richard M. Cyert, "Oligopoly and the Business Cycle," Journal of Political Economy 63 (February 1955): 41–51; Bjarke Fog, "How Are Cartel Prices Determined?" Journal of Industrial Economics 5 (November 1956): 16–23; R. F. Harrod, "Imperfect Competition and the Trade Cycle," Review of Economics and Statistics 18 (February 1936): 84–88; John Palmer, "Some Economic Conditions Conducive to Collusion," Journal of Economic Issues 6 (June 1972): 29–38; Richard A. Posner, Antitrust Law: An Economic Perspective (Chicago: University of Chicago Press, 1976); and George J. Stigler, "A Theory of Oligopoly," Journal of Political Economy 72 (February 1964): 44–62. On the incentive to seek government protection during contractions, see, for example, Ellis

W. Hawley, *The New Deal and the Problem of Monopoly* (Princeton, N.J.: Princeton University Press, 1966); Thor Hultgren and Merton R. Peck, *Costs, Prices, and Profits: Their Cyclical Relations* (New York: Columbia University Press, 1965); Fritz Machlup, *The Political Economy of Monopoly* (Baltimore, Md.: Johns Hopkins University Press, 1952); and Fritz Voight, "German Experience with Cartels and Their Control During Pre-War and Post-War Periods," in J. P. Miller, ed., *Competition, Cartels, and Their Control* (Amsterdam: North Holland, 1962), pp. 169–213.

5. For the anticonsumer view of Robinson-Patman, see Richard A. Posner, *The Robinson-Patman Act: Federal Regulation of Price Differences* (Washington, D.C.: American Enterprise Institute, 1976), and U.S. Department of Justice, *Report on the Robinson-Patman Act* (Washington, D.C.: Government Printing Office, 1977).

6. Peltzman, "Toward a More General Theory of Regulation," pp. 224–25.

7. Ibid., p. 225.

8. Thomas Moore suggests a variant of Peltzman's model that also generates procyclical benefits for producers. He argues that because "both buyers and sellers prefer stable prices over rapidly fluctuating ones . . . regulation tends, therefore, to fix nominal prices." Moore's hypothesis does not, however, lead to predictions about the level of general regulatory activity over the business cycle. His argument implies only that consumers benefit in expansions because regulation prevents prices from rising as much as they might and that producers gain in contractions because regulation prevents prices from falling as rapidly as they otherwise would. See Thomas G. Moore, "The Applied Theory of Regulation: Political Economy at the Interstate Commerce Commission, a Comment on the Alexis Paper," *Public Choice* 39 (1982): 29–32.

9. Jack Hirschleifer, "Comment," *Journal of Law and Economics* 19 (August 1976): 243.

10. In examining the origins of the Robinson-Patman Act, Tom Ross found evidence that grocery chains suffered wealth reductions, that food brokers benefited, and that there was no significant effect on the market value of grocery manufacturers or other chains. Moreover, the wealth effects of Robinson-Patman enforcement were found by Ross to be substantial and largely associated with issuance of a complaint, not the ultimate outcome of the case. See Tom Ross, "Winners and Losers Under the Robinson-Patman Act," *Journal of Law and Economics* 27 (October 1984): 243–72.

11. Posner, *Robinson-Patman Act*.

12. Ross, "Winners and Losers."

13. The important event was the decision in Federal Trade Commission v. Cement Institute, 333 U.S. 683 (1948), which held that the commission could, under Section 5 of the FTC Act, challenge practices that offend the Sherman Act.

14. Posner, *Robinson-Patman Act*, p. 25.

15. Our data are available on request.

16. Since the non-Robinson-Patman series covers the period 1915–1981, a Robinson-Patman dummy variable, RPDUM, was included as a regressor. RPDUM is equal to unity for the years beginning 1937 and is zero otherwise.

17. For example, see William F. Shughart II and Robert D. Tollison, "Antitrust Recidivism in Federal Trade Commission Data: 1914–1982" (Chapter 12 in this volume).

18. George J. Stigler, *The Citizen and the State* (Chicago: University of Chicago Press, 1975), p. 183.

Chapter 7

Dual Enforcement of the Antitrust Laws

RICHARD S. HIGGINS,

WILLIAM F. SHUGHART II, &

ROBERT D. TOLLISON

RECENT criticism of the Federal Trade Commission (FTC) has again raised the debate about whether the current system of dual antitrust law enforcement by the FTC and Department of Justice is efficient or leads to wasteful duplication.[1] Most of the controversy deals with the issue of the quality of output, that is, the relative number of "good" and "bad" cases under the current bureaucratic structure compared with some idealized benchmark that might exist with a single antitrust agency. In short, much of the discussion does not focus on dual enforcement, as such, but on the nature of the FTC's authority versus that of the Justice Department. For example, much weight is placed on the fact that the FTC's mandate combines both a judicial and a prosecutorial role, whereas the Justice Department's functions are limited to the latter. Importance is also given to the FTC's budgetary independence in contrast to the Justice Department's status within the executive branch.

In this paper we approach the issue of dual antitrust enforcement not as legal critics but as positive economists. We develop a model that shows that independent dual enforcement leads to more antitrust activity at a lower unit cost than would obtain with a single agency. On the other hand, if the agencies collude, as they appear to do under present institutional arrangements, dual

We benefited from comments on an earlier draft by Robert Mackay, Dennis Mueller, and Bruce Yandle. The views expressed in this paper are those of the authors and do not necessarily reflect those of the Federal Trade Commission, individual commissioners, or other staff.

enforcement leads to less antitrust activity and is more costly than it otherwise would be. Empirical tests using historical agency budgets and case production figures fail to refute the model's predictions.

Our model abstracts from the quality issue mentioned above. We are only concerned with aggregate antitrust law enforcement activity as a function of the degree of competition between the two agencies. By assuming case quality to be constant, we avoid unnecessarily complicated normative judgments and focus on the amount of antitrust activity and its costs.

To provide some institutional background for our analysis, we review common criticisms and defenses of dual enforcement in the first section below. Our positive theory of dual enforcement is presented next, followed by an empirical test of the theory. We offer some brief concluding remarks in the last section.

PROS AND CONS OF DUAL ENFORCEMENT

Critics of existing dual antitrust law enforcement have focused their attacks on the FTC's organizational structure and broad enforcement authority and on the potential waste of resources arising from having two governmental agencies performing the same function. Proponents of dual enforcement see advantages in most of these same institutional arrangements. In this section we summarize the salient points in the dual enforcement debate.

Commission Structure and Organization

A prominent 1960s critic of the FTC, the American Bar Association (ABA), noted that:

> the idea of creating an administrative agency to operate in the antitrust field arose out of a concern that federal district judges, unequipped with a staff of fact-finders, evaluators, and economists, would not be able to apply the antitrust laws effectively to halt the growth of anticompetitive practices and at the same time not unduly interfere with vigorous economic growth.[2]

Whatever efficiencies may be gained from combining prosecutorial and judicial functions under one roof, such an arrangement clearly provides the potential for conflict of interest. Succinctly put, "FTC cases are tried largely within the FTC itself, with five commissioners first bringing the charges and later adjudging guilt or innocence."[3]

Conflicts are most likely to arise in so-called test cases where attempts are made to create new law. As former commissioner Philip Elman put it: "while there is no bias or prejudgment of guilt in the classic sense, there is an inescapable predisposition in favor of the agency position, as set forth in the complaint . . . While a test case may be and usually is vigorously contested, the result—at least in the agency phase—is likely to be a foregone conclusion."[4]

Recent events belie Elman's assumption of no prejudgment. General Mills, a respondent to the commission's recently dismissed "shared monopoly" case, moved to disqualify then-chairman Michael Pertschuk on the basis of his alleged public statement that "winning the cereal case would be an enormous help." Although the commission ultimately voted to deny General Mills' motion, Pertschuk was disqualified from participating in the FTC's Children's Advertising rulemaking proceedings in November 1978 on a finding by the District Court of the District of Columbia that he had "conclusively prejudged factual issues." In January 1979 an FTC cease-and-desist order was overturned because of "Commissioner [Calvin J.] Collier's adjudicative participation in the case."[5]

It should be noted that one commentator sees advantages in the FTC's dual functions in the sense that "as an enforcement agency, as well as an adjudicator, the Commission makes policy decisions and provides both the opportunity for judicial actions and input to the judicial process."[6] However, the majority of dual enforcement critics appear to concur with Richard Posner's judgment:

> It is too much to expect men of ordinary character and competence to be able to judge impartially in cases that they are responsible for having instituted in the first place. An agency that dismissed many of the complaints that it issued would stand condemned of having squandered the taxpayer's money on meritless causes. Besides, commissioners who lack the tenure, the high status, and the freedom from other duties that federal judges enjoy cannot realistically be expected to perform the judicial function as well; and they do not.[7]

An important consequence of the commission's joint prosecutorial and judicial roles is that the arrangement appears to lengthen the law-enforcement process and therefore raise the costs to respondents of antitrust litigation. In essence, alleged violators face additional proceedings before the FTC that they would not face if the same practices were challenged by the Justice Department. Specifically, complaints issued by the commission in its prosecutorial role are first litigated before a hearing examiner, whose decision is then automatically appealed to the commission, which then acts as judge. If the commission finds in favor of complaint counsel, only then may the FTC decision be appealed to the federal courts. In contrast, Justice Department allegations go to federal court immediately. Posner found that "the use of administrative proceedings to enforce the antitrust laws has not contributed to expedition—rather the contrary." Examining all federal antitrust cases between 1930 and 1964, he discovered that "the average length of FTC cases in which the respondent exercised his right of judicial review is far greater than the average length of litigated Department of Justice cases; and the length of FTC cases reviewed by the Supreme Court is greater than that of Department of Justice cases reviewed by the Court."[8]

A further criticism of the commission's structure and organization concerns the agency's independence from the executive branch. This line of attack views the agency as a creature of Congress having the primary function of creating wealth transfers within the polity:

> [T]he FTC can be understood only as a political institution. As such it offers no reason to expect its actions to make sense from the standpoint of market analysis—and they do not. Congress needs the Commission as an institution to which to refer complaints from its constituents about all the tedious ills of life that can, plausibly or not, be blamed on the business community. It is not to be supposed that Congress expects the FTC to respond to these complaints in any way that seriously interferes with the operation of the market. The Commission's real function is (or at least was intended to be) to relieve the Congressman of blame when no satisfaction is produced for the constituent—as, in the vast majority of cases, it cannot be.[9]

Empirical evidence in support of this proposition is given by Roger Faith, Donald Leavens, and Robert Tollison in Chapter 2 of this volume. Moreover, Barry Weingast and Mark Moran propose that even so-called runaway bureaucracies reflect the influence of congressmen serving on agency oversight committees, who "protect the bureaus under their jurisdiction for the benefit of their constituencies."[10]

The commission's budgetary independence is thought by some to be advantageous in freeing the agency from presidential pressure. For example, Robert Pitofsky asserts that this freedom allows the FTC to bring controversial cases and to take on tough political opponents.[11]

Commission Enforcement Authority

A second major element in the dual enforcement debate concerns the broad language of the commission's legislative authority, Section 5 of the FTC Act, which states that "unfair methods of competition in commerce and unfair or deceptive acts or practices in commerce are hereby declared illegal." To its critics, the statute's vagueness allows the FTC to "roam at large, extending at will the frontiers of antitrust."[12] The situation is exacerbated by the fact that, unlike the Justice Department, the commission has the power neither to impose criminal sanctions on law violators nor "to issue interlocutory cease-and-desist orders on the basis of a *prima facie* case."[13]

The discretion given to the FTC by Section 5 was designed by Congress to avoid enumeration of all possible trade restraints.[14] Proponents of dual enforcement argue that vagueness of Section 5 is a virtue in the sense that Congress could not have been expected to foresee in 1914 all of the possible anticompetitive practices that would be utilized by imaginative law violators. From this point of view, the "unfair" standard of the FTC Act provides the flexibility needed by law-enforcement officials to deal with future problems. To the criticism that flexibility encourages vague standards, FTC proponents respond that since the courts ultimately determine legal standards, aberrant interpretations by the commission will never attain the status of enforceable precedent.

In contrast, virtually all of the commission's critics note that whatever elements were thought desirable in such flexibility have remained unused. In 1969 both the ABA Commission and the "President's Task Force Report on Productivity and Competition" criticized the FTC's case-selection record.[15] In particular, "if the measure of quality of FTC performance in the antitrust area is whether the agency has broken new ground and made new law by resort to its unique administrative resources, it seems clear that the record is largely one of missed opportunities."[16] The dominant view is that the commission has brought far too many Robinson-Patman price-discrimination matters, to the exclusion of cases that would have had beneficial effects on competition.[17]

Waste from Overlapping Authorities

The debate over the extent to which dual enforcement leads to resource waste has a venerable history in the legal literature. As early as 1925, only ten years after passage of the FTC Act, the National Industrial Conference Board (NICB) complained that the commission's vigorous program of resale price maintenance prosecutions had encroached on an area of antitrust law enforcement that Congress did not intend to be in its purview. The board went on to recommend that:

> in order to bring about a more logical and efficacious distribution of functions, and thereby contribute to the expedition of Federal Trade Commission procedure in its proper sphere, [it seems necessary] to provide by law that whenever the Commission secures evidence pointing to a violation of the Sherman Act it shall transmit the same to the Department of Justice, with such recommendations as it may deem suitable.[18]

Criticisms such as that of the NICB apparently had little practical effect on interagency rivalry. However, mutual action to delimit respective fields of authority followed a 1948 Supreme Court decision, which held that the commission could condemn conduct under Section 5 that offends the Sherman Act, and that filing of a Justice Department suit did not require termination of pending FTC proceedings.[19] In June of the same year, an interagency liaison agreement established a formal mechanism for allocating cases among the two law-enforcement bodies.[20] The liaison agreement clearly represents an important event in antitrust law enforcement. In particular, as a point of transition from independent dual to collusive dual enforcement, it supplies the conditions for a natural experiment of which we take advantage in the empirical work reported in the next section.

The FTC–Justice Department case-allocation system is not without its critics. J. B. Sloan believes that the exchange of information about respondents taking place within the liaison framework "raises substantial constitutional questions, including issues of due process and self-incrimination," and D. L. Roll cites instances in which the interagency competition for cases has caused unwarranted administrative delays. In contrast, A. D. Neale and D. G. Goyder describe the liaison system as a "well-established mechanism for avoiding duplication," and Robert Katzmann notes that the two agencies have generally avoided major confrontations over their jurisdictions: "Usually, one agency will automatically grant clearance to the other to pursue an investigation, unless the contemplated action duplicates or interferes with a case that it is already conducting."[21]

Some critics have contended that the potential for wasted resources is less serious than the uncertain legal standards that business faces because of dual enforcement. T. J. McGrew argues that dual antitrust policies force "the business community to risk being caught between two conflicting federal agencies."[22] In the arguments of some critics it is difficult to separate condemnation of the dual-enforcement concept from condemnation of FTC performance. For example, E. E. Vaill sees no place in modern society for a system in which if an alleged violator "happens to draw the Justice Department, he will be accorded a federal court trial and due process, but if he draws the FTC, he will be relegated to a quasi-judicial procedure, where his rights are not so great."[23]

In summary, major questions about the efficacy of dual antitrust law enforcement remain unresolved. Both supporters and opponents of bureaucratic competition have found elements in the FTC's organizational structure, its broad enforcement authority, and the rivalrous jurisdictions of the two agencies that are consistent with their own particular views. With few exceptions, however, the debate has focused on normative issues—the relative number of "good" and "bad" cases under the current system—rather than on the amount of antitrust activity and its cost. We now turn to a more formal treatment of dual enforcement.

THE MODEL

In this section we construct a model of dual enforcement and contrast the testable implications with those derived from a model of single-agency (collusive) behavior. The model rests on the following assumptions:

1. There is no quality competition; the quality of each agency's output is identical and fixed.
2. Both agencies have identical cost functions, $C(X_1)$ and $C(X_2)$, and the production cost for each agency is functionally independent of the other's output. Initially, we assume that average cost, c, is constant; we subsequently drop this assumption.
3. There is a functional relationship between aggregate budgetary appropriations, R, and the aggregate output level, $X = X_1 + X_2$. Further, it is assumed that $R(X)/X$ is linear and negatively sloped; the "demand" curve is linear.
4. Each agency receives appropriations in proportion to its output share subject to the "demand" curve implicit in $R(X_1 + X_2)$.
5. Each agency treats the output of the other as a parameter and maximizes its appropriations subject to a break-even constraint. This makes our model the revenue-maximizing analogue of the Cournot duopoly model.
6. We derive reaction functions for each agency and assume that a Nash equilibrium describes independent dual-agency enforcement activities.

The model we postulate is one particular description of the rivalry between two government agencies producing the same output. Some of the assumptions, such as linear cost and demand functions, simplify the analysis without compromising its applicability. Other assumptions are more fundamental, reflecting a specific analytical depiction of the appropriations process. For example, we suppose that the two agencies answer to one appropriations "committee"—that is, the agencies share the same demand curve. As a matter of fact, the FTC and the Antitrust Division receive their funding from different sources. However, since Congress is not oblivious to the fact that two agencies are producing antitrust output and that revenues are scarce, the ultimate appropriations to the two agencies are not independent. In lieu of a more complete explanation of how appropriations are actually made, we assume that the two agencies compete along the same demand curve.

Furthermore, of the various mechanisms of appropriating funds that could be postulated, we suppose that the agencies behave according to the Cournot output conjectures, and we define equilibrium as the output vector that is identical regardless of the sequential order of the offers. Other assumptions could have been supposed, leading perhaps to different results.

In particular, we have adopted William Niskanen's seminal treatment of government bureaus as budget maximizers, but we have not retained his assumption that the agencies make all-or-none offers to their sponsors.[24] It is unclear how such all-or-none offers are consistent with equilibrium in a competitive environment.[25] Notwithstanding the all-or-none alternative, we stick with the Cournot model because it offers a straightforward way to obtain testable implications about bureaucratic competition. Finally, for the special case of FTC–Justice Department competition, we attain further simplification by omitting interagency differences that arise from commission and bureau organizational structures.[26]

In Niskanen's single-bureau model, two cases are distinguished depending on demand and cost conditions. On the one hand, if marginal revenue vanishes at an output above the agency's break-even output, the single agency will sell output at its cost of production (Case I). On the other hand, if the revenue-maximizing output is not constrained by costs, there will be "fat" in the agency's budget (Case II). In the latter case the agency will not produce with least-cost input combinations. Instead, costs will be overstated, and the agency will receive more appropriations than its output warrants. Of course, to some extent, budgeting oversight and management information systems will enable the appropriations committee to estimate the agency's production cost. Nevertheless, under the demand and cost conditions described for Case II, there is a clear tendency for agencies to produce output inefficiently.

Cases I and II

The conditions described in Cases I and II are also important to distinguish when deriving implications from the dual agency model. Case I (revenue-maximizing output constrained by cost) is relatively uninteresting, at least for constant cost. In Case I the reaction functions coincide. Each reaction function has slope equal to -1, and regardless of how appropriations are allocated between the two agencies, total output, $X_1 + X_2$, is equal to X^*, where $R(X^*) = C(X^*)$. In Case I dual enforcement and single-agency enforcement yield the same results, and there is no fat in either agency's budget.

In Case II (revenue-maximizing output not constrained by costs) the optimization problem for Agency I is different depending on the given value of

Agency II's output. By assumption, for $X_2=0$ the break-even constraint does not bind Agency I. As a consequence, there is a range of values of X_2, $0 \leq X_2 \leq X_2'$, over which the constraint is not binding. For values of $X_2 > X_2'$, Agency I maximizes its appropriations subject to the break-even constraint. The reaction function for Agency I is found by splicing the two reaction functions defined by the marginal conditions associated with the unconstrained and the constrained optimization problems. (Because we assume identical cost functions, derivation of the reaction function for Agency II is symmetric to that for Agency I.)

For $X_2 \leq X_2'$, Agency I maximizes:

$$X_1 R(X_1+X)/(X_1+X_2). \tag{1}$$

The expression in (1) is average appropriations times Agency I's output, or Agency I's share of appropriations. The marginal condition is:

$$a-2bX_1-bX_2=0, \tag{2}$$

where $R(X)/X=a-bX$. The expression on the left-hand side in (2) is the marginal revenue for Agency I, holding X_2 constant.

In Figure 7.1, Agency I's output choice is depicted for three arbitrary values of X_2, $X_2^0=0$, $X_2=X_2^1$ and $X_2=X_2^2$. The revenue-maximizing value of X_1 is found by subtracting horizontally the fixed levels of X_2 from demand, constructing the residual demand curves and the corresponding marginal revenue curves, and finding the zeroes of the respective marginal revenue functions. This yields the corresponding outputs, X_1^0, X_1^1, and X_1^2, depicted in Figure 7.1.

The reaction function defined by (2) is depicted in Figure 7.2. Of course, as observed above, the reaction function is only applicable for $X_2 \leq X_2'$. Inspection of Figure 7.1 reveals that Agency I cannot cover cost if it produces X_1^2 in response to X_2^2 for Agency II. In other words, (1) is an incorrect specification of Agency I's optimization problem when $X_2=X_2^2$ since $X_2^2 > X_2'$. For $X_2 > X_2'$, Agency I's maximization of appropriations is constrained by cost; the reaction function in Figure 7.2 only applies for $X_2 \leq X_2'$.

For $X_2 > X_2'$ agency I maximizes:

$$X_1 R(X_1+X_2)/(X_1+X_2), \tag{3}$$

subject to

$$X_1 R(X_1+X_2)/(X_1+X_2) \geq C(X_1). \qquad (4)$$

Because the constraint is binding, the marginal condition is simply:

$$R(X_1+X_2) = c(X_1+X_2). \qquad (5)$$

The reaction function defined by (5) is a straight line between $(X^*,0)$ and $(0,X^*)$, where X^* is the "competitive" output.

In Figure 7.3, the two reaction functions corresponding to unconstrained and constrained maximization are depicted. The point of intersection of the reaction curves in Figure 7.3 occurs at X_2, where the maximization problem for Agency I switches from an unconstrained problem to one bound by the break-

FIGURE 7.1
OUTPUT CHOICES BY AGENCY I FOR THREE VALUES OF AGENCY II OUTPUT

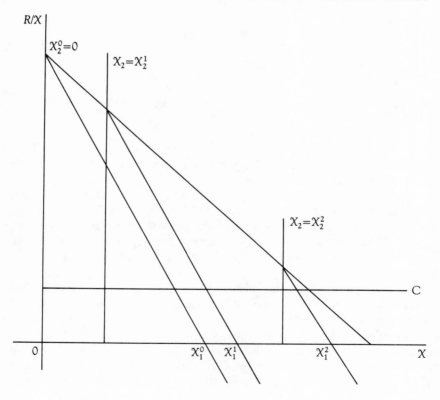

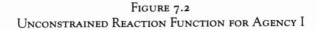

FIGURE 7.2
UNCONSTRAINED REACTION FUNCTION FOR AGENCY I

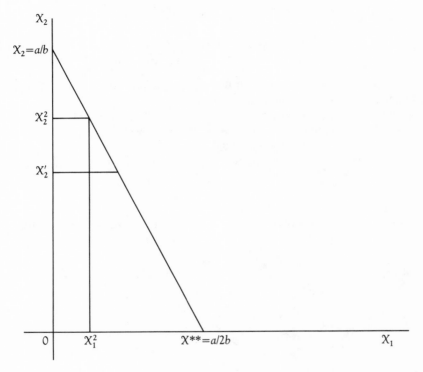

even constraint. Thus, the reaction function that applies for Agency I for all X_2 is depicted in Figure 7.3 by the cross-hatched line segments.

To find the equilibrium outputs for the two agencies under independent dual enforcement, we find the intersection of the overall reaction functions for the two agencies. By the symmetry of the problems for the two agencies, Agency II's reaction function is the inverse of Agency I's reaction function. These are depicted respectively in Figure 7.4 by the circled and cross-hatched lines.

In Figure 7.4 an equilibrium obtains along the reaction functions defined by the marginal conditions from unconstrained maximization. A different result occurs when the value of marginal cost is relatively high. For high values of c, the values of the switching points, X_2' and X_1' ($X_2' = X_1'$), are smaller.[27] The effect is to shift the reaction function for the constrained maximization problem, the 45-degree line between $(X^*, 0)$ and $(0, X^*)$, back toward the origin in Figure 7.4. If c is large enough, the equilibrium outputs will be defined not by

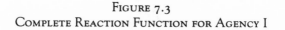

FIGURE 7.3
COMPLETE REACTION FUNCTION FOR AGENCY I

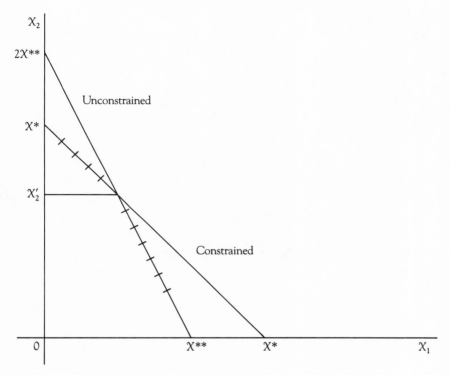

the intersection of the "unconstrained" reaction functions, but along the "constrained" reaction functions that coincide.

Implications

Regardless of whether the equilibrium outputs are determined by the constrained or the unconstrained reaction functions, we are able to show that independent dual enforcement leads to more aggregate output than single enforcement. We are also able to show that output per budget dollar is greater under independent dual enforcement than under single enforcement. Furthermore, abstracting from the costs of collusion so that the collusive output is identical to single-agency output, we see that independent dual enforcement leads to more output (and more output per dollar) than joint dual enforcement. This proposition is tested in the next section, where we compare empirical

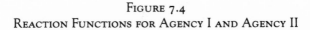

FIGURE 7.4
REACTION FUNCTIONS FOR AGENCY I AND AGENCY II

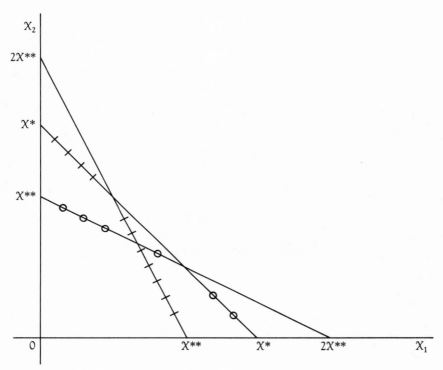

evidence on antitrust activity by the FTC and the Department of Justice before and after the liaison agreement of 1948.

Suppose first that equilibrium obtains at the intersection of the unconstrained reaction functions. Equilibrium is defined by:

$$a - 2bX_1 - bX_2 = 0, \text{ and}$$
$$a - bX_1 - 2bX_2 = 0. \tag{6}$$

Each agency supplies $a/3b$ units of output for a total of $2a/3b$. In contrast, the joint revenue-maximizing output is defined by:

$$a - 2b(X_1 + X_2) = 0. \tag{7}$$

From (7) we see that each agency produces some portion of $a/2b$. Total output under dual enforcement, $2a/3b$, exceeds single-agency output, $a/2b$, by $a/6b$.

Furthermore, since there is fat in the budget for both these equilibrium magnitudes, costs will rise to meet revenues, and output per dollar is therefore measured by the reciprocal of average appropriations. Because average revenue is a declining function of output and output is larger under independent dual enforcement, output per dollar is greater with independent dual enforcement than with single-agency enforcement.

If, however, the cost constraint is binding on the agencies in equilibrium, equilibrium output is determined by:

$$R(X_1+X_2)=c(X_1+X_2). \tag{8}$$

In this case single-agency enforcement leads either to the same total output or to less total output as independent dual enforcement. Specifically, when the joint revenue-maximizing output, X^{**}, exceeds the competitive output, X^*, total output is the same in each case. Alternatively, when X^* exceeds X^{**} but is also less than the total output implied by independent unconstrained maximization, single-agency output is less than independent dual-agency output.

In the standard market model, if collusion costs are zero, identical outputs obtain under joint- and single-firm production. Similarly, in the case of agency behavior, the single-agency solution can be attained by collusive agreement in which the two agencies divide up the market. If dual agencies succeed in halving the demand curve, then each, in appearance, can act independently to achieve the joint revenue maximum. Consequently, in either of the two cases of equilibrium described above, under independent dual enforcement, output and output per budget dollar are at least as large under independent dual enforcement as under collusive dual enforcement. Furthermore, in contrast to collusive and single-agency enforcement, dual-agency rivalry forces the competitive output in one set of cost and revenue configurations.

Increasing Average Cost

We now show that relaxing our previous assumption—that production cost is constant—does not alter our comparative assessment of independent and collusive dual enforcement. There are two differences between the constant- and increasing-cost cases. First, with increasing cost, when the cost constraint binds the two agencies' equilibrium output choices, the equilibrium output shares are unique. Recall that under these circumstances with constant cost, total output satisfies $R(X^*)=C(X^*)$, but individual agency shares are indeterminate. Second, with increasing cost single-agency output may differ from the output chosen by colluding dual agencies; under constant cost these outputs are identical.

Just as in the case of constant cost, equilibrium outputs are determined by reaction functions implied by constrained or unconstrained revenue maximization for each agency, depending on whether average cost is high or low. However, in the case of increasing cost, how rapidly average cost rises also matters. In general, the reaction function for each agency under the increasing cost assumption will consist of portions of both the unconstrained- and constrained-reaction functions, just as with constant cost. We next look at the only instance of any significant difference between the two cost assumptions, which occurs when equilibrium output is constrained by the break-even condition.

Each agency maximizes:

$$X_i R(X_i+X_j)/(X_i+X_j) \qquad i=1,2; \, j \neq i, \tag{9}$$

subject to:

$$X_i R(X_i+X_j)/(X_i+X_j) = C(X_i). \tag{10}$$

The marginal conditions are:

$$\begin{aligned} a-b(X_1+X_2) &= C(X_1)/X_1, \text{ and} \\ a-b(X_1+X_2) &= C(X_2)/X_2. \end{aligned} \tag{11}$$

Assuming that average cost is a linear function, $c+dX$, each equation in (11) defines a linear reaction function with respective slopes, $-(d+b)/b$ and $-b/(d+b)$. (In the constant-cost case $d=0$, and the slopes are identically equal to -1.)

The joint solution of (11) is unique, and it is depicted in Figure 7.5. Since (11) implies equal average cost for the two agencies, equilibrium aggregate output is found by summing horizontally the average-cost functions for the two agencies and equating the aggregate "supply" price to demand price.

Inspection of Figure 7.5 reveals the different implications about output under independent dual enforcement, collusive dual enforcement, and single-agency enforcement. Under the demand and supply conditions depicted, output X' would be chosen by a single agency; output X^{**} would be chosen by two agencies acting jointly (that is, dividing the market equally between them); and output X^* would be chosen by independent dual agencies. Clearly, $X^* > X^{**} > X'$.

It is true that different cost and demand configurations may alter the results, but not in any essential way. For example, if X^{**} were greater than X^*, X^{**} could not be an equilibrium under any of the regimes since the break-even constraint would be violated. In this case, collusive dual enforcement and

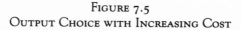

FIGURE 7.5
OUTPUT CHOICE WITH INCREASING COST

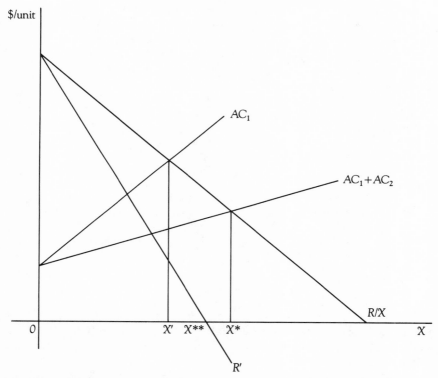

independent dual enforcement would yield the same output. Or, if X' were greater than X^{**}, single-agency and collusive dual-agency equilibrium output would still be greater than X^{**}.

In sum, we have found that by relaxing the constant-cost assumption, independent dual-agency output is at least as great as collusive dual-agency output and always greater than single-agency output. Moreover, output per dollar under collusion will at most be as large as output per dollar with independent dual enforcement.

EMPIRICAL EVIDENCE

Under conditions of either constant or increasing cost, our positive theory of dual enforcement predicts that output (and output per budget dollar) will be at least as large under independent dual enforcement as under collusive dual

TABLE 7.1
INDUSTRY AND VIOLATION ALLOCATIONS UNDER
THE 1948 LIAISON AGREEMENT

FTC	Antitrust Division
Brewing: monopolization and price discrimination	Brewing: acquisitions
Auto parts: monopolization and acquisitions	Automobile industry: monopolization and dealer relations
Tires, batteries, and accessories: distribution	Tires: manufacturing
Cement	Steel (primary)
Shopping centers: trade restraints	Aviation
Department stores: acquisitions	Newspapers: acquisitions
Health care	Aluminum
Food and food distribution	Patents and know-how (with some major exceptions)
Petroleum: monopolization	Communications
Copiers/business machines	Banking and securities
Franchising	Computers
Textile mill products: acquisitions	International agreements
Dairy industry: acquisitions	

SOURCE: Roll, "Dual Enforcement of the Antitrust Laws," p. 2080.

enforcement or enforcement by a single agency. In this section we test the model's main prediction by contrasting FTC and Justice Department antitrust activity over time.

The historical development of U.S. antitrust institutions—especially the events of 1948—supplies the conditions for a natural experiment. Between 1890 and 1914 the Department of Justice was the sole antitrust agency, having responsibility for enforcing the Sherman Act; dual enforcement began in 1914 when the FTC Act was passed. A period of 34 years followed in which the commission and Antitrust Division respectively and independently enforced the FTC and Sherman Acts, and they had joint responsibility for seeing that the provisions of the Clayton Act were obeyed. In 1948 the Cement Institute decision and a formal liaison agreement between the two antitrust enforcement units ushered in a period of information exchange and case allocation that effectively turned antitrust law institutions into a system of collusive dual enforcement.

The independence of the two agencies prior to 1948 is illustrated by the confrontation that occurred between the commission and Justice Department in separate investigations of the Aluminum Company of America.[28] In October 1924 the FTC wrote to the attorney general concerning evidence in its possession that Alcoa was continuing to violate the provisions of a 1912 consent decree. Because the statute of limitations would become operative within one year, the commission began another investigation, but when the new evidence was requested by the Justice Department, "it was refused unless *written* consent was given by the Aluminum Company."[29] The attorney general subsequently began his own investigation, but by the time the interagency dispute had gone on for two months, the Senate intervened to halt any inquiry into Alcoa's alleged consent decree violations. In January 1926 the Senate Judiciary Committee began an investigation of the two agencies' handling of the case, described by Thomas Blaisdell as "the amazing spectacle of a congressional committee's investigation of the Department of Justice's investigation of the Federal Trade Commission's investigation of the Aluminum Company of America."[30] Similarly, "the lack of coordination of Commission activities with those of the Attorney General have never appeared to worse advantage" than in their contemporaneous investigations of RCA during the 1920s.[31]

The principal features of the 1948 liaison agreement are a division of enforcement responsibility according to industry of respondent and, to a lesser extent, according to type of violation. The major areas of responsibility given in Table 7.1 are suggestive of the rather detailed allotments made under the liaison agreement. Case allocations are handled through a procedure in which one agency grants "clearance" to the other. In the liaison process consideration is usually given to prior experience with the industry or respondent in question, with the exception that criminal violations are handled exclusively by the Justice Department.

THE DATA

In order to test the predictions of our dual enforcement model, we obtained a time series of FTC and Antitrust Division budgets. (The data are given in Table 7.2.) FTC appropriations were available for each fiscal year from 1915 through 1981. Unfortunately, the Antitrust Division series is not as extensive because its appropriations were not listed as a separate line item in the Justice Department budget until 1932.

As a surrogate for agency output, we chose to use the annual number of antitrust cases instituted. Antitrust Division matters are given by Posner for the years 1890 to 1969.[32] Figures for 1970 through 1981 were obtained from the most recent issue of the Commerce Clearing House's *Trade Regulation Reporter* (4 [1982]). FTC cases in which a complaint was issued or a consent order was executed were derived from the commission's "Matter Listing by Respondent," which is maintained by the Office of the Secretary, Inquiry and Search Branch.

TABLE 7.2
ANNUAL BUDGETARY APPROPRIATIONS
FOR THE FTC, 1915–1981,
AND ANTITRUST DIVISION, 1932–1981
(DOLLARS IN THOUSANDS)

Fiscal Year	FTC	Antitrust Division	Fiscal Year	FTC	Antitrust Division
1915	184		1948	2,970	2,400
1916	431		1949	3,621	3,572
1917	567		1950	3,723	3,750
1918	1,609		1951	3,892	3,750
1919	1,754		1952	4,314	3,421
1920	1,306		1953	4,179	3,200
1921	1,032		1954	4,054	3,500
1922	1,026		1955	4,129	3,148
1923	974		1956	4,549	3,396
1924	1,010		1957	5,550	3,539
1925	1,010		1958	6,186	3,912
1926	1,008		1959	6,488	4,131
1927	997		1960	6,840	4,500
1928	984		1961	8,010	5,074
1929	1,163		1962	10,345	5,873
1930	1,496		1963	11,472	6,218
1931	1,863		1964	12,215	6,599
1932	1,817	204	1965	13,475	7,072
1933	1,427	150	1966	13,863	7,175
1934	1,314	154	1967	14,378	7,495
1935	2,097	415	1968	15,281	7,820
1936	2,035	420	1969	16,900	8,352
1937	1,939	435	1970	20,889	10,026
1938	1,996	414	1971	22,490	11,079
1939	2,283	789	1972	25,189	12,268
1940	2,346	1,309	1973	28,974	12,836
1941	2,300	1,324	1974	32,496	14,790
1942	2,360	2,325	1975	38,983	18,253
1943	2,050	1,800	1976	47,199	22,239
1944	2,083	1,760	1977	54,680	27,706
1945	2,059	1,540	1978	62,100	32,371
1946	2,174	1,875	1979	65,300	37,508
1947	2,975	2,089	1980	66,059	43,544
			1981	70,774	44,862

SOURCES: Federal Trade Commission; Division of Budget and Finance; and *Budget of the United States Government*, respective years.

The Results

The data were initially divided into four time periods. The years 1890–1914 represented an era of single-agency enforcement; 1915–1931 was a time of independent dual enforcement, but for which Antitrust Division budgets were unavailable; complete data were obtained for the independent dual enforcement period of 1932–1948; and 1949–1981 represented a period of collusive dual enforcement.

Mean annual case output, real budgets, and output per real budget dollar are given for each of the four periods in Table 7.3. Data unavailability makes it difficult to evaluate the transition from single-agency to independent dual antitrust law enforcement. Prior to 1915, however, the Justice Department instituted, on average, just over six Sherman Act cases per year. Entry by the FTC in 1914 raised the department's average annual case output to nearly 10.5 cases. The fact that total antitrust activity rose to about 127 cases per year gives some support to our prediction that output under independent dual enforcement will be at least as large as under single-agency enforcement.

The most striking comparison is between the independent dual enforcement era of 1932–1948 and the post-1948 collusive dual enforcement period. Total antitrust activity remained roughly the same (239 cases per year in 1932–1948 and 249 cases per year in 1949–1981), but average cases per budget dollar fell dramatically. The liaison agreement appears to have reduced the output per dollar of both agencies by half. The decline is statistically significant at the 1 percent level for each agency separately and for aggregate case output per budget dollar.

As a further test of the model's predictions, we regressed 1932–1981 agency and aggregate budgets on case output, real gross national product (GNP), and a dummy variable for collusion. GNP measures the overall level of transactions in the economy and serves as a proxy for the supply of potential antitrust violations. The case activity variable on the right-hand side of the regression equation is a primitive measure of the benefits to consumers and producers of antitrust regulation. The *ceteris paribus* relation between budgets and output can thus be viewed as indicating the amount society is willing to pay for antitrust regulation.[33] The collusion dummy variable is given a value of 1 for the years following 1948, and therefore accounts for budgetary effects arising from the FTC–Justice Department liaison agreement. The predictions of our model will be supported if the coefficient on the dummy variable has a positive sign.

The budget and output data were transformed logarithmically, and the regressions were estimated using generalized least squares to adjust for the

TABLE 7.3
ANTITRUST OUTPUT, REAL BUDGETS,
AND OUTPUT PER REAL BUDGET DOLLAR, ANNUAL AVERAGES, 1890–1981
(DOLLARS IN THOUSANDS)

Time Period	FTC			ANTITRUST DIVISION			AGGREGATE ACTIVITY		
	Cases	Real Budget	Cases Per Dollar	Cases	Real Budget	Cases Per Dollar	Cases	Real Budget	Cases Per Dollar
1890–1914	—	—	—	6.08	N/A	N/A	6.08	N/A	N/A
1915–1931	117.06	$ 3,246.06	0.0334	10.47	N/A	N/A	127.53	N/A	N/A
1932–1948	214.18	6,401.38	0.0319	25.06	$ 3,110.18	0.0081	239.24	$ 9,511.56	0.0252
1949–1981	199.48	19,188.30	0.0157	49.24	10,798.40	0.0049	248.72	29,986.70	0.0083

autocorrelation that was present in ordinary least squares estimates. The results are reported in Table 7.4.

In row 1 variations in aggregate case output, real GNP, and the liaison dummy variable explain 66 percent of the variation in aggregate antitrust budgets. The coefficient on the dummy variable is positive and significantly different from zero at the 10 percent level. When real GNP is dropped as an explanatory variable in row 2, the liaison dummy variable coefficient reaches significance at the 1 percent level. Overall, aggregate antitrust budgets appear to be relatively insensitive to changes in either case output or GNP.

Qualitatively similar results are obtained when separate regressions are run for each law-enforcement agency. The FTC estimates in rows 3 and 4 mirror those for aggregate antitrust activity. For the Antitrust Division, however, the dummy variable coefficient is significantly different from zero only when real GNP is omitted. Moreover, in contrast to the previous results, the Antitrust Division displays a positive and significant *ceteris paribus* relation between appropriations and caseload. These findings suggest that the 1948 liaison agreement had a greater impact on the FTC than on the Justice Department. That is, the budget "fat" that our model predicted would arise from collusive dual enforcement appears to have been disproportionately garnered by the FTC.

In summary, the empirical results in this section provide broad support for our dual-agency enforcement model. The significant increase in antitrust activity following the entry of the FTC in 1914 is consistent with the prediction that output under independent dual enforcement will be at least as large as under single-agency enforcement. In addition, we found that the 1948 FTC–Justice Department liaison agreement, which led to cartel-like information exchanges and output allocations, caused antitrust case production per budget dollar to fall by half. Finally, regression estimates showed a *ceteris paribus* increase in the sum of FTC and Justice Department budgetary appropriations as a result of the transition from independent to collusive dual enforcement, with most of the collusive gains accruing to the FTC.

CONCLUDING REMARKS

We have modeled the competition between government agencies having identical responsibilities and analyzed the special case of dual antitrust law enforcement by the Justice Department and the FTC. We find that, as in the private sector, competition limits output restrictions and disciplines cost decisions. Our theory predicts that output, however measured, will be larger and produced at a lower unit cost under independent dual enforcement than under single-agency or collusive dual enforcement. Empirical tests using

Table 7.4
Regression Results
(Logged Annual Data, 1932–1981)

Dependent Variable	C	Aggregate Cases	FTC Cases	Antitrust Division Cases	Real GNP	Liaison Dummy	ρ̂	R²
Aggregate Budget:	3.6358	0.0418 (0.80)			0.8970 (6.59)***	0.2407 (1.86)*	0.7618	0.659
	9.2083	0.0727 (1.34)				0.4390 (3.20)**	0.9091	0.203
FTC Budget:	4.9415		0.0133 (0.33)		0.6620 (3.89)***	0.2222 (1.72)*	0.8703	0.363
	9.1898		0.0223 (0.55)			0.2900 (2.26)**	0.9306	0.104
Antitrust Division Budget:	−0.5572			0.1892 (3.07)***	1.3221 (8.93)***	0.0177 (0.12)	0.3548	0.892
	6.7987			0.3552 (4.23)***		1.0178 (5.45)***	0.5115	0.619

Notes: t-values in parentheses; ρ is the estimated autocorrelation coefficient. Asterisks denote significance at the 1 percent (***), 5 percent (**), and 10 percent (*) levels.

historical antitrust agency budgets and case-production figures do not refute the model's main predictions. The implications of our analysis are quite straightforward and have general applicability. With respect to the antitrust agencies, more enforcement activity could be obtained at a lower unit cost if the 1948 FTC–Justice Department liaison agreement were abandoned. Far from resulting in wasteful duplication, bureaucratic competition leads to more efficient resource use. Empirically, we found that aggregate case production was roughly the same under independent and collusive dual enforcement, but that cases per budget dollar were more than twice as high prior to the 1948 liaison arrangement. Put another way, collusive dual enforcement resulted in the same amount of antitrust activity as competitive enforcement, but at twice the cost in real budget dollars.

We recognize that some would view the increased case output predicted by our model under independent dual enforcement as "bad" rather than as "good." For example, William Baxter has expressed the opinion that the preference of economists for competition is misplaced when applied to law-enforcement activities: "It is not at all clear to me that we ought to have more antitrust intervention by the government than we have had in the last twenty years."[34] His concern was that more cases would not necessarily mean better cases. Although we abstracted from this normative issue in the theoretical work, our empirical results indicate that the efficiency effect from antitrust-enforcement competition far outweighs the output effect. Our findings are therefore not particularly sensitive to case quality considerations.

Our results do provide support for Niskanen's contention that "the passion of reformers to consolidate bureaus with similar output . . . seems diabolically designed to . . . increase the inefficiency (and, not incidentally, the budget) of the bureaucracy."[35] The "fat" in agency budgets associated with collusive dual enforcement appears as rents in payments to the inputs used in antitrust case production. That is, following implementation of the 1948 liaison agreement, the two agencies employed relatively more attorneys, economists, and other inputs per case than would have been used in the absence of collusion.

Our findings can be extended to other bureaucratic situations. More efficient output will be obtained if government goods and services are produced competitively. Examples include allowing the various armed services to bid for the right to supply national defense, establishing an alternative postal service, and providing for a dual Coast Guard. In government, as in most other markets, monopoly will not be preferable on efficiency grounds to competition. The public interest is better served through competition than by well-meaning efforts to hire more better-qualified, good-intentioned bureaucrats.

Finally, the importance of our analysis for the dual enforcement debate is transparent. Dual enforcement has not existed since 1948. For the last three and a half decades, interagency collusion has effectively given us a single antitrust-law-enforcement institution.

NOTES

1. See, for example, Ernest Gellhorn, "Two's a Crowd: The FTC's Redundant Antitrust Powers," *Regulation* 5 (November–December 1981): 32–42; "Debate: The Federal Trade Commission Under Attack: Should the Commission's Role Be Changed?" *Antitrust Law Journal* 49 (1982): 1481; Murray Weidenbaum et al., "On Saving the Kingdom—Advice for the President-Elect from Eight Regulatory Experts," *Regulation* 4 (November–December 1980): 14; "Proposed Budget Cuts Fuel Debate Over FTC's Role, *Legal Times of Washington* 3 (February 23, 1981): 1; and Milton Handler, "Reforming the Antitrust Laws—Dual Enforcement, FTC's Mission," *New York Law Journal* 188 (April 18, 1982): 4.

2. American Bar Association, *Report of the American Bar Association Commission to Study the Federal Trade Commission* (Chicago, 1969), pp. 406–7 (hereafter cited as *ABA Report*). Other advantages cited by the ABA are the FTC's wide powers to investigate and require submission of reports, its opportunity to decide antitrust questions through industry-wide rulemaking activities rather than through a case-by-case approach, and "the power to issue studies and reports to the President, Congress, and the public can illuminate antitrust issues and evaluate the need for additional legislation."

3. E. E. Vaill, "The Federal Trade Commission: Should It Continue as Both Prosecutor and Judge in Antitrust Proceedings?" *Southwestern University Law Review* 10 (1978): 764.

4. Ibid., p. 770.

5. Ibid., pp. 765–66. The 1979 conflict arose over the fact that Collier had served as FTC counsel in American General Ins. Co. v. FTC, 496 F.2d 197 (5th Cir. 1974) and as commissioner in American General Ins. Co. v. FTC, 589 F.2d 462 (9th Cir. 1979).

6. Thomas E. Kauper, "Competition Policy and the Institutions of Antitrust," *South Dakota Law Review* 23 (Winter 1978): 17–18.

7. *ABA Report*, p. 440.

8. Richard A. Posner, "A Statistical Study of Antitrust Enforcement, *Journal of Law and Economics* 13 (October 1970): 377–81.

9. Wesley J. Liebeler, "The Role of the Federal Trade Commission, Proceedings of the Symposium: Changing Perspectives in Antitrust Litigation," *Southwestern University Law Review* 12 (1980–1981): 229.

10. Barry R. Weingast and Mark J. Moran, "The Myth of the Runaway Bureaucracy—The Case of the FTC," *Regulation* 6 (May–June 1982): 33.

11. "Debate: The FTC Under Attack," p. 1497.

12. Handler, "Reforming the Antitrust Laws."

13. U.S. Congress, Senate, Committee on the Judiciary, *Report on Regulatory Agencies to the President-Elect*, Report prepared by James M. Landis, 86th Cong., 2d sess., 1960, p. 50. See also Gellhorn, "Two's a Crowd," p. 32.

14. *ABA Report*, p. 436.

15. "President's Task Force Report on Productivity and Competition" (hereafter cited as "Stigler Report"), Appendix to U.S. Congress, House Committee on Interstate and Foreign Commerce, *Hearings Before the Special Subcommittee on Small Business and the Robinson-Patman Act*, 91st Cong., 1st sess., October 7–9, 1969.

16. *ABA Report*, p. 407.

17. "Stigler Report," p. 275.

18. See Gilbert H. Montague, "The Commission's Jurisdiction over Practices in Restraint of Trade: A Large-scale Method of Mass Enforcement of the Antitrust Laws," *George Washington Law Review* 8 (January–February 1940): 385–86.

19. Federal Trade Commission v. Cement Institute, 333 U.S. 683 (1948).

20. D. L. Roll, "Dual Enforcement of the Antitrust Laws by the Department of Justice and the FTC: The Liaison Procedure," *The Business Lawyer* 31 (July 1975): 2075.

21. See J. B. Sloan, "Antitrust: Shared Information Between the FTC and the Department of Justice," *Brigham Young University Law Review* 4 (1979): 883; Roll, "Dual Enforcement of Antitrust Laws"; A. D. Neale and D. G. Goyder, *The Antitrust Laws of the U.S.A.*, 3d ed. (London: Cambridge University Press, 1980), p. 373; and Robert A. Katzmann, *Regulatory Bureaucracy: The Federal Trade Commission and Antitrust Policy* (Cambridge, Mass.: MIT Press, 1980), p. 293.

22. T. J. McGrew, "Antitrust Enforcement Has More Staff Than Policy," *Legal Times of Washington* 4 (October 12, 1981): 11.

23. Vaill, "FTC: Both Prosecutor and Judge?" pp. 793–94.

24. William A. Niskanen, "Nonmarket Decision Making: The Peculiar Economics of Bureaucracy," *American Economic Review* 58 (May 1968): 293. See also Niskanen's *Bureaucracy and Representative Government* (Chicago: Aldine-Atherton, 1971), and his "Bureaucrats and Politicians," *Journal of Law and Economics* 18 (December 1975): 617.

25. See Robert J. Mackay and Carylyn L. Weaver, "Agenda Control by Budget Maximizers in a Multi-Bureau Setting," *Public Choice* 37 (1981): 447. They describe an equilibrium with all-or-none offers. In such models, budget "fat" (rents) accrues to the bureau's sponsor, usually the congressional oversight committee, while in our framework rents are imputed in the payments to bureaucratic inputs.

26. Such differences imply that the private rewards from additional regulation "cannot be captured in increased salary by commissioners *as much as* they can by bureaucratic officials" (emphasis in the original). R. D. Eckert, "On the Incentives of Regulators: The Case of Taxicabs," *Public Choice* 14 (1973): 86.

27. That $dX'_2/dc < 0$ can be shown by solving $a - 2bX_1 - bX_2 = 0$ and $a - bX_1 - bX_2 = c$ simultaneously for X'_2 and differentiating with respect to c. There is also a symmetric solution for X'_1.

28. This discussion draws heavily on the material in Thomas C. Blaisdell, *The Federal Trade Commission: An Experiment in the Control of Business* (New York: Columbia University Press, 1932).

29. Ibid., p. 90; emphasis in the original.

30. Ibid., p. 241.

31. Ibid., p. 243.

32. Posner, "Statistical Study of Antitrust Enforcement," p. 366. Posner's evidence (see p. 372) also reveals that it would be inappropriate to include private antitrust suits in our measure of aggregate antitrust activity. He reports, for example, that two-thirds (986 out of 1,456) of the private suits brought between 1946 and 1963 followed an Antitrust Division judgment. That is, civil plaintiffs often free ride on Justice Department complaints by suing for treble damages under the Sherman Act after respondents have been found guilty in a government case. Moreover, a lot of double-counting appears in the available data because a single Justice Department suit may give rise to more than one private action. Therefore, "one does not know how many separate violations have been attacked by private suits."

33. See George J. Stigler, "The Process of Economic Regulation," *Antitrust Bulletin* 17 (1972): 207.

34. "Debate: The FTC Under Attack," pp. 1495–96.

35. Niskanen, "Nonmarket Decision Making," pp. 300–301.

Chapter 8

Truth and Consequences: The Federal Trade Commission's Ad Substantiation Program

RICHARD S. HIGGINS & FRED S. McCHESNEY

As THE economic theory of regulation has developed, a better understanding of the distribution of gains and losses from government intervention in the marketplace has emerged. George Stigler's original contribution reversed the hypothesis that regulation remedies externalities or other supposed market failures and suggested, instead, that the "victims" of regulation are more frequently its beneficiaries.[1] Sam Peltzman demonstrated more precisely regulators' utility trade-offs in allocating favorable treatment between regulated firms and consumers.[2] Other recent contributions have stressed the diversity of interests among producers.[3] Thus, regulation may benefit some producers, not just at consumers' expense, but to the detriment of their industry rivals as well.

This paper uses an economic model of regulation to examine some of the allocative and distributive consequences of the Federal Trade Commission's (FTC) "advertising substantiation" doctrine. The ad substantiation doctrine grew out of a series of commission actions in the early 1970s that sharply altered the focus of advertising regulation at the FTC. Rather than prove after

We received helpful comments on earlier drafts from Ronald Bond, Gerard Butters, David Haddock, Cotton Lindsay, Robert Mackay, Michael Maloney, Steven Marston, Robert McCormick, John Peterman, William Shughart, Robert Tollison, and Bruce Yandle. Research and computational assistance from Susan Campbell, Kim Garman, and Kathleen McChesney is also gratefully acknowledged. The views expressed in this paper are those of the authors and do not necessarily represent those of the Federal Trade Commission, individual commissioners, or other staff.

the fact that their advertising claims were true, as the FTC had traditionally required, advertisers thenceforth were required to possess a "reasonable basis" for advertising claims *prior* to making them. The FTC now enjoins advertising claims it finds unsubstantiated in the light of the evidence available at the time the claims were made.

The first section of this paper explains the origins and workings of the substantiation doctrine in greater detail, noting also the FTC's unusual role in enforcing private, self-regulatory substantiation requirements in the advertising industry. The second section contrasts two hypotheses of advertising regulation: the public-interest explanation of regulation to correct market failure, and the economic explanation of regulation as a rent-creating device to benefit some producers at others' expense. It is hypothesized that increasing advertisers' fixed costs by requiring substantiation *ex ante* enables the FTC and private regulators to create rents, but only for some producers. The third section introduces empirical evidence based on stock price data that the ad substantiation program has significantly increased the values of large advertisers and advertising agencies. The fourth section tests the contrasting implications of the economic and the public-interest models. This is followed by a summary and conclusion.

Advertising Substantiation Doctrine

Origins of Ad Substantiation

To analyze the impact of the FTC's ad substantiation doctrine, one must first be aware of substantiation's origins, its institutional counterparts in the private sector, and of the FTC's regulatory program to ensure compliance with its substantiation requirement.[4] Before substantiation, the FTC had long brought cases against allegedly deceptive advertising. The commission's authority to challenge alleged deception derives from the 1938 amendment to Section 5 of the FTC Act that outlaws "unfair and deceptive acts and practices." Deceptive advertising cases essentially entail two elements: commission interpretation of the claims made in the advertisements, and determination of the claims' "capacity to deceive."[5] The federal courts, which hear appeals from FTC rulings, traditionally defer to the commission's interpretation of advertising claims and its determination of their truthfulness.[6]

After decades of challenging advertisements as deceptive, the commission announced in April 1970 that it would sue Pfizer, Inc. for advertising claims about its "Unburn" sunburn lotion, charging that they were unsubstantiated. For the first time, the issue was not an ad's truth or falsity *ex post*, which had been the test in traditional deception cases. Rather, the commission was challenging whether Pfizer had and relied on adequate evidence *ex ante* in making the claims. In our theory section below we show how this new approach to advertising regulation increases the cost of advertising, *ceteris paribus*, which allows us to distinguish empirically the public-interest and economic models of FTC advertising regulation.

The commission's break with its more traditional method of regulating advertising proceeded in several stages. In December 1970, Ralph Nader's Center for the Study of Responsive Law petitioned the commission for a trade regulation rule requiring national advertisers routinely to submit to the commission the documents substantiating advertising claims. Commission staff proposed such a rule some months later but, in June 1971, the FTC announced its refusal to initiate a rulemaking. Instead, it adopted a resolution requiring advertisers to submit relevant substantiation materials to the commission only on demand. The submission program distinguished factual (objective and empirically verifiable) from nonfactual ("puffing") claims, and it required substantiation only for the former. The submissions were not to be used to generate cases, but would be made public to inform consumers of unsubstantiated claims and to encourage competitors to challenge them.[7]

Several industries were selected and required to submit substantiation for all factual claims. The results of these "industry rounds" were disappointing. The expected consumer interest and competitor challenges never materialized, while an avalanche of paper descended on the commission. The FTC was unable to evaluate much of the substantiation because it was too technical or complex (which doubtless dampened any consumer interest as well).[8] In the meantime, the FTC administrative law judge presiding in the Pfizer case ruled that Pfizer's advertising did not violate Section 5.

While its staff was unsuccessfully arguing the Pfizer suit in the administrative proceeding and conducting rounds of various industries, the commission itself had never ruled judicially whether failure to possess and rely on prior substantiation violated Section 5, even if the ad claims were true. Full commission endorsement of ad substantiation did not come until July 1972, in the commission's opinion regarding Pfizer, which reversed the holding of the administrative law judge on this point.[9]

Subsequently, the elements of the substantiation doctrine have remained as they were established by the commission in the Pfizer case. Under Section 5, it is unfair and deceptive to make an advertising claim for a product without possessing a "reasonable basis" for the claim.[10] The commission explicitly held that substantiation must exist prior to dissemination of the claim: "the fact that [a] test was not conducted *prior* to making the affirmative product claims . . . precludes it from being considered as a defense."[11] In other words, a claim might be true, but that would not defeat liability.[12]

Enforcing Substantiation

Following its determination in the Pfizer case, the FTC began to issue more complaints under Section 5 for alleged lack of substantiation. The commission modified the program in late 1973, formally abandoning the consumer-information goal of substantiation and, instead, making substantiation part of its law-enforcement program. From 1973 through 1983, the substantiation program resulted in over a dozen litigated matters and over 100 consents. Indeed, substantiation, not falsity, has been the principal focus of FTC advertising regulation.

The penalty for deceptive advertising is the same today as it was before the Pfizer decision. Violation of Section 5 through inadequate substantiation subjects the advertiser to a cease-and-desist order. The order carries no monetary penalty, but advertisers incur the costs of litigation and adverse publicity, and sometimes the cost of interrupting a productive advertising campaign. Violation of an outstanding order, however, is punished by civil penalties.[13] Further, the advertising agency hired by an advertiser has almost always been held liable once the client-advertiser's liability has been established, on the theory that the agency is a partner in designing, preparing, and running the typical advertising campaign and so shares responsibility for required substantiation. The commission does not sue the media that broadcast or print the offending ads, however.

The FTC is not alone in regulating advertising via substantiation. In July 1971 the advertising industry established its own self-regulatory system. It consists of two parts: the National Advertising Division (NAD), established as part of the Council of Better Business Bureaus, and the National Advertising Review Board (NARB). The NAD investigates ads either on its own initiative or on complaints from competitors or consumers. From its inception until 1983 the NAD investigated almost 2,000 ads.[14] Most of its investigations involve allegedly inadequate substantiation. An adverse determination by the NAD requires modification or removal of the offending ad; between 1971 and 1983, 52 percent of the ads investigated had to be modified or discontinued. Adverse NAD determinations can be appealed to the NARB.

The NAD/NARB was founded by three advertising trade associations: the Association of National Advertisers, the American Association of Advertising Agencies (4A's), and the American Advertising Federation. These associations represent large advertisers and ad agencies. (Membership in the 4A's, for example, is explicitly restricted to firms with demonstrable experience and a record of past business; newer, smaller firms are therefore ineligible.)[15] These founding industry groups also dominate the self-regulatory process. For example, NARB membership is established to include 60 percent advertisers, 20 percent representatives of advertising agencies, and 20 percent nonindustry members. It hears appeals in panels of five, with the same ratios of representation on each panel—that is, four from the industry and one outsider. Advertisers and agencies also provide all of the funding for the NAD/NARB.[16]

It is noteworthy that the television networks and broadcasters and other media are not involved in the NAD/NARB system. Indeed, the industry complains about the media's failure to join it in regulating advertising. Television networks' "continuity departments" conduct their own review of ads, but are more concerned with matters of taste and morals than about substantiation.[17] Other media (such as radio, newspapers, and magazines) apparently ignore substantiation altogether.[18]

Also noteworthy is the complementary relationship between the FTC and the NAD/NARB. Private self-regulation of substantiation reduces the commission's caseload and so leads to speedier resolution of substantiation contests. One director of the commission's Bureau of Consumer Protection (which enforces the ad substantiation doctrine) has publicly praised the NAD/NARB as having helped to "relieve us of much of the burden in the regulatory area."[19] At the same time, the FTC provides services of importance to the self-regulatory scheme. Its presence reduces any private worries about antitrust violations in collectively enforcing industry sanctions. This is useful, as it is recognized that the industry domination of self-regulation may be viewed as anticompetitive. More important, the FTC is the ultimate enforcer for the private self-regulators: it "provides the teeth for industry's own self-regulatory procedures."[20] In the event that an advertiser refuses to modify or withdraw an ad following an adverse determination, NAD/NARB procedures require that the matter be referred to the government, with a request for corrective action.[21]

Thus, not only has the commission devised and enforced its own substantiation requirement, but it has also allowed private advertisers collectively to establish their own program, for which the commission is the enforcer of last resort. Disentangling the separate effects of government and private regulation is impossible, since the two systems make similar substantiation demands of sellers and arose at the same time. The discussion of the economic effects of the FTC's substantiation doctrine that follows refers not only to the commission's own program but also to the private self-regulatory system with which it cooperates.

An Economic Analysis of FTC Advertising Regulation

This section sets out two different hypotheses about the design and effects of FTC advertising regulation. The implications of the public-interest hypothesis, which is premised on cost-effective repair of market failure, are contrasted with those of the wealth-redistribution hypothesis. The section also explains how the FTC's adoption in 1972 of the ad substantiation doctrine provides the basis for empirical tests of the competing hypotheses about FTC advertising regulation.

Advertising Regulation: Two Hypotheses

Advertising conveys information directly and indirectly to consumers about the utility per dollar they can expect from use of the advertised product. Indirectly, the mere volume of advertising can convey valuable information to consumers and, directly, the specific factual content of advertising can provide consumers valuable information about products and sellers.[22]

The ostensible purpose of FTC advertising regulation is to raise the information content of factual advertising by penalizing firms engaged in false or deceptive advertising. A policy of penalizing false or deceptive advertising on a case-by-case basis raises the cost to firms from misleading consumers. The result is that while there may be less advertising overall, the value of the advertising that remains is greater than the value of the advertising supplied in the absence of regulation. Under this view, an information-market failure is remedied by the public enforcement of promises made through advertising, and product demand is increased.

The major oversight in this version of FTC advertising regulation is that more truthful advertising has costs as well as benefits. Neglect of the cost of advertising regulation stems from the naive premise that advertising is, with certainty, either true or false (or deceptive or nondeceptive). When factual advertising claims are either true or false there is no cost to consumers, other than the direct cost of public enforcement, of deterring false claims. However, when truth and falsity are seen as an economic problem concerning the efficient level of accuracy, the situation is much changed. In general, advertising claims are more or less true. Greater accuracy about product and seller performance benefits consumers, but greater accuracy entails additional cost.

When we scrutinize advertising regulation in the context of "more or less," instead of "all or none," the effect of advertising regulation on consumer welfare is more ambiguous. Were we to imagine the FTC raising the level of accuracy in particular types of ads, there would be two opposing effects. Demand price would rise as the accuracy of advertising was increased from regulation and perhaps from the fact that advertising would no longer be subject to adverse selection. Simultaneously, the supply price of advertising would increase on account of the higher cost of achieving the level of accuracy required by the FTC. Efficient enforcement of truth in advertising would require increased accuracy up to the point where the marginal increase in demand price was just matched by the marginal increase in supply price.

The ability of the regulator to influence the output margin through its choice of the required level of accuracy implies that advertising regulation could be used to restrict output of advertised products. Moreover, if the cost of achieving the required levels of accuracy is largely a fixed cost independent of a firm's output rate, unit cost will rise more for firms with relatively small market share. As a consequence, inframarginal firms will gain from a restriction of market output.

In practice, the cost of greater accuracy is largely independent of output. The FTC's determination that advertising claims are deceptive is a rough-and-ready solution to a complex statistical decision problem. If the FTC were to correctly weigh the marginal benefits of accuracy against the marginal cost of producing accuracy, the appropriate level of accuracy would be positively related to unit sales, *ceteris paribus*. However, what the FTC typically does is to contrast the expected cost of chilling truthful claims and the expected cost of permitting false ones. In this calculus, the decision depends critically on two costs: the costs to a typical consumer of a foregone benefit, and the costs of an erroneous purchase. Thus, the appropriate advertising claim, according to the FTC, is largely independent of output.

If, as we assume, the cost of accuracy required by the FTC is independent of output, the FTC can raise the value of inframarginal firms to the detriment of consumers by requiring inefficiently high levels of accuracy in advertising. As the required level of accuracy is raised beyond the efficient level, the supply price at the output margin rises more than demand price and more than inframarginal supply price. Thus, FTC advertising regulation can be used to create rents for inframarginal firms. The welfare loss stems from a restriction in output due to the exit of firms whose additional receipts at the higher price are insufficient to cover the added cost of greater accuracy. There would be no incentive to offset this by entry.

The firms that gain from FTC advertising regulation are those best situated to cover the additional cost of greater accuracy, or which are better able to avoid this cost through the use of substitute inputs. On two counts we hypothesize that the beneficiaries are firms with relatively large market shares. First, they are more likely, all else being equal, to collect through the higher price an amount sufficient to cover the lump sum cost of substantiation. Second, firms with relatively large market shares are the successful firms. These are the firms with established reputations for providing top utility per dollar to consumers and are presumably better able to advertise effectively without factual advertising than are their low-reputation competitors.[23] By merely reminding consumers of their names and demonstrating their credibility with advertising "levels," these firms can more easily than their smaller competitors avoid the FTC's accuracy requirements by resorting to "nonfactual" advertising.[24]

Our hypothesis about advertising regulation is an example of "raising rivals' costs."[25] Achieving the goal of output restriction by raising rivals' costs typically requires government intervention or protection. For example, Oliver Williamson cites the case of capital-intensive firms conspiring with a government-protected monopoly supplier of labor services to raise the wage rate.[26] Similarly, we hypothesize that the FTC's sanction and enforcement of the apparently beneficent goal of greater truth in advertising raises the cost of advertising for firms with small market shares and little reputation capital relative to these firms' more established rivals.

In the case of advertising, as in Williamson's case study, the cooperation of upstream suppliers is entailed. The large advertisers and the established ad agencies jointly enforce substantiation standards through a government sanctioned self-regulatory scheme in which the FTC is the enforcer of last resort against recalcitrant member and nonmember competitors.[27] The member ad agencies stand to gain in several possible ways. First, the demand for ad agency services—and for the advice of marketing experts and lawyers familiar with FTC requirements—may rise as greater accuracy in factual advertising is required.[28] Second, as in the case of advertisers as a group, the larger ad agencies may have a comparative advantage over their country cousins in providing advertising that will pass FTC scrutiny—especially since the advent of the Pfizer doctrine, which has emphasized the need for scientific survey research and clinical tests. Third, the private regulatory mechanism enforced by the advertiser and ad agency associations may raise the cost to advertisers of using nonmember ad agency service by pressing for FTC investigations of fringe firm advertising.

Our hypothesis of the design and effect of FTC advertising regulation contrasts sharply with the public-interest version. In the latter, small and large firms alike benefit from advertising regulation. If there is any relative effect at all predicted by the public-interest hypothesis, it is that small firms and new entrants gain, since FTC regulation reduces the value of firms' reputations as a mechanism for assuring accuracy.[29] Moreover, according to the public-interest story, the demand for advertising rises and the market output margin is extended, as public enforcement of advertising promises cost-effectively corrects market failure. Finally, the overall level of truth in advertising rises, as both the amount of factual advertising and the level of accuracy in factual advertising rises.

According to our hypothesis, advertising regulation reduces output and raises price, redistributing wealth from consumers to firms with large market share. The firms with large market shares and substantial reputations gain relative to the firms with small market shares and little or no reputations.[30] Also, the large ad agencies, which were the founders of advertising self-regulation, are predicted to gain from FTC regulation. The demand for advertising overall may rise or fall, and though the level of truth in factual advertising that remains in the face of FTC regulation will be greater, the amount of factual advertising may be smaller. Thus, the overall level of accuracy in factual advertising is ambiguous.

Finally, the two hypotheses about FTC advertising regulation have different implications for FTC case-by-case enforcement. According to our hypothesis, the FTC's ability to redistribute wealth in a market depends on dispersion in firms' market shares. Conversely, if firms had equal market shares the cost of greater levels of required accuracy would not fall differentially on firms and wealth could not be redistributed by raising accuracy. A finding that case incidence is positively related to dispersion in firm shares, *ceteris paribus*, is inconsistent with the public-interest hypothesis. The latter predicts that the number of small unestablished firms governs case incidence, if it predicts anything at all.

AD SUBSTANTIATION: THE BASIS FOR EMPIRICAL TEST

It is agreed between proponents and opponents of FTC advertising regulation that the prior substantiation doctrine, established by the Pfizer decision in 1972, has enhanced the FTC's control over truthfulness in factual advertising.[31] Thus, the commission's adoption of prior substantiation provides a natural experiment that enables us to test our hypothesis about the effects of FTC advertising regulation. In short, if ad substantiation enhanced the FTC's ability to regulate truth in advertising, it also enhanced the FTC's ability to redistribute wealth from consumers to inframarginal firms.

Ad substantiation necessarily raises the cost to firms of deceptive advertising, as defined by the FTC, *ceteris paribus*. It accomplishes this additional deterrence—that is, in addition to the deterrence achieved through traditional FTC advertising regulation—by substituting an *ex ante* standard of deception for an *ex post* standard. Before the Pfizer decision, firms were allowed to present evidence gathered after the FTC initiated an investigation that their claims were not false or deceptive. After Pfizer, post-claim evidence about the accuracy of the firm's claims became irrelevant. Since Pfizer, advertisers are liable for lacking a "reasonable basis" for its claims prior to making them.

Since the probability that a firm's advertising is investigated by the FTC is less than one, firms were more free before than after the Pfizer decision to allocate information-gathering inputs after a claim was made. That is, for the same level of accuracy required by the commission and all other things being equal, the prior substantiation doctrine is more onerous than the traditional deception doctrine. Alternatively, for the same enforcement effort the FTC is better able to impose standards of accuracy in advertising and, hence, better able to control the distribution of wealth in product markets. Thus, the advent of ad substantiation causes the regulatory equilibrium to shift toward greater accuracy requirements.[32] In both the timing and choice of evidentiary inputs, ad substantiation forces advertisers off their expansion path of least-cost input combinations and forces them to produce truth in ways dictated by the FTC. Accordingly, our hypothesis about advertising regulation predicts that ad substantiation increases wealth for inframarginal firms and reduces consumer welfare.

EMPIRICAL EVIDENCE

Effects on Firms' Stock Prices

The hypotheses of advertising regulation, and ad substantiation in particular, that we have articulated suggest straightforward tests based on stock market data. Our hypothesis predicts that firm wealth will change with the advent of ad substantiation. Specifically, wealth changes will be positively related to the firm's market share, with a positive wealth change for the biggest firm and a negative wealth change for the smallest. Our hypothesis makes a similar prediction for ad agency wealth. In contrast, the public-interest hypothesis predicts that the relationship between wealth change and market share is negative. On the issue of ad agency wealth, the public-interest hypothesis is silent about relative effects, but predicts ad agency wealth will rise in general.

Lacking small-firm data, our stock market tests of the effect of ad substantiation on large firm wealth and large ad agency wealth are not dispositive. In short, a wealth increase for the largest firms is consistent with both hypotheses. Thus, in addition to the estimation of the wealth effects of ad substantiation on the firms with the largest market share and on the largest ad agencies, we tested a strong prediction of the public-interest hypothesis. Specifically, the public-interest hypothesis predicts that the demand for advertising will rise overall with the inception of the ad substantiation doctrine. Hence, the value of media firms should increase with the advent of ad substantiation. In contrast, our hypothesis is silent about ad substantiation's effects on media firm wealth.

In summary, our stock-market tests assess the wealth effects of ad substantiation on the firms with largest market share across a number of consumer goods markets, on the largest ad agencies, and on a portfolio of publicly traded media firms.

Financial market analysis is used here to measure the effects on advertisers, ad agencies, and media firms of the FTC's shift in advertising regulation from falsity *ex post* to substantiation *ex ante*. Financial market analysis is based on the efficient market theory of finance.[33] Security prices at a given moment in time reflect all available information and discounted expected future returns, including risk adjustments. As new information affecting a security is received, the resulting wealth effect is reflected in the security's price. The wealth effect of a regulatory change expected to affect a firm's revenues and costs into the future is captured in the present price of the firm's securities as information of the regulatory change develops.

In financial market analysis, then, a principal concern is the timing of events that alter present values. A time "window" is investigated if a series of events contributed to changing expectations. In the case of ad substantiation, the FTC first signaled the policy change away from deception when it announced in April 1970 its intention to file a complaint against Pfizer (which it in fact did three months later). At that time, a Pfizer spokesman was quoted in the *Wall Street Journal* as saying that the FTC was "seeking to establish new legal theories that have no precedent in cases that have been decided by the courts or by the FTC."[34] This was apparently the first public mention of substantiation; a review of the financial and advertising press in 1969 and 1970 discloses no earlier reference to it.

Thus, any adjustment in firms' values would date from April 1970.[35] The appropriate end of the time window is harder to select. Market adjustment to substantiation must have been affected by establishment of the NAD/NARB system of self-regulation in 1971. However, at almost the same time the FTC seemed to back away from required substantiation when it denied the Nader rulemaking petition and when its administrative law judge dismissed the commission's Pfizer complaint. Only with the commission's own Pfizer opinion in July 1972 was it clear that the commission itself would legally require substantiation, and also that the NAD/NARB could look to the FTC for enforcement. The relevant time window for measuring the value changes of firms affected by substantiation is therefore from April 1970 to July 1972. Although this provides a relatively lengthy adjustment period, the possibility of confounding the effects of substantiation with those of other events during the period was controlled, as explained below.

Advertisers' Returns

We began our investigation of wealth changes due to the new substantiation requirement with an examination of monthly rates of return for large advertisers in two categories: drugs and toiletries, and home products (for example, televisions and furniture) and building products. Within these product categories, for each of 79 subclasses (markets) defined by Leading National Advertisers, the largest firm in total 1970 advertising expenditures was selected.[36] This produced a portfolio of 54 firms (some firms were leaders in more than one market). The equally weighted portfolio's monthly rate of return was regressed on the monthly returns for an equally weighted market portfolio of stocks traded on the New York Stock Exchange (NYSE), as reported by the Center for Research in Securities Prices, and on a dummy variable for the time of adjustment to the new substantiation requirement.[37] The dummy was coded 1 for the period April 1970 to July 1972, zero otherwise.

The results are shown in Table 8.1. The coefficient for the market portfolio return is significant and positive, as one would predict.[38] The equation explains most of the variation in the dependent variable. Notably, the coefficient for the time of adjustment to the ad substantiation program shows that substantiation had a positive effect on the value of the market leaders, significant at the 5 percent level. These firms experienced an estimated abnormal monthly increase in their rates of return of almost 1 percent for over 28 months.

Clearly the evidence supports the hypothesis that substantiation increased the wealth of larger advertisers. This is the result unequivocally predicted by the redistribution model.

TABLE 8.1

REGRESSION COEFFICIENTS FOR THE
EFFECTS OF ADVERTISING SUBSTANTIATION ON
RETURNS TO PORTFOLIO OF LEADING ADVERTISERS

	Coefficient (t-statistic)
Intercept	−.002 (−1.10)
Market Return	.691[a] (12.78)
Event Dummy	.009[b] (1.71)
F = 182.58[a]	
R^2 = .78	
Durbin-Watson = 2.26	

NOTES: a. Significant at .01 in one-tailed test.

b. Significant at .05 in one-tailed test.

SOURCE: Estimates from monthly returns tape (1964–1978), Center for Research in Securities Prices.

TABLE 8.2

REGRESSION COEFFICIENTS FOR THE
EFFECTS OF ADVERTISING SUBSTANTIATION ON RETURNS TO
PORTFOLIO OF NYSE-TRADED ADVERTISING AGENCIES

	Coefficient (t-statistic)
Intercept	−.0057 (−1.01)
Market Return	.954a (12.67)
Event Dummy	.0287b (2.15)
F=82.06a R²=.51 Durbin-Watson=2.30	

NOTES: a. Significant at .01 in one-tailed test.

   b. Significant at .025 in one-tailed test.

SOURCE: Estimates from monthly returns tape (1965–1978), Center for Research in Securities Prices.

Advertising Agencies' Returns

We next tested the effects of the FTC ad substantiation policy on a four-firm portfolio of large advertising agencies, the only agencies traded on the NYSE and for which data are readily available.[39] The portfolio's equally weighted monthly rate of return was regressed on an equally weighted market portfolio of all NYSE firms and a dummy variable for the substantiation adjustment period, with the results shown in Table 8.2. Again, the coefficient for the event dummy is positive and significant at .05, strongly supporting the hypothesis that the introduction of substantiation increased the wealth of the large agencies, the result predicted by the economic model of regulatory redistribution, but ambiguous under the market-failure model.

The size of the event coefficient is somewhat startling. It shows a *monthly* increase in the large advertising agencies' common stock prices over the 28-month adjustment period of almost 3 percent. Though similarly large wealth effects from advertising regulation have been found before,[40] the large effect here raises a question whether relevant explanatory variables have been overlooked, a possibility increased by the relatively lengthy time window. We controlled for this possibility in several ways.[41] In particular, we obtained data on prices for all national media.[42] The price data should reflect the effect of any exogenous changes in the advertising industry, whatever the source or the medium affected. Table 8.3 shows the results of including media price data in the model. The media variable itself is positive and significant. More important, by controlling for media prices the estimated effect and significance of ad substantiation on the performance of the ad agency portfolio increases considerably. For the period April 1970 to July 1972, the estimated monthly increase in portfolio returns due to substantiation rises by almost one percentage point when media price data are included.

Controlling for media prices only reinforces our confidence that substantiation has significantly increased the wealth of large agencies, as the economic model predicts. We caution, however, that the magnitude of substantiation's estimated wealth effect is high. Refinement of the model may reduce the size of the wealth effect but not, we believe, its sign or significance. Also, as we have noted, the ad agency results are consistent with both hypotheses.

Media Firms' Returns

The market-failure and economic hypotheses of ad substantiation have competing implications for the effects of substantiation on the value of the advertising media. The former predicts that substantiation, by efficiently repairing market failure, would raise the value of advertising and so would increase the value of advertising media. Under the economic hypothesis, the

TABLE 8.3

REGRESSION COEFFICIENTS FOR THE EFFECTS OF
ADVERTISING SUBSTANTIATION AND MEDIA PRICES ON
RETURNS TO PORTFOLIO OF NYSE-TRADED ADVERTISING AGENCIES

	Coefficient (t-statistic)
Intercept	$-.0712$[a]
	(-2.54)
Market Return	$.947$[a]
	(12.69)
Event Dummy	$.0382$[a]
	(2.79)
Media Price	$5.32 \times 10-4$[a]
	(2.38)
$F=58.24$[a]	
$R^2=.53$	
Durbin-Watson$=2.38$	

NOTE: a. Significant at .01 in one-tailed test.

SOURCE: Estimates from monthly returns tape (1965–1978), Center for Research in Securities Prices.

TABLE 8.4
REGRESSION COEFFICIENTS FOR THE
EFFECTS OF ADVERTISING SUBSTANTIATION ON RETURNS TO
PORTFOLIO OF NYSE-TRADED MEDIA FIRMS

	Coefficient *(t-statistic)*
Intercept	−.0019
	(−.144)
Market Return	1.12[a]
	(31.28)
Media Prices	.00003
	(.295)
Event Dummy	.0077
	(1.18)
F=327.35[a]	
R²=.86	
Durbin-Watson=1.80	

NOTE: a. Significant at .01.

SOURCE: Estimates from monthly returns tape (1964–1978), Center for Research in Securities Prices.

wealth of media firms is unpredictable, a function of unknown elasticities and demand shifts.

To test advertising's effect on the media, we constructed an equally weighted portfolio of media (television, radio, newspaper, periodical, and outdoor advertising) firms whose stocks are traded on the NYSE.[43] As before, the monthly returns to the portfolio were regressed on the monthly returns to a market portfolio and a dummy variable for the ad substantiation adjustment period. The results are shown in Table 8.4. The equation explains almost all the variation in the dependent variable, but the coefficient for the substantiation period does not differ significantly from zero.

This result is consistent with the economic model, but inconsistent with that of the market-failure hypothesis. While no one of the stock-market tests clearly distinguishes between the economic and public-interest models, the total configuration of advertiser, ad agency, and media wealth changes is consistent only with the economic model. The public-interest hypothesis does not unambiguously predict large-firm wealth increases, and one of its testable implications—that of increasing media wealth—is refuted.

Incidence of FTC Substantiation Cases

The two hypotheses about ad substantiation have opposing implications for the way in which the FTC implements the program. The economic model hypothesizes that substantiation exists to redistribute wealth. The necessary condition for the FTC to redistribute wealth is a differential advantage of large firms with high brand name capital to spread the costs of substantiation and to substitute away from the kinds of claims likely to attract FTC suspicion. Thus the economic model predicts that the FTC will bring more ad substantiation cases in those product markets where firm market share and reputation are more diverse, since that diversity gives the FTC greater power to redistribute wealth. In contrast, the market-failure model predicts that diversity of firm market share and reputation in a market has no effect on case incidence, *ceteris paribus*. Instead, the market-failure model emphasizes the supply of unsubstantiated advertising as a major predictor of ad substantiation case incidence. The latter prediction does not distinguish the two models, however. The economic model does not deny that the FTC may target markets possibly prone to market failure, but it maintains that the FTC's interest in such markets is inversely related to the degree of uniformity of firm market size and reputation there.

To distinguish these two hypotheses we specify a regression model with case incidence as the dependent variable, and, as independent variables, average firm market size (reputation) and coefficient of variation of firm market size (reputation). To assure that variation in firm market size and reputation is not merely reflecting the number of low-reputation firms in the market (another indicator of the extent of market failure), we also hold constant the number of low-reputation firms.[44] The market-failure model predicts that the number of low-reputation firms matters (positively) as does the mean (negatively), but that variation does not. The economic model predicts that variation matters (positively) and is silent about the sign of the effect of mean firm market size and reputation and the number of low-reputation firms. The economic model does predict, however, that if the mean significantly affects case incidence the magnitude of the effect is positively related to diversity of firm size in the market.

For appropriately defined product markets, there are no perfect measures of the firms' market size and reputation. As in the stock market analysis of advertisers' returns, we adopted Leading National Advertisers' product subclasses to define markets, and we used as proxies for firm output and reputation in each market a firm's 1970 total advertising expenditure.[45] The mean and coefficient of variation for firm advertising expenditures in each market was computed. We included two alternative measures of low-reputation firms in the market: the number of firms with advertising expenditures less than a standard deviation below the mean, and the number of firms in a market with 1970 sales in all markets below $1 million. To define the dependent variable, we assigned FTC ad substantiation cases and consent orders from 1972 to 1980 to the relevant market.

The results of regressing case incidence on the mean and coefficient of

TABLE 8.5
INCIDENCE OF FTC AD SUBSTANTIATION CASES
AS A FUNCTION OF FIRM'S ADVERTISING VOLUME, 1972–1980

	Coefficient (t-statistic)	
Intercept	−.391	−.399
	(−.81)	(−.85)
Mean advertising expenditures	2.5×10^{-5}	2.1×10^{-5}
	(.21)	(.18)
Coefficient of variation for advertising expenditures	.464[a]	.474[a]
	(1.69)	(1.95)
Number of firms with advertising expenditures less than a standard deviation below mean	−.001 (−.18)	
Number of firms with total sales below $1 million		−.003
		(−.30)
F	1.71	1.73
R^2	.07	.07

NOTE: a. Significant at .05 in one-tailed test.
SOURCE: See note 36.

variation of advertising expenditures and the alternate measures of small, low-reputation firms are shown in Table 8.5. The only estimated parameter of significance is the coefficient of variation, and its positive sign is correctly predicted by the economic hypothesis.[46] The test results refute the principal implication of the public-interest model: that the number of small, low-reputation firms is of any significance.[47]

We constructed an alternative measure of the mean and variation of firms' reputations within a product market, based on the number of specific products in a market that firms advertise.[48] Breadth of product line works like repeat purchases to discipline the truthfulness of firms' advertising claims. The ability to earn additional returns on capital built up in a brand name is perhaps the principal incentive for a firm to diversify its product line. Investment in broader product lines should thus be positively correlated with brand name capital.

For each market we computed the average per-firm number of products advertised, as well as the coefficient of variation. We regressed the number of FTC ad substantiation cases in a product market on the resulting mean and coefficient of variation, also including the alternative measures of the number of low-reputation firms. The estimates appear in Table 8.6.[49] As in Table 8.5, the sign and significance of the coefficient of variation is correctly predicted by the economic model.[50]

TABLE 8.6
INCIDENCE OF FTC AD SUBSTANTIATION CASES
AS A FUNCTION OF FIRM'S PRODUCT DIVERSITY, 1972–1980

	Coefficient (t-statistic)	
Intercept	.047	.111
	(.09)	(.22)
Mean product lines	−.254	−2.81
	(−.94)	(−1.01)
Coefficient of variation	1.151[a]	1.218[b]
	(1.92)	(2.03)
Number of firms with advertising expenditures less than a standard deviation below mean	.004 (.80)	
Number of firms with total sales		.004
		(.48)
F	1.98	1.83
R^2	.08	.07

NOTES: a. Significant at .05 in one-tailed test.
         b. Significant at .025 in one-tailed test.
SOURCE: See note 36.

The case-incidence test results support rejection of the null hypothesis that variation of firms' reputations and sizes does not matter for FTC case selection. Diversity is shown to influence case incidence positively. Overall, the results are fully consistent with the economic model of ad substantiation and inconsistent with the market-failure model.

CONCLUSION

Upon his arrival at the FTC, Chairman James C. Miller III publicly questioned the commission's prior substantiation doctrine and sought comment on it. Television and radio networks, newspapers, and other media voiced no reaction. But to the surprise of many, Miller's suggestions that the program be re-examined met with a "frosty reception" from advertisers and ad agencies, with the result that "the ad industry is carrying the burden of defending tough law enforcement from the assaults of [the] FTC chairman."[51] "One ad industry leader after another warned [Miller] that the industry sees no reason to tamper with the existing obligation for prior substantiation."[52]

Of particular interest has been the reaction of the three organizations that organized and now operate the private, self-regulatory NAD/NARB system.

The Association of National Advertisers, the American Association of Advertising Agencies, and the American Advertising Federation have all underscored their commitment to the FTC's prior substantiation program.[53] "[A]t his meeting with leaders of all three ad industry associations, [Miller] was told once again that the industry is not interested in anything which questions the advertiser's responsibility to have prior substantiation in hand."[54]

Once again, the regulated implore for regulation. This article suggests why. Using an economic model of regulation, we noted the wealth transfer potential in the FTC's prior substantiation requirement and found that the principal requisite for successfully transferring wealth among producers—significant variation in reputation and size among firms in a given market—is in fact conducive to more substantiation cases. The wealth transfers from ad substantiation are reflected in the tests showing significant increases in stock prices for large advertisers during the period of adjustment to the new regulation, and especially in the extraordinary jump in large advertising agencies' stock prices during that period. However, media firms have apparently been unaffected by the regulatory shift to substantiation. Together these findings are consistent with the view that the substantiation doctrine is used to redistribute wealth from marginal to inframarginal firms, as predicted by the economic theory of regulation.

In sum, the market-failure view of ad substantiation is unable to explain the total configuration of wealth changes and the incidence of cases brought by the FTC. According to the evidence, the redistribution model is better substantiated.

NOTES

1. George J. Stigler, "The Theory of Economic Regulation," *Bell Journal of Economics and Management Science* 2 (Spring 1971): 3–21.

2. Sam Peltzman, "Toward a More General Theory of Regulation," *Journal of Law and Economics* 19 (August 1976): 211–48.

3. Howard P. Marvel, "Factory Regulation: A Reinterpretation of Early English Experience," *Journal of Law and Economics* 20 (October 1977): 379–402; Ronald H. Coase, "Payola in Radio and Television Broadcasting," *Journal of Law and Economics* 22 (October 1979): 269–328; Michael T. Maloney and Robert E. McCormick, "A Positive Theory of Environmental Quality Regulation," *Journal of Law and Economics* 25 (April 1982): 99–123; and Sharon Oster, "The Strategic Use of Regulatory Investment by Industry Sub-Groups," *Economic Inquiry* 20 (October 1982): 604–17.

4. For background and overviews of the ad substantiation program, see Dorothy Cohen, "The FTC's Advertising Substantiation Program," *Journal of Marketing* 44 (Winter 1980): 26–35; Robert Pitofsky, "The FTC Ad Substantiation Program," *Georgetown Law Journal* 61 (July 1973): 1427–52; and Robert Pitofsky, "Beyond Nader:

Consumer Protection and the Regulation of Advertising," *Harvard Law Review* 90 (1977): 661–701.

5. See, for example, Charles of the Ritz Distributors Corp. v. FTC, 143 F.2d 676 (2d Cir. 1944). See also American Home Products Corp. v. FTC, 695 F.2d 681, 695–702 (3d Cir. 1982).

6. See, for example, FTC v. Colgate-Palmolive Co., 380 U.S. 374, 384–85 (1965).

7. *Wall Street Journal*, June 11, 1971.

8. Stanley E. Cohen, "Ad Industry Goes Only Partway with Miller," *Advertising Age*, November 1, 1982.

9. In re Pfizer, Inc., 81 FTC 23 (1972).

10. Although the Pfizer holding was based solely on Section 5 unfairness, lack of prior substantiation has also been held deceptive under Section 5. National Dynamics Corp. v. Federal Trade Commission, 82 FTC 488 (1973), aff'd, 492 F.2d 1333 (2d Cir.), cert. denied, 419 U.S. 993 (1976).

11. In re Pfizer, Inc., 81 FTC 67 (emphasis in original).

12. Richard A. Posner, *Regulation of Advertising by the FTC* (Washington, D.C.: American Enterprise Institute, 1973).

13. Interestingly, more than half the recidivism at the FTC has involved violation of advertising orders. Penalties assessed typically run between $10,000 and $100,000, but may be higher. See the papers in this volume by Shughart and Tollison (Chapter 12) and Altrogge and Shughart (Chapter 11).

14. See National Advertising Review Board, *Self-Regulation of National Advertising* (NAD Case Report, July 15, 1983).

15. See two publications by the American Association of Advertising Agencies: *Advertising Agencies: What They Are, What They Do, and How They Do It* (New York, 1976), and "Qualifications for Membership," in *1982/83 Roster and Organization of the 4A's* (New York, 1982), pp. 11–14.

16. Priscilla LaBarbera, "Advertising Self-Regulation: An Evaluation," *MSU Business Topics* (Summer 1980).

17. Bill Arams, "The Networks Censor TV Ads for Taste and Deceptiveness," *Wall Street Journal*, September 30, 1982, p. 33.

18. National Advertising Review Board, *Advertising Self-Regulation and Its Interaction with Consumers* (New York: A.B. Primer, n.d.).

19. LaBarbera, *Advertising Self-Regulation*, p. 59.

20. "Will ANA Heed Call of FTC's Muris?" *Advertising Age*, November 15, 1982, p. 3. See also Howard A. Bell, "Self-Regulation by the Advertising Industry," *California Management Review* 16 (Spring 1974): 58–63.

21. NARB, *Self-Regulation of National Advertising*; Richard L. Gordon, "Substantiation Proposals Emerge," *Advertising Age*, July 18, 1983.

22. Philip Nelson, "Information and Consumer Behavior," *Journal of Political Economy* 78 (March–April 1970): 311–29; Philip Nelson, "Advertising as Information," *Journal of Political Economy* 82 (July–August 1974): 729–54.

23. Lester G. Telser, "A Theory of Self-Enforcing Agreements," *Journal of Business* 53 (January 1980): 27–44; Benjamin V. Klein and Keith B. Leffler, "The Role of Market

Forces in Assuring Contractual Performance," *Journal of Political Economy* 89 (August 1981): 615–41.

24. John A. Healey, "The Federal Trade Commission Advertising Substantiation Program and Changes in the Context of Advertising in Selected Industries" (Ph.D. diss., University of California at Los Angeles, 1978).

25. Steven C. Salop and David T. Scheffman, "Raising Rivals' Costs," *American Economic Review* 73 (May 1983): 267–71; Steven Salop, David Scheffman, and Warren Schwartz, "Raising Rivals' Costs in a Rent-Seeking Society," in *The Political Economy of Regulation* (Washington, D.C.: FTC, 1985).

26. Oliver E. Williamson, "Wage Rates as a Barrier to Entry: The Pennington Case in Perspective," *Quarterly Journal of Economics* 82 (February 1968): 85–116. See also Michael T. Maloney, Robert E. McCormick, and Robert D. Tollison, "Achieving Cartel Profits Through Unionization," *Southern Economic Journal* 46 (October 1979): 628–35.

27. At the Securities and Exchange Commission (SEC), government sanction of an industry cartel is even more explicit. The National Association of Securities Dealers enforces reasonable basis requirements for profitability claims made by securities dealers and investment advisers, with the SEC as court of appeal.

28. John Monsarrat, *The Case of the Full Service Agency* (New York: American Association of Advertising Agencies, 1971); Francesco U. Nicosia, *Advertising Management and Society* (New York: McGraw-Hill, 1974).

29. The magnitude of the reputation investments is shown by the exceptional goodwill losses suffered by firms sued by the FTC for advertising violations. Sam Peltzman, "The Effects of FTC Advertising Regulation," *Journal of Law and Economics* 24 (December 1981): 403–48.

30. It is important to differentiate our hypothesis from one investigated by Peltzman ("Effects of FTC Advertising Regulation"). Our hypothesis is that the ad substantiation program raised the value of firms with large market shares relative to those with small market shares; Peltzman assessed the effects of specific cases on the respondent firm's market value. Our hypothesis allows that FTC complaints against large firms will reduce these firms' values while they benefit from the ad substantiation program.

31. In re Pfizer, Inc., 81 FTC 58; Posner, *Regulation of Advertising*.

32. The most recent substantiation cases, for example, have held certain advertising claims unsubstantiated unless backed by well-controlled clinical studies (and no other sort of evidence) and unless there are at least two such studies to support the claims. See American Home Products Corp. v. FTC; Sterling Drug, 102 FTC 395 (1983); and Bristol-Myers, 102 FTC 21 (1983).

33. G. William Schwert, "Measuring the Effects of Regulation: Evidence from the Capital Markets," *Journal of Law and Economics* 24 (April 1981): 121–58.

34. "Pfizer's Advertising of Sunburn Reliever Is Challenged by FTC," *Wall Street Journal*, April 14, 1970.

35. Also well publicized was the Nader petition, filed with the commission in December 1970, that sought a rulemaking to require submission for public disclosure of all substantiation material. By that time, however, the market adjustment process should have been well underway.

36. Leading National Advertisers, Inc., *LNA Multi-Media Report Class/Brand $* (New York, January–December 1970); Media Records, Inc., *Expenditures of National Advertisers in Newspapers* (New York, 1970); and "Network and Spot Radio Advertisers Estimated Expenditures: National and Regional Advertising, First Quarter–Fourth Quarter," *Radio Expenditure Report* (Larchmont, N.Y., 1970).

37. The portfolios for both the dependent and the independent variables exclude dividends. However, see note 41 below.

38. We also tested for the stability of the beta coefficient on the market portfolio return variable, and found that the introduction of the ad substantiation program caused no significant shift in the beta coefficient.

39. The firms were: (1) Interpublic Group of Companies, Inc. (a conglomerate of agencies, including McCann-Erickson); (2) J. Walter Thompson Co.; (3) Foote, Cone and Belding Inc.; and (4) Wells, Rich, Greene, Inc. In 1982 these firms ranked numbers 2, 4, 8, and 24 respectively in advertising agency market share, with a combined share of 16 percent. The first observation is in 1965, when the first public ownership of advertising agencies occurred. Most advertising agencies are not publicly traded, but rather are employee-owned corporations akin to professional firms in other service industries (such as law and accounting). There is no reason to expect that substantiation would affect large publicly held agencies differently from large nonpublicly owned firms. Although the NYSE agencies used in our tests are among the largest in the industry, many quite large and well-known agencies are privately held (for example, Benton and Bowles; Dancer FitzGerald Sample, Inc.; and Young and Rubicam).

40. The magnitude of the wealth effects is reminiscent of Peltzman's findings in a related area, the negative wealth effects to a particular company when the FTC sues it over its advertising. He termed the estimated wealth losses "amazing" and "astounding." See Peltzman, "Effects of FTC Advertising Regulation," p. 418.

41. The financial and advertising press for 1969–1970 was reviewed to see whether any exogenous shocks other than the onset of substantiation might have affected industry returns during this period. None were found. In a second attempt to control for other exogenous changes affecting ad agency returns, we constructed a new dependent variable: monthly returns to a portfolio of television network common stock. We regressed it on the overall market return variable and included the residuals from that regression in the ad agency regressions. The demand for advertising agency services is derived from the demand for advertising, all other things equal. Exogenous changes increasing the demand for television networks' advertising time would be closely correlated with the demand for ad agencies' services. The network residuals, representing network profitability not explained by overall market changes, are thus a proxy for unidentified exogenous shocks that could account for abnormal agency profits. The residual variable was not significant in the agency regressions, however, and its inclusion had little effect on the size and none on the significance of the ad substantiation coefficient.

The coefficients presented in Table 8.2 use equally weighted returns without dividends for the advertising agency and market portfolio variables. To be certain that this did not account for the magnitude of the wealth effects shown in the table, the regressions were also run with these variables defined to include dividends. There were no important differences in the size or significance of the coefficients when dividends were included.

42. The data are equally weighted composite indices (1967=100) for almost all advertising media: magazines, newspapers, network and spot television, network and spot radio, and outdoor advertising. The data were collected by the advertising agency McCann-Erickson and reported annually. Monthly figures were derived by treating annual changes as linear progressions.

43. The firms are those listed under Standard Industrial Classification codes 4832 (radio broadcasting), 4833 (television broadcasting), 2711 (newspapers), 2721 (periodicals), and 7312 (outdoor advertising services).

44. We also estimated mean-variance models without the number of low-reputation firms as an independent variable, with results equivalent to those presented below.

45. There are several theoretical and empirical problems with using a firm's advertising expenditures as a proxy for its size or reputation in a market. (See Thomas T. Nagle, "Do Advertising-Profitability Studies Really Show That Advertising Creates a Barrier to Entry?" *Journal of Law and Economics* 24 [October 1981]: 333–49.) For example, in the advertising-profitability literature, a critical issue is the appropriate depreciation rate for advertising capital. For our purposes, whether advertising is a current or capital expense is irrelevant so long as depreciation rates do not vary substantially across products. In fact, there is evidence that retention rates differ across products. (See Yoram Peles, "Rates of Amortization of Advertising Expenditures," *Journal of Political Economy* 79 [1971]:1032–58, and Jean J. Lambin, *Advertising Competition and Market Conduct in Oligopoly Over Time* [New York: American Elsevier, 1976].) The unavailability of a sufficiently large set of product-specific estimates of depreciation rates precluded adjustment of advertising expenditures in our product sample. However, we were able to apply a crude test based on evidence that depreciation rates are higher for durable goods. When we estimated the regression model in this section on the subsample, drugs and toiletries, we got results identical to those for the full sample, which included many markets for durables.

46. The case-incidence random variable is truncated at zero, and there are a substantial number of product markets with zero case incidence. We corrected for potential bias in the two regression models of Table 8.5 using TOBIT. Qualitatively, we obtained results identical to those in Table 8.5. Besides the intercept, only the coefficient of variation is statistically significant, with estimated t-values of 1.92 and 2.06, respectively. Quantitatively, consistent estimators of these coefficients yield larger point estimates: 2.000 instead of .464 and 1.903 instead of .474.

47. The measure of mean size and reputation does have a significant negative effect, as predicted by the public-interest model. Specifically, although the coefficients on the mean in Table 8.5 are not significant, the mean also appears in the denominator of the coefficient of variation term, which has a positive and significant influence on case incidence. We observe, however, that the partial derivative with respect to mean approaches zero as the variance approaches zero, the result predicted by the economic model.

We also estimated the regression models of Table 8.5 by including total market advertising expenditures as a regressor. The results do not support the public-interest model any more than those in Table 8.5. However, the significance of the variation coefficient was reduced to .08 in a one-tailed test. (Total advertising affects case incidence positively, but the effect is statistically insignificant.)

48. Our previous test of the mean and variation used advertising expenditure data for 1970, a year that captures the state of the markets when ad substantiation began. Unfortunately, the data required to construct the product-line measure of reputation were only available to us for 1976. To some extent our measure of market characteristics may thus have already been affected by the ad substantiation program. We note, however, that when we regressed cases on the mean and variance of Leading National Advertisers' advertising expenditures for 1976, we got results virtually identical to those in Table 8.5, which used 1970 data.

49. We also regressed cases on the mean/variance pairs for advertising expenditures and product line simultaneously. The variance terms have the predicted positive sign, but their individual statistical significance is marginal. The one-tailed levels of significance are .07 and .08.

50. As noted above, the positive coefficient on the coefficient of variation implies that the mean has a negative effect which diminishes as the standard deviation diminishes. See note 47 above.

51. S. Cohen, "Ad Industry Goes Only Partway with Miller."

52. Richard L. Gordon, "Miller Asks for Ad Rule Review," *Advertising Age*, October 25, 1982.

53. Gordon, "Substantiation Proposals Emerge."

54. S. Cohen, "Ad Industry Goes Only Partway with Miller."

Chapter 9

Settlement vs. Litigation in Antitrust Enforcement

JAMES LANGENFELD & ROBERT A. ROGOWSKY

A VARIETY of goals are attributed to the antitrust laws, including protecting small business, combating industrial concentration, and, as Senator John Sherman claimed in 1890, preventing the business arrangements that "advance the cost to the consumer."[1] Although it is possible that each of these goals has guided antitrust policy, from an economist's point of view, efficiency and social welfare maximization should motivate antitrust enforcement. In fact, antitrust laws appear to have been promulgated with these latter two goals in mind.[2]

Have antitrust officials been motivated by welfare maximization or by some combination of other goals? Many efforts have been made to uncover the determinants of the government's antitrust prosecution. Some have tried, with only limited success, to correlate antitrust prosecution with industries that appear to generate substantial efficiency or "dead-weight" losses.[3] Other, more recent efforts have attempted to identify the forces driving antitrust enforcement by looking to the constituency or constituencies served. For instance, these forces could be: (1) serving the public interest by enhancing efficiency and maximizing welfare; (2) protecting small business; (3) advancing antitrust bureaucrats' interest by increasing their budget; (4) protecting the antitrust bar's source of income; or (5) serving the whim of key congressional leaders.[4] In

The conclusions set forth in this paper are those of the authors and do not necessarily represent those of the Federal Trade Commission.

general, these research efforts have not met with much success, at least in part because it is difficult to formulate testable hypotheses that can distinguish the most powerful explanation from the competing theories.

One approach to testing the motivation of antitrust enforcement is to consider the decision of the antitrust agencies to settle or to litigate. A growing literature has set out the settlement process and its implications,[5] and some have applied bargaining models to antitrust. Richard Posner, for instance, has designed a model to predict how a rational, utility-maximizing antitrust agency would divide its attention among cases with different characteristics. Extending his model to the settlement process, Posner predicts that the larger the ratio of the defendant's stake to the agency's stake, the more likely the parties will settle.[6]

While helping to explain the distribution of small and large cases in rational enforcement, models such as Posner's do not adequately address the question of whether the agencies are maximizing welfare in the decision to settle or litigate. This paper presents a partial equilibrium framework for estimating whether antitrust officials have employed settlements in a manner consistent with social welfare maximization. Combining data on Federal Trade Commission (FTC) and Antitrust Division of the Department of Justice merger cases with the most plausible set of assumptions about the relationship between settlement and unremedied monopoly losses, we find the antitrust agencies have not responded to changes in the size of monopoly losses as welfare maximization would dictate. The results are, however, consistent with a relatively naive model of welfare maximization, suggesting the agencies may attempt to maximize welfare, but are simply misguided. There is also evidence that more cases may be litigated merely in response to larger agency budgets, bringing the misguided agency model into some question and lending some credence to other models of agency behavior.

Efficient Merger Relief: A Benefit/Cost Tradeoff

Consumer welfare is reduced when the competitive conditions in a market are undermined by mergers or by industry practices that facilitate collusion.[7] In particular, persistent noncompetitive behavior in an oligopolistic industry leads to inefficiencies and the misallocation of resources. The loss can come, of course, from a cartel colluding on prices or from dominate-firm price leadership (both leading to inefficiencies, that is, dead-weight loss), from predatory behavior by the largest firm(s) against smaller rivals, from X-inefficiencies generated by noncompetitive firms, or from "unfair" redistribution of income to firm owners from consumers.[8] For our purposes, it is sufficient to lump the likely losses under the label "monopoly loss." The benefit to society of merger remedy, therefore, comes from the repair of competitive injury due to the merger and the elimination of the monopoly loss—not merely the victory in court of an antitrust agency providing anticompetitive behavior.

The benefit to society of antimerger enforcement must be weighed against its direct and indirect costs. Enforcement is a direct cost, the loss to society of the opportunity cost of resources diverted to challenging mergers. The total direct cost of enforcement must include the financial burden on the prosecution and on the respondents, the latter pulling resources directly from the firms involved and the former pulling resources from the economy at large.

The existence of enforcement costs raises the possibility that obtaining less than full relief may be efficient. By its very nature, the give and take in the settlement process will generally not achieve successful litigation's relatively complete remedy to an antitrust problem. Nevertheless, negotiated settlements may provide the welfare-maximizing remedy. Successful pretrial bargaining avoids the costs of litigation and ensures at least a partial safeguard of competition.

Moreover, the time required to obtain relief is critical in comparing the partial remedy from settlement to the fuller remedy obtained through litigation. Successful litigation will generally not achieve relief as quickly as settlement, and the benefits of full relief in the future must be discounted. Obtaining full relief is also not a certainty, and the benefits of litigation must be expressed as the expected value of the outcome of the trial; that is, a welfare-maximizing agency must average the gain to society if litigation is successful with the loss if litigation is unsuccessful, each weighted by their respective probability. Therefore, the welfare-maximizing agency should compare the discounted present value of the expected benefits of pursuing full relief to the discounted present value of partial relief through settlement, which is obtained more quickly and with certainty.

THE MODEL

Definitions and Assumptions

To analyze the trade-off between litigation and settlement, we develop a model that a "rational" welfare-maximizing government antitrust agency should consider when deciding to accept a settlement or push forward to litigation. We first define the concepts discussed in the last section, list assumptions, and then sketch a partial equilibrium model of welfare-maximizing antitrust enforcement. The model enables us to identify variables that should concern the antitrust agencies and to understand how changes in these variables should affect the proportion of cases settled and litigated. Let

C_L = Monopoly loss if the merger is allowed to stand (dead weight loss + X-efficiency loss) at each point in time, t, relative to the competitive outcome. It is assumed that any private litigation costs would be included in this cost and, in the absence of litigation, these costs would become rents to the owners of the firm.

C_S = Monopoly loss of a negotiated settlement at each point in time, t, relative to the competitive outcome. This is the monopoly loss that would remain after the best partial relief obtained in settlement discussions.

C_A = Administrative cost of litigating at each point in time, t. Specifically, these costs are the difference between total cost of obtaining a consent decree and the total administrative cost of litigating a case.

δ = The probability of winning the case and obtaining full relief necessary to eliminate monopoly loss ($0 < \delta < 1$).

r = Interest rate (social discount rate).

T = The expected amount of time between the agency decision whether to settle or to litigate, and the final court decision if the case is litigated.[9]

L = Discounted, expected total cost to society of litigating.

S = Discounted, expected total cost to society of settling.

For simplicity, all costs (C_L, C_S, C_A) are assumed constant over time. Because the cost of monopoly power is likely to decrease with time, C_L and C_S are probably upper bounds.[10] Note also that, although the merging firms may know their merger will create monopoly power or achieve efficiencies, in general the government will not know this with certainty. Again, for simplicity we assume that the government knows there is a monopoly loss in cases that present a litigation or settlement decision. This could be modified by an expected value calculation based on the subjective probability of a violation, but so long as society is risk-neutral between winning and losing in monopoly losses, and so long as errors are distributed randomly and independently, no bias will result from our simplification.

We also assume that the agency must either accept the "best" settlement available in $t=0$ or litigate. A multiperiod bargaining game characterized by a Bayesian Nash equilibrium can be used to determine when the final offers are made for settlement, similar to that employed by Robert Cooter and Stephen Marks.[11] As they show, under the proper assumptions on bargaining strategy, the multiperiod model collapses to the single period model we use.

Finally, we assume case independence (that is, no deterrence or precedent effects) and successful litigation will fully remedy the monopoly loss, C_L. These assumptions should not limit the generality of C_L, because the value of deterrence is most likely a monotonic function of monopoly loss and therefore C_L can be redefined as a reduction in monopoly loss that includes the value of deterrence.

The Decision Rule and Comparative Static Effects

At some juncture in the investigation of a potential antitrust violation, the rational welfare-maximizing antitrust agency must choose either settlement or litigation, depending on which is less costly to society. The antitrust agency's decision to accept settlement or to litigate will result in one of three possible states: litigate and win; litigate and lose; or settle.

The expected total cost to society of litigating the case is the discounted administrative cost plus the expected monopoly loss of litigation. Under the risk neutrality assumption, the expected monopoly loss of litigation is the present value of monopoly losses that accrue prior to winning the case and obtaining the remedy, plus the present value of monopoly losses that remain when a case is lost, each weighted by their respective probabilities. Formally, the discounted expected loss to society of litigating (L) is:

$$L = \int_0^T C_A \cdot e^{-rt} dt + \delta \int_0^T C_L \cdot e^{-rt} dt + (1-\delta) \int_0^\infty C_L \cdot e^{-rt} dt \qquad (1)$$

where the first term on the right-hand side is the present value of administrative cost if the case is litigated until period T, the second term is the expected monopoly loss prior to T, and the third is the expected monopoly loss if the case is litigated and lost.

The total discounted cost of settling to society in $t=0$ can be expressed as

$$S = \int_0^\infty C_S \cdot e^{-rt} dt \approx \frac{C_S}{r}. \qquad (2)$$

Note that in equation (2), the settlement cost continues into the indefinite future; this is also true for the monopoly loss when the agencies litigate but do not win (the third term in [1]). However, both the administrative costs of prosecution and the monopoly loss (first two terms in [1]) end when the courts impose a correct remedy in time period T.

We can define a settlement/litigation decision function as

$$D=L/S. \tag{3}$$

If $D > 1$, the agency should settle out of court, because the expected cost of litigation is larger than the cost of settlement. If $D < 1$, then the agency should litigate the case because the costs of settlement are higher. When $D = 1$, the agency should be indifferent between litigation and settlement, because the expected costs are the same.

For cases with D near one, small changes in some of the independent variables should affect the decision to settle or litigate. As D increases, cases where the agency is indifferent between prosecution and litigation—and cases that had previously just fallen into the litigation category—should be settled instead. When D decreases, cases about which antitrust officials would be otherwise indifferent—or cases marginally favoring settlement—should now be prosecuted.

To see how D changes in response to each of the variables, substitute (1) and (2) into (3), and simplify the expression by substituting $\int_0^T e^{-rt} dt = (1/r)(1 - e^{-rt})$. This yields

$$D = \frac{(1 - e^{-rt})C_A + (1 - \delta e^{-rt})C_L}{C_S}. \tag{3'}$$

By partially differentiating (3') with respect to each independent variable, we can then identify the impact a change in each variable should have on D, *ceteris paribus*, and therefore on the proportion of cases settled and litigated.

Differentiating D with respect to T, the expected length of time for an adjudication, yields $\partial D/\partial T > 0$. Therefore, the longer the expected court battle, the greater the incentive for the welfare-maximizing public agency to settle. This would predict that defendants in antitrust suits would tend to delay court action if they knew the agency's decision function. Hiring prestigious legal counsel may signal the intention of the defendants to wage a lengthy court battle, if necessary, and may bias the agency's calculations in favor of settlement.

Not surprisingly, an increase in the agency's probability of winning decreases the incentive for the agency to settle ($\partial D/\partial \delta < 0$). We would expect private firms to try to reduce δ, perhaps by increasing their expenditures on legal counsel. Higher expenditures on legal counsel by the defendants tend to reduce their likelihood of losing once a case is brought, and would thus increase the likelihood of settlement favorable to them.

As interest rates increase, the present value of costs associated with both settlement and prosecution decrease. However, $\partial D/\partial r > 0$, indicating settlement costs are reduced more than litigation costs, so as interest rates rise a larger proportion of cases should be settled. To understand this result, consider the cases with D near one. Until the adjudication is finally resolved during T, the expected value of litigation per period of time (monopoly loss, C_L, plus administrative costs, C_A) is greater for these cases than the monopoly loss per time period (C_S) if the cases were settled. After period T, the expected value of the monopoly loss associated with litigation is equal to the unremedied monopoly loss, reduced by the probability that the agency wins in T. With D approximately one, this lower expected monopoly loss per time period after T must be less than the settlement loss after T to offset the higher costs of litigation prior to T. An increase in the interest rate always reduces the value of future costs more than current costs due to the compounding effect in present value calculations. Hence an increase in the interest rate will reduce the higher costs of settlement after T by proportionately more than it will reduce the higher costs of litigation before T. The relatively higher litigation costs make settlement relatively more attractive than litigation to a welfare-maximizing (loss-minimizing) agency.

Of particular interest to the antitrust agency is the effect of the size of the potential losses of settlement and the size of the expected loss with litigation. It is easily shown—holding monopoly losses (C_L) and administrative costs (C_A) constant—that the larger the cost to society of the best available settlement (C_S), the smaller the proportion of cases that should be settled ($\partial D/\partial C_S > 0$). Similarly, holding settlement costs constant, an increase in either the monopoly loss expected from the merger or administrative costs of litigation will increase the desirability of settlement. However, these results critically depend on the assumption that these variables are not systematically related to each other—an assumption that does not fully express the role of the defendant firms in the litigation-settlement decision.

Defendant firms make a litigation-settlement calculation similar to that of the rational agency. The defendants weigh the cost of settling (the value of the reduced monopoly rents of settlement) against litigation costs (the expected value of monopoly rents discounted by the possibility of losing the trial). The defendant's best offer to the antitrust agency, C_S, will also be a function of other variables important to the agency. Our results would therefore be biased if we rely exclusively on the simple independence assumption. This bias will be small if we make certain critical variables endogenous, such as the probability of victorious litigation.

Relaxing the naive assumption of strict independence can expand the inquiry into a bargaining model (as posited by Cooter and Marks) or lead to a joint maximization model between litigator and defendant (according to Posner). In this paper we do not attempt this expansion, because our focus is deriving testable hypotheses about the actions of government agencies. However, we can capture the most important interrelationships between the variables that should concern rational, welfare-maximizing antitrust agencies. First, bargaining theory tells us the cost of the settlement (C_S) in each time period is generally an increasing function of the size of monopoly costs (C_L). Therefore, let $C_S=(1-\alpha)C_L$ where α is the proportion of monopoly loss reduced by settlement. If the unconstrained monopoly cost is greater than the loss due to settlement (as one would hope), then $0<\alpha<1$. Second, our empirical work suggests that the probability of victory in antitrust cases is a function of proxies for monopoly costs (see Appendix), so $\delta=\delta(C_L)$, where the probability of agency victory is an increasing function of the unremedied monopoly loss.

The impact of a change in monopoly loss becomes more complex under these more realistic assumptions. Incorporating these two assumptions into (3'), a change in the size of the potential monopoly loss (and therefore settlement costs) now yields

$$\frac{\partial D}{\partial C_L}=(1-\alpha)^{-1}\left[(e^{-rt}-1)\frac{C_A}{C_L^2}-\frac{\partial\delta}{\partial C_L}\cdot e^{-rt}\right] \qquad (4)$$

where $\partial\delta/\partial C_L$ is the change in the probability of victory with respect to a change in unconstrained monopoly loss. We now see that an increase in unconstrained monopoly loss leads to more litigation ($\partial D/\partial C_L<0$) when the change in the agency's probability of victory in litigation due to unremedial monopoly loss is positive or zero ($\partial\delta/\partial C_L\geq0$).

Testing Whether or Not
Antitrust Agencies Maximize Welfare

The partial equilibrium model sketched above can be used to test empirically whether or not the antitrust agencies have settled the optimal number of cases. To do this, we estimate an econometric model with a binary dependent variable defined as one for cases that were settled and zero for litigated cases, and with the independent variables that should affect the litigation settlement decision—that is, proxies for monopoly loss, the interest rate, and duration of the case.[12] To pick up any institutional bias we also add a dummy variable for the agency that brought the case (if an FTC case, $AG=1$). The initial year of the investigation is included to pick up any secular trend in the settlement or litigation process.

The government filed over 260 cases under Section 7 of the Clayton Act from 1968 through 1981. Of these, over 100 have been dismissed or are still pending. Our sample is drawn from the matters during this period where a complaint was filed and the case terminated either by a consent decree or by adjudication. The sample then includes all completed horizontal, vertical, and conglomerate (potential competition) merger cases where data are available for the relevant variables; only the nearly 50 banking cases brought by the Department of Justice are excluded.

The qualitative dependent variable in our model implies estimation by ordinary least squares (OLS) or a linear probability model will give a hetero-skedastic error term, resulting in a loss of efficiency and the possibility of predicted values outside of the zero–one range. Instead, we use a probit probability model. To estimate the nonlinear cumulative normal transform of the probit model, we use a standard maximum likelihood (ML) estimating technique. The results of two specifications of the model are presented in Table 9.1. The table includes the ML coefficients and the change in the probability of litigation due to a change in each independent variable. The latter corre-spond to the coefficients obtained in an OLS model and are evaluated at the mean of the dependent variable in all specifications.

As our model of welfare-maximizing antitrust officials predicts, the longer the duration of the case (MO), the more likely the case was litigated rather than settled (significantly different from zero at .01 level for the two-tail t test). A one-month increase in case length implies an increase in the probability of litigation by about .009. This result is not surprising and is consistent with most models of the settlement or litigation decision.

The interest rate enters with a positive sign in both specifications (signifi-cant at the 10 percent level in estimate [1]). This result is also consistent with a rational, welfare-maximizing agency, although the low level of significance limits the certainty we can place on the result. Apparently the antitrust agencies realize that as interest rates increase, the value of waiting for the benefits of full relief shrinks relative to partial relief obtained by an immediate settlement.

Cardinal measures of remedied or partially remedied monopoly loss (C_L and C_S) do not exist. Nonetheless, monopoly loss should be a function of the industry structure, the volume of sales of the companies involved in the merger, and the difficult-to-measure market characteristics such as barriers to entry. We tried various proxies for monopoly loss, but in many cases we were limited by the information available in the record. When sales of either the acquiring or acquired firms are introduced in our estimation (see Table 9.1, specification [2]), neither is significantly different from zero. To the extent the volume of sales represents potential monopoly loss due to the merger, the Justice Depart-ment and the FTC have not implemented any systematic relationship between monopoly loss and the litigation or settlement decision. The four firm con-centration fares little better in explaining the settlement decision, as shown in specification (1) of Table 9.1. However, the market shares of the acquired and

TABLE 9.1
PROBIT ANALYSIS OF THE LITIGATION OR SETTLEMENT DECISION
(DEPENDENT VARIABLE=0 IF LITIGATED, 1 IF SETTLED)

Variable	Coefficient Estimate	Standard Error	Partial Derivative of the Probability, Evaluated at the Mean of the Dependent Variable
(1) Constant (C)	13.975	5.576***	—
Market share, acquiring firm (MS1)	.035	.016**	.012
Market share, acquired firm (MS2)	.023	.013*	.008
Four-firm concentration ratio (CR4)	−.015	.010	−.005
Duration of case in months (MO)	−.025	.006***	−.009
Nominal interest rate (R)	.343	.196*	.120
Agency (AG)	−.247	.302	−.086
Year case began (YR)	−.203	.089**	−.071
(−2.0)×log of likelihood ratio =31.3, 7 degrees of freedom.			
(2) C	4.519	5.237	—
Sales, acquiring firm	.000004	.001	.000001
Sales, acquired firm	−.00017	.001	−.001
MO	.023	.006***	.008
R	.125	.224	.044
AG	−.535	.320*	−.186
YR	−.051	.089	−.018
(−2.0)×log of likelihood ratio=22.5, 6 degrees of freedom.			

NOTES: For the two-tail t test, asterisks denote that the coefficient is significantly different from zero at the 1 percent (***), 5 percent (**), and 10 percent (*) confidence levels. The number of observations for (1) is 111, for (2) is 98.

acquiring firms have a consistent and significant impact, which indicates that the larger the monopoly loss, the larger the probability that a case will be settled rather than litigated.[13] This is consistent with the simple model of welfare maximization, where the probability of victory and the size of the monopoly loss associated with a settlement are assumed independent of the unremedied monopoly loss. In fact, the FTC and the Justice Department may have made this simplistic assumption when evaluating the impact of the size of consumer harm on settlement or litigation decision.

However, if we employ the more realistic assumptions used to derive equation (4), we find that the agencies have acted diametrically opposed to consumer interests. In particular, recall that if the probability of victory increases with a larger expected monopoly loss, and if settlement costs are proportional to the monopoly loss, then a welfare-maximizing agency will increase the proportion of cases it litigates—*not* decrease the proportion as the simple model predicts and as our results indicate.

The elasticity of the probability of victory with respect to a change in the market share of the acquiring company is positive, and it falls in the elastic range $(\partial d/\partial C_L \cdot C_L/d = 1.63)$.[14] In other words, as long as market share is a good proxy for potential monopoly loss, then the larger the potential monopoly loss, the more likely the agency is to win in litigation. Therefore equation (4) is negative. Thus, agencies should litigate a higher proportion of the cases that have larger monopoly losses, contrary to what they appear to have done.

The other variables in our empirical model are also of interest, although they do not directly test the welfare-maximization model. The negative coefficient on Agency (AG) in Table 9.1 suggests, albeit weakly, that the FTC on average is more likely to litigate than the Justice Department. It is surprising that any difference in the litigation or settlement outcome would exist if both enforce the merger law with an eye to maximizing consumer welfare. The FTC is an independent commission with different adjudication procedures than the Justice Department (which is part of the executive branch). It is possible that different institutional incentives may encourage or enable more litigation at the FTC.

The last independent variable, the year the case was litigated, is introduced to pick up any secular trends in the litigation or settlement decision. It is consistently positive and frequently significant at the 5 percent confidence level, implying that there has been a trend toward litigating a higher proportion of cases over time. This result may explain why we observe a much smaller percentage of cases being won by the antitrust agencies in our sample than in the pre-1969 sample discussed by George Priest and Benjamin Klein. As these authors point out, prior to 1969 both the FTC and the Justice Department won 81 percent of their cases—far more than the Klein and Priest model of wealth maximizing litigants predicts.[15] In our sample, 45 percent of the cases were won by the agencies, suggesting that the case selection by the agencies changed during the 1970s and that the agencies may be selecting cases in a manner more consistent with Priest and Klein's model—and thus less consistent with Posner's version of the budget constraint model or the model that agencies select cases for litigation to maximize the number of agency victories.

To test an alternative to our welfare-maximizing model, we added a budget variable to the estimating equation. The variable is equal to the inflation-adjusted annual budget for one of the agencies, depending on which agency brought the case. The results shown in Table 9.2 are representative of various

TABLE 9.2
PROBIT ANALYSIS OF THE LITIGATION OR
SETTLEMENT DECISION WITH BUDGET VARIABLE
(DEPENDENT VARIABLE=0 IF LITIGATED, 1 IF SETTLED)

Variable	Coefficient Estimate	Standard Error	Partial Derivative of the Probability, Evaluated at the Mean of the Dependent Variable
C	1.799	.991*	—
Agency budget	−.000041	.000027	−.143
MS1	.037	.017**	.129
MS2	.028	.014**	.097
CR4	−.013	.010	−.045
MO	−.023	.005***	−.081
R	.111	.136	.039

(−2.0)×log of likelihood ratio=27.6, 6 degrees of freedom.

NOTES: See Table 9.1 and text for variable definitions. Asterisks denote that the coefficient is significantly different from zero at the 1 percent (***), 5 percent (**), and 10 percent (*) confidence levels. There are 112 observations.

specifications of the model that include the budget. As can be seen in this specification, the other variables we use are basically unaffected by the addition of the FTC or Justice Department budgets. The budget variable is not significant at normal confidence levels for the two-tail t test, although it is negative and significant at the 10 percent level for the one-tail t test. This weak relationship suggests that if the agencies' budgets are increased, the agencies will tend to litigate more cases. There is nothing in our model to indicate that such a relationship is optimal behavior on the part of the agencies. However, a budget increase will lower the antitrust officials' perceived administrative costs of litigation, assuming those officials always spend all of the money allotted them by Congress. Under these circumstances, significant increases in the budget of the agencies are unlikely to lead to an optimal proportion of litigated and settled cases, but are more likely to lead to too many cases being litigated. Moreover, the rapid expansion of Justice Department and FTC budgets during the 1970s may have initiated the trend from too high a proportion of victories prior to 1969 to a proportion of victories smaller than predicted by the Priest and Klein model. More theoretical and empirical research is needed before this last hypothesis can be confirmed.

Conclusion

In testing a model of a welfare-maximizing antitrust agency, we find that in several respects the FTC and Justice Department act consistently with the promotion of economic efficiency and welfare maximization. However, the most realistic model we test suggests that in at least one aspect—the effect of unremedied monopoly loss on the probability of litigation—the antitrust agencies' actions have not been those of a social welfare-maximizing agency. Between 1969 and 1981 the agencies' behavior in this critical aspect of the settlement or litigation decision may simply have been the naive response of administrators who intended to maximize social welfare, but who did not fully realize the complex nature of the problem. However, there is also some evidence that more litigation may have been the result of increased budgets during the 1970s, not necessarily the result of agencies attempting to welfare maximize. More research will be needed to distinguish between these two possibilities and to develop alternative models of agency behavior that better explain how the settlement or litigation decision is made.

Appendix

The relationship between the probability of victory and the proxies for monopoly loss was also tested with a probit analysis. These results are presented in Table 9.3. The market share of the acquiring firm has a highly significant influence on the probability of victory. Evaluating this effect at the mean of the probability of victory and market share, the elasticity is 1.63.

Both year and agency variables are significant at the 10 percent level, showing that the FTC tends to win a higher percentage of its cases than the Justice Department. According to our estimate, the Justice Department and the FTC both seem to be losing more cases as time passes.

Notes

1. Hans Thorelli, *The Federal Antitrust Policy* (Baltimore, Md.: Johns Hopkins University Press, 1954), p. 168. See also Robert H. Lande, "Wealth Transfers as the Original and Primary Concern of Antitrust: The Efficiency Interpretation Challenged," *Hastings Law Journal* 34 (September 1982): 65–151.

2. Robert H. Bork, "The Legislative Intent and the Policy of the Sherman Act," *Journal of Law and Economics* 9 (1966): 7–48; Kenneth G. Elzinga, "Goals of Antitrust,"

TABLE 9.3

PROBIT ANALYSIS OF THE PROBABILITY

OF THE AGENCIES WINNING LITIGATION

(DEPENDENT VARIABLE = 1 IF CASE WON BY AGENCY, 0 IF LOST)

Variable	Coefficient	Standard Error	Partial Derivative of the Probability, Evaluated at the Mean of the Dependent Variable
Constant	35.300	16.174***	—
MS1	.185	.064***	.069
MS2	−.013	.049	−.005
MO	.0005	.012	.0002
R	−.138	.616	−.052
AG	1.772	1.036*	.664
YR	−.515	.266*	−.193
(−2.0)×log of likelihood ratio = 31.4.			

NOTES: See Table 9.1 and text for variable definitions. Asterisks denote that the coefficient is significantly different from zero at the 1 percent (***) and 10 percent (*) confidence levels. There are 40 observations.

University of Pennsylvania Law Review 125 (1977): 1191–1213; Timothy J. Muris, "The Efficiency Defense Under Section 7 of the Clayton Act," *Case Western Reserve Law Journal* 30 (1980): 381–432.

3. William Long, Richard Schramm, and Robert Tollison, "The Determinants of Antitrust Activity," *Journal of Law and Economics* 16 (1973): 351–64. See also Robert Masson and Robert Reynolds, "Statistical Studies of Antitrust Enforcement: A Critique" (Paper delivered before the American Statistical Society, 1977).

4. See William Baxter, "The Political Economy of Antitrust," in Robert D. Tollison, ed., *The Political Economy of Antitrust: Principal Paper by William Baxter* (Lexington, Mass.: Lexington Books, 1980); Kenneth W. Clarkson and Timothy J. Muris, eds., *The Federal Trade Commission Since 1970: Economic Regulation and Bureaucratic Behavior* (Cambridge, Eng.: Cambridge University Press, 1981); and Barry R. Weingast and Mark J. Moran, "Bureaucratic Discretion or Congressional Control? Regulatory Policymaking by the Federal Trade Commission" (Chapter 3 of this volume).

5. Alan Friedman, "An Analysis of Settlement," *Stanford Law Review* 22 (1969): 67–100; Jay Gould, "The Economics of Legal Conflict," *Journal of Legal Studies* 2 (1973): 279–300; William Landes and Richard Posner, "Adjudication as a Private Good," *Journal of Legal Studies* 8 (1979): 235–84; Richard A. Posner, "The Behavior of Administrative Agencies," *Journal of Legal Studies* 1 (1972): 305–347; Robert Cooter and Stephen Marks, with Robert Mnooking, "Bargaining in the Shadow of the Law: A Testable Model of Strategic Behavior," *Journal of Legal Studies* 11 (1982): 225–53;

George Priest and Benjamin Klein, "The Selection of Disputes for Litigation," *Journal of Legal Studies* 13 (1984): 1–76.

6. Posner, "Behavior of Administrative Agencies," p. 318. See also Baxter, "Political Economy of Antitrust." Posner argues that the prospect of a large loss induces the defendant to make a relatively generous offer that the agency finds acceptable, because the agency has little to gain from litigation.

7. There are three types of merger violations. First, horizontal mergers can directly increase concentration. Second, a challenge to the purchase of a substantial factor in the market by a "potential entrant" rests on the theory that the acquiring firm, on the verge of entry, holds in check the collusive tendencies of the firms already in the industry. Third, vertical mergers are challenged on the grounds of foreclosure of sources of supply and customers and because vertical integration can increase barriers to entry.

8. See F. M. Scherer, *Industrial Market Structure and Economic Performance*, 2d ed. (Chicago: Rand McNally, 1980), pp. 460–71.

9. Technically, this is when remedy is achieved, but we will assume compliance time is the same in both litigation and settlement.

10. It is reasonable to expect the market mechanisms over time to erode any market power obtained due to the merger as rivals react, entry occurs, and economic and technological conditions change. Scherer, *Industrial Market Structure*, pp. 114–17. As market power is eroded, the economic benefit from the antitrust intervention is also diminished.

11. Cooter and Marks, "Bargaining in the Shadow of the Law."

12. See also Posner, "Behavior of Administrative Law," and Cooter and Marks, "Bargaining in the Shadow of the Law."

13. This conclusion assumes that market structure is a good proxy for monopoly loss, as suggested in the 1984 Department of Justice *Merger Guidelines*. This assumption is subject to significant controversy, which we do not address in this chapter.

14. This is drawn from the empirical work in the Appendix.

15. See Priest and Klein, "Selection of Disputes," pp. 52–54. If the gains to each party are equal, Klein and Priest's model predicts litigation will occur only if the probability of winning is close to 0.5.

Chapter 10

The Pyrrhic Victories
of Section 7:
A Political Economy Approach

ROBERT A. ROGOWSKY

CRITICIZING federal antitrust enforcement has been popular sport for most of this century. From every angle, antitrust has been scrutinized and found wanting. An abundant literature dissects "significant" cases to point out specific failures.[1] Attempts to correlate antitrust enforcement with crude estimates of monopoly and welfare loss in the economy find enforcement misguided.[2] A separate literature analyzes the effectiveness of antimerger enforcement measured by equity value of the merging firms.[3] These studies consistently find no evidence that federal enforcement effectively targets mergers that will lead to monopoly power.[4] Studies evaluating the effectiveness of relief accomplished in monopoly and merger cases have uniformly found that even when they win the opinions, the agencies consistently lose the decrees.[5] Repair of competitive injury—society's desired antitrust output—is given short shrift by the agencies.

Two recent studies by the author, requiring detailed case-by-case analysis of the entire antimerger caseload of the Federal Trade Commission (FTC) and the Justice Department's Antitrust Division from 1968 through 1982, bring a more detailed view of the nature of antitrust enforcement. The first study examined how closely merger policy followed the Justice Department's 1968 merger guidelines.[6] Of the horizontal and vertical merger cases brought after 1967,

The author would like to thank William Breit, Ken Elzinga, and Fred McChesney for helpful comments. The conclusions set forth in this paper are those of the author and do not necessarily reflect those of the Federal Trade Commission or of individual commissioners.

fully 21 percent fell below the market share standards. More important, the cases could not be justified by the special exceptions outlined in the guidelines, which indicated a trend toward concentration or the acquisition of a particularly "disruptive" force in the market.[7] Nor could they be explained by other extenuating circumstances, such as high concentration, size of the firms, particularly high entry barriers, a history of price-fixing or other special characteristics, or mergers involving leading firms.

Evidence from the caseload suggests no reliable quantitative benchmarks guiding enforcement. Mergers of small firms with small market shares, with no significant impediments to entry, and in deconcentrating markets have been attacked rather consistently.[8]

Limiting prosecution by setting market-share benchmarks is of little use when prosecutors can define the markets within which those numerical benchmarks are calculated. The markets in many above-guideline cases are suspect: for instance, independent bookstores in Cleveland, artificial Christmas trees over two feet tall, importation and sale of bananas in Los Angeles, or retail frozen dessert pies.[9] If bagged dry-mix concrete in the Washington/ Baltimore area, beer production in Kentucky, or "quality" frozen dinner entrees,[10] in fact, too narrowly confine the true areas of effective competition, the caseload appears even worse than the numbers suggest.

The second study looked at the backside of merger enforcement—that is, what was done to repair the competitive injury.[11] One hundred and four cases filed since 1968 achieved relief, or efforts were terminated by 1981. Judged on the independence, viability, and competitive effectiveness of the divested assets, the relief in each case was rated "successful," "sufficient," "deficient," or "unsuccessful." Sixty-eight of the 104 cases fell into the deficient or unsuccessful categories. Incorporating time into the evaluation of the remedy (on average, the government required more than five years to undo a merger), nearly 70 percent of the cases fell into the unsuccessful category; an additional 21 percent were rated deficient.

A second part of the study focused on the subsample of cases where substantial relief was achieved. A single criterion—barriers to entry—was used to judge the economic merit of each case. By this measure only a dozen cases were not shown to be devoid of any economic merit. (A little research into any of these is likely to eliminate them as well.) The point is clear: merger enforcement since 1968 has left unlawful acquisitions largely unrepaired, and thankfully so, since the vast majority of the mergers would not lessen competition at all, let alone lessen competition substantially.

Efforts to discern an economic explanation for poor relief were unsuccessful.[12] Ordinary least squares estimation was used to investigate factors that prolong relief. Probit and multinominal logit estimation regressed effectiveness rankings against various models based on structural variables. No systematic influences were found on relief stemming from the structure of the firms or conditions of the market. The data could only indicate that the Justice Department tends to get more successful compliance, but that overall, compliance has gotten worse over time.

The bulk of antitrust enforcement is unnecessary and unsatisfactory. Many cases are plainly ludicrous. Moreover, the government has been imposing remedies in antitrust cases for more than 70 years. Nevertheless, efforts to remedy anticompetitive mergers persistently prove disappointing. Lacking an explanation based on the economic factors of the cases, attention must focus on institutional factors driving the agencies. This paper argues a bureaucracy theory of antitrust output that explains the peculiar caseload and ineffective relief characterizing antitrust for so many decades.

Bureaucratic Management of Antitrust

A rapidly growing literature investigates decisionmaking in public agencies.[13] Most analyses set up "the bureaucrat" as the agency decisionmaker, maximizing a single variable, monotonic, twice differentiable utility function.[14] Imperfect control by the public allows the bureaucrat discretion over the output of the agency. Typically, the bureaucrat's goal variable is the budget, the size of the bureau (staff), or an output-residual combination that allows for utility extracted in the form of costly expenses such as perquisites, salary, or lobbying activity.[15] In this framework the productivity and output of the bureau is geared toward specific goal maximization. Yet, perhaps the most useful insight into the theory of public bureaucracy is that organizations are hierarchies of decisionmakers, each with his own set of goals and motives.[16] "The bureaucrat" is only the last stage in the hierarchy.

In a large organization, authority must be delegated and information processed at relatively low levels in the structure. Goal distortion occurs as self-interested utility maximizers at each level make decisions and generate information for final decisionmakers at higher levels. Information reaching top management strongly reflects the biases of the lower-level managers who furnish it. The bounded rationality of the top-level decisionmakers resulting from the vast amount of information necessary to make fully informed decisions permits a nontrivial degree of discretion to arise at each level of the hierarchy. Outcomes are biased toward the maintenance or extension of the internal organization. Bureaucratic decisionmakers are constrained from below by the preferences of the staff and their control over information.

Roger Faith, Donald Leavens, and Robert Tollison (Chapter 2 of this volume) and Barry Weingast and Mark Moran (Chapter 3) have added legislative influence to bureaucratic decisionmaking. Their findings dispute the traditional bureaucratic approach, which sees agencies as having substantial discretion due to inadequate congressional control. Both studies find, as Weingast and Moran put it, "significant and important influences by the relevant Congressional subcommittees."

In fact, it is quite clear that legislative influence is present and can be detected in agency actions. However, these studies focus on relatively gross measurements of congressional control. Faith et al. focus on the number of favorable decisions (that is, dismissals in regions represented by congressmen in committees with some type of direct influence over the FTC). Weingast and Moran look at how the political leanings of the influential committees (that is, ADA rating) altered the composition of the aggregate FTC caseload. For instance, a higher average ADA rating among influential committees brought more consumer-oriented cases, such as under the Fair Credit Reporting Act. Hence, while congressional influence is real, that influence appears in a crude form, either in particular favors or in broad swings in the direction of activity. Within this constraint, there is still substantial leeway for bureaucratic discretion. As a consequence, bureaucratic decisionmaking is influenced from above—by congressional oversight—and from below—by the heavy reliance bureaucrats must place on their staffs.

Cotton Lindsay further improves our understanding of bureaucratic behavior by distinguishing between visible and invisible bureau output.[17] This distinction helps explain the limits of congressional oversight. Congress is presumably interested in pleasing its constituents, and this means getting as much output as possible at the least cost. In other words, productivity is Congress' goal for its agencies.

When bureaucratic output is difficult to measure, Congress must estimate productivity through some crude output proxy. Astute bureaucrats will divert resources to the production of the attributes that will be monitored from those that will not. Increasing the visible output of the bureau increases the perceived effectiveness of the agency. The diminution of the invisible output, that for which the bureau was actually established, does not substantially diminish the perceived value of the bureau's effort. Consumers of the agency's product can influence the bureau's revenue stream only through the political system. So long as Congress sees the visible output being supplied, and possibly increased, appropriations will continue and probably increase.[18]

Combined with the separate incentives of the individuals within the organization, the incentive for bureaucrats to pursue visible output can lead to substantial divergence from the original goals of the agency and the expectations of its constituency. The primary function of this paper is not to extend the theory of bureaucracy. Its purpose is to consider the machinery of antitrust enforcement in light of what is known about bureaucratic behavior and to learn why the federal agencies persistently generate poor cases and ineffective relief. The two antitrust agencies are composed of the staff attorneys, the middle managers overseeing the case generation and litigation functions of the staff, and the top-level decisionmakers. Final prosecution and policy decisions are made at this last level. The following section outlines the incentive structure for staff attorneys and for the different levels of management. It is shown that case selection and remedy are victims of the reward system in the bureaucracy.

Staff Attorneys

Staff attorneys in either agency are the front line in case generation. They uncover cases, conduct investigations, recommend filing of complaints, conduct litigation and settlement negotiations, and recommend and justify closing cases. The vast amounts of information generated in each case and the inability of managers to assimilate and scrutinize all the information gives the staff great sway in determining the overall caseload, the ultimate outcome of those cases, and, of course, the remedy achieved.

What motivates antitrust staff attorneys? Generally they fall into the category James Wilson calls "professionals" or that Leonard Riessman calls "functional bureaucrats."[19] These professionals seek and receive recognition and reward, tangible and intangible, from professional colleagues outside the government agency. Accomplishment is measured in terms of the professional quality of job performance, not in terms of bureaucratic goals. "The bureaucracy imposes certain well-defined limitations upon him, but within these he is professionally biased."[20]

Most entering attorneys see the government as a stepping-stone to more lucrative antitrust practice in the private bar. Government experience is valued not only for providing knowledge of antitrust laws and trial experience, but also because attorneys learn about the preferences and operating routines of the agencies. This knowledge is highly marketable. "In short, they viewed government service not as an ultimate career objective, but as a means to an end—a career in the private bar."[21]

The statistics bear this out. Between 1970 and 1976 the annual turnover rate of attorneys at the FTC ranged from 13 to 25 percent; 90 percent had a tenure of four years or less. At the end of fiscal 1976, there were only twenty of the nearly two hundred attorneys whose service dated from 1969. Eighty-nine percent of all attorneys who joined the commission between 1972 and 1975 expected (in July of 1976) to leave within two years.[22] Suzanne Weaver finds similar turnover rates for the Antitrust Division. In 1949 no departing attorneys were recorded as having left for private law firms or industry; in 1959, the figure was 4 out of 17; by 1964, 16 of 21 left for the private bar.[23]

The "professional" staff attorney recognizes that he does little to increase his own brand name capital by seriously striving to maximize consumer welfare, the "invisible" output of the agency, even if he could measure it. Instead, the antitrust prosecutor's output is measured by cases brought and completed (including settlements). Cases are the visible output by which enforcement productivity is measured and brand name capital created. Investigations, legal research, and development of legal and economic theories for large cases may be visible to immediate superiors in the bureau, but not easily visible to the outside profession—the future employers. Attorneys want maximum exposure to the private bar through trial time and settlement negotiations. Courtroom experience is especially valuable.[24]

Several consequences important for antitrust enforcement and remedy derive from the professional orientation of staff attorneys. Enthusiasm is focused on proving liability as attorneys demonstrate their legal talents in the courtroom or in settlement negotiations.[25] The invisible output is of less value and will receive less time. Attorneys may even shun these goals, since cases of substantial economic merit are frequently large structural matters requiring much effort with little visible output to show for it.[26] The small, simple cases attract lawyers, "cases that can be investigated and prosecuted in a reasonably brief period of time with maximum display of legal acumen."[27] Maximum exposure to the private bar and bolstering of one's prosecution record comes through being in charge of a case. For the young, entrepreneurial trial attorney, proprietary rights are most likely kept in a relatively small case concerning a straightforward violation.

It is, as one attorney suggested, easier to play the "market shares game," where one or both parties is a relatively small manufacturer concentrated in a local geographic market and in an easily recognized industry or product market. In such mergers, the small, local concentrated markets are identified quickly. It is easy to file the complaint, wrest some sort of settlement, dump it onto the compliance section, and go on to others.[28] Complaints by competitors reinforce this tendency by making cases easier to justify. Small firms especially fear the prospects of aggressive competition and predatory possibilities from national producers taking over local rivals. Industries "going national"—such as brewing, linen services, and vending, where large national companies are acquiring small and relatively inefficient local producers—are favorite targets. Economic theory might not recommend protecting these small competitors; utility-maximizing antitrust prosecutors can find it very attractive.

The implications for remedy are equally clear. The reward structure pushes attorneys toward visible output, but consumer welfare is an invisible output. The direct returns to staff attorneys from efforts expended in this direction are lower than in new case generation, and remedy tends to become an incidental part of a case.

The reward system that detours staff around consumer-welfare outcomes need not drive case selection and remedies. Safeguards can be imposed by a consumer-welfare-maximizing management, such as standards and procedures that enforce full consideration of remedies. In fact, the incentive structure of the managers and the top decisionmakers reinforces the biases found in the staff. It is to the bureaucratic structure nurturing poor case selection and ineffective relief that we now turn.

Managers

Both the FTC and Antitrust Division have similar bureaucratic layers above staff attorneys. Section chiefs in the Antitrust Division direct and supervise the staff. Above the section chiefs is the director of operations, who reviews and processes requests for complaint. Finally, there is the assistant attorney general in charge of the Antitrust Division.

At the FTC the legal staff is divided into "shops," each headed by an assistant director reporting to the bureau director. Above all, and separated necessarily because of their judicial role, are the five commissioners. Cases are generated by staff and assistant directors but must pass through an evaluation committee (headed by the bureau director), which can decide to initiate or expand investigations, request compulsory process (subpoena power), or recommend a complaint to the commission.

Middle management (that is, the section chiefs of the Antitrust Division and assistant directors of the FTC) maximize a utility function with pecuniary and nonpecuniary elements. One nonpecuniary element is the recognition received as a result of aggressive and successful prosecution.[29] Recognition comes from managing a productive shop and enforcing the laws through active prosecution.

Output is measured by the number of successful challenges to unlawful mergers. Certainly skilled handling of a large, well-publicized merger may be superior to a single small merger in terms of visible output. It will also absorb more resources. A section chief or assistant director will want to minimize the percentage of staff bogged down in large, complicated structural matters when for the same resources many less complex cases could be tackled. It is logical, and found to be true by both Weaver and Katzmann, that section chiefs and assistant directors are significant forces for case generation. They are eager to find cases, authorize investigations, and ensure that these investigations bear "prosecutorial fruit."[30]

The commissioners and assistant attorney generals are the chief prosecutors (that is, the decisionmaking "bureaucrat" set up in analyses of bureaucratic behavior). Each is ultimately responsible for the decision to file complaints and close cases, accept the relief proposed in consent decrees, and enforce compliance with remedy orders handed down by the courts. They frequently come to the government with an eye toward implementing pet beliefs about antitrust.[31] Innovative prosecutorial directions are usually born with substantial fanfare. Expectations are raised and cases must be brought, even dubious ones. Above all, however, each is entrusted with upholding the antitrust statutes. These forces combine to create a substantial incentive to file cases.

In summary, whatever antitrust bureaucrats maximize, it is purchased through the budget. The budget, in turn, is maximized by offering substantial visible output. In the case of the antitrust agencies, visible output means aggressive prosecution. Congress cannot directly measure the economic welfare generated by antitrust enforcement. Except for a few cases of notoriety, such as the Antitrust Division suit against IBM Corporation or the Mobile-Marathon merger challenged by the FTC, the consumer welfare gained through antitrust is estimated by the sheer number of cases brought by each agency. A large number of cases demonstrates a need for more funding to carry on the work of the agency and to expand into new and innovative areas. Each level of the antitrust bureaucracy has an incentive to maximize the visible output—that is, to generate cases.[32]

IMPLICATIONS FOR REMEDY

Several predictions fall logically from the antitrust bureaucracies' incentive structure: (1) case generation outweighs proper case selection to address true market problems;[33] (2) proving liability in a given case is more important than formulating and implementing effective relief; and (3) the disposition of cases will always accord with maximizing the visible output of the agency—that is, any resolution that contributes to visible output is preferred to a failure or dropping of a case. The first prediction is well answered in the abundant literature criticizing antitrust. The remainder of this section focuses on the second two predictions.

Overemphasis on Liability

Two encounters neatly summarize why antitrust officials have failed to emphasize relief adequately. Explained one attorney: "We spent so much time proving the violation that we never got around to devising a remedy. We put together about three paragraphs at the end of the [trial] brief." Another candid litigator noted: "I really don't care what happens to the assets after the trial; that's not my department."[34]

The attitude is built into the structure of the agencies. In 1978, for instance, the Antitrust Division had roughly 390 attorneys. Seventeen, or approximately 4 percent, were assigned to the Judgment Section, which oversees compliance. Since some litigation comes from the Judgment Section, the number of attorneys actively enforcing orders is even smaller. In that year, the FTC's Bureau of Competition included approximately 210 attorneys. About sixteen, or 7.5 percent, worked in the Compliance Division.

One of the most glaring examples of misplaced emphasis is found in the El Paso Natural Gas case, in which the Justice Department was reprimanded by the Supreme Court for failure to develop and pursue adequate relief.[35] In the words of one participant:

> Divestiture hearings began [in] 1967, with intervention granted at the outset to 29 new parties, which included most of the western states and all of the customers of El Paso. There were also ten applicants to acquire the new company who, although not admitted as parties, were required by the Court to fully present their respective qualifications, test the El Paso plan, develop an alternative divestiture plan, and detail how they would operate the new company and particularly how they intended to reinstitute competition in the relevant markets. The Court was required to put such reliance and burden on the applicants because the Justice Department failed to provide the much-needed assistance required by the Court. Despite the recent public chastisement of the [Justice] Department by the Supreme Court for "knuckling under" in the first divestiture proceeding . . . Justice provided only one lawyer with no staff support or prior familiarity with the case. This lawyer, known as "lone government counsel," while competent and diligent, was completely outgunned by El Paso's battery of experienced counsel and large staff support.

Subsequent divestiture efforts were lengthy in part because "the lack of government assistance and the Supreme Court directives materially reduced the required flexibility and resourcefulness of the court to meet the complex issues and circumstances."[36]

It is worth noting the incentive structures that concern the formulation of remedies facing opposing counsel. While complaint counsel generally tend to emphasize liability over remedy, counsel for respondents are paid to minimize the impact, or harm, of the government's challenge. Either victory in the courts or minimal relief measures will accomplish this end. It follows that counsel for respondents will more diligently emphasize their alternative remedy proposals, wresting a degree of victory on remedy from the jaws of defeat on liability. Over 20 percent of the government's legal victories in antimerger cases since 1968 ended with either token divestiture or no structural relief at all; the remedy in more than 65 percent of the cases could be branded deficient.[37]

Judicial Reluctance to Impose Effective Relief

The courts have been charged with undue reluctance to reorganize corporate entities as an antitrust remedy. This reluctance, it is claimed, is because some courts believe that structural relief is overly punitive and that relief directed at the conduct alone is sufficiently effective in dissipating illegal market power.[38]

The consumer-welfare benefits of restoring workable competition by reorganizing corporations are indirect, even abstract. The direct losses to the firm, its employees, and its shareholders are tangible and can appear more compelling. When, as in the case of El Paso, the more difficult argument for consumer welfare is undertaken lightly by the prosecuting agency, it is not surprising that the substantial efforts marshalled by respondents might sway judges toward less drastic and possibly less effective relief measures.[39]

Are the courts, in fact, reluctant to use structural relief? Base on antimerger enforcement between 1968 and 1982, the answer is no. In seventeen antimerger cases that reached a litigated order since 1968 (excluding preliminary injunctions), all but one ordered some form of divestiture.[40] Of these, 70 percent ordered full or virtually full divestiture. One other ordered the creation of a new firm from the scrambled assets of the merged companies. In contrast, only 30 percent of the consent decrees accepted by antitrust officials have approached full divestiture. Sixty percent of the consent decrees accepted partial divestiture. Half of them accepted divestiture of less than half the acquired assets. About 13 percent of the consented partial divestitures could be described as *de minimis*—divesting less than 10 percent of the acquired assets. Another 10 percent resulted in no structural relief at all. One might conclude that the courts have feared reorganizing firms only in the sense that they preferred full divestiture of the acquired, market-tested entity over the piecemeal divestitures and regulatory relief frequently accepted by antitrust officials in their many consent decrees.[41]

Weak or Meritless Cases

The predominance of cases lacking any substantive economic merit goes a long way toward explaining the poor relief found in the sample. A case with no economic merit is not automatically doomed to weak relief. Even a procompetitive merger can be undone. However, many instances of relief rated deficient or unsuccessful by structural criteria are hampered by poorly designed orders, unmarketable assets, substantially changed market condition, or other factors that reflect squarely on the economic merits of the case.

A simple and common scenario ties the weak case, partial divestiture, and consent decrees into ineffective relief. A merger is challenged. Initial estimates of the concentration ratios and market shares meet the merger guidelines. Initial findings, however, may not hold. Alleged relevant product market may prove unrealistic, or the economic conditions may change or are inadequately understood. In the Converse Rubber Corp. case, for example, the Justice Department negotiated a divestiture that was destined to fail because foreign competition was "murdering the hell" out of domestic firms.[42]

Government antitrust attorneys will avoid bringing to trial an exceptionally weak case. As one veteran enforcer put it: "Many young attorneys do not want to take the cases they have to trial, to face high-powered defense counsel and industry experts. As the trial nears, settlement becomes more attractive."[43] Similarly, to avoid a record of embarrassing losses, the management structure will support expeditious disposal of weak cases.

In cases involving the asphalt roofing industry, the FTC accepted the divestiture of only one of three acquired asphalt roofing plants. Competition was certainly undamaged by the merger or diminutive remedy, since there has been "substantial and almost continual entry at least since 1960." At least eight de novo entries occurred between 1960 and 1973. After that, the pace quickened; four new firms entered by 1978, with more considering entry. It was shown that single-plant firms have cost advantages over multiplant firms. Firms were entering with capital investments no greater than $1 million (although one new entrant began production in Alabama, the heart of the violated geographic market, with $2.4 million).[44] The FTC decided that the sale of the Alabama plant to another asphalt roofing manufacturer was preferable to trial or dismissal.

Small market share makes a case weak on both economic and legal grounds, and complaint counsel may be reluctant to risk losing it in court. A paltry divestiture might seem preferable to trial in a case like Bohack, Inc., where 2.6 percent of the market acquired 0.9 percent; or Walter Kidde, where a firm with 6.3 percent of the lockset production joined with 2.9 percent; or Occidental Petroleum, where less than 1 percent of capacity picked up 6.4 percent of the diamonium phosphate market.[45] In each of these cases the government settled for small partial divestitures.[46]

Complaint counsel may hesitate to litigate an acquisition of obsolete assets. In the Western Farmers suit, the processing plant could not meet the latest health standards. The divestiture order was eventually rescinded and the plant razed. In the case of Movielab, the acquired assets had been made obsolete by new technology; a court-appointed trustee was unable to dispose of them. The divestiture of the theaters in the General Cinema decision was abandoned for several reasons, among them the fact that nearly thirteen new rival theaters (with 30 new screens) entered during the four years of divestiture efforts. More important, as one economist in the Antitrust Division noted, "the high cost of operating old, large structures in the downtown area, makes the operation of [these] downtown theaters unprofitable under terms of the current leases." As another example, the Justice Department challenged the acquisition by G. Heileman Brewing of three breweries, alleging that Kentucky constituted a relevant geographic market. After considering the theory for a year, complaint counsel accepted an offer to divest a trade name and/or capacity equal to roughly one-third that of one of the three acquired plants. More recently, in the Crane Company settlement, the cement plant targeted for divestiture was eventually sold to the nation's largest cement producer. The horizontal divestiture was justified on the grounds that the purchaser had the expertise and financial resources to rebuild the obsolete facility.[47]

Another indication that any settlement may be preferable to litigation might be the length of time between the filing of the complaint and the settlement order. A case that drags on for years without reaching trial, especially a rather straightforward horizontal merger, is withheld from court for some reason. Defendants are typically blamed for manipulating the adjudication process to prolong cases. That argument is not always persuasive, since many matters never get beyond settlement negotiations.

Consider the two separate challenges against acquisitions by Leggett and Platt (LP).[48] In 1968 and 1969, LP acquired two bedspring and innerspring manufacturers in Cincinnati and Detroit. LP had annual "springs" sales east of the Rockies of approximately $12 million. The sales of the acquired firm totaled $5.4 million. A complaint was filed in early 1971 (charging, among other things, that the acquisition would permit LP multiplant economies of scale). In 1972 LP, with annual metal bed-rail sales of $1.4 million, acquired Metal Bed-Rail Company of Lexington, North Carolina, with sales of $1.9 million. In January 1978 both cases were settled.

The bed-rail merger left the owner of the acquired company the largest stockholder and on the board of directors of LP. His intransigence (he "would not sit still for the divestiture of his company"[49]) turned the Justice Department to replacement relief: a single plant in Oklahoma, sans any marketing and distribution system necessary to sell the product. In the sister case, the Cincinnati plant was ordered divested. New entry had caused the business to decay and in 1980 the plant sold as vacant real estate.

It is unlikely that any defendant wants to divest unlawfully acquired assets, hence the legal process to force divestiture. Yet some cases seem destined never to see the courtroom. Why was LP allowed to "negotiate" for up to seven years before being "forced" to divest minor assets? In other cases, why was Guardian Industries allowed to negotiate for three years before having to divest five auto-glass shops in the Cleveland area? Parker-Hannifen held the Schulz Tool and Manufacturing Company five years under a hold-separate order before it agreed to divest sixteen separate component lines. Walter Kidde settled after five years for the sale of machinery for a single product line of locksets and lock assemblies. Kaiser Steel negotiated for three and a half years before agreeing to keep the acquired assets but charge "reasonable" prices. The Antitrust Division negotiated for over five years before United Artists Theatres agreed to divest within five years 24 theaters of 85 acquired in the New York metropolitan area.[50]

Minimal relief settlements play an important role in the antitrust bureaucracy. Bureaucracies fear failure and criticism. This fear can reveal itself in "persistence behavior." Once a program like an antitrust case has been started, there is a natural resistance to terminating it. Sunk costs need to be justified; the decision to proceed is transformed into a commitment to succeed, whatever the cost. "Sequential decisionmaking procedures, designed to permit project review on the merits, if they exist at all, are often overwhelmed by partisan appeals due to the tie-in of advocacy and administration."[51]

Staff attorneys who have invested time in an investigation are reluctant to close it without some visible output, even where the merits do not justify action.[52] This persistence finds favor in the antitrust bureaucracies because the agencies are similarly biased. "If the . . . administrative system has committed itself in advance to the correctness and efficiency of its reform, it cannot tolerate learning of failure."[53]

In simple terms, any case is better than no case. Antitrust agencies cannot expect to justify increased appropriations with a record dominated by legal defeats and closed investigations. Nor do they have to try. Consent decrees are a way to avoid litigating meritless cases without losing any output—a sort of "easy victory" policy.[54] Respondents, complaint counsel, and the enforcing agency are all better off. The effect on consumer welfare is less clear.

The settlement of the Nestle Alimentana case is a stark example.[55] In 1973 Nestle acquired the Stouffer Corporation for over $100 million. The FTC alleged that Nestle, through its subsidiary Libby, was a potential entrant into a national "frozen entree" product market and into a secondary "quality frozen entree" submarket. Six years later Nestle agreed to divest within one year a frozen-prepared-foods facility in Wisconsin. The plant had been used solely as a cold storage warehouse since 1973. It was sold for $10 million to a processor of canned and frozen vegetables.

The divestiture had virtually no relevance to the alleged violation, was of extremely small proportions, and involved a minor storage facility that had never been a part of Stouffer. The justification for the relief was made clear, however, by staff counsel arguing for the settlement:

> By any standard, the relief falls short of effective remedy in an unlawful acquisition case. When one considers, however, that after almost six years of

investigation the staff has failed to develop evidence of unlawful adverse competitive effect and the case stands on the threshold of dismissal, the relief obtained is better than no relief at all. It is in this spirit that the proposed settlement is tendered to the Commission.[56]

It was also in this spirit that the consent was accepted.

After exhaustive and unsuccessful efforts to develop either a theory or evidence of any adverse effect, why was the case not dismissed? Dismissals are failures. The consent allowed the case to be counted in the successfully completed settlements category. If the same bureaucratic rationale can be attributed to the majority of consent settlements of small proportions, of obsolete assets, or in declining or aggressively competitive industries, the pervasiveness of the motive becomes clear.

CONCLUSION

Enforcement bureaus have aggressively and persistently attacked small mergers, acquisitions of obsolete assets, and mergers in industries where the possibility of injury to competition is exceedingly slight. Moreover, agencies have historically been ineffective in repairing what injury to competition they do uncover. These perplexing phenomena are in large part explained by the mechanism that generates them. The popular convention that bureaucrats are inefficient and ineffective is misleading. It is important to identify what output antitrust bureaucrats are trying to produce. It is evident that the antitrust agencies and their officials, like good entrepreneurs, have been quite successful at generating the output that maximizes their own welfare. This is not necessarily the output that maximizes consumer welfare.

NOTES

1. As just one recent example, see Ernest Gellhorn, "Regulatory Reform and the Federal Trade Commission's Antitrust Jurisdiction," *Tennessee Law Review* 49 (1982): 471–510.

2. William Long, Richard Schramm, and Robert Tollison, "The Determinants of Antitrust Activity," *Journal of Law and Economics* 16 (1973): 351–64; John Siegfried, "The Determinants of Antitrust Activity," *Journal of Law and Economics* 18 (1975): 559–81. Some valid criticisms of the methodology appear in Robert Masson and Robert Reynolds, "Statistical Studies of Antitrust Enforcement: A Critique" (Paper delivered before the American Statistical Society, 1977).

3. J. C. Ellert, "Antitrust Law Enforcement and the Behavior of Stock Prices," *Journal of Finance* 715 (1976): 715–32; R. Stillman, "Examining Antitrust Policy

Toward Horizontal Mergers," *Journal of Financial Economics* 11 (1983): 225–40; B. E. Eckbo, "Horizontal Mergers, Collusion, and Stockholder Wealth," *Journal of Financial Economics* 11 (1983): 241–73; P. Wier, "The Cost of Antimerger Lawsuits," *Journal of Financial Economics* 11 (1983): 207–24.

4. Stock value indicators cannot distinguish between monopoly power and efficiency effects. Eckbo, "Horizontal Mergers," compares merger announcement impact with federal challenge impact and finds the former significant where the latter is not. He concludes that the merger releases valuable technological information while the government challenge is perceived as not harming the status of the firms.

5. The important studies include: Walter Adams, "Dissolution, Divorcement, and Divestiture: The Pyrrhic Victories of Antitrust," *Indiana Law Journal* 27 (Fall 1951): 1–36; Joseph Brodley, "Statement Before the National Commission to Review Antitrust Laws and Procedures," Mimeographed (Washington, D.C., October 26, 1978); Carl Kaysen, *United States v. United Shoe Machinery Corporation: An Economic Analysis of an Antitrust Case* (Cambridge, Mass.: Harvard University Press, 1956); Kenneth G. Elzinga, "The Antimerger Law: Pyrrhic Victories?" *Journal of Law and Economics* 12 (1969): 43–78; Milton Goldberg, "The Consent Decree: Its Formulation and Use," Occasional Paper no. 8 (East Lansing: Graduate School of Business, Michigan State University, 1962); Warren Greenberg, "Section 7 Relief," Unpublished manuscript (Federal Trade Commission, 1974); Kevin O'Conner, "The Divestiture Remedy in Sherman Act Section 2 Cases," *Harvard Journal of Legislation* 13 (1976): 698–775; Malcolm R. Pfunder, Daniel Plaine, and David Whittemore, "Compliance with Divestiture Orders Under Section 7 of the Clayton Act: An Analysis of the Relief Obtained," *Antitrust Bulletin* 17 (1972): 19–180; National Commission to Review the Antitrust Laws and Procedure, *Report to the President* (Washington, D.C.: GPO, January 22, 1979), pp. 114–39; Robert A. Rogowsky, "An Economic Study of Antimerger Remedies" (Ph.D. diss., University of Virginia, May 1982).

6. Robert A. Rogowsky, "The Department of Justice Merger Guidelines: A Study in the Application of the Rule," *Research in Law and Economics* 6 (1984): 135–66.

7. U.S. Department of Justice, Antitrust Division, "Merger Guidelines," Washington, D.C., May 30, 1968.

8. For instance, in 1968 the FTC challenged the merger of two grocery retailers in New York City. One controlled 2.9 percent of the market and the other held 0.9 percent. The complaint recognized that in the nine preceding years the four-firm concentration ratio had declined from 41 percent to 34 percent. Nevertheless, the commission feared that the merger might slow the on-going process of deconcentration in the market. To make the point, we can jump to 1981. The commission filed a complaint and imposed a relief order on two grocery retailers in Los Angeles with a combined market share of 8.5 percent.

9. See, for example, United States v. Higbee Corp., 1971 Trade Cases ¶73,685; United States v. American Technical Industries, 1974 Trade Cases ¶74,873; In re United Fruit Co., 82 FTC 53 (1973); and United States v. Mrs. Smith's Pies, 440 F.Supp. 220 (1976).

10. See, for example, United States v. Flintkote, 1980-1 Trade Cases ¶64,032;

United States v. G. Heileman Brewing Co., 1973 Trade Cases ¶74,550; and In re Nestle Alimentana S.A., 94 FTC 122 (1979).

11. Robert A. Rogowsky, "The Economic Effectiveness of Section 7 Relief," *Antitrust Bulletin* 31 (Spring 1986): 187–233.

12. Ibid.

13. The literature goes back to Ludwig von Mises, *Bureaucracy* (New Haven, Conn.: Yale University Press, 1944), but modern analysis starts with William A. Niskanen, *Bureaucracy and Representative Government* (Chicago: Aldine-Atherton, 1971).

14. See, for example, Louis De Alessi, "An Economic Analysis of Government Ownership and Regulation," *Public Choice* 19 (1974): 1–42.

15. See Niskanen, *Bureaucracy*; Oliver E. Williamson, *The Economics of Discretionary Behavior: Managerial Objectives and the Theory of the Firm* (Englewood Cliffs, N.J.: Prentice-Hall, 1964); and Jean-Luc Migué and Gérard Bélanger, "Toward a General Theory of Managerial Discretion," *Public Choice* 17 (1974): 27–43.

16. See Kalman Cohen and Richard M. Cyert, *Theory of the Firm*, 2d ed. (Englewood Cliffs, N.J.: Prentice-Hall, 1975), ch. 17, and R. Joseph Monsen and Anthony Downs, "Large Managerial Firms," *Journal of Political Economy* 73 (1965): 221–36.

17. Cotton M. Lindsay, "A Theory of Government Enterprise," *Journal of Political Economy* 84 (October 1976): 1061–76.

18. See Kenneth W. Clarkson, "Legislative Constraints," in Kenneth W. Clarkson and Timothy J. Muris, eds., *The Federal Trade Commission Since 1970: Economic Regulation and Bureaucratic Behavior* (Cambridge, Eng.: Cambridge University Press, 1981). Clarkson concludes that "in addition to Congress's limited powers to control individual programs of the Commission, individual members, facing numerous competing interests, will lack the incentive to control most F.T.C. activities" (p. 32).

19. James Q. Wilson, *The Politics of Regulation* (New York: Basic Books, 1980), p. 379; Leonard Reissman, "A Study of Role Conceptions in Bureaucracy," *Social Forces* 27 (March 1949): 305–10. Two studies have examined in depth the antitrust-enforcement bureaucracies and found characteristics among the bulk of staff attorneys that support the assumptions made here. Suzanne Weaver, *Decision to Prosecute: Organization and Public Policy in the Antitrust Division* (Cambridge, Mass.: MIT Press, 1977); Robert A. Katzmann, *Regulatory Bureaucracy: The Federal Trade Commission and Antitrust Policy* (Cambridge, Mass.: MIT Press, 1980). See also Kenneth W. Clarkson and Timothy J. Muris, "Commission Performance, Incentives, and Behavior," in Clarkson and Muris, *Federal Trade Commission Since 1970*.

20. Reissman, "Role Conceptions in Bureaucracy," p. 309.

21. Weaver, *Decision to Prosecute*, pp. 39–40, 76.

22. See Clarkson and Muris, "Commission Performance, Incentives, and Behavior," p. 300.

23. Ibid., p. 185 n.7.

24. Katzmann, *Regulatory Bureaucracy*, p. 61, quotes one attorney: "For me, each complaint is an opportunity, a vehicle which someday could take me into the courtroom. I want to go to trial so badly that there are times when I overstate the possibilities which the particular matter might offer."

25. Attorneys with no intention of leaving the agency—in Wilson's terms the

"careerists"—have a reward structure similar to that of the "professionals." Reissman, "Role Conceptions in Bureaucracy," finds these "specialist bureaucrats" much like the functional bureaucrats but exhibiting a greater identification with the bureaucracy and the people in it. Generally more conservative about the rules and regulations, they nevertheless share goals similar to those of the "functional" attorneys: visible output—investigations, cases, and legal victories—to obtain promotions and positions of managerial responsibility within the bureau.

26. Katzmann, *Regulatory Bureaucracy*, found that attorneys "who are convinced that their advancement depends on the securing of trial experience, resist assignment to structural matters, which generally do not reach the courtroom for several years" (p. 29).

27. Wilson, *Politics of Regulation*, p. 379.

28. For instance, the court denied a preliminary injunction in United States v. Tidewater Marine (1968 Trade Cases ¶72,447), finding "virtually no barriers whatsoever to entry. Financing is readily available and anyone with a knowledge of boats or the oil industry, which knowledge abounds in this area, can enter the business with a capital investment as low as $5,000." Several hundred small firms had entered. Many large oil service companies also had begun servicing their own and other offshore drillers. The court found "no probability that the merger will lessen competition."

The Antitrust Division, undaunted, filed a complaint. Three and a half years later, the Justice Department settled for the divestiture of eight boats within three years. Forty-seven vessels had been acquired. The divestiture order intended to maintain capacity in the Gulf of Mexico market but ultimately reduced it. This fact is incidental since at the time of settlement, it was recognized that because "the market for such boats in the Gulf of Mexico was greatly depressed due to the diminished need for their services," the defendant would have trouble divesting itself of the eight boats. (Memorandum to Judgment Section File, "U.S. v. Tidewater Marine Services," June 1, 1972.)

American Cyanamid, 82 FTC 1220 (1973), is another example. In April 1971 Cyanamid acquired Shulton, Inc., manufacturer of a broad range of men's fragrance products, other men's toiletries, women's cosmetics and toiletries, and perfumes, among other products. Cyanamid was not a competitor, but its distribution network and heavy advertising outlays were believed to make it a potential entrant into the industry. There are no barriers to entry in the industry. Between 1973 and 1979 there were 38 new women's and 36 new men's entries into the fragrances market. (Victor Cohen, "American Cyanamid Company, Docket No. C-2381," Memorandum, n.d.) These entrants introduced approximately 112 (62 percent) of the fragrances introduced during that period. Suppliers do not need facilities since production is commonly contracted out. In 1973 the FTC settled for divestiture of two fragrance product lines: Burley and Manpower. The assets were sold a year later to Armour-Dial, a horizontal competitor with Shulton. Armour had substantial advertising expenditures and, of course, a large distribution network.

29. Nonpecuniary returns can easily be monetized by attorneys who can capture the quasi-rents of prestige and reputation.

30. As one attorney put it, "It is not the section chiefs who give you trouble. After all, they're 'in on it' to some extent" (Weaver, *Decision to Prosecute*, p. 101).

31. Such as Donald Baker's emphasis on challenging bank mergers, Donald Turner's interest in large structural cases, and Michael Pertschuk's interest in rulemaking.

32. The rule is not perfect, as is evident from the appointees under the Reagan administration. James C. Miller III, chairman of the FTC, and William Baxter, assistant attorney general of the Antitrust Division, entered their respective positions intent on limiting unnecessary and misguided antitrust enforcement efforts. Hence their incentives were to reduce the number of cases and, especially on the part of Miller, reduce the size and budget of the agency. On the other hand, see BNA *Regulatory and Legal Developments*, no. 139 (July 20, 1982): 19–21, in which Thomas Campbell, then director of the FTC's Bureau of Competition, discusses the most recent "big campaign to generate more cases."

33. United States v. American Steamship (1970 Trade Cases ¶73,233) and United States v. American Shipbuilding (1971 Trade Cases ¶74,261) offer striking examples of how small a part the economic merits can play in the decision to prosecute. In 1969 the largest bulk shipper on the Great Lakes, American Steamship Company (ASC), acquired the third and fifth largest self-loading bulk shippers, Reiss Steamship Company and Gartland Steamship Company, respectively. At first blush this merger had the appearance of a strong antitrust case. The acquisition bought ASC fifteen ships, increasing its revenue about $14 million and its market share about seven percentage points.

After being challenged by the FTC, ASC agreed to sell either the acquired Reiss Steamship Company or the eleven Reiss ships or equivalent ships in type and tonnage to those formerly owned by Reiss. Later the order was modified to allow ASC to sell fourteen ships, seven of which would be traded in to the rival American Shipbuilding Company as partial payment for a single new ship under construction. In the end, four others were sold to competitors, two for scrap, and another declared unfit for duty on the Great Lakes.

The rather dismal relief in this case is neither surprising nor important to preserving competition. The ships averaged 65 years of service and were less than one-third the size of competing vessels. Two had been out of service since 1968. In addition, the aging fleet was facing severe competition from Canadian ships and foreign ocean-going vessels entering through the St. Lawrence Seaway (which had captured more than 25 percent of the total tonnage on the Great Lakes). Substantial competition was felt from the railroads as well. Costs were rising and profits were suffering; Gartland experienced losses for the two years prior to the merger. Reiss' marginal profits were declining. By 1970 Congress amended the Merchant Marine Act of 1936 to promote cooperative efforts among domestic shippers toward replacement and modernization of the domestic fleet.

Nevertheless, when American Shipbuilding subsequently acquired nine vessels from Litton Systems, Inc., the Antitrust Division challenged that merger also, but felt that divestiture of any three would suffice (1971 Trade Cases ¶74,621).

34. For further discussion see U.S. General Accounting Office, *Closer Controls and Better Data Could Improve Antitrust Enforcement* (Washington, D.C., 1980), especially pp. 24–25.

35. United States v. El Paso Natural Gas Co., 376 U.S. 651 (1964). The story is told

by David Watkiss from his experience as chief counsel for the ultimately successful applicant for the purchase of the divested assets in that matter. See David K. Watkiss, "Statement Before the National Commission to Review Antitrust Laws and Procedures (NCRALP)," Mimeographed (Washington, D.C., September 12, 1978), pp. 4–5. The case was also noted in *Report to the President*, p. 125 n.34.

36. Watkiss, "Statement Before the NCRALP," p. 5.

37. Rogowsky, "Section 7 Relief."

38. *Report to the President*, p. 117.

39. Kaysen, *U.S. v. United Shoe Machinery*, concluded that "the natural tendencies of courts to be cautious in their approach to antitrust remedies is reinforced by the ill-considered and poorly presented plans which are often the contribution of the government to the proceedings on relief"; the government's relief case was "sketchy, poorly prepared, and failed to come to grips with any of the problems involved" (p. 343). Goldberg, "Consent Decree," p. 50, concedes that the courts are reluctant to provide effective divestiture or dissolution remedies, but he also points out that is true in part because of the gap in economic theory, poor presentation, and the lack of economic sophistication on the part of the government.

40. See Rogowsky, "Section 7 Relief." In the one exception, In re Litton Industries, Inc., 82 FTC 793 (1973), the commission ordered full divestiture and then vacated that order upon recommendation of the administrative law judge. It was shown that the merger would enhance competition.

41. Looking at an earlier sample of monopoly cases, Goldberg observed that consent decrees seldom include dissolution provisions. Goldberg, "Consent Decree," p. 55.

42. M. E. Jaffee, "U.S. v. Converse Rubber Corp.," Memorandum to Judgment Section File, July 1, 1976. The plant finally divested in 1977 and had gone under by 1980. United States v. Converse Rubber Corp., 1972 Trade Cases ¶74,101.

43. Interview with Charles McAleer, Special Negotiator, Antitrust Division, Washington, D.C., October 9, 1978.

44. See In re Bird and Sons, Inc., 87 FTC 411 (1976); Alan Fisher, "Analysis of the Asphalt Roofing Industry," Memorandum (Federal Trade Commission, April 1980), pp. 15–16; and In re Jim Walter Corp., 90 FTC 671, 704–6 (1977).

45. Since these data are taken from the respective complaints, they represent the maximum likely market shares assuming complaint counsel's alleged product markets. These instances do not stand alone. In sixteen cases the acquired company had 5 percent market share or less. Over 60 percent of this latter group were acquired by firms with 10 percent of the market or less. In re Bohack, Inc., 74 FTC 640 (1968); In re Walter Kidde and Co., 87 FTC 1401 (1976); In re Occidental Petroleum Corp., 74 FTC 1191 (1968). For an expansion on this topic, see Rogowsky, "Merger Guidelines."

The Walter Kidde settlement divested about 1.3 percent of the market, including a product line on which the patent had just expired. In the Occidental Petroleum case, that company had acquired Hooker Chemical in what the complaint termed a time of "temporary overcapacity" in diamonium phosphate, due in large part to "a recent invasion in the industry by petroleum companies" (p. 1194). One of the two diamonium phosphate plants ordered divested was closed for four years. At the time of the divestiture, overproduction and overcapacity were depressing prices and profits.

Despite substantial investment to start up the closed plant, it was shut down again in January 1976, "pending substantial improvement in market conditions for that product" (Beker Industries Corporation, *Annual Report*, 1977, p. 3).

46. For details, see Rogowsky, "Antimerger Remedies," appendix.

47. For details on all of these cases, see United States v. Western Farmers Association, Civ. No. 8150 (W.D. Washington, 1969); United States v. Movielab, 1974 Trade Cases ¶75,033; United States v. General Cinema, 4-71 Civ. 473 (D.C. Minnesota, 4th, 1973); Affidavit of Daniel Kelley, "U.S. v. General Cinema 4-71 Civ. 473," January 21, 1977; U.S. v. G. Heileman Brewing; and FTC v. In re Crane Co., 93 FTC 459 (1979).

48. United States v. Leggett and Platt, Inc., 1979-1 Trade Cases ¶62,453 and ¶62,610.

49. Interview with John Wilson, Judgment Section, Antitrust Division, October 10, 1978.

50. See United States v. Guardian Industries, 1976 Trade Cases ¶60,932; United States v. Parker-Hannifen, 1976 Trade Cases ¶61,099; In re Walter Kidde; In re Kaiser Steel Corp., 82 FTC 493 (1973); and United States v. United Artists Theatres Circuit, Inc., Civ. No. 71-C-609 (E.D.N.Y., 1976).

51. Oliver E. Williamson, *Markets and Hierarchies* (New York: The Free Press, 1975), pp. 121–22. See also Monsen and Downs, "Managerial Firms," p. 231.

52. Clarkson and Muris, "Commission Performance, Incentives, and Behavior," p. 291.

53. D. T. Campbell, "Reforms as Experiments," *American Psychologist* 24 (1969): 410; cited in Williamson, *Markets and Hierarchies*, p. 121.

54. See Rogowsky, "Merger Guidelines," p. 141.

55. In re Nestle Alimentana.

56. Memorandum to the Federal Trade Commission, "Nestle Alimentana, S.A. et al., Docket No. 9003" (n.d.), p. 23.

Chapter 11

The Regressive Nature of Civil Penalties

PHYLLIS ALTROGGE

& WILLIAM F. SHUGHART II

THE Federal Trade Commission (FTC), which enforces the Clayton, Sherman, and FTC Acts, has statutory authority to seek civil penalties in district court against firms found in violation of the commission's rules and orders. Although fines may be imposed on firms found not in compliance with certain antitrust orders, civil penalties have heretofore been assessed by the FTC only in consumer-protection matters. The provisions of the law that authorize such penalties are vague with respect to how the commission should determine the size of the fines it assesses; these provisions state only that penalties shall not exceed $10,000 for each violation, each day of noncompliance constituting a separate violation. In arriving at the total amount, the commission is instructed to consider "the degree of culpability, history of prior such conduct, ability to pay, effect on ability to continue to do business, and such other matters as justice may require."[1] Thus, the commission has substantial discretion in using fines as an enforcement device.

Most previous discussions of enforcement strategies for civil violations omit details about the implementation of monetary remedies. For example, Gary Becker, in his theoretical work on crime in general, pointed out that in

This paper was previously published under the same title in *International Review of Law and Economics* 4 (June 1984): 55–66. We are grateful to Robert Tollison, Richard Higgins, and two anonymous referees for comments on an earlier draft. The usual caveat applies. The views expressed here are those of the authors and do not necessarily represent those of the Federal Trade Commission, individual commissioners, or other staff.

focusing on optimal policies he had paid little attention to actual policies, although he believed a positive correspondence might exist between optimal and actual strategies.[2] In contrast, George Stigler suspected the difference between optimal and actual enforcement policies might be substantial for civil violations. As an example, he singled out the FTC's enforcement of truthful labeling for furs and textiles. According to Stigler, the commission in its annual report recites "scandals corrected and others still unrepressed, but neither offers nor possesses a criterion by which to determine the correct scale of its activities."[3]

Although much empirical work has been done in the area of criminal violations, we are not aware of any studies that have looked at civil violations.[4] There are no empirical analyses directed toward identifying whether the way in which civil penalties are actually assessed is consistent with optimal enforcement or even with the professed goals of the law-enforcement agencies. Nor have there been any tests of the responsiveness of offenders to changes in the allocation of enforcement resources and to the type and severity of punishment.[5]

In this paper we offer evidence on the factors that have entered into the determination of civil penalty amounts assessed historically by the FTC in its consumer-protection mission. Specifically, we test a prediction derived from the Stigler-Peltzman theory of regulation that penalty assessments by the FTC will reflect the relative success of interest groups in influencing commission policy. One proposition is that the concentrated interests of large firms will tend to dominate the more diffuse interests of small firms and consumers in the remedy phase of regulatory proceedings. In addition, we examine the popular view that small business is the FTC's primary constituency. In the process of our examination, we are able to shed some light on the implicit methodology employed by the commission to calculate civil monetary penalties.

Based on data derived from 57 civil penalty cases before the commission between 1979 and 1981, we find evidence that suggests monetary fines transfer wealth from small to large firms. That is, although civil penalty amounts are found to be influenced by commission judgments of culpability and ability to pay, and most firms violating previous cease-and-desist orders pay higher fines than first offenders or nonrespondents, the majority of the variation in civil penalty amounts is explained by variations in firm size, where size is measured by sales. Moreover, an increase in firm size results in a less than proportional increase in penalty, *ceteris paribus*. Thus, civil penalties operate as a regressive tax on law violators through which small firms are fined proportionately greater amounts than large firms.

The paper is organized as follows. In the next section we outline the elements of the interest-group theory of regulation from which we derive our main testable hypothesis. The data and empirical results are described in the third section, which is followed by some concluding remarks.

REGULATORY AGENCIES AS WEALTH BROKERS

In his extension of Stigler's theory of regulation, Sam Peltzman posits a vote-maximizing regulator who trades off producer and consumer interests when setting a regulated price or imposing a regulatory tax.[6] Specifically, the regulator seeks to maximize his political majority subject to the constraint that high prices (lower regulatory taxes) generate greater producer support but antagonize consumers, and vice versa. Given this trade-off, the theory implies that neither group achieves all that it wants from regulation in the sense that the price-tax combination consistent with political equilibrium maximizes neither producer nor consumer surplus.

There are additional forces at work in the interest-group model, however. In particular, "the regulator's choice problem is not limited to selecting the appropriate size of an interest group to benefit or tax; it includes selection of an appropriate structure of benefits and costs." Thus, the regulator may choose to "exploit differences within the group that, taken as a whole, either wins or loses." Peltzman observes that even if the regulator is constrained by "due process" considerations, such constraints will typically not require gains or losses to be distributed equally among the members of the relevant group.[7]

The Stigler-Peltzman theory of regulation implies that, even if we presuppose that in enforcing consumer-protection laws the FTC has chosen to benefit consumers at the expense of producers, the losses imposed on sellers need not be distributed equally. In particular, if the concentrated interests of large firms outweigh the more diffuse interests of small sellers in the regulatory process, the latter will bear a larger proportion of the costs of regulation. Under this interpretation, the structure of civil fines would approximate a regressive tax on sales in which, other things being equal, civil penalty amounts rise less than proportionately with firm size.

The distributional effects of regulation have been described elsewhere. For example, the penchant of regulatory agencies to adopt technology-specific environmental quality regulations in preference to effluent fees or pollution permits has been explained on the basis of the rents accruing to a subset of firms in the affected industry.[8] Others have noted the benefits of child labor laws to certain segments of the work force.[9]

In sum, our principal hypothesis is that civil penalty assessments by the FTC are responsive to the pressures exerted by interest groups. The most straightforward prediction of the Stigler-Peltzman model is that the concentrated interests of large firms will tend to dominate the interests of small firms and consumers. However, an alternate view exists that the principal constituency of the FTC is small business.[10] If this hypothesis is correct we would expect to see disproportionately high civil penalties imposed on large firms. The following section offers empirical evidence on these hypotheses.

EMPIRICAL DETERMINANTS
OF CIVIL PENALTIES

The commission interprets its rather broad enforcement mandate as requiring that it adopt a "flexible judicial" approach in assessing civil penalties.[11] According to this approach, monetary fine determinations are made on the basis of certain statutory, judicial, and practical requirements that attempt to balance the sometimes conflicting goals of deterrence, consumer compensation, and industry guidance.

In this section we investigate empirically the factors that enter into the determination of civil penalty amounts by the FTC. To do so we estimate a multiple regression model, which permits us to test for the effect of firm size on the amount of penalty imposed. Our model also includes explanatory variables that account for other factors entering into the fine-setting process. Specifically, we develop proxies for the commission's statutory instruction to consider degree of guilt, history of prior violations, and ability to pay.

The regression model has the following form.

$$
\begin{aligned}
\text{PENALTY} = b_0 &+ b_1 \text{ SALES} + b_2 \text{ SALES 51} + b_3 \text{ I51} + b_4 \text{ SUBSID} + b_5 \text{ ABLE} \\
&+ b_6 \text{ INST} + b_7 \text{ LARGE} + b_8 \text{ GUILT} + b_9 \text{ OTHER} \\
&+ b_{10} \text{ PROG I06} + b_{11} \text{ PROG L03} + e,
\end{aligned}
$$

where

> SALES = annual sales of respondents;
>
> SALES 51 = sales of firms violating Section 5(1) of the FTC Act;
>
> I51 = Section 5(1) dummy variable ($=1$ if violation of Section 5[1], $=0$ otherwise);
>
> SUBSID = subsidiary dummy variable ($=1$ if case involves a subsidiary of a larger firm, $=0$ otherwise);
>
> ABLE = ability-to-pay dummy variable ($=1$ if firm considered able to pay, $=0$ otherwise);
>
> INST = installment dummy variable ($=1$ if fine paid in installments, $=0$ otherwise);

LARGE=injury dummy variable (=1 if violation thought to cause "large" consumer injury, =0 otherwise);

GUILT=culpability dummy variable (=1 if respondent acted in bad faith, =0 otherwise);

OTHER=remedy dummy variable (=1 if other remedies imposed, =0 otherwise);

PROG I06=program code dummy variable, (=1 if program I06, =0 otherwise);

PROG L03=program code dummy variable (=1 if program L03, =0 otherwise); and

e=regression error term.

In the regression model, sales serve as a proxy for firm size. Although one would expect a positive relationship between size of firm and size of penalty under a variety of hypotheses, our main interest is in the magnitude of the coefficient on SALES. In particular, we transform the sales variable log-arithmically to estimate the elasticity of civil penalty amounts with respect to firm size. By doing so we are able to gauge whether fines rise proportionately, less than proportionately, or more than proportionately with sales.

A coefficient on SALES statistically different from unity implies that civil penalty amounts are not assessed proportionately across firms, *ceteris paribus*. If the coefficient is less than unity, a 1 percent increase in firm size leads to a less than 1 percent increase in penalty. This result would lend support to the hypothesis that small firms bear disproportionately higher fines. On the other hand, a coefficient greater than unity would imply that large firms pay higher penalties, *ceteris paribus*. That is, a 1 percent increase in sales leads to a more than 1 percent increase in fines.

We divide sales into several categories according to the FTC Act section violated to account for differences in statutory authority for assessing penalties and for the type of violation involved. In particular, civil penalties may be assessed under three different provisions of the FTC Act. Under Section 5(1), the commission may impose penalties on firms that are directly subject to and found in violation of outstanding FTC cease-and-desist orders. In addition, in 1975 the Magnuson-Moss Warranty and Federal Trade Commission Improvements Act provided more sweeping authority for imposition of civil penalties: under Section 5(m)(1)(A), firms found to be in violation of commission rules and statutes are subject to fine; and under Section 5(m)(1)(B), firms can be penalized if they are found to be knowingly in violation of a commission cease-and-desist order even if they are not themselves directly subject to it.[12]

Penalties administered under Section 5(m) might be expected to be less than those under Section 5(1). This is because many of the rules and statutes subject to Section 5(m)(1)(A) are relatively new and respondents may have benefited from some educational grace period. In addition, the constitutionality of Section 5(m)(1)(B) has not been clearly established. Moreover, the knowledge standard required for conviction under the three provisions also differs, with Section 5(1) having the lowest knowledge requirement and Section 5(m)(1)(B) the highest. Because a low standard concerning a firm's knowledge about existing commission orders raises the probability of conviction, Section 5(1) respondents may incur lower penalties than those subject to Section 5(m). Therefore, it is difficult to predict a priori the effect these different statutory authorities may have on the size of civil penalties. The two sales variables, SALES and SALES 51, along with the Section 5(1) dummy variable, I51, permit us to test whether the commission treats these provisions differently—that is, whether the regression slope and intercept differ according to statutory authority.

SUBSID indicates whether the sales data are for a corporate subsidiary or for a company as a whole. This dummy variable allows us to make inferences about alternative enforcement strategies in the case of multiproduct firms. If one assumes that private economic gain relates most directly to the revenue from the product line involved in the violation, then bringing cases against subsidiaries would be consistent with a deterrence strategy.[13] In contrast, if subsidiary status is associated with larger fines, a concern with ability to pay could be inferred.

Inclusion of the variables ABLE and INST provide a more direct test of the ability-to-pay proposition. In particular, ABLE is assigned a value of unity if the respondent was considered able to pay a monetary fine, and INST indicates the presence of an arrangement to pay the penalty in installments. Inability to pay or necessity for a series of payments might indicate that the respondent's financial condition was viewed as weak, perhaps inducing the commission to lower the total size of the penalty.

LARGE denotes violations considered to have caused substantial consumer injury. Such violations would be expected to increase civil penalty amounts, *ceteris paribus*. Moreover, the FTC Act requires the commission to consider degree of culpability in assessing fines. For purposes of this study, GUILT is lesser or greater according to whether the respondent was said to have acted in good or bad faith, with larger penalties expected to be assessed in the latter case, other things being equal. (Instances of bad faith included those respondents with a history of noncompliance and firms violating more than one rule, statute, or order.)

Civil penalties are often accompanied by other types of relief, notably injunctions, consumer redress, or some informational requirement such as notifying customers of their rights under a trade regulation rule. These additional remedies also impose costs on the firm, contributing in part to removal of the economic gain from noncompliance and in part to deterrence of future violations. The variable OTHER denotes the presence or absence of additional remedial measures that may lead to a reduction in the size of the fine so as to hold constant the total cost to the firm of the entire relief package.

In addition to the above considerations, the type of violation may also affect the size of the penalty. For example, if the commission pursues a goal of historical consistency, we would expect penalties to fall within a given range for similar types of infractions, with values within the range varying according to mitigating or aggravating circumstances. To test for such an effect we classified the civil penalty cases on the basis of the consumer-protection program area in which enforcement action was initiated. There were ten such program areas for the cases in our sample. The two that we focus on—cigarette advertising practices and enforcement of the Equal Credit Opportunity Act— are the only two program areas found to differ significantly from the mean.

The Data

To test empirically the relative importance of firm size, statutory authority, and other factors in assessing monetary fines, we examined the complaint files on 57 civil penalty cases before the commission between 1979 and 1981. (Respondents and civil penalty amounts are listed in the Appendix.)[14] Where possible, the relevant data were derived from staff memoranda and other internal documents, since such information was relied on by the commission in reaching its decisions on guilt and in establishing civil penalty amounts. In the case of sales, however, observations on thirteen respondents were missing from commission documents; data from company annual reports were therefore obtained to fill the gaps.[15]

Information on some of the qualitative explanatory variables included in the regression was not always available for every case. The staff memoranda may have discussed consumer injury in one case, culpability in another, and ability to pay in still another. Rarely were all mitigating and aggravating circumstances covered in the context of any single respondent. Such missing observation problems were handled by the method of modified zero-order regression.[16]

Sample statistics by FTC program area are listed in Table 11.1. The smallest civil penalty assessed by the commission between 1979 and 1981 was $1,000; the largest was $1,750,000. On average, the heaviest fines were imposed for violations of outstanding orders (compliance matters) and for Equal Credit Opportunity Act infractions. Deceptive sales practices drew the smallest average penalties.

TABLE 11.1
SAMPLE CIVIL PENALTIES BY FTC PROGRAM AREA, 1979–1981

Program Area	Number of Cases	Average Penalty	Standard Deviation
Cigarette advertising practices	6	97,000	7,144
Deceptive sales practices	4	10,000	0
Business opportunities, franchising	1	25,000	—
Children's advertising	1	100,000	—
General credit practices	8	51,000	36,198
Equal Credit Opportunity Act	4	115,000	88,412
Credit information	14	36,600	22,636
Rule and statute enforcement	5	21,000	4,183
Compliance	14	161,000	459,561[a]

NOTE: a. The high variation in the Compliance program area is because it included both the highest (Reader's Digest, $1,750,000) and the lowest (R. Paron, $1,000 and Tri-West Construction, $2,000) penalties.

The Results

Our empirical model suggests that civil penalty amounts are a positive function of firm size as measured by sales and are also affected by mitigating and aggravating circumstances reflecting company financial condition, extent of consumer injury, degree of culpability, imposition of other remedial requirements, and institutional factors associated with statutory authority and type of violation. The positive effect of firm size on penalty amount is expected to be inelastic (that is, the coefficient on SALES is expected to be less than one) if, other things being equal, the concentrated interests of large firms dominate regulatory decisionmaking.

The regression results are presented in Table 11.2.[17] Overall, variations in the explanatory variables explain 85 percent of the variation in civil penalty amounts. With the exception of the extent of consumer injury, all parameter estimates are significantly different from zero at the 1 percent level.[18]

Sales and FTC Act Authority. Firm size is apparently an important consideration in setting civil penalty amounts. (In fact, variations in sales alone explain 58 percent of the variation in monetary fines.)[19] The coefficient on SALES indicates that a 1 percent increase in firm size results in a .23 percent increase in penalty amount for Section 5(m) violations, suggesting

TABLE 11.2

REGRESSION RESULTS FOR CIVIL PENALTIES ASSESSED BY THE
FTC IN CONSUMER PROTECTION MATTERS, 1979–1981
(DEPENDENT VARIABLE: LOGARITHM OF CIVIL PENALTY AMOUNT)

Independent Variable	Parameter Estimate	Standard Error	Relative Effect
Intercept	4.84***	0.60	
Log sales	0.23***	0.04	0.23[a]
Log sales for Sec. 5(l)	0.18***	0.06	0.41[b]
Sec. 5(l) intercept diff.	−2.69***	0.96	−0.96[c]
Subsidiary of larger firm	0.75***	0.24	1.05
Able to pay	0.56***	0.26	0.69
Installment payment	0.60***	0.20	0.79
Large consumer injury	0.04	0.32	—
Culpability	0.72***	0.26	0.99
Other remedial actions	0.57***	0.17	0.73
Program Code I06	−1.62***	0.44	−0.82
Program Code L03	−1.00***	0.37	−0.66
R^2=0.85, N=57			

NOTES: *** Statistically significant at the 1 percent level.

a. The slope of the sales function for Sec. 5(m) violations.

b. The slope of the sales function for Sec. 5(l) violations, equal to the sum of the parameter estimates for log sales and log sales for Sec. 5(l).

c. See Note 20.

that the penalty burden falls disproportionately on smaller respondents. The coefficient is significantly less than unity at the 1 percent level.

The sales effect also differs according to which section of the FTC Act was the source of authority for the penalty assessment. The results indicate that the marginal effect of sales on penalty size is larger for Section 5(1) matters, *ceteris paribus*, with each 1 percent increase in sales resulting in a .41 percent increase in the size of the fine. No significant difference between penalties assessed in Section 5(m)(1)(A) and Section 5(m)(1)(B) matters was apparent, however.

For small firms, Section 5(m) violators (of orders against other firms or of commission rules) incurred relatively larger penalties than violators of Section 5(1) (those directly subject to commission orders), but the reverse was true for larger firms, specifically those with sales of over $4 million in 1981 dollars, which included most of the firms in the sample. Overall, our findings are consistent with the interpretation that violators of the recently legislated Section 5(m) did indeed enjoy a grace period during the sample period. Moreover, considering the relatively high probability of conviction for violating a previous order under Section 5(1), along with the relatively high penalty amounts assessed for such violations, one can conclude that the expected cost to respondents of Section 5(1) charges is much greater than that for Section 5(m) infractions.

The results also show that the existence of a parent company had a significant effect on the absolute size of the penalty. For such firms the fine was more than twice as high at each sales level than for firms that were not subsidiaries of a larger corporation.[20] The absolutely larger penalties for subsidiaries are not enough to offset the overall regressivity in the penalty rate, however.

Ability to Pay.   When financial condition was discussed in internal commission documents and the respondent was judged able to pay, the fine tended to be almost 70 percent higher than when the firm was considered unable to pay. This finding, together with the significance of subsidiary status discussed above, suggests that ability to pay is an important determinant of civil penalty amounts.

The conjecture that penalty payment by installments might be a sign of financial weakness and therefore be associated with reduced fines is not supported by the regression estimates. In particular, fines paid by installment were almost 80 percent larger than those penalties paid in a lump sum, indicating that installment arrangements are a device for assessing greater fines than otherwise.[21]

Consumer Injury.   Judgments concerning the degree of consumer injury caused by a particular violation had no impact on civil penalty amounts, other things being equal. It is interesting to note, however, that when any judgment was made about consumer injury, whether large or small, fines were *lower* by more than 60 percent than when the subject was not addressed at all in commission documents.[22]

Culpability.   Firms with a history of noncompliance, those found in violation of more than one rule, statute, or order, and other companies showing bad faith in dealing with the commission faced fines more than double the amount imposed on "good behavers." The fact that this variable was significant despite the inclusion of separate information on Section 5(1) violations suggests that companies judged by the commission staff to be acting in bad faith increase their liability substantially. (Section 5[1] infractions involve repeat offenders by definition.)

Other Remedial Provisions.   The inclusion of additional relief measures in civil penalty cases tends to raise the amount of the fine rather than reduce it.

When other remedies were imposed along with fines to form a larger relief package, the expected size of the penalty was increased by 73 percent. This suggests that consumer compensation and nonmonetary remedies serve as complements to and not substitutes for direct fines.

Type of Violation. The regression model tested for the existence of consistency and predictability among types of violations by including dummy variables for the commission program areas responsible for bringing each of the cases. Differences between program areas would indicate that consistency within specific types of violations was an important concern in setting penalty size. The results did not support this conjecture for eight of the ten program areas covered by our sample. However, the means of two program areas (cigarette advertising practices and the Equal Credit Opportunity Act) were significantly lower, the former by more than 80 percent, the latter by more than 60 percent, after controlling for other variables. Thus, penalties assessed within these two areas tend to be more consistent from violation to violation than the fines imposed in the other FTC program areas.

In sum, the regression model explains quite well the factors that enter into the determination of civil penalty amounts. It is important to keep in mind, however, that the qualitative data were derived from internal FTC documents. The possibility exists that when the penalty was relatively large, claims of large consumer injury, significant culpability, and adequate ability to pay were invoked as an afterthought to justify imposing a large fine, and conversely when the penalty was relatively small. Our results nevertheless provide evidence that in setting civil penalties the FTC places a disproportionate burden on small firms.

Concluding Remarks

In this paper we have reported results from an empirical analysis of the factors that enter into the determination of civil penalties assessed by the FTC in its consumer-protection mission. Based on data derived from 57 civil penalty cases before the commission between 1979 and 1981, we found evidence that suggests monetary fines transfer wealth from small firms to large firms. In particular, nearly 60 percent of the variation in civil penalty amounts was explained by variations in firm size alone, where size was measured by sales.

Moreover, an increase in firm size resulted in a less than proportional increase in penalty, *ceteris paribus*. This is consistent with the Stigler-Peltzman hypothesis that the concentrated interests of large firms will tend to dominate the more diffuse interests of small business. However, a regressive penalty structure might be consistent with a rational enforcement policy if the expected net returns to actions that are in violation of FTC rules and orders are relatively greater for small firms or if the probability of detection and conviction increases as the size of the offending firm increases. Greater expected returns in relative terms to small firms might come about if larger firms were more constrained by market forces to maintain the integrity of their products. Market forces in many instances provide an implicit guarantee of quality by punishing firms through loss of future sales for degrading quality.[23] Such a market check may be more effective for larger firms if they have significantly greater investments in intangible assets, such as brand name capital that could be destroyed by loss of consumer confidence in their products. Small firms, in contrast, would have less to lose from "hit and run" tactics if they have relatively fewer intangible assets at stake, especially if, as is often the case, they operate in industries with no significant economies of scale. Additionally, greater visibility of large violators may increase the probability of detection, so that if the objective is to maintain a constant degree of deterrence across firms, penalties would increase less than in direct proportion to private benefit as an offset to the increasing probability of detection for larger violators.

These reasons suggest that it may be optimal for the FTC to impose relatively large penalties on small firms, since maximization of social welfare requires that penalties be just large enough to achieve the desired degree of compliance. However, the disparity may simply reflect greater bargaining skills or better legal counsel for larger corporations.[24] Whatever the explanation for this observed regressivity, the fact remains that the penalty structure for the FTC's consumer-protection mission is disproportionately weighted against smaller firms.

We also found that judgments concerning respondents' ability to pay and their degree of culpability were important in explaining the size of fines. That is, violators that were subsidiaries of larger companies or were otherwise thought to be able to bear monetary penalties paid higher fines than did other respondents. Firms acting in bad faith or showing a history of noncompliance also faced stiffer penalties than first offenders or good behavers. Moreover, other relief measures appeared to serve as complements to and not substitutes for direct monetary fines. Finally, neither the extent of consumer injury caused by a violation nor a concern with consistency within particular types of infractions appeared to be given much consideration in setting civil penalty amounts.

In sum, our results cast doubt on the popular view that small business is the FTC's main constituency. We find that in the case of the civil penalties assessed by the commission in consumer-protection matters, large firms tend to bear a disproportionately smaller share of the costs of regulation. We are therefore able to offer support to the Stigler-Peltzman interest-group theory.

Appendix:
Cases Included in Sample with Size of Civil Penalty

Respondents	Civil Penalty	Respondents	Civil Penalty
1. A. Abraham	$ 25,000	30. Modern Home	$ 10,000
2. American Brands	100,000	31. Mod-Maid Imports	25,000
3. Amoco (Standard Ind.)	200,000	32. Montgomery Ward	175,000
4. Associated Dry Goods	75,000	33. National Siding	10,000
5. Atlantic Hosiery	16,000	34. Nationwide	10,000
6. Atlantic Industries	10,000	35. Neighborhood Periodicals	150,000
7. Britene Internat'l Textiles	20,000	36. Phillip Morris	100,000
8. Brown and Williamson	100,000	37. Pulte Home	70,000
9. Budget Marketing	125,000	38. Radiology Consultant	30,000
10. Cadence Industries	50,000	39. Reader's Digest	1,750,000
11. Capital Credit	75,000	40. Ricardo Pagnini	20,000
12. Centex (Midwest)	50,000	41. R. J. Reynolds	100,000
13. Collectron and Telechek	65,000	42. RJR Foods	70,000
14. Credit Rating Bureau	10,000	43. R. Paron	1,000
15. Crosland	20,000	44. Scarborough	50,000
16. Dixieland	10,000	45. Sure Products	30,000
17. Downing	10,000	46. Tasemkins Furniture	20,000
18. Edward W. Scott	10,000	47. Tri-Texas, Inc.	25,000
19. Exxon	100,000	48. Tri-West Construction	2,000
20. General Mills	100,000	49. United Corp.	15,000
21. Georgia Telco	10,000	50. Universal Collection	90,000
22. Hylton	28,000	51. U.S. Homes	90,000
23. Intaltex	15,000	52. Van Schaack	30,000
24. Ivy International	25,000	53. Virginia Builders	30,000
25. Kettler	25,000	54. Wauwatosa Realty	15,000
26. Lawson Hill	15,000	55. Westminster	50,000
27. Liggett	82,500	56. Yeonas	25,000
28. Lorillard	100,000	57. Young Ford, Inc.	10,000
29. Maralco Enterprises	15,000		

Notes

1. Section 5(m)(1)(c) of the FTC Act, *Statutes at Large*, vol. 88 (1975), *U.S. Code*, vol. 15 (1975).

2. Gary S. Becker, "Crime and Punishment: An Economic Approach," *Journal of Political Economy* 76 (March–April 1968): 169–207.

3. George J. Stigler, "The Optimum Enforcement of Laws," *Journal of Political Economy* 78 (May–June 1970): 526–36.

4. For recent empirical work on criminal violations, see Isaac Ehrlich, "Capital Punishment and Deterrence: Some Further Thoughts and Additional Evidence," *Journal of Political Economy* 85 (August 1977): 741–88; and Gary Becker and W. M. Landes, eds., *Essays in the Economics of Crime and Punishment* (New York: Columbia University Press, 1974).

5. See Colin Diver, "The Assessment and Mitigation of Civil Money Penalties by Federal Administrative Agencies," *Columbia Law Review* 79 (December 1979): 1436–1502.

6. Sam Peltzman, "Toward a More General Theory of Regulation," *Journal of Law and Economics* 19 (August 1976): 211–40. See also George J. Stigler, "The Theory of Economic Regulation," *Bell Journal of Economics and Management Science* 2 (Spring 1971): 3–21.

7. Peltzman, "Toward a More General Theory," pp. 218–19.

8. Michael T. Maloney and Robert E. McCormick, "A Positive Theory of Environmental Quality Regulation," *Journal of Law and Economics* 25 (April 1982): 99–123.

9. See Howard P. Marvel, "Factory Regulation: A Reinterpretation of Early English Experience," *Journal of Law and Economics* 20 (October 1977): 379–402; and Gary Anderson and Robert Tollison, "A Rent-Seeking Explanation of the British Factory Acts," in David C. Colander, ed., *Neoclassical Political Economy* (Cambridge, Mass.: Ballinger, 1984), pp. 187–201.

10. This view has been described with respect to the FTC's antitrust enforcement efforts in Robert D. Tollison, ed., *The Political Economy of Antitrust: Principal Paper by William Baxter* (Lexington, Mass.: Lexington Books, 1980). A hypothesis that large corporations are at a legal disadvantage as a result of more stringent enforcement by regulatory agencies and the antagonism of public-interest groups has been advanced by B. Peter Pashigan, "A Theory of Prevention and Legal Defense with an Application to the Legal Costs of Companies," *Journal of Law and Economics* 25 (October 1982): 247–70.

11. U.S. Federal Trade Commission, *Civil Penalties: Policy Review Session* (Washington, D.C., July 1982).

12. See David O. Bickart, "Civil Penalties Under Section 5(m) of the Federal Trade Commission Act," *University of Chicago Law Review* 44 (Summer 1977): 761–803.

13. By levying fines proportional to the sales of the product line involved in the offense rather than to sales of the entire firm, firms' incentives at the margin for committing offenses are not distorted. Penalties levied according to firm-wide sales might encourage firm-wide violations.

14. There were actually 66 civil penalty cases during the 1979–1981 period. Four were excluded from our sample because sales data were not available. These were Haband Company ($30,000 penalty), Macmen Financial Services ($20,000 penalty), National Talent Associates ($25,000 penalty), and Womack Nursery ($10,000 penalty). Five other cases were excluded either because their files were missing or because the matters were still active: J. B. Williams ($75,000 penalty), Sydney N. Floer-

sheim ($75,000 penalty), Korman Corp. ($35,000 penalty), Paul Ramage ($10,000 penalty), and National Dynamics ($100,000 penalty).

15. Sales data were generally for the most recent year in which the violation was said to have occurred.

16. See Jan Kmenta, *Elements of Econometrics* (New York: Macmillan, 1971), pp. 336–44.

17. Sales and penalty values were deflated by the consumer price index and then transformed by taking natural logarithms.

18. The results therefore do not display the symptoms of multicollinearity (relatively high correlations between independent variables), a frequent problem with three or more dummy variables.

19. Based on a regression of the log of penalty amount on the log of sales by itself.

20. For dummy variables the relative effect is measured by $g=\exp(b-0.5v_b^2(b))-1$, where b is the estimated regression coefficient, v_b is the estimate of its variance, and $100g$ measures the percentage impact of the dummy variable on the dependent variable. For a discussion of this method, see Peter Kennedy, "Estimation with Correctly Interpreted Dummy Variables in Semilogarithmic Equations," *American Economic Review* 71 (September 1981): 801.

21. Since in none of the cases did installments extend beyond three years, the absolutely larger fines are not the result of present value calculations. Indeed, in at least one case an interest rate of 6 percent was added to the penalty.

22. From the zero order regression method, discussed in Kmenta, *Elements of Econometrics*.

23. See Benjamin V. Klein and Keith B. Leffler, "The Role of Market Forces in Assuring Contractual Performance," *Journal of Political Economy* 89 (August 1981): 615–41.

24. One of the referees drew our attention to Donald Black's suggestion that large organizations are more immune from the law than their smaller counterparts. See Donald Black, *The Behavior of Law* (New York: Academic Press, 1976).

Chapter 12

Antitrust Recidivism in Federal Trade Commission Data: 1914–1982

WILLIAM F. SHUGHART II

& ROBERT D. TOLLISON

APPROXIMATELY 23 percent of the law-enforcement actions brought by the Federal Trade Commission (FTC) involve repeat offenders. Although this figure is small in comparison to the recidivism rates commonly observed among convicted felons, firms that are charged more than once with antitrust violations account for a nontrivial proportion (nearly one-fourth) of historical agency output.

What type of inferences can be drawn with respect to recidivists who violate the antitrust laws and other trade statutes and rules? Competing explanations include an absence of effective remedies, the existence of a group of industries whose structural characteristics or other economic data are conducive to noncompetitive behavior by incumbent firms, and the presence of law-enforcement institutions and incentives that lower the costs of challenging the practices of firms that have previously been involved in legal proceedings with the agency.

In this paper we provide data about cases involving firms that repeatedly violate the laws enforced by the FTC. Although the available data are not of sufficient detail to permit statistical tests that would distinguish among the competing hypotheses, the evidence does allow us to consider which of the

We benefited from comments by William Baxter, Richard Higgins, James C. Miller III, Dennis Mueller, John Peterman, and Gordon Tullock. The views expressed here are those of the authors and do not necessarily reflect those of the Federal Trade Commission, individual commissioners, or other staff.

explanations appears most plausible. Our analysis is in the spirit of related work by George Stigler, Richard Posner, and G. A. Hay and D. Kelley.

Stigler focused on assessing the general effects of the antitrust laws on aggregate concentration, on the frequency of horizontal mergers, and on the prevalence of collusion.[1] Using data covering roughly 1890 to 1960 and contrasting concentration levels in selected industries in the United States with corresponding figures for the United Kingdom, Stigler found that the Sherman Act had only modest effects on the market shares of leading firms. Similar conclusions were reached for the antimerger laws, but the Sherman Act did seem to have eliminated the most efficient methods of collusion. One of Stigler's main points, however, was the poor quality of existing data, which made it difficult for him to draw strong *ceteris paribus* inferences.

Posner examined data on virtually all antitrust activity occurring after the passage of the Sherman Act in 1890.[2] In particular, he considered indicia such as the number of cases filed by various enforcement agencies, including those at the federal and state levels; the length of proceedings; "success" records; and the violations, remedies, and industries involved. Overall, Posner concluded that "antitrust enforcement is inefficient, and the first step toward improvement must be . . . a much greater interest in the dry subject of this paper, antitrust statistics."[3]

Posner also calculated a recidivism rate from cases brought by the Justice Department between 1964 and 1968. He found "that 46 of the 320 corporations that were convicted of a criminal violation of the antitrust laws" during this period had previously been convicted. Because of data deficiencies, however, Posner felt that the true percentage of recidivists was "undoubtedly higher" than the 14 percent he estimated from his restricted sample. The FTC data that we report in the next section below confirm Posner's impression.[4]

Hay and Kelley limited their analysis to a study of horizontal price-fixing cases brought by the Justice Department's Antitrust Division.[5] "All Section 1 criminal cases which were filed and won in trial or settled by *nolo contendere* pleas from January 1963 to December 1972 were examined."[6] They considered whether the facts in these proceedings were consistent with the factors that economic theory suggests facilitate collusion. The findings of their study support a structure-conduct link for price-fixing conspiracies and indicate that "industries colluding at one point in time often can be found to be colluding at later points in time, in spite of antitrust action in the interim." Hay and Kelley conclude that "applying dissolution to habitual offenders may provide the publicity needed to raise further the perceived cost of violating the antitrust laws and thus force compliance by firms in industries prone to conspiracy."[7]

The data we present cover every law-enforcement action brought by the FTC from 1914 to early 1982. As such, the evidence provides a broad view of repeat offenses under the traditional antitrust statutes enforced by the agency, the FTC and Clayton Acts, as well as consumer-protection laws such as the Truth-in-Lending, Fair Credit Reporting, Wool, and Fur Acts.[8] The next section below contains a detailed description of the data and offers broad categorizations of information about recidivism over time, including the violations most likely to be involved in repeat offenses, consumer products and services most often sold by multiple violators, and elapsed time between offenses. In the third section it is argued that the pattern of FTC recidivism is more consistent with an agency-driven rather than a firm-driven hypothesis; concluding remarks follow.

RECIDIVISM DATA

Data on FTC recidivists were extracted from the commission's "Matter Listing by Respondent," maintained by the Office of the Secretary, Inquiry and Search Branch. This magnetic tape listing, current through the period ending March 31, 1982, is organized alphabetically by respondent name and contains coded summaries of each law-enforcement action brought by the attorney staff. We would be happy to share our data set with any interested reader.

Between 1914 and early 1982, the FTC brought 12,244 cases that proceeded beyond the investigation stage; 9,159 of these involved administrative litigation, and 3,085 were settled by consent order. Recidivists accounted for 2,830 of these law-enforcement actions, 2,217 of which reached the point of hearings before an administrative law judge; 613 cases ended in a consent decree. Overall, repeat offenders were involved in 4,096 matters. In addition to administrative litigation and consents, recidivists were the subject of 512 investigations and 19 other matter types; 735 of the actions could not be classified because of missing data. This information is summarized in Table 12.1.[9]

During the 67 years covered by the data, 1,217 firms had been charged with multiple violations and those charges had reached a hearing before an administrative law judge or a consent decree settlement. On average, therefore, each recidivist was involved in 2.3 law-enforcement actions (2,830 cases divided by 1,217 firms). Overall, the typical firm in the population of FTC respondents faced 1.2 complaints (12,244 cases divided by 10,631 firms).

If we use as a measure of success the carrying forward of a matter to either a negotiated or a litigated settlement, then the commission's staff was successful more than two-thirds of the time when dealing with repeat offenders. Further evidence of this sort is found in the observation that 2,018 of the 2,830 recidivist law-enforcement actions were classified as compliance matters, which involved questions of firms' adherence to earlier consent or administrative orders. Thus, 16 percentage points of the overall 23 percent recidivism

TABLE 12.1
FTC MATTERS INVOLVING REPEAT OFFENDERS, 1914–1982

Matter Type	Frequency	Cumulative Frequency	Percent	Cumulative Percent
Unknown	735	735	17.94	17.94
Investigations	512	1,247	12.50	30.44
(Initial phase)	(160)			
(Full phase)	(352)			
Projects	18	1,265	0.44	30.88
Consents	613	1,878	14.97	45.85
Administrative litigation	2,217	4,095	54.13	99.98
External court	1	4,096	0.02	100.00

SOURCE: Federal Trade Commission.

rate were attributable to violations of previous commission prescriptions, and 7 percentage points resulted from novel enforcement efforts.

Such a success criterion would be appropriate if we were interested in gauging the extent to which case selection is influenced by the incentive of attorneys to develop courtroom and bargaining skills that are later transferable to the private sector. The data are also consistent with the theory of government enterprise put forth by Cotton Lindsay.[10] Lindsay notes that in monitoring the performance of bureaucratic organizations, Congress lacks "the convenient yardstick of profit." Oversight is necessarily limited to observation of visible agency output. To the extent that "Congress will decline to fund output which it cannot measure," FTC attorneys may have an incentive to "produce" highly visible consent orders and docketed cases, the least costly of which in terms of commission resources are probably those involving compliance issues.

The distinction between compliance and novel repeat offenses is not important for the purpose of defining a true recidivism rate for FTC respondents, which we have calculated to be 23 percent. That is, recidivism legitimately arises when a firm repeatedly violates an existing order or when it faces antitrust complaints in more than one separate matter. Posner's conjecture that the true antitrust recidivism rate was higher than 14 percent is therefore correct when the FTC data are analyzed in these terms.

The broader issue that we seek to address concerns the general efficacy of antitrust law enforcement. To this end we first present evidence on the statutes infringed by repeat offenders and the specific violations with which they were charged. We next investigate the distribution of recidivists across product classes and examine the way in which repeat offenses occur over time. Finally, we present several case studies of firms that exhibit the highest recidivism rates.

Statutes Violated by Recidivists

The Federal Trade Commission Act of 1914 (as amended by the Wheeler-Lea Act of 1938) provides the legislative basis for the agency's antitrust and consumer-protection activities. Section 5 states that "unfair methods of competition in commerce and unfair or deceptive acts or practices in commerce are hereby declared illegal." Because of its broad language, it is not surprising that the majority of commission enforcement actions are brought under Section 5. Traditional antitrust matters are handled by the commission's Bureau of Competition and are generally brought either under Section 5 or the Clayton Act, which was also passed in 1914 and later amended. The broad provisions of Section 5 of the FTC Act are also enforced by the commission's Bureau of Consumer Protection.

Four Clayton Act provisions have been enforced by the FTC. Section 2 makes illegal the practice of price discrimination, but, as A. D. Neale and D. G. Goyder note, few such cases were brought successfully prior to passage of the Robinson-Patman Act in 1936.[11] The main provisions of that amendment were embodied in Clayton Act Section 2(a), which prohibits price discrimination in favor of large buyers "where the effect of such discrimination may be substantially to lessen competition or tend to create a monopoly in any line of commerce." Sections 2(c) through 2(e) prohibit, respectively, discrimination through brokerage commissions, promotional payments, or promotional services and facilities. Section 2(f) makes it illegal for anyone knowingly to induce or receive a discrimination in price.

The Robinson-Patman Act also contained a criminal provision that became Section 3 of the Clayton Act. This section provides fines and imprisonment for parties found guilty of price discrimination or for those involved in selling goods at "unreasonably low prices for the purpose of destroying competition or eliminating a competitor." Section 3 also declares tying arrangements and exclusive dealing to be illegal.[12]

Two other provisions of the Clayton Act are worth noting. Section 7 prohibits mergers and acquisitions that "tend to create a monopoly in any line of commerce." Initially, only acquisitions of stock or other share capital fell under Section 7, and this loophole was not closed until 1950, when the Celler-Kefauver Act modified the Clayton language to account for mergers through the purchase of physical assets.[13] Finally, Section 8 bans so-called interlocking directorates where the same person serves as a director of two or more competing corporations, one of which has "capital, surplus, and undivided profits" totaling more than $1 million.

As can be seen in Table 12.2, over 89 percent of matters involving repeat offenders that reached the hearing or consent stage were brought under

TABLE 12.2

STATUTES VIOLATED BY REPEAT OFFENDERS, 1914–1982

Statute	Frequency	Cumulative Frequency	Percent	Cumulative Percent
Clayton Act	297	297	10.49	10.49
(Section 2)	(254)			
[2a]	[89]			
[2c]	[15]			
[2d]	[112]			
[2e]	[4]			
[2f]	[34]			
(Section 3)	(6)			
(Section 7)	(29)			
(Section 8)	(8)			
FTC Act Section 5	2,525	2,822	89.22	99.71
(Competition)	(416)			
(Consumer Protection)	(2,109)			
Wool Act	1	2,823	0.04	99.75
Unknown	7	2,830	0.25	100.00

NOTE: Includes only those cases reaching the hearing or consent stage.

SOURCE: Federal Trade Commission.

Section 5 of the FTC Act. Robinson-Patman violations accounted for just under 9 percent of FTC cases against recidivists, with Section 7 (antimerger) and Section 8 (interlocking directorates) matters contributing a relatively small portion of alleged Clayton Act infractions.

Specific Violations

Table 12.3 contains more detailed information about the activities of repeat offenders. Although in many instances firms are charged with multiple infractions, we focus on the key subject area listed in the complaints against recidivists. The majority of actions are brought by the Bureau of Consumer Protection, the bulk of which entail advertising practices matters. In fact, well over half of all repeat offenses fall into the advertising category.

Behavioral violations represent the primary area of recidivism in more traditional antitrust actions. The majority of these consist of price discrimination matters, with other practices—such as price-fixing, tie-in sales, and exclusive dealing—forming a relatively small part of recidivist cases. Repeat offenders also seem rarely to engage in monopolization attempts. They are

TABLE 12.3
PRINCIPAL VIOLATIONS OF REPEAT OFFENDERS, 1914–1982

Violation	Frequency	Cumulative Frequency	Percent	Cumulative Percent
I. *Competition Matters*				
Monopolization	125	125	4.42	4.42
(General)	(68)			
(Attempt to monopolize)	(50)			
(Single-company monopoly)	(7)			
Mergers	5	130	0.18	4.60
Interlocks	8	138	0.28	4.88
Behavioral Violations	564	702	19.93	24.81
(General)	(261)			
(Horizontal price-fixing)	(3)			
(Tying arrangements)	(5)			
(Price discrimination-leverage)	(6)			
(Exclusive dealing)	(11)			
(Discriminatory practices)	(119)			
(Price discrimination)	(46)			
(Service/promotional allowances)	(111)			
(Sales below cost)	(2)			
Unclassified	156	858	5.51	30.32
II. *Consumer Protection Matters*				
Advertising	1,587	2,445	56.08	86.40
(General)	(2)			
(Nondisclosure)	(110)			
(Unsubstantiated claim)	(38)			
(Endorsements)	(50)			
(Miscellaneous)	(1,387)			
Credit/Financing	18	2,463	0.64	87.04
(General)	(8)			
(Misrepresented charges)	(1)			
(Other unfair practices)	(4)			
(Other deceptive practices)	(5)			
False Claims/Deceptive Sales	340	2,803	12.01	99.05
(General)	(71)			
(Deceptive packaging)	(106)			
(Deceptive pricing)	(25)			
(Deceptive repairs)	(1)			
(Misrep. business opportunity)	(1)			
(Misrep. salesman's status)	(5)			
(Other unfair selling)	(6)			
(Misrepresentation)	(33)			
(Door-to-door sales)	(92)			
Failure to Perform	1	2,804	0.04	99.09
Unfair Debt Collection	4	2,808	0.14	99.23
Unfair Practices N.E.C.	4	2,812	0.14	99.37
Violations of Special Statutes	8	2,820	0.28	99.65
Compliance Matters	10	2,830	0.35	100.00
(Fictitious prices)	(3)			
(Passing off of name/goods)	(3)			
(Spurious samples)	(1)			
(False claims)	(3)			

NOTE: Includes only those cases reaching the hearing or consent stage.
SOURCE: Federal Trade Commission.

TABLE 12.4
GOODS AND SERVICES SOLD BY REPEAT OFFENDERS, 1914–1982

Product Class	Frequency	Cumulative Frequency	Percent	Cumulative Percent
Apparel/accessories	655	655	23.15	23.15
Automobiles	185	840	6.54	29.68
Business/education	119	959	4.21	33.89
Floor coverings	28	987	0.99	34.88
Foods and beverages	321	1.308	11.34	46.22
Home repair services/products	119	1,427	4.21	50.42
Household appliances, large	24	1,451	0.85	51.27
Household appliances, small	38	1,489	1.34	52.62
Household furnishings	126	1,615	4.45	57.07
Household operations and products	11	1,626	0.39	57.46
Household supplies and products	50	1,676	1.77	59.22
Housing	2	1,678	0.07	59.29
Kitchen products	38	1,716	1.34	60.64
Lawn/garden products	53	1,769	1.87	62.51
Medical care and services	4	1,773	0.14	62.65
Medical supplies and devices	286	2,059	10.11	72.76
Personal care	231	2,290	8.16	80.92
Pet supplies	9	2,299	0.32	81.24
Publications	81	2,380	2.86	84.10
Recreation	364	2,744	12.86	96.96
Stationery	36	2,780	1.27	98.23
Transportation	1	2,781	0.04	98.27
Misc. products and services	2	2,783	0.07	98.34
Credit services	47	2,830	1.66	100.00

NOTE: Includes only those cases reaching the hearing or consent stage.
SOURCE: Federal Trade Commission.

much more likely to be charged with unfair and deceptive advertising claims or to have violated other standards about how they may represent their goods.

Given the nature of the violations that repeat offenders are most often charged with, what products and services are most likely to be involved? Table 12.4 provides an answer to this question.

Recidivism is most often found among firms in the apparel and accessories industry. Representative products in this class include clothing of all types, footwear, jewelry, and watches. Relatively high repeat-offense rates also occur among firms that produce goods and services used in recreation activities. Examples of such products are art supplies, cameras, hotels and motels, movies, radios, stereos, television sets, and travel agencies. Firms selling food and beverage products rank third among repeat offenders, closely followed by medical supply retailers—druggists, opticians, and denturists—and personal-care product companies that sell cosmetics, hair care items, shaving gear, and tobacco.

In Table 12.5 we match repeat violations and industries for the major violation categories contained in Table 12.3. With few exceptions, advertising violations are the largest class of offenses for recidivists in every industry. Looking across product classes, firms exhibiting the highest levels of repeated product misrepresentation and other false claims are in apparel, medical supplies, and recreation businesses. Competition matters (columns 1 and 2 in Table 12.5) are most likely to occur in the foods, personal care, recreation, autos, and apparel classes. Reading across violations, traditional antitrust matters dominate as a source of repeat offenses in only a few selected industries: food and beverage sellers, firms in the household operations and household supplies categories, and medical care providers.[14]

Recidivism over Time

Table 12.6 lists the number of commission actions dealing with repeat offenses occurring in each year since passage of the FTC Act. In constructing this table (and Table 12.7 to follow), the data were sorted by respondent name and by year in which the case was opened. The first case against each recidivist was then deleted, yielding a population of 1,596 matters. For a given year the frequency count therefore represents the number of cases brought against firms that had until then been charged with one or more law violations. All other tables utilize the full data set containing 2,830 observations.

Clearly, a firm must have been charged with an initial law violation before there is a possibility of subsequent violations. In consequence, relatively few repeat offenses were recorded in the first two decades of the commission's existence. High numbers of repeat offenses follow passage of the Robinson-Patman Act in 1936, with 329 recidivist matters occurring during the next nine years. The late 1950s and early 1960s contained the largest number of repeat offenses. Over 39 percent of all recidivism matters were brought between 1957 and 1964; half of all complaints against repeat offenders were issued from 1957 to 1977. On average, the commission opened 25 repeat-offense cases each year.

An important characteristic of the recidivism time series is the significant decline in case openings during the 1970s. In fact, no complaints involving recidivists have been issued since 1977. A possible explanation for this phenomenon is that the late 1960s was a period of organizational crisis for the commission. Internal reforms followed severe public criticism of the agency's performance by the American Bar Association, Ralph Nader, and President

TABLE 12.5
REPEAT VIOLATIONS BY PRODUCT CLASS, 1914–1982

Product Class	Monopoli- zation	Behavioral Violations	Advertising	False Claims	Other	Total
Apparel	1	65	446	112	31	655
Autos	19	64	91	5	6	185
Bus./ed.	0	24	76	13	6	119
Floors	0	6	15	6	1	28
Foods	49	124	65	14	69	321
Home repair	10	24	68	5	12	119
HH appliances, L	0	6	15	1	2	24
HH appliances, S	0	2	31	3	2	38
HH furnishings	1	5	72	43	5	126
HH operations	3	7	1	0	0	11
HH supplies	8	22	19	1	0	50
Housing	0	0	2	0	0	2
Kitchen	0	1	25	8	4	38
Lawn/garden	4	3	40	3	3	53
Medical care	0	3	1	0	0	4
Medical supplies	3	22	249	2	10	286
Personal care	7	85	95	34	10	231
Pet supplies	0	0	9	0	0	9
Publications	4	29	36	2	10	81
Recreation	16	70	179	49	50	364
Stationery	0	2	23	8	3	36
Transportation	0	0	0	0	1	1
Misc. products	0	0	1	1	0	2
Credit	0	0	28	5	14	47
Total	125	564	1,587	340	214	2,830

NOTE: Includes only those cases reaching the hearing or consent stage.
SOURCE: Federal Trade Commission.

Nixon.[15] The recidivism data undoubtedly reflect the FTC's renewed efforts to bring "big" cases and, perhaps, a Nader-induced shift from litigation to regulation.

To put the information in Table 12.6 in perspective, we obtained data on the total number of FTC matters for which a complaint or consent order was issued during each year and calculated annual recidivism rates—that is, the percentage of cases brought during the year involving firms that had previously been before the FTC.[16] The results appear in Table 12.7. As expected, the proportion of cases involving repeat offenders was relatively low in the com-

TABLE 12.6
ANNUAL NUMBER OF REPEAT OFFENDERS, 1917–1977

Year	Frequency	Cumulative Frequency	Percent	Cumulative Percent
1917	1	1	0.06	0.06
1918	3	4	0.19	0.25
1919	13	17	0.82	1.07
1920	10	27	0.63	1.69
1921	14	41	0.88	2.57
1922	9	50	0.56	3.13
1923	31	81	1.94	5.08
1924	17	98	1.07	6.14
1925	6	104	0.38	6.52
1926	6	110	0.38	6.89
1927	10	120	0.63	7.52
1928	4	124	0.25	7.77
1929	12	136	0.75	8.52
1930	7	143	0.44	8.96
1931	4	147	0.25	9.21
1932	6	153	0.38	9.59
1933	6	159	0.38	9.96
1934	7	166	0.44	10.40
1935	36	202	2.26	12.66
1936	28	230	1.75	14.41
1937	28	258	1.75	16.17
1938	48	306	3.01	19.17
1939	11	317	0.69	19.86
1940	50	367	3.13	22.99
1941	32	399	2.01	25.00
1942	46	445	2.88	27.88
1943	50	495	3.13	31.02
1944	36	531	2.26	33.27
1945	17	548	1.07	34.34
1946	10	558	0.63	34.96
1947	9	567	0.56	35.53
1948	24	591	1.50	37.03
1949	10	601	0.63	37.66
1950	30	631	1.88	39.54
1951	15	646	0.94	40.48
1952	21	667	1.32	41.79
1953	21	688	1.32	43.11
1954	13	701	0.82	43.92
1955	23	724	1.44	45.36
1956	28	752	1.75	47.12
1957	63	815	3.95	51.07
1958	75	890	4.70	55.76
1959	106	996	6.64	62.41
1960	111	1,107	6.96	69.36
1961	56	1,163	3.51	72.87
1962	84	1,247	5.26	78.13
1963	73	1,320	4.57	82.71
1964	70	1,390	4.39	87.09
1965	28	1,418	1.75	88.85
1966	31	1,449	1.94	90.79
1967	35	1,484	2.19	92.98
1968	43	1,527	2.69	95.68
1969	33	1,560	2.07	97.74
1970	20	1,580	1.25	99.00
1971	6	1,586	0.38	99.37
1972	0	1,586	0.00	99.37
1973	0	1,586	0.00	99.37
1974	1	1,587	0.06	99.44
1975	1	1,588	0.06	99.50
1976	7	1,595	0.44	99.94
1977	1	1,596	0.06	100.00

NOTE: Includes only those cases reaching hearing or consent stage.
SOURCE: Federal Trade Commission.

TABLE 12.7
ANNUAL RECIDIVISM RATES, 1916–1977

Year	No. of FTC Matters	Matters Involving Recidivists	Percent	Year	No. of FTC Matters	Matters Involving Recidivists	Percent
1916	5	0	0.0	1947	48	9	18.7
1917	25	1	4.0	1948	107	24	22.4
1918	206	3	1.5	1949	98	10	10.2
1919	312	13	4.2	1950	106	30	28.3
1920	152	10	6.6	1951	105	15	14.3
1921	160	14	8.7	1952	134	21	15.7
1922	93	9	9.7	1953	81	21	25.9
1923	154	31	20.1	1954	126	13	10.3
1924	147	17	11.6	1955	199	23	11.6
1925	105	6	5.7	1956	221	28	12.7
1926	76	6	7.9	1957	320	63	19.7
1927	55	10	18.2	1958	323	75	23.2
1928	63	4	6.3	1959	368	106	28.8
1929	195	12	6.2	1960	560	111	19.8
1930	141	7	5.0	1961	239	56	23.4
1931	101	4	4.0	1962	329	84	25.5
1932	93	6	6.5	1963	445	73	16.4
1933	61	6	9.8	1964	240	70	29.2
1934	131	7	5.3	1965	178	28	15.7
1935	401	36	9.0	1966	174	31	17.8
1936	351	28	8.0	1967	156	35	22.4
1937	262	28	10.7	1968	211	43	20.4
1938	393	48	12.2	1969	226	30	13.3
1939	300	11	3.7	1970	194	20	10.3
1940	460	50	10.9	1971	333	6	1.8
1941	220	32	14.5	1972	246	0	0.0
1942	222	46	20.7	1973	183	0	0.0
1943	225	50	22.2	1974	191	1	0.5
1944	153	36	23.5	1975	222	1	0.4
1945	150	17	11.3	1976	79[a]	7	8.9
1946	64	10	15.6	1977	19[b]	1	5.3

NOTES: a. Complaints through 11/12/76, consent orders through 7/12/76.

b. Unfair competition complaints and consent orders only.

SOURCES: Commerce Clearing House, *Trade Regulation Reporter*, vol. 3 (New York: Commerce Clearing House, 1977), pp. 24,001–25,803; and Federal Trade Commission.

mission's early years. By 1923, however, the recidivism rate had reached 20 percent, indicating perhaps that behavior consistent with the Lindsay hypothesis—bureaucratic output will contain few elements that are "invisible" to Congress—tended to arise fairly quickly. The highest recidivism rates occurred in the 1950s and 1960s. Over 100 of the complaints issued in 1959 and 1960 involved firms that had previously been charged with violating the laws enforced by the FTC. Nearly 30 percent of commission activity in 1964 was devoted to repeat offenders. Relatively low recidivism rates have been the rule since 1969.[17]

Table 12.8 presents more detailed information about the time series of repeat violations, including the first offenses of eventual recidivists. In general, both traditional antitrust and consumer-protection recidivism follow a similar pattern. Whenever the number of matters involving recidivists rises during a given time period, the increase does not seem to be attributable to a particular type of violation. The two eras of relatively high recidivism—the decade following 1936 and the late 1950s to mid-1960s—were also times of historically great numbers of repeat offenses in actions involving both behavioral violations and advertising infractions.[18]

The data in Table 12.9 provide information about the mean time between offenses. The average recidivist is charged with violating the law every 10.8 years. Over 9 percent of repeat offenses occur in the same year (zero in the table), and half occur within nine years following the initial violation. On rare occasions firms are charged with subsequent violations up to 61 years after an earlier infraction. In general, however, the chance of repeat offenses is highest within the first one or two years following a previous violation.

Prominent Recidivists

Table 12.10 contains a list of those companies charged with five or more law violations by the FTC between 1914 and early 1982. The listed firms can be broadly characterized as some of the leading and most successful industrial companies in the United States, prominent drug and cosmetics firms, and relatively small clothiers. To capture the flavor of antitrust recidivism, we sketch the case histories of six prominent repeat offenders.

American Tobacco. Three separate complaints were issued against the American Tobacco Company in September 1922, charging the firm with using resale price maintenance in the sale of cigars and other tobacco products. Similar charges were simultaneously brought against Liggett and Myers, P. Lorillard, and the Tobacco Products Corporation. Cease-and-desist orders were issued against all respondents in May 1923. Identical complaints were again voted out by the commission in February, March, and April 1923, but

TABLE 12.8
VIOLATIONS OF REPEAT OFFENDERS, BY YEAR, 1917–1977

Year	Monopoli-zation	Behavioral Violations	Advertising	False Claims	Other	Total
1917	0	3	0	0	1	4
1918	3	18	3	0	1	25
1919	14	21	3	2	0	40
1920	1	8	6	0	3	18
1921	2	6	18	2	0	28
1922	0	15	6	2	3	26
1923	2	35	11	3	3	54
1924	4	22	9	0	5	40
1925	3	4	9	6	1	23
1926	0	0	10	1	2	13
1927	2	1	12	4	0	19
1928	1	2	7	2	0	12
1929	2	4	23	3	0	32
1930	0	1	10	5	12	28
1931	1	0	13	1	0	15
1932	0	0	21	2	4	27
1933	0	0	8	4	0	12
1934	0	2	17	9	1	29
1935	2	3	34	21	14	74
1936	3	20	32	14	11	80
1937	2	8	34	10	16	70
1938	2	21	48	18	5	94
1939	0	3	14	2	0	19
1940	1	17	73	10	9	110
1941	1	6	34	6	8	55
1942	0	16	33	7	13	69
1943	0	4	55	10	6	75
1944	4	3	44	8	0	59
1945	0	4	29	4	0	37
1946	1	8	6	1	3	19
1947	0	3	9	1	1	14
1948	0	18	11	0	8	37
1949	0	6	11	5	2	24
1950	7	2	38	10	2	59
1951	4	5	18	8	0	35
1952	1	10	18	8	5	42
1953	1	2	33	9	3	48
1954	6	2	13	7	1	29
1955	2	13	26	15	7	63
1956	2	18	40	6	6	72
1957	4	33	76	14	9	136
1958	3	24	95	6	1	129
1959	21	47	93	23	1	185
1960	9	33	88	24	8	162
1961	4	7	48	9	4	72
1962	2	39	62	6	4	113
1963	2	19	64	0	6	91
1964	0	7	75	4	7	93
1965	1	5	22	2	0	30
1966	1	5	21	4	0	31
1967	2	4	19	14	2	41
1968	0	1	36	2	7	46
1969	1	0	28	3	2	34
1970	1	2	13	2	2	20
1971	0	3	3	1	0	7
1972	0	0	0	0	0	0
1973	0	0	0	0	0	0
1974	0	0	1	0	0	1
1975	0	0	0	1	0	1
1976	0	0	1	0	6	7
1977	0	0	1	0	0	1

NOTE: Includes only those cases reaching hearing or consent stage.

SOURCE: Federal Trade Commission.

TABLE 12.9
ELAPSED TIME BETWEEN OFFENSES, IN YEARS, 1914–1977

Elapsed Time (years)	Percent	Cumulative Percent	Elapsed Time (years)	Percent	Cumulative Percent
0	9.59	9.59	26	1.25	90.47
1	9.53	19.12	27	1.00	91.47
2	7.90	27.02	28	0.82	92.29
3	5.71	32.73	29	0.69	92.98
4	5.83	38.56	30	0.88	93.86
5	5.27	43.82	31	0.82	94.67
6	4.39	48.21	32	1.07	95.74
7	3.01	51.22	33	0.44	96.18
8	2.88	54.11	34	0.44	96.61
9	3.45	57.56	35	0.31	96.93
10	2.32	59.88	36	0.31	97.24
11	2.01	61.88	37	0.63	97.87
12	2.38	64.26	38	0.56	98.43
13	2.01	66.27	39	0.50	98.93
14	1.94	68.21	40	0.25	99.19
15	2.26	70.47	41	0.06	99.25
16	3.07	73.54	42	0.00	99.25
17	2.07	75.61	43	0.25	99.50
18	2.07	77.68	44	0.06	99.56
19	2.32	80.00	45	0.06	99.62
20	2.26	82.26	46	0.06	99.69
21	1.51	83.76	47	0.13	99.81
22	1.76	85.52			
23	1.19	86.71	53	0.13	99.94
24	1.25	87.96			
25	1.25	89.22	61	0.06	100.00

NOTES: Table indicates time between matter opening dates for those cases reaching the hearing or consent stage. Mean=10.8 years; standard deviation=10.4; coefficient of variation=0.97.
SOURCE: Federal Trade Commission.

were dismissed with prejudice on June 30, 1925, on a finding that the practices had been discontinued. Allegations that the tobacco companies had engaged in a conspiracy to maintain fixed retail prices were the subject of two May 1923 complaints and one June 1923 complaint. All three were dismissed with prejudice a year later. American Tobacco was next the subject of FTC action in August 1942, when the commission alleged that the firm had made misrepresentations about its cigarettes. Litigation dragged on for nine years, ending in

TABLE 12.10
MAJOR REPEAT OFFENDERS, 1914–1982

Company	No. of Matters
American Tobacco	12
Armour and Co.	8
B. D. Ritholtz	7
Borden Co.	5
Bristol-Myers	6
Firestone Tire and Rubber	6
General Electric	6
General Foods	6
General Motors	7
H. Greenberg	7
Helena Rubinstein	5
J. Weiss	5
L. Brown	5
Liggett and Myers	5
M. Cohen	8
McKesson and Robbins	5
Montgomery Ward	9
N. Shure Co.	5
National Dairy Products Corp.	7
National Silver Co.	7
P. Lorillard Co.	9
Pittsburgh Plate Glass Co.	5
Procter and Gamble	6
S. Cohen	5
S. Levy	6
Shell	5
Standard Brands Inc.	5
Standard Oil	11
Sterling Drug	6
Swift and Co.	6
Westinghouse Electric	6

NOTE: Includes only those cases reaching hearing or consent stage.
SOURCE: Federal Trade Commission.

June 1951 when American Tobacco was ordered to cease and desist its product misrepresentations. Finally, a Clayton Act Section 2 complaint was voted out in June 1957, based on charges that the company had made illegal payments to chain stores selling smoking tobaccos. The allegations were settled by a consent order in September 1959.

General Motors.   GM, the country's largest manufacturer of automobiles, became the subject of an FTC complaint issued in November 1936 that charged its subsidiary, GM Acceptance Corporation, with miscellaneous deceptive advertising practices. In particular, GM was alleged to have made false and misleading representations as to the amount of interest charged to car buyers under deferred payment plans. The matter reached a hearing before an administrative law judge. In December 1939 the commission ordered GM to cease and desist its illegal practices. In June of the following year, GM Sales Corporation became involved in administrative litigation on charges of monopolistic tendencies as to auto parts and supplies, and in July 1937 a complaint was issued alleging that GM Sales Division had engaged in deceptive advertising by misrepresenting automobile prices.

GM's next three experiences with administrative hearings occurred in March 1942, November 1948, and December 1955. Behavioral violations (price discrimination in the sale of auto parts and accessories) were the subject of the 1948 matter; the other two complaints again centered on deceptive advertising. First, GM was ordered to cease alleged misrepresentations about the effectiveness of fog lamps. Then GM was charged with falsely claiming "genuine Chevrolet" replacement parts as superior to similar parts sold by competitors. A final hearing took place in March 1976, involving a compliance charge that GM and other automakers had unlawfully passed off their names in violation of a 1965 order that prohibited camera trickery in auto glass television commercials.

In addition to seven hearings, GM has been the subject of a dozen investigations over the past twenty years. Violations that have never been proved include nondisclosure of material facts, unfair creditor remedies, conspiracy to monopolize, price discrimination, unfair contracts, and deceptive pricing.

Montgomery Ward.   The FTC first complained of Montgomery Ward's behavior in May 1920, alleging that the retailer had advertised liquid cement as containing no coal tar when in fact it did. In 1936 the firm was named as a respondent to a complaint issued against Bird and Son, Inc. that contained price discrimination allegations. Then, in January 1941, the commission voted to charge Ward with misrepresenting the efficacy of reducing belts. Other advertising allegations quickly followed in November 1941, February 1942, March 1942, September 1943, and October 1945. These complaints alleged misrepresentations concerning fabric garments as having been made from animal pelts, the quality of chicks, the therapeutic value of cosmetic creams, "Dr. Pierce's Purgative Pellets," and radio receiving sets, respectively. Infractions of advertising standards were again the subject of a December 1960 complaint that charged Ward with making fictitious pricing and savings claims for its automobile tires. Finally, a February 1964 complaint alleged that the retailer had falsely claimed its automotive equipment to be guaranteed unconditionally. All of the charges against Montgomery Ward were settled by the issuance of cease-and-desist orders.

S. Cohen.   Cohen, a seller of apparel and accessories, ran afoul of advertising and Robinson-Patman standards between 1950 and 1968. Cohen's first advertising infraction occurred in May 1950 and concerned charges that he made use of illegal lottery methods in the sale of miscellaneous goods. In November 1958 he was named as a respondent to a complaint against Coleman Fashion Shop, alleging that the parties had advertised furs at fictitious prices. The following year, Cohen was charged with having used unlawful practices (exaggerating the wool content of apparel) in door-to-door sales of men's and boys' clothing. In July 1964 Cohen consented to cease alleged discrimination in the payment of promotional allowances, and in December 1968 he entered into a consent agreement to settle allegations of misbranding and falsely invoicing and guaranteeing furs.

Standard Oil.   FTC action against Standard Oil began in April 1918, when Standard Oil of Indiana was charged with violating FTC Act Section 5 by offering price cuts in certain geographic areas and with violating Clayton Act Section 2 by conditioning discounts on nonuse of competitors' goods in the sale of petroleum products. A cease-and-desist order was issued on July 21, 1919. In May 1918 Sohio and Standard Oil of Indiana were alleged to have disparaged competitors' products for the purpose of inducing customers to break contracts, and to have used price discrimination schemes to effect the same end. These complaints were later vacated for lack of evidence. Standard Oil of New York faced two FTC complaints: A challenge of its acquisition of Magnolia Petroleum Company in April 1918, which was subsequently dismissed, and May 1918 allegations of illegal tying (loaning equipment to gasoline dealers on the condition that they use only Standard petroleum products) and exclusive dealing, which were reversed in 1921. Illegal tying complaints similar to those against Standard Oil of New York were issued for Standard Oil of New Jersey in July 1919 and for Standard Oil of Kentucky in September 1919. Both of these were eventually set aside. However, Standard Oil of Kentucky was soon back before the commission as a result of a June 1923 complaint that the firm had participated in a conspiracy to fix and maintain resale prices in the sale of gasoline. In November 1925 Standard Oil of Kentucky was again charged with engaging in resale price maintenance, this time in the sale of stoves and heaters. The former complaint resulted in a cease-and-desist order; the latter was dismissed.

The next event for Standard Oil was a November 1940 price discrimination complaint. Lengthy litigation on this issue resulted in several order modifications that were reversed by the Supreme Court in January 1951 and remanded to the commission. Further reconsiderations ended in vacating the FTC order in 1956, an action that was ultimately affirmed by the Supreme Court on January 27, 1958. A May 1950 price discrimination complaint against Atlas Supply Company involving the sale of tires and automobile accessories named Standard Oil of Indiana, Standard Oil of Kentucky, Standard Oil of New Jersey, Sohio, and Socal as respondents. The commission prevailed and issued a cease-and-desist order the following year. Most recently, Standard Oil of Indiana was charged with entering into illegal price-fixing agreements with certain of its lessee-dealers. Hearings before an administrative law judge were held following the August 1959 complaint, and a decision finding for the commission was rendered on December 28, 1964.

Sterling Drug. Sterling Drug Incorporated was involved in two commission complaints during the 1940s. In October 1944 Sterling was charged with making misrepresentations about yeast tablets, and a June 1946 complaint alleged that the firm had made false claims about aspirin and cosmetics. A cease-and-desist order was issued in the second matter; the commission found against Sterling in the first. In March 1961 the commission challenged Sterling's claim that Bayer Aspirin had "fast" pain-relieving qualities, but this complaint was withdrawn in April 1965. In another matter, in June 1962 charges of illegal promotional payments resulted in a declaratory order. Returning to Sterling's advertising claims about aspirin, extensive litigation followed a January 1963 complaint. The commission's request for a preliminary injunction against Sterling was denied by the New York District Court in March 1963. In August 1969 hearings were held on allegations that Sterling's acquisition of a health and beauty aid company violated Clayton Act Section 7. An initial decision to dismiss the complaint was rendered in May 1971, but it was remanded on appeal for additional document discovery. Finally, Sterling entered into a consent agreement in May 1968 to settle allegations that it had made false claims about the performance of ionized yeast and similar drug preparations.

AGENCY- V. FIRM-DRIVEN RECIDIVISM

At the beginning of this paper we noted that there are several competing hypotheses about antitrust recidivism. These include an absence of effective remedies, structural characteristics of industries or other factors that are conducive to repeated violations by incumbent firms, and the existence of law-enforcement incentives that make it less costly to challenge firms that have previously been accused of violations. From our point of view the most interesting question is whether repeat offenses are firm-driven or agency-driven. That is, we do not accept the benign assumptions commonly made in the literature that antitrust agencies operate in the public interest and that needed improvements can be made by employing better people to do a better job. Rather, we focus here on the effects of bureaucratic incentives. The available data do not allow us to construct statistical tests that might distinguish between these competing explanations. However, several suggestive pieces of information can be gleaned from the evidence.

First, although the mean elapsed time between repeated offenses is ten years, the largest probabilities of subsequent law violations occur within two years of a previous offense. This fact appears to be consistent with the hypothesis of agency-driven recidivism in the following way. Most commission attorneys specialize in the law pertaining to particular types of violations and in industry-specific cases. For example, the Bureau of Competition has legal divisions that focus on petroleum, natural resources, food, transportation, and health-care matters. Representative divisions in the Bureau of Consumer Protection include marketing abuses, advertising practices, product reliability, food and drug advertising, and credit practices. To the extent that attorneys develop statute- or industry-specific human capital, it will be less costly for them to challenge recidivists than to seek out novel violations or offenders. Many repeat violations appear to occur within a time period that is shorter than the average length of tenure for commission attorneys.[19]

The incentive structure faced by commission attorneys has been examined by Robert Katzmann, who notes that the ultimate career goal of most legal staff members is a job with a prestigious law firm. Courtroom experience while employed by the government is an important method of achieving this end. Such employee perceptions mean that bureau managers will find that "structural matters and industry-wide cases threaten the morale of the staff attorneys because they often involve years of tedious investigation before they reach the trial stage." In consequence, the Bureau of Competition director and his upper-level executives may support "the opening of a number of easily prosecuted matters, which may have little value to the consumer . . . in an effort to satisfy the staff's perceived needs."[20]

Recidivist matters have several characteristics that are compatible with attorneys' career goals. In particular, complaints against previous offenders draw on the staff's industry-specific capital. Moreover, because much of the relevant economic data about the respondent have been gathered in earlier investigations, subsequent cases can proceed through internal review processes and reach the trial stage more quickly than matters involving first offenders. Such tendencies are reinforced by the fact that the salary structure for FTC attorneys may be competitive only at entry-level positions and that the commission's incentive to produce visible output is not compatible with the protracted investigations and litigation associated with the pursuit of "big" cases.

The data are not consistent with firm-driven recidivism in the sense that most industries exhibiting high numbers of repeat offenders are not among those normally considered to be either highly concentrated or to have characteristics that facilitate collusion among incumbent firms. In particular, firms producing products such as apparel and accessories, recreation equipment, and food and beverages are not usually thought of as being a source of substantial social-welfare loss. Automobile and petroleum companies may be exceptions to this conclusion.

Further support for agency-driven recidivism is found in the relatively high number of repeat offenses following passage of the Robinson-Patman Act. This statute, widely condemned by economists as preventing lower prices to consumers, apparently led to a substantial number of repeated violations. It is not obvious, however, that enforcement efforts conferred any real benefits on society, especially since most price discrimination recidivism seems to have occurred among small firms in unconcentrated industries.

Such evidence is consistent with the idea that the commission and other regulatory agencies are in the business of creating wealth transfers and are therefore only nominally concerned with promoting economic efficiency. For example, Barry Weingast and Mark Moran propose that even so-called runaway bureaucracies reflect the influence of congressmen serving on agency oversight committees who "protect the bureaus under their jurisdiction for the benefit of their constituencies."[21]

It is somewhat noteworthy to find that an overwhelming proportion of repeat offenses involve alleged deceptive advertising violations. Again, several competing explanations can be suggested, but not resolved. Commission enforcement guidelines in this area generally allow advertisers a "first bite." That is, initial deceptive claims are challenged, but penalties are normally imposed only for second and subsequent infractions. Moreover, a common remedy for deceptive advertising is to "fence in" a firm by extending cease-and-desist orders to other products not directly the source of law violation allegations. Both agency practices increase the probability of recidivism. First, firms can rationally commit a first offense with the knowledge that they will suffer no monetary penalty until the next violation. Second, the existence of standing cease-and-desist orders covering all of a firm's products lowers the costs to commission attorneys of challenging subsequent ads and practices.

In addition to the "first bite" doctrine, the relatively high rates of deceptive advertising recidivism may be attributable to the fact that regulatory standards in this area are particularly murky, implying that enforcement efforts will appear capricious. The suggestion here is that cases tend to be brought in areas where there is mutual uncertainty about the law. More importantly, Sam Peltzman's research indicates that firms whose advertising claims are successfully challenged by the FTC suffer substantial reductions in their ability to attract first-time buyers.[22] Peltzman also finds that the capital value of such firms falls by more than the value of the challenged brand's entire advertising capital.

If commission action destroys the brand name capital of advertisers, then agency-driven recidivism is promoted in the following way. Suppose that the challenged advertising copy was not viewed as false or deceptive by all first-time and loyal customers. During the time when the firm is attempting to repair its image through the introduction of claims that conform to FTC requirements, it may be rational in an expected value sense to continue using the old advertising copy for the purpose of retaining the business of undeceived buyers. In such a transitional period the firm chooses the mix of old and new claims that equates the marginal benefit of sales to customers who buy on the basis of the challenged advertising copy with the expected marginal cost of subsequent FTC penalties. The advertiser thus becomes a recidivist in order to repurchase its brand name capital. Clearly, the more capricious the original FTC complaint, the more likely the firm is to risk later offenses.

A further source of agency-driven recidivism may be the use by rival firms of the FTC's law-enforcement powers as a competitive weapon. For example, in 1971 a group of advertising agencies formed the National Advertising Division (NAD) of the Council of Better Business Bureaus as a self-regulation mechanism. In addition to operating its own monitoring program, the NAD accepts complaints about national advertising from any source, including consumers, competitors, and local Better Business Bureaus. Advertisers whose claims are found to be misleading and who disagree with the NAD's decision may appeal to the National Advertising Review Board (NARB), which attempts to arbitrate the dispute. Cases that cannot be resolved internally are referred by the NARB to the FTC for further action.[23]

The NAD/NARB process is clearly a cartelizing device that relies on the FTC to enforce its agreement. Between June 1971 and April 1980, 931 of the 1,697 complaints received by the NAD came from competitors and from its own monitoring program.[24] We suspect that advertisers having a comparative advantage in cheating on the cartel and fringe (non-NAD-member) firms are the ones most likely to be repeatedly turned over to the FTC by the ad agency group. Other candidates for referral to the FTC are firms introducing new products and those conducting particularly successful ad campaigns. Agency-driven recidivism is promoted because it is likely that firms will be repeatedly turned over for government discipline by the NAD/NARB until the gains from cheating on the cartel are offset by FTC penalties. Data on the source of FTC deceptive advertising complaints are unfortunately not available for testing this hypothesis, however.

SUMMARY AND CONCLUSIONS

In this paper we have provided detailed information about firms that are charged more than once with violating the laws enforced by the FTC. The data covered every law-enforcement action brought by the FTC from 1914 to early 1982. Focusing on the matters reaching the administrative hearing or consent stage, we found that the proportion of FTC activity accounted for by recidivists was approximately 23 percent.

Not surprisingly, the majority of repeat offenses involved violations of Section 5 of the FTC Act, which provides a broad legislative basis for the agency's antitrust and consumer-protection activities. Nine percent of repeat offenses concerned infractions of the Robinson-Patman Act (Section 2 and 3 of the Clayton Act). Relatively few repeat offenses were brought under anti-merger laws or other miscellaneous statutes enforced by the commission.

Strictly speaking, the "antitrust" recidivism addressed in this paper is consumer-protection recidivism. Over half of the repeat offenses involve advertising violations. Firms are rarely charged with multiple monopolization attempts, although 20 percent of the recidivist cases dealt with behavioral violations, the majority of which were price discrimination charges. Repeat offenders are much more likely to be charged with unfair or deceptive advertising claims or to violate standards about how they may represent their goods.

Recidivism is most often found among firms in the apparel and accessories industry. Relatively high repeat-offense rates also occur among businesses that produce goods used in recreation activities. Food and beverage firms, medical product sellers, and personal-care products companies are also prominent repeat offenders. Behavioral violations dominate as a source of repeat offenses among medical care providers and food and beverage sellers; advertising violations predominate in most other categories.

One question that remains unanswered in this paper is whether an examination of Department of Justice case files would reveal recidivism rates similar to those found in FTC data.[25] Differences between the two agencies may arise because the attorney general has primary responsibility for enforcing the Sherman Act and because that agency has the power to impose criminal sanctions on antitrust law violators. Offsetting these differences are a 1948 ruling that allows the FTC, under Section 5, to condemn conduct that offends the Sherman Act, and an interagency agreement of the same year that established a mechanism for allocating cases among the two law-enforcement bodies. An answer to this question is left as a task for future study.[26]

The evidence available from FTC data seems to be more consistent with the hypothesis that the relatively high rates of antitrust recidivism we have observed are due to the presence of law-enforcement institutions and incentives that make it less costly for the commission to challenge the practices of repeat offenders, rather than arising from the behavior of the firms themselves. No matter which theory is ultimately found to explain repeat offenses, however, one conclusion is clear: if one accepts the premise that each administrative complaint arose from business practices that were reasonably likely to be found anticompetitive, then the antitrust laws have been quite ineffective in deterring subsequent violations, since almost one-fourth of FTC activity is devoted to repeat offenders.

This result has an important implication about the efficacy of antitrust policy. A large part of the argument in favor of antitrust is that a single case can deter many other firms from committing similar violations, that is, "the ghost of Senator Sherman is an ex officio member of the board of directors of every large company."[27] Yet, our evidence suggests that even convicted firms may not be effectively deterred from repeating earlier violations. This would seem to weaken the support for bringing such cases. Perhaps enforcement efforts should be focused on those industries and violations where recidivist probabilities are low.

Notes

1. George J. Stigler, "The Economic Effects of the Antitrust Laws," *Journal of Law and Economics* 9 (October 1966): 225–58.

2. Richard A. Posner, "A Statistical Study of Antitrust Law Enforcement," *Journal of Law and Economics* 13 (October 1970): 365–419.

3. Ibid., p. 419.

4. Ibid., pp. 394–95.

5. G. A. Hay and D. Kelley, "An Empirical Survey of Price-Fixing Conspiracies," *Journal of Law and Economics* 17 (April 1974): 13–38.

6. Ibid., p. 18. Emphasis in the original.

7. Ibid., p. 28.

8. Other laws enforced by the FTC include the Fair Debt Collection, Trademark, Export Trade, Fair Packaging-Labeling, Consumer Leasing, Hobby Protection, Textile, Fair Credit Billing, and Fair Credit Opportunity Acts.

9. Initial phase investigations are preliminary inquiries into allegations brought by consumers or competitors. By definition, these activities cannot consume more than 100 professional workhours. Authorization to conduct a full-phase investigation requires commission approval and is usually accompanied by a request for subpoena

power. Projects consist of industry-wide monitoring or testing activities that may or may not lead to formal legal action. Examples include the FTC's cigarette testing program and surveys to determine the effects of trade regulation rules. The "unknown" category does not include actions reaching the hearing or consent stage, which are the primary focus of this paper. These two matter types can be separately identified by the fact that FTC matter numbers are preceded by a "C" for consent orders and a "D" for administrative hearings ("docketed matters"). Thus, the fact that we cannot categorize 735 of the initial and full phase investigations, projects, and external court actions does not affect the results presented in Table 12.1.

10. Cotton M. Lindsay, "A Theory of Government Enterprise," *Journal of Political Economy* 84 (October 1976): 1061–76.

11. A. D. Neale and D. G. Goyder, *The Antitrust Laws of the U.S.A.*, 3d ed. (London: Cambridge University Press, 1980), p. 4.

12. Ibid., p. 244.

13. Ibid., pp. 184–85.

14. The household operations category includes heating and air-conditioning suppliers, burglar prevention and fire equipment products, and firms in the telephone and utilities industries.

15. Robert A. Katzmann, *Regulatory Bureaucracy: The Federal Trade Commission and Antitrust Policy* (Cambridge, Mass.: MIT Press, 1980), p. 2.

16. Docketed matters and consent orders are given serially in Commerce Clearing House, *Trade Regulation Reporter*, vol. 3 (New York: Commerce Clearing House, 1977).

17. One method of evaluating the significance of the observed recidivism time series in Table 12.7 would be to compare it with a baseline series constructed under the assumption that FTC cases are generated by chance. In particular, suppose that in a given year the attorney staff randomly chooses firms one at a time from the population, n, of business concerns in operation, issues a complaint, and then returns the respondent to the pool of potential violators. The process continues until the year's enforcement budget is exhausted at k cases. The probability, p, that all k complaints are issued against different firms is given by the formula: $p = n!/[(n-k)!n^k]$. The probability that at least one firm will be chosen twice is therefore $(1-p)$.

As an example, in 1917 there were 1,733,000 business concerns in operation (U.S. Department of Commerce, Bureau of the Census, *Historical Statistics of the United States, Colonial Times to 1970*, vol. 2 [Washington, D.C.: Government Printing Office, 1975], p. 912), and the commission brought 25 cases that reached the hearing or consent stage. The probability of observing *any* repeat offenses during the year was $1 - (1,733,000)!/[(1,732,975)!(1,733,000)^{25}]$, which is vanishingly small. By using this process, duly noting that n grows over time and making adjustments for the fact that firms selected in one year have a greater chance of being selected again in later years than firms not previously chosen, one could construct a baseline recidivism series. Because the probability of repeat offenses arising randomly is quite small, however, it is clear that the FTC data were generated by a systematic process. Explanations for the nonrandomness are sought in the third section, "Agency- v. Firm-Driven Recidivism."

18. This is probably to be expected as a result of internal rivalry between the Bureaus of Competition and Consumer Protection.

19. See Meredith Associates, "Report to the Chairman, Federal Trade Commission: Attorney and Attorney Manager Recruitment, Selection, and Retention," Mimeographed (July 1976).

20. Katzmann, *Regulatory Bureaucracy*, p. 83.

21. If the commission's budgetary appropriations are tied to the number of cases it brings, regardless of the benefits to consumers, the agency will have an incentive to ignore the returns to society of antitrust law enforcement and to challenge previous violators repeatedly. One explanation of agency-driven recidivism is therefore that the potential benefits to consumers of complaints brought by the commission receive less weight in the case selection process than the "private" benefits to the FTC. Thus, the commission enforces the laws Congress wants it to enforce, whether or not those statutes comport with economic efficiency in some abstract sense. This argument is discussed by Barry R. Weingast and Mark J. Moran, "The Myth of the Runaway Bureaucracy—The Case of the FTC," *Regulation* 6 (May–June 1982): 37–38. See also Kenneth W. Clarkson and Timothy J. Muris, eds., *The Federal Trade Commission Since 1970: Economic Regulation and Bureaucratic Behavior* (Cambridge, Eng.: Cambridge University Press, 1981); and Roger L. Faith, Donald R. Leavens, and Robert D. Tollison, "Antitrust Pork Barrel" (Chapter 2 in this volume).

22. Sam Peltzman, "The Effects of FTC Advertising Regulation," *Journal of Law and Economics* 24 (December 1981): 403–48.

23. Priscilla LaBarbera, "Advertising Self-Regulation: An Evaluation," *MSU Business Topics* (Summer 1980): 55–63. See also Richard A. Posner, *Regulation of Advertising by the FTC* (Washington, D.C.: American Enterprise Institute, 1973).

24. LaBarbera, "Advertising Self-Regulation," p. 59.

25. A Justice Department recidivism rate can be calculated from data given by J. M. Clabault and M. Block, *Sherman Act Indictments, 1955–1980*, vol. 2 (New York: Federal Legal Publications, 1981), pp. 905–32. Between July 1955 and February 1980, the Justice Department instituted 616 cases alleging Sherman Act violations. Offenders charged with and convicted of four or more of these infractions accounted for 99 of these matters, or 16.1 percent of the department's Sherman Act indictments. Recidivism rates ranged from zero percent in 1969 and 1979 to 47 percent in 1956. By arbitrarily selecting four multiple violations as their criterion for recidivism, the Clabault and Block data undoubtedly underestimate the true extent to which Justice Department law-enforcement activity involves repeat offenders.

26. See Federal Trade Commission v. Cement Institute, 333 U.S. 683 (1948). Neale and Goyder, *Antitrust Laws of the U.S.A.*, p. 373, describe the interagency liaison agreement as a "well-established" system of avoiding duplication.

27. George J. Stigler, "Monopoly and Oligopoly by Merger," *American Economic Review* 40 (May 1950): 23–34, p. 32.

Part III

Internal Management and Budgeting at the Federal Trade Commission

Chapter 13

Chairman Choice and Output Effects: The FTC Experience

BRUCE YANDLE

IN THE study of regulation, attention has been focused sharply on the character, effects, and causes of regulation and on the evolution of legal frameworks in which regulatory bodies and those affected by them operate.[1] Along with these broader issues, subsidiary questions have been investigated, such as the pros and cons of independent commissions managed by collegial bodies versus administrative units directed by politically appointed administrators.[2] However, there has been little analysis of regulatory organizations that focuses on how they function in a managerial sense, how production is organized, and how costs and output might be related to the management structure of those organizations.[3]

This paper focuses on these issues. Indeed, its purpose is to report an analysis of a small part of the larger question of management structure, namely, the effect on an independent regulatory agency's operations when the method of selecting the chief executive—the chairman—is changed. The application of what is learned from the analysis may extend beyond the somewhat narrow confines of regulatory commissions. Indeed, the comparison of management

The opinions expressed here are solely those of the author and do not necessarily represent the views of the Federal Trade Commission, its staff, or any individual commissioner. The author expresses appreciation for comments by Robert Mackay, Richard Higgins, Bill Shughart, and Tim Muris; thanks are also expressed to Frank Curtin for computer assistance.

institutions may provide insight to many not-for-profit firms whose decisions are made by voting managements.

Some theoretical analysis is required to frame the issues associated with this analysis. That component of the paper comes first. Two kinds of data are then reported in sections that follow. The first are historical data, a story about the Federal Trade Commission (FTC) which, having been organized in 1914, is the second oldest independent regulatory agency in the federal government. The agency's history provides a laboratory for the analysis, since two distinct methods have been used for naming chairmen of the FTC. The second kind of data presented relate to FTC production and costs. In that section, a statistical analysis of management change on cost and output is reported. Finally, a brief summary concludes the paper.

A Theory of
Commission-Managed Enterprises

The commission-managed political enterprise is a peculiar version of the theoretical firm, though it shares certain attributes with complex private-sector organizations.[4] For example, a political commission and certain branch offices and plants of private firms each receive annual budgets and must generally operate within their limits. Both public-sector and private-sector organizations make plans, argue for projects and programs before a larger bureaucracy, and return the residuals of their budgets to headquarters organizations.

It is generally accepted that private-sector managers are offered economic incentives that are geared to the performance of their particular production units. Quite often, a private-sector manager who directs production shares in the savings or profits produced through that effort, whereby the sharing occurs after accounting period records have been tallied. Moreover, while a private-sector manager who operates with some independence from headquarters may have some discretion in determining the range and mix of output, modern theorists tell us that the agency costs related to that independence will be minimized through competitive market forces.

Unlike the remote private-sector managing agent and his enterprise, commissioners and commissions have no clear-cut reward structure in their management contracts, though the larger political mechanism of which they are a part definitely applies sanctions based on their performance.[5] Residuals can be created by commissioner action, but the resulting resources must be used in the production of products approved by the larger political bodies that have oversight responsibility. Furthermore, the discretion that may be exercised by commissioners when determining a range and mix of output is arguably biased. For example, if production decisions are made on the basis of majority vote, the median voter will determine outcomes. If there is a chair-man with strong legal authority to determine policy and make management decisions, he can provide incentives that alter the behavior of the staff. With agenda-setting capabilities exerted by a chairman, production decisions will be less affected by the preferences of the other commission members, although their influence will still be felt.

Just as with labor-managed firms, or under rules of codetermination in the private sector, a commission-managed political enterprise will be subject to the strivings of key staff members.[6] Since most public-sector organizations provide tenure and other strong entitlements to staff, but not to politically appointed senior managers, workers within a commission organization are somewhat favorably situated to influence production. They can affect the agenda of actions considered by the voting commissioners, create residuals, and quickly transform them into rewarding activities, so long as the resulting mix and level of output is acceptable to those who ultimately monitor agency output. Unlike the private-sector counterpart, which might also be managed partly by em-ployees, a federal commission generally operates as a monopolist. There are few, if any, competitive forces that might dependably minimize the agency costs associated with worker-directed production.

In any case, managers of a commission, whether they be staff, commis-sioners, a strong chairman, or some combination of these, are described here as striving to select production points on a transformation surface. Given some continuous production relationship and fully employed resources, consistent with an annually determined budget constraint, the ultimate question be-comes whose preferences will prevail.

The transformation locus in Figure 13.1 illustrates the problem. Given two kinds of activities available to it, R_1 and R_2, the commission may vote and, in conjunction with staff, who may have influenced the agenda, determine output combination 1, where U^m is a median voter indifference curve.

With voting and strongly diverging views, rules requiring some political balance among named commissioners may dampen swings along the transfor-mation surface that might occur otherwise as turnover takes place among the commissioners. Even with that institutional arrangement, one might still expect to observe a "hunting" behavior as different median voters influence production decisions. However, abrupt changes in direction would not likely be observed unless external forces somehow intervene and dictate some policy changes.

If a strong chairman form of management were put in place, along with other commissioners who also vote, decisions about production could be influenced in two ways. First, the sole authority of the chairman to name key staff and to reward staff would tend to bring staff behavior in line with the

FIGURE 13.1
DETERMINATION OF OUTPUT MIX

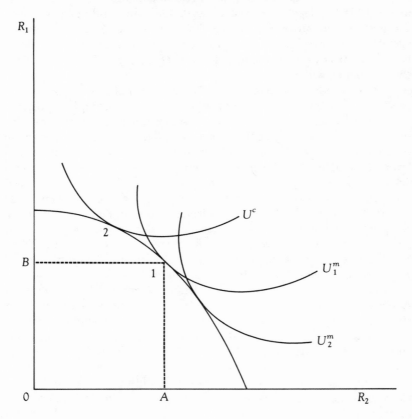

preferences of the chairman. Those key employees will determine the kinds of products to produce, organize the output, and determine its rate of production. The use of residuals, though limited, could be applied more effectively by a chairman-manager. Second, decisions about internal operations made by the chairman, without the needed approval of the voting commissioners, would influence production.

In terms of Figure 13.1, point 2 might reflect the preferences of an individual commissioner-chairman. However, if all decisions, even those regarding staff and management, are controlled by voting commissioners with equal influence on staff, point 2 would not obtain. Point 1, the commission-determined equilibrium described earlier, will prevail. If a change in management rules occurs, naming the commissioner who prefers point 2 as chairman and giving the chairman authority over staff and management policy, a rapid adjustment in the direction of point 2 would be expected to follow, even in a voting environment.

Adjustments in output always generate costs. The larger the rate of movement along the production surface in any given time period, the larger the observed costs will be. However, once a strong chairman has made adjustments, one would expect costs to fall as the previous "hunting" effects associated with decisionmaking by strict voting would be dampened.

There is one further point that might be offered to explain the enhanced ability of a strong chairman to affect the path of production for a federal regulatory commission. Under a strong chairman regime, politics matters to a greater extent than under the weaker system. That is, a chairman appointed by the president, for example, has predictably strong political allegiance to the president and his party. Other commissioners named by presidents with the same party affiliation would be expected to show greater interest in the chairman's views than in a situation where the chairmanship was rotated annually by majority vote of the commissioners, all of whom having been nominated by presidents at one time or another. Productivity, therefore, is arguably enhanced when a chairman and the majority of a commission hold allegiances to presidents of the same political party.

THE HISTORICAL DATA

The FTC officially began business on March 16, 1915. Heralded by one of its sponsoring senators as an independent commission, "removed as far as possible from political influence," and constituted of five commissioners of which "not more than three . . . [were] of the same political party," the agency was nonetheless a major instrument of President Woodrow Wilson.[7] Indeed, the FTC was the legal incarnation of Wilson's "interstate trade commission," a much-debated element in his campaign for the presidency.[8]

While the issue of independence, the meaning of the concept, and the tension associated with it would never go away, that first commission tackled an obvious problem at its first official meeting. They needed a chairman, and no precise criteria had been established for making the selection. It was clear, however, that the commission would elect one of its own members to serve as chief. It was not clear what the responsibilities, term of office, or method of selection would be.

By resolution, the five commissioners named as chairman Joseph E. Davies, a Democrat and the former chief administrative officer of the old Bureau of Corporations, which was absorbed by the FTC. The resolution named Davies chairman for a full seven-year term.[9] Each of the other commissioners held staggered terms of from three to six years. However, recognizing that their action implied that none but Davies would have the honor of serving as chairman, the commissioners soon brought the issue back to the table, took another action setting the term of office to one year, and then limited the chairman's authority to presiding at official meetings. All issues of policy and management were to be decided by the full commission. The FTC thus had its first chairman, a procedure for operating, and was on its way. As it turned out, Davies held office from March 16, 1915, to June 30, 1916, and was followed by Edward W. Hurley, a Democrat businessman from Illinois and one of the original five commissioners. The chairman's slot then rotated annually among commissioners until 1950, when changes in administrative law altered the selection process by instituting a system of presidential selection.[10]

Studies of the FTC's operations over the period 1915–1949 report efforts by presidents to override the collegial form of management used by the independent commissioners.[11] The FTC's history is replete with incidents of actions by Congress that reversed the directions and actions taken by the sitting commissioners.

For example, President Wilson, the father of the agency, was clearly and somewhat understandably active in the operation of the commission during its first few years.[12] Presidents Harding and Coolidge called for presidential dominance of all independent commissions and even went so far as to obtain signed and undated letters of resignation from their appointees.[13] Later, President Franklin Roosevelt obtained control of at least one independent commission by abolishing it and reconstituting a similar one staffed with his appointees.[14]

It was Franklin Roosevelt's effort to gain control of the FTC, however, that led to a definitive statement of just what independence means. In his first year in office, Roosevelt took action to remove William E. Humphrey, chairman of the FTC and a Coolidge appointee. He was successfully removed, and a Democrat was appointed to replace him, but the removal did not go smoothly. Indeed, the government was sued by Humphrey's executor, Humphrey having died soon after removal, and the case was heard by the Supreme Court.

The court's opinion, in favor of Humphrey, found his removal an illegal use of presidential authority and ordered payment of the deceased commissioner's past salary. The court opinion went on to give a statement clarifying the meaning of independence:[15]

> The authority of Congress, in creating quasi-legislative or quasi-judicial agencies, to require them to act in discharge of their duties independently of executive control cannot well be doubted; and that authority includes, as an appropriate incident, power to fix the period during which they shall continue in office, and to forbid their removal except for cause in the meantime.

For it is quite evident that one who holds his office only during the pleasure of another, cannot be depended upon to maintain an attitude of independence against the latter's will.

The debate about the status of the independent commissions and executive control of them did not end with the Humphrey decision. Indeed, reports on the status of commissions by task forces and transition teams have continually raised the issue. Marver Bernstein reports that since 1937 five major governmental studies have reviewed the independent commissions and called for reform.[16] While these five reports included the FTC in their analysis, the agency has been the subject of two additional studies, one by the American Bar Association at the behest of President Nixon and another by associates of Ralph Nader, both written in 1969.[17]

It was the result of one of the government-wide studies—the Hoover Commission report of 1949—that led to changes in the method used for selecting chairmen of commissions and simultaneously increased sharply the authority of chairmen over fellow commissioners in managing their agencies. The changes did not come without debate and controversy, however. Statements from the Supreme Court's Humphrey decision were recalled in Senate debate on the proposals. Representatives of regulated industries and sitting commissioners themselves generally opposed the changes.[18] There was one exception to the opposition, however: the commissioners of the FTC felt that changes would be relatively unimportant and would brook no particular effect on agency operations.

In terms of this brief history, the management structure of the FTC can be divided into two periods: 1915–1949, a period of full commission voting with a weak chairman form of management, strong attempts by presidents to intervene in agency operations, and rotating chairmen with no management authority; and 1950–1975, a period of full commission voting with a strong chairman form of management and chairmen with management and agenda-setting authority who have been named by the president.

The first period, fraught with the early problems of organizing, determining direction, and coping with unusual issues associated with World War I, was one in which presidents and Congress intervened in agency operations. In the first few years, President Wilson was, in a sense, the managing officer of the FTC. The second period, distinctly different from the first, has been affected by a different management system, though external pressures on the commission have arguably been just as severe. In any case, changes in chairmen, especially when the party affiliation of the chairman changes, should produce significant observable effects on agency operations.

The predicted effects on agency output costs associated with the second managerial regime, relative to the first, should be observed in: (1) lower instability in output costs in the second period—that is, less hunting for equilibrium output; (2) sharp increases in costs in association with newly appointed chairmen when political philosophies also change; and (3) long periods of declining costs during the tenure of a single political party.

OUTPUT AND COST

To examine the effects of the different decisionmaking processes that have prevailed at the FTC, data on total actions taken by the sitting commissioners are used as a measure of output.[19] The data were assembled for the years 1916 through 1975, a year marked by an abrupt change in FTC procedures and rulemaking for consumer-oriented rulemaking that came at the behest of Congress.[20] Prior to 1975, commission activity can be described crudely as being case-by-case in orientation.

Total actions by year were divided by total agency employment to compensate for changing budgets, as reflected by workyears, and to give a kind of real average cost of output. Calculations were then made of year-to-year relative changes in workyears per action.

To test for differences in the two periods, 1915–1949 and 1950–1975, when the commission was first managed by voting commissioners with annually elected chairmen and when chairmen were appointed by the president, a means test was calculated using absolute annual percentage changes in workyears per action. This test was to determine if hunting—year-to-year changes—occurred in the first period to a greater degree than in the second. Put differently, the test examines costs to see if they were more stable over the second period relative to the first.

The mean absolute percentage change in average cost was 48.0 percent in the pre-1950 period, with a standard deviation of 38.6. The statistics for the post-1950 period were a mean of 29.6 percent and a standard deviation of 34.1 percent. The two means were significantly different at the 10 percent level of confidence.

The two series were then examined to identify outliers—that is, absolute percentage changes in average cost that were more than one standard deviation from the mean. Four observations were identified in the first period: 1916–1917, 1919–1920, 1940–1941, and 1945–1946, with each period arguably associated with adjustments to or from war conditions.

Outliers observed in the second series included 1961 and 1964, with the first observation associated with a change in chairman and party affiliation. The years with new chairmen of different parties from their successors were then examined in the second period. Such years were 1953, 1961, and 1970. Recalling that the mean plus one standard deviation for the series is 63.7, the percent increase in costs for the three years was 58 percent in 1953, 176 percent in 1961, and 32 percent in 1970. The behavior of average costs in the post-1950 period was also found interesting in another way. After the change in chairman and party in 1953, when costs rose 58 percent, average costs fell for seven years thereafter, or until a new chairman was appointed. Average costs jumped in 1961 and then fell or were stable for five of the next eight years, rising 32 percent in 1970 with the appointment of a new chairman.

There were five chairmen appointed in the second period who were of the same party as their predecessors. The years were 1950, 1955, 1959, 1969, and 1973. Average costs fell in the first four years mentioned and rose 33 percent in 1973.

In short, an examination of the data supports the proposition that the change in the commission decisionmaking process had a distinct effect on agency production and costs. Costs increased at the time when a new chairman and party was named, and then costs fell. Relative to the first period, costs were generally more stable in the second. When a new chairman was appointed who was of the same party as the previous chairman, costs fell in four of five instances. In each instance, the change in cost was less than one standard deviation from the mean.

Some Final Thoughts

This article has examined the cost effects generated for a commission-managed regulatory agency when the method of selecting the chief executive officer—the chairman—has changed. In the development of the analysis, a theory of the commission-managed firm was first presented. In that discussion, several propositions regarding decisionmaking and costs were developed.

These propositions were used as a basis for examining historical data for the FTC and were then subjected to statistical testing. On the basis of the findings, one can conclude that the method by which chairmen are selected matters for commission-managed agencies. That is, costs behave differently when a system of rotating chairmen is used, whereby all matters of business are decided on the basis of commission vote, as opposed to a system whereby chairmen of a voting commission are appointed by outside authority and given responsibility for managing the agency. Although the evidence suggests that costs behave differently under the two management systems, there is still no basis to conclude that one system is to be preferred over the other. To make such a judgment would require the Herculean assignment of estimating and comparing the value of commission output over the time period discussed, a task that is far beyond the scope of this paper. It is possible, however, to conclude that if the output of collectively managed firms is desired, stronger decisionmakers have a positive effect.

NOTES

1. Of course, the literature on regulation is voluminous, to say the least. Examples of each aspect of the literature mentioned here can be gleaned easily from almost any issue of *Regulation* magazine or from any volume of the *Journal of Law and Economics*.

2. Discussions of this issue are confined primarily to studies in administrative law. For example, see Richard G. Dixon, Jr., "The Independent Commissions and Political Responsibility," *Administrative Law Review* 27, no. 1 (Winter 1975): 1–16; Emmette S. Redford, "Regulation Revisited," *Administrative Law Review* 28, no. 3 (Summer 1976): 543–68; Kenneth J. Meier, "The Impact of Regulatory Organization Structure: IRCs or RAs?" *Southern Review of Public Administration* (1980): 427–43; Marver H. Bernstein, "Independent Regulatory Agencies: A Perspective on Their Reform," *The Annals* 402 (March 1972): 14–26; and Roger C. Cramton, "Regulatory Structure and Regulatory Performance: A Critique of the Ash Council Report," *Public Administration Review* (July–August 1972): 284–91.

3. Other research on FTC budgets and their relationship to the political process includes Kathleen A. Kemp, "Instability in Budgeting for Federal Regulatory Agencies," *Social Science Quarterly* 63, no. 4 (December 1982): 643–60.

4. The theoretical analysis here contains component thoughts similar to those in Roger D. Congleton, "A Model of Assymetric Bureaucratic Inertia and Bias," *Public Choice* 39, no. 3 (1982): 421–25.

5. The essence of the analysis of legislatures and special interests by economists is found in Robert E. McCormick and Robert D. Tollison, *Politicians, Legislators, and the Economy: An Inquiry into the Interest Group Theory of Government* (Boston: Nijhoff, 1981). Other examples are found in W. Mark Crain and Robert D. Tollison, "Constitutional Change in an Interest Group Perspective," *Journal of Legal Studies* 8 (January 1979): 165–75, and W. Mark Crain and Robert D. Tollison, "Legislative Size and Voting Rules," *Journal of Legal Studies* 6 (1977): 235–40. The research reported by Roger Faith, Donald Leavens, and Robert Tollison in Chapter 2 of this volume supports one aspect of this notion. They examined FTC actions and found these to occur less frequently in the regions of congressmen who sit on FTC-related committees. Another analysis especially pertinent to the FTC is found in Barry R. Weingast and Mark J. Moran, "The Myth of the Runaway Bureaucracy—The Case of the FTC," *Regulation* 6 (May–June 1982): 33–38.

6. Analysis of codetermination and industrial democracy is found in Eirik G. Furubotn, "Decisionmaking Under Labor Management: The Commitment Mechanism Revisited," *Zeitschrift für die gesamte Staatswissenschaft* 135 (1979): 216–27; Eirik Furubotn and Svetozar Pejovich, *The Economics of Property Rights* (Cambridge, Mass.: Ballinger, 1975); and Rex L. Cottle, Hugh H. Macaulay, and Bruce Yandle, *Labor and Property Rights in California Agriculture* (College Station: Texas A&M Press, 1982), ch. 5. William Niskanen discusses trades between operating bureaus and budget au-

thorities, and an over-expansion of output, with cost minimization. (For the first, primitive model, see William A. Niskanen, *Bureaucracy and Representative Government* [Chicago: Aldine-Atherton, 1971]. A later model is developed by Niskanen in "Bureaucrats and Politicians," *Journal of Law and Economics* 18 [December 1975]: 617–43.) A relevant discussion by Richard A. Posner on strivings by FTC staff is found in his dissenting comment in "Report of the ABA Commission to Study the FTC," *BNA Antitrust and Trade Regulation Reports*, Special Supplement no. 427 (September 15, 1979): 115–18. Kenneth W. Clarkson and Timothy Muris discuss internal agency incentives and external controls placed on the agency in their chapter, "Commission Performance, Incentives, and Behavior," in Kenneth W. Clarkson and Timothy J. Muris, eds., *The Federal Trade Commission Since 1970: Economic Regulation and Bureaucratic Behavior* (Cambridge, Eng.: Cambridge University Press, 1981). Oliver E. Williamson also discusses bureaucratic behavior in *The Economics of Discretionary Behavior: Managerial Objectives and the Theory of the Firm* (Englewood Cliffs, N.J.: Prentice-Hall, 1964).

7. The quotations are from the Interstate Commerce Committee's Report to the Senate (Senate Report No. 597, 63d Cong., 2d sess., 1914) and are found in A. Everette MacIntyre and Paul Rand Dixon, "The Federal Trade Commission After 50 Years," *Federal Law Journal* 24 (1964): 388.

8. Woodrow Wilson campaigned for the presidency on his "New Freedom" platform, which included an independent commission for assuring that competition would prevail. For discussion of this, see Thomas Lane Moore III, "The Establishment of a 'New Freedom' Policy: The Federal Trade Commission, 1912–1918" (Ph.D. diss., University of Alabama, 1980).

9. Ibid., pp. 72–73.

10. It is interesting that the chairman's slot rotated without obvious regard for the dominant party affiliation of the commission majority or the administration in office. An examination of tenures by chairmen suggests no particular pattern of selection. Of 33 chairmen in the pre-1950 period, eighteen were of the party represented by the majority of the commissioners.

11. T. L. Moore's dissertation, "Establishment of a 'New Freedom' Policy," is replete with examples of President Wilson's guiding influence. Other examples are found in Marver H. Bernstein, *Regulating Business by Independent Commission* (Princeton, N.J.: Princeton University Press, 1955), pp. 131–36, and Susan Wagner, *The Federal Trade Commission* (New York: Praeger, 1971), pp. 212–15.

12. T. L. Moore, "Establishment of a 'New Freedom' Policy."

13. See Bernstein, *Regulating Business*, p. 132.

14. The commission abolished was the Federal Radio Commission, which was replaced by the Federal Communications Commission. For discussion, see Bernstein, *Regulating Business*, p. 110.

15. Discussion of the Humphrey incident is found in MacIntyre and Dixon, "Federal Trade Commission After 50 Years," p. 418.

16. The reports are: The President's Committee on Administrative Management (1937), the First Hoover Commission Report (1949), The Second Hoover Commission

Report (1955), The Landis Report (1960), and the Ash Report (1971). See Bernstein, "Independent Regulatory Agencies."

17. "Report of the ABA Commission to Study the FTC"; Edward F. Cox, Robert C. Fellmeth, and John E. Schulz, *The Nader Report on the Federal Trade Commission* (New York: Richard W. Baron, 1969).

18. See Bernstein, *Regulating Business*, pp. 136–37.

19. The data on all actions taken by the sitting commissioners, by year, for 1916–1975 are reported in Table 12.7 of this volume.

20. The passage of the Magnuson-Moss Warranty/FTC Improvements Act in 1974 marked a major turning point for the agency in terms of industry-wide rulemaking. The act established a highly structured procedure for developing rules that would apply to entire industries and prompted the agency to embark on such rulemaking activity, reducing significantly the number of actions heard by the commission.

Chapter 14

The FTC Budget Process: Zero-Based Budgeting by Committee

ROBERT J. MACKAY

FROM 1977 until 1983, a unique voting scheme was used by the Federal Trade Commission (FTC) for determining its collective priorities during the annual budgetary process. The FTC's many activities were organized into decision units with three possible funding levels and plans for action specified for each unit. Each commissioner was asked to provide a ranking of the decision-unit increments, arraying the increments in decreasing order of priority and assigning each a point score based on a modified Borda count. The commission's collective priority ranking was then obtained by summing the scores for each increment over all commissioners and arraying the increments in order of their total scores. Each step in the ranking implied a particular budget, with the total cost equal to the cumulative cost of all the included increments. Finally, the imposition of an overall funding level by the Office of Management and Budget (OMB) led to a choice of a recommended budget with a specified mix of activities.

This paper examines the underlying logic and normative properties of this decisionmaking procedure and highlights its advantages and disadvantages

The author would like to thank Ron Bond, Richard Higgins, James Miller III, Nic Tideman, Robert Tollison, James Williams, and Bruce Yandle for helpful discussions during the preparation of the first draft of this paper. The initial research for this paper was conducted while the author was a consultant to the Office of the Executive Director, Federal Trade Commission. As a result, it is important to note that the views expressed in this paper do not necessarily represent the views of the commission or of any individual commissioner.

relative to alternative procedures.[1] Two analytical perspectives are utilized. First, the procedure is examined under the assumption that all commissioners behave in a sincere fashion, truthfully reporting their budgetary priorities. Second, the procedure is examined at a strategically deeper level by considering the incentives for commissioners to vote in a sophisticated fashion so as to bias budgetary outcomes toward their own conception of the "public interest." In each case, the likely influence of this procedure on final budgetary outcomes is also considered.

THE BUDGETARY PROCESS AT THE FTC: PROCEDURES AND LOGIC

The formal aspects of the budget procedures used at the FTC can be conveyed with a fairly simple and hypothetical example. Suppose there were three commissioners making budgetary choices for three decision units (maintaining competition, consumer protection, and economics) with three possible funding levels for each unit (minimum, current [or base], and expanded).[2] The decision packages would be defined on an incremental basis and each funding level or increment would be associated with a prespecified set of activities. With the assistance of the executive director and the bureau directors, a commissioner would evaluate the decision packages and provide his or her priority ranking of the activity levels.

More precisely, a commissioner would be asked to rank all activity levels for all decision units by arraying them in decreasing order of priority, thus identifying the relative priority assigned to each decision-package increment. A commissioner's ranking would be conveyed by assigning a certain number of 5's, 4's, 3's, 2's, and 1's to the increments, with the highest priority increments (that is, those that should receive funding before any other set of increments) being assigned 5's and the lowest priority increments (that is, those that should be the last to receive funding) being assigned 1's. The only procedural restriction on the allocation of these points is that the minimum level of a particular activity must be ranked at least as high as the current level of the same activity, which, in turn, may be ranked at least as high as the expanded level of that activity. The minimum level of one activity could be ranked lower than the current or expanded level of another activity.

The diverse "priorities" of the individual commissioners would then be aggregated into a single priority ranking for the commission by summing the scores for each decision-package increment over all commissioners and arraying the increments in order of their total score. Each step in the priority ranking would correspond to a particular budget involving that increment and all prior increments with a total cost equal to the cumulative cost of all the

TABLE 14.1
ANALYSIS OF COMMISSIONERS' RANKING

DECISION PACKAGE			COMMISSIONERS' PRIORITY			
Decision Unit	*Level*	*$*	*I*	*II*	*III*	*Total*
A: Maintaining	AM	100	5	5	5	15
competition	AC	25	3	4	4	11
	AE	25	1	2	3	6
B: Consumer	BM	100	4	5	5	14
protection	BC	25	3	4	2	9
	BE	25	2	3	1	6
C: Economics	CM	50	5	3	4	12
	CC	15	4	2	3	9
	CE	15	2	1	2	5

included increments. With this statement of the commission's priorities, the imposition of an overall funding level, by the OMB or Congress, would lead in a natural way to a choice of a budget with a specific mix of activities included. Different funding levels would result in a different mix of activities being included.

This discussion can be made more concrete with the help of Tables 14.1 and 14.2. The commissioners are denoted by I, II, and III; the decision units are A, B, and C; and the funding increments by M, C, and E. Table 14.1 shows the incremental cost of each activity level and the priority ranking for each of the commissioners. The scores assigned by all commissioners for each increment have been totaled to obtain that increment's relative score.

Table 14.2 displays the commission's priority ranking that would result from these procedures. It also shows the cost of each increment and the cumulative cost as one moves down the ranking to lower priority increments. If the OMB were to impose an overall funding level of $300, then this limit combined with the commission's statement of priorities would lead to an implied budget of AM, BM, CM, AC, and BC—that is, minimum-level funding for all three decision units along with current-level funding for units A and B. This budget choice could be represented more simply as (AC, BC, CM) since the approval of current-level funding implies that minimum level funding has been approved.

As the present example clearly indicates, the budget procedures at the FTC involved: (1) a sequential and incremental approach to the construction of a final budget rather than a total approach based on a direct comparison of all alternative budgets that could be constructed from the set of proposed

TABLE 14.2

COMMISSION'S PRIORITY RANKING AS DEFINED BY FTC BUDGET PROCEDURES

	Decision Unit Level	Relative Score	Amount	Cumulative Amount
	AM	15	$100	$100
	BM	14	100	200
	CM	12	50	250
	AC	11	25	275
OMB mark	BC	9	25	300
	CC	9	15	315
	AE	6	25	340
	BE	6	25	365
	CE	5	15	380

increments; (2) an attempt to articulate and extract individual priorities or "preferences" independently of possible constraints on the overall funding level; and (3) the determination of the commission's *collective* priorities through the aggregation of individual commissioners' priorities by means of a system of point voting. The basic logic underlying these procedures is that the budget process can be broken down into two, essentially separate, stages: first, the internal articulation of the commission's priorities; and second, the external determination of an overall constraint on the level of funding. The commission's priority ranking and the funding constraint then combines to produce a specific budget choice.

For the commissioners, as participants in the budget process, these procedures had a clear practical appeal. They were straightforward and seemed to greatly reduce the scale and complexity of the decision problem at hand. The commissioners were required to rank only the individual decision units, rather than all possible budgets that might be constructed from various combinations of these units.[3] These procedures simplified matters even further by not requiring the commissioners to provide a full ordinal ranking of the decision units; instead, they only had to divide the units into five priority classes. On bounded rationality grounds, then, the procedures seemed quite attractive, since they apparently imposed a minimum of decisionmaking costs. They also seemed to enhance communication, since each commissioner was given the opportunity to convey his or her felt priorities to the other commissioners as well as to the staff of the commission. Finally, the procedures had a certain intuitive appeal given the obvious analogy to the way an individual decisionmaker might go about making the same choices; instead, however, they incorporated the *average* judgment, values, and expertise of a diverse group of decisionmakers.[4]

THE BUDGET PROCESS
WITH SINCERE BEHAVIOR

Despite the apparent advantages of these procedures, their basic structure—an incremental approach based on point voting—raises several concerns. First, does the incremental approach to the construction of a budget through a priority ranking of individual decision units lead to the same outcome as a total approach based on a direct ranking or comparison of alternative budgets? This is a property that one might expect of individual decisionmaking, so the question of whether or not it is true of these collective decisionmaking procedures warrants some interest and attention. Second, and relatedly, are these procedures likely to lead to policy outcomes that are acceptable to a majority of the commissioners? In other words, how do these procedures square with various normative notions of majority rule? Finally, are there any hidden or unconscious procedural influences in the current budget process? Does the process have a tendency to be systematically biased in favor of or against certain types or sizes of projects?[5]

Insight into these basic issues can be obtained through an examination of the following example, which builds on but modifies the previous one. Suppose that the three decision units are each being considered for two possible funding levels—a minimum level and a current level. In addition, suppose that the incremental cost for each minimum level is $100 and for each current level is $50. The commissioners' estimates of the incremental social benefits from decision-unit increments are shown in Table 14.3. Incremental benefit-cost ratios, denoted **r**, have been calculated using the information provided and are also shown in Table 14.3.

In this example, commissioners II and III assign the same priorities to the decision-unit increments although their estimates of the incremental benefit-cost ratios are somewhat different. Commissioner I, by contrast, would assign roughly the opposite priorities. Suppose each commissioner behaves sincerely and reports his true priority ranking. The priority rankings would then be as shown in Table 14.4, where a commissioner's first priority is assigned a score of 6 while the lowest priority is assigned a score of 1. The score for each decision-unit increment is summed across all commissioners and is shown in the fourth column.

The commission's collective priority ranking, as defined by an incremental Borda count, is shown in Table 14.5 along with the cost and cumulative cost of

TABLE 14.3

COMMISSIONERS' VALUATION OF DECISION-UNIT FUNDING LEVELS

Decision Unit		I		II		III	
Level	Cost	ISB[a]	ρ[b]	ISB	ρ	ISB	ρ
AM	$100	$150	1.5	$125	1.25	$120	1.2
AC	50	70	1.4	60	1.2	55	1.1
BM	$100	$145	1.45	$165	1.65	$160	1.6
BC	50	65	1.3	78	1.56	75	1.5
CM	$100	$125	1.25	$ 80	1.8	$170	1.7
CC	50	55	1.1	80	1.6	78	1.56

NOTES: a. ISB=Incremental Social Benefits.

b. ρ=Incremental Social Benefit to Cost Ratio.

each increment. If the overall funding level were $300, then the implied choice of a final budget would be (AM, BM, CM). All the minimum levels would be funded with no current levels funded.

What is to be made of this outcome? To what extent can it be said to reflect the commissioners' preferences? One plausible way of addressing this question is to compare this outcome with the outcome that would result from applying a Borda count to the commissioners' rankings of all possible budgets that could be formed from this set of increments.[6] This alternative procedure immediately suggests itself once one focuses on the fact that the actual procedures require commissioners to rank *individual* decision units as candidates for stages in the construction of a final budget, when, presumably, what commissioners care about is the makeup of the final budget, not what particular units were

TABLE 14.4

ANALYSIS OF THE COMMISSIONERS' RANKING

Decision Unit Level	COMMISSIONERS' PRIORITY			
	I	II	III	Total
AM	6	2	2	10
AC	4	1	1	6
BM	5	5	5	15
BC	3	3	3	9
CM	2	6	6	12
CC	1	4	4	9

TABLE 14.5
COMMISSION'S PRIORITY RANKING AS DEFINED BY A BORDA COUNT

	Decision Unit Level	Relative Score	Amount	Cumulative Amount
	BM	15	$100	$100
	CM	12	100	200
OMB	AM	10	100	300
mark	BC	9	50	350
	CC	9	50	400
	AC	6	50	450

given higher priority. Fortunately, the scale of this example is small enough so that the required calculations to make the comparison are feasible.

Assuming that the commissioners view the decision units as independent of one another (that is, there are no significant substitutability or complementary relationships between the decision units in either production or consumption), then it is possible to calculate the net social benefits resulting from a particular budget by simply summing the net social benefits derived from its parts.[7] Table 14.6 lists all possible budgets—all 26 of them excluding the zero budget—along with the net social benefits each commissioner estimates for that budget and its ranking in his preference ordering. Under a Borda count, a commissioner's most preferred budget is assigned a score of 26 and the least preferred budget is assigned a score of 1. If a commissioner is indifferent between any budgets, they each receive the average of the sum of the scores they would get if they occupied the same position in the commissioner's ranking but were not tied.

The commission's ranking of budgets, as defined by the Borda count, is shown in Table 14.7. If the overall funding level is $300, then this procedure leads to a budget choice of (BC, CC) rather than (AM, BM, CM), as would be chosen under the actual procedures used. Quite clearly then, the procedures based on an incremental approach are not, as might have been hoped, simply a computational shortcut for obtaining the same results as the more comprehensive procedure. In other words, the incremental approach and the total approach do not necessarily lead to the same policy outcomes when starting from the same underlying set of preferences and constraints.

Which approach is better? There is no easy answer to this question. Both approaches have a certain intuitive appeal by analogies with the theory of individual decisionmaking. However, is there anything more attractive about the outcome (BC, CC) than the outcome (AM, BM, CM)? One way to answer this question would be to let the commissioners directly compare the options.

TABLE 14.6

COMMISSIONERS' RANKINGS AND VALUATIONS OF BUDGETS

Budget Levels	I		II		III	
	NSB[a]	Rank	NSB	Rank	NSB	Rank
(AC,BC,CC)	$160	26.0	$238	26.0	$208	26.0
(AC,BC,CM)	155	25.0	208	23.0	180	22.0
(AC,BM,CC)	145	24.0	210	24.0	183	23.5
(AC,BM,CM)	140	22.5	180	19.0	155	17.5
(AM,BC,CC)	140	22.5	228	25.0	203	25.0
(AM,BC,CM)	135	21.0	198	20.0	175	20.0
(AM,BM,CC)	125	19.0	200	21.5	178	21.0
(AM,BM,CM)	120	18.0	170	16.5	150	16.0
(AC,BC)	130	20.0	128	12.0	110	12.0
(AC,BM)	115	17.0	100	7.0	85	6.5
(AM,BC)	110	16.0	118	10.5	105	11.0
(AM,BM)	95	13.5	90	5.5	80	5.0
(AC,CC)	100	15.0	145	14.5	123	14.0
(AC,CM)	95	13.5	115	10.5	95	9.0
(AM,CC)	80	10.0	135	13.0	118	13.0
(AM,CM)	75	8.5	105	8.0	90	8.0
(BC,CC)	90	12.0	203	21.5	183	23.5
(BC,CM)	85	11.0	173	16.5	115	17.5
(BM,CC)	75	8.5	175	18.0	158	19.0
(BM,CM)	70	6.5	145	14.5	130	15.0
(AC)	70	6.5	35	2.0	25	2.0
(AM)	50	4.0	25	1.0	20	1.0
(BC)	60	5.0	93	5.5	85	6.5
(BM)	45	3.0	65	3.0	60	3.0
(CC)	30	2.0	110	9.0	98	10.0
(CM)	25	1.0	80	4.0	70	4.0

NOTE: a. NSB=Net Social Benefit.

Suppose that the commission, faced with the current dilemma, was allowed to choose between the budgetary outcomes in a direct vote.[8] Which budget would win? An examination of Table 14.6 reveals that commissioners II and III both prefer (BC, CC) to (AM, BM, CM) and, hence, it would be chosen by a 2 to 1 margin. It is important to be aware, then, that the incremental procedures can lead to a policy outcome that a majority of the commissioners view as inferior to some feasible alternative.

This result, however, is not simply a peculiar property of the incremental nature of the procedures. Instead, it is a basic property of the Borda count or,

TABLE 14.7
COMMISSION'S RANKING OF BUDGETS AS DEFINED BY A BORDA COUNT

	Budget Levels	Relative Score	Amount	
	(AC,BC,CC)	78.0	$450	
	(AM,BC,CC)	72.5	400	
	(AC,BM,CC)	71.5	400	
	(AC,BC,CM)	70.0	400	
	(AM,BM,CC)	61.5	350	
	(AM,BC,CM)	61.0	350	
OMB	(AC,BM,CM)	59.0	350	infeasible
mark	(BC,CC)	57.0	300	feasible
	(AM,BM,CM)	50.5	300	
	(BM,CC)	45.5	250	
	(BC,CM)	45.0	250	
	(AC,BC)	44.0	300	
	(AC,CC)	43.5	300	
	(AM,BC)	37.5	250	
	(AM,CC)	36.0	250	
	(BM,CM)	36.0	200	
	(AC,CM)	33.0	250	
	(AC,BM)	30.5	250	
	(AM,CM)	24.5	200	
	(AM,BM)	24.0	200	
	(CC)	21.0	150	
	(BC)	17.0	150	
	(AC)	10.5	150	
	(BM)	9.0	100	
	(CM)	9.0	100	
	(AM)	6.0	100	

for that matter, most any weighted voting scheme. Note that the Borda count applied to the set of all possible budgets actually ranks certain budgets higher than other budgets that are capable of defeating them in a majority rule election. In the present example, the Borda count ranks (AM, BM, CM) higher than both (BM, CC) and (BC, CM), although either of these budgets is preferred to the former budget by both commissioners II and III (see Table 14.6).

The Borda count tends to work against "extreme" options—those highly favored by some, even a majority, but also highly opposed by a significant minority—and searches instead for a "compromise" option—one ranked *relatively* high by all the commissioners. Depending on one's philosophical position (or, more likely, one's position on the issues), this characteristic of point voting may be viewed as either an advantage or disadvantage. For some, it provides partial protection from the "tyranny of the majority." For others, it involves a fundamental subversion of basic notions of majority rule.[9]

At a philosophically less fundamental level, the incremental approach appears to have a tendency to include minimum-level funding for each of the decision units, while the total approach appears to more easily allow for comparisons and trade-offs between minimum levels and combinations of current levels of funding. In actual practice, moreover, minimum-level funding for all decision units on the menu seemed virtually assured. The incremental nature of the budget process, the incommensurate sizes of the funding increments, and the coarseness in the scoring of the rankings all mitigated against a systematic and coherent comparison and trade-off of minimum-level funding for some units against packages of current- and expanded-level funding for others.

There is one further difficulty with the incremental procedures that should be addressed before moving on to examine strategic considerations. In the present example, the commissioners were assumed to form their ranking by using their estimates of the social benefit to cost ratio for the decision-unit increments as a measure of priority. Unfortunately, this criterion may lead to certain difficulties when the projects are discrete (that is, when fractional increments are not possible) and of significantly different sizes. To illustrate the difficulties involved, suppose that the OMB were willing to support an overall funding level of $350 instead of $300. Does the priority ranking in Table 14.4 for, say, commissioner I reveal the best choice of budget? Unfortunately, the answer is no. If the decision-unit increments were not discrete, then the best choice would be (AC, BC) plus half of CM, with a cumulative net social benefit of $142.5; however, this option is simply not available. Instead, in order for commissioner I to find the best budget, he must scan all possible uses of $350. In this case, the best use of $350 is to spend it on (AC, BM, CM), with a cumulative net social benefit of $140.

The problem here is analogous to the classic capital budgeting problem facing a firm with discrete investment projects and either an externally or internally imposed financing constraint.[10] In this case, the firm cannot simply choose all projects with an expected rate of return greater than or equal to the interest rate or cost of funds. As the literature on the theory of finance indicates, it is generally not possible under these circumstances to pick a single best criterion for ranking investment projects. This difficulty also strikes at the heart of the logic underlying the incremental procedures, since it implies that there may not be a coherent way to state priorities or to rank decision units independently of the budget constraint that might ultimately be imposed.

The Budget Process
with Sophisticated Behavior

The analysis in the previous section was predicted on the assumption that the commissioners behaved in a sincere manner, truthfully reporting their felt preferences or budget priorities as if they alone determined the collective outcome. They did not try to read the priorities of other commissioners and then manipulate the FTC's priority ranking by misreporting their true priorities. By contrast, the analysis of this section examines the extent to which there are incentives, implicit in these procedures, for commissioners to behave in a sophisticated or strategic fashion, drawing on their personal knowledge of other commissioners' priorities in an attempt to manipulate commission decisions in the direction of their own conception of the public interest.[11] In addition, this section examines the likely effect of these incentives on the commission's budgetary decisions and on the meaning that can be attached to the priorities revealed in the process. The issue of strategic manipulation is especially important in the context of a small and ongoing committee, such as the commission. In this case, all the members are reasonably well informed about the preferences of their fellow members and each member is likely to be significant in determining the collective outcome.[12]

A First Approximation

To gain some initial insight into how sophisticated voting might proceed under these procedures, consider the following highly simplified example of the budget process. Suppose there are five decision units, denoted A, B, C, D, and E, being considered for an expanded level of funding, but only three of the five can be funded under the planning level proposed by the OMB. The budget increments are the same for all units, and if a unit's budget is not expanded it receives base-level funding. (Historically, this example is somewhat dated.) Moreover, suppose the commissioners can state a consistent priority ranking of the decision units, based on an expected social benefit to cost ratio. For this example, the commissioners' true priority rankings are assumed to be as shown in Table 14.8.A and are denoted by S_I, S_{II}, and S_{III}.

As established in the previous section, the sincere voting strategies involve each commissioner reporting his true priority ranking. The sincere voting decision results from applying a Borda count to the sincere situation. The sincere decision, based on the commission's priority ranking, is shown in Table 14.8.A and leads to expanded-level funding for units A, B, and D; C and E fall below the mark and, thus, only receive base-level funding.

TABLE 14.8
PRIORITY RANKING WITH SOPHISTICATED VOTING

COMMISSIONERS' PRIORITY RANKINGS			FTC's PRIORITY RANKING

A. Sincere Situations, S

Priority	S_I	S_{II}	S_{III}	Score
1st	A	B	A	A=14
2d	B	A	B	B=13
3d	C	D	D	D= 8 {planning
4th	D	E	C	C= 6 {level
5th	E	C	E	E= 4

B. Situation, S'

Priority	S_I^*	S_{II}	S_{III}	Score
1st	C	B	A	A=13
2d	A	A	B	B=12
3d	B	D	D	C= 8 {planning
4th	E	E	C	D= 7 {level
5th	D	C	E	E= 5

C. Situation, S″

Priority	S_I^*	S_{II}^*	S_{III}	Score
1st	C	D	A	A=12
2d	A	B	B	B=11
3d	B	A	D	D= 9 {planning
4th	E	E	C	C= 8 {level
5th	D	C	E	E= 5

D. Situation, S‴

Priority	S_I^*	S_{II}	S_{III}^*	Score
1st	C	B	D	A=12
2d	A	A	A	B=11
3d	B	D	B	D= 9 {planning
4th	E	E	E	C= 7 {level
5th	D	C	C	E= 6

E. Sophisticated Situation, S*

Priority	S_I^*	S_{II}^*	S_{III}^*	Score
1st	C	D	D	A=11
2d	A	B	A	D=11
3d	B	A	B	B=10 {planning
4th	E	E	E	C= 7 {level
5th	D	C	C	E= 6

What are the incentives for the commissioners to adopt sophisticated voting strategies relative to the sincere situation? Drawing on the analysis of Richard Niemi and A. Frank, sophisticated voting strategies can be determined in an intuitive and iterative manner as follows:[13]

(1) Commissioners consider the current voting situation and the outcome implied by that situation. To start, the current situation is sincere voting by all commissioners.

(2) Each commissioner determines whether he can improve the outcome by altering his own ranking while assuming that all other rankings remain the same.

(3) If no commissioner can improve the outcome, the current situation contains the sophisticated strategies and the sophisticated outcome. If only one commissioner can improve the outcome, he changes his ranking accordingly and the process reverts to step (1). If two commissioners can improve the outcome, then there is a two-person game in which each commissioner has two strategies: revealing the current ranking or revealing the altered ranking. If there is a dominant strategy for one or both of the commissioners, the rankings are changed accordingly and the process reverts to step (1). If there is no dominant strategy, the sophisticated outcome is indeterminate.

This definition can be applied to the present example to determine sophisticated voting strategies.

Starting with the sincere situation, S, as the current situation, commissioners II and III have no incentive to change their rankings since they cannot improve on the sincere outcome—they are getting their first three choices. Commissioner I, however, can improve the outcome by adopting the strategy $S*$ in which he tries to raise his third choice over the line by raising it to the top of his ranking and simultaneously tries to push the third choice of the other commissioners, D, below the line by lowering it to the bottom of his ranking. The new situation, S', is given by (S_I^*, S_{II}, S_{III}), and is shown in Table 14.8.B. If commissioner I is the only one to act strategically by misrepresenting his preferences, he can manipulate the commission's decision. The effect of the manipulation is to make a majority of the commissioners worse off.

This situation, though, is not a sophisticated voting equilibrium. It is necessary to check and see if commissioners II and/or III can improve the outcome by also behaving strategically and misrepresenting their preferences. Consider commissioner II first. Relative to situation S', can he improve the outcome if commissioners I and III do not change their strategies? Yes, he can. By adopting the strategy S_{II}^*, in which he raises D to the top of his ranking and lowers A and B a rank, he can create the new situation, S'', which is given by

(S_I^*, S_{II}^*, S_{III}) and is shown in Table 14.8.C. Note that commissioner II cannot lower C's score, since he was already ranking C last in his sincere strategy. There is no way he can punish C any further. Nevertheless, the outcome that would result from this new situation involves raising D back over the line and dropping C back below the line. Commissioner II has a clear and strong incentive to also misrepresent his preferences.

What about commissioner III? Relative to situation S', he too can improve the outcome by adopting the strategy S_{III}^*, in which he raises D to the top of his ranking and lowers C to the bottom. This change would create a new situation, S''', given by (S_I^*, S_{II}, S_{III}^*) as shown in Table 14.8.D. The outcome is a clear improvement for commissioner III.

Relative to situation S', then, both commissioners II and III have an incentive to change their strategies, assuming the other two commissioners do not change their strategies. Commissioners II and III are in a two-person game in which each must decide whether to behave sincerely or sophisticatedly, taking account of the possibility that the other commissioner may also behave sincerely or sophisticatedly. In this example, fortunately, the dominant strategy for commissioner II is to misrepresent his preferences regardless of whether or not commissioner III also chooses to do so. The same is true for commissioner III with respect to commissioner II's actions. If both commissioners II and III follow their dominant strategies, the situation becomes S^*, given by (S_I^*, S_{II}^*, S_{III}^*) as shown in Table 14.8.E.

As it turns out, these strategies are the sophisticated voting strategies and S^* is the sophisticated voting situation. None of the commissioners can improve on this situation by altering their strategies. Commissioner I cannot reward C and punish D any further. Similarly, commissioners II and III cannot reward D or punish C any further. The sophisticated voting decision, therefore, is a budget including expanded-level funding for units A, B, and D.

Several features of this example are worth noting. First, the sophisticated voting strategies and the sincere voting strategies are quite different for all three commissioners. In spite of these differences, the sophisticated budget is the same as the sincere budget. Although the final budgets are the same, the commissioners' priority rankings are different in the two cases.

Second, these results raise questions about the meaning of the commission's priority ranking. With sophisticated voting, are the details of the commission's ranking to be taken seriously as a measure of priority? For example, is D of equal priority as A and of higher priority than B? This is hardly the case if the sincere rankings are to be believed.

Third, this example clearly illustrates the difficulties that uninformed "outsiders"—such as bureau directors, staff in each decision unit, and others—may face in trying to interpret the *stated* priorities of individual commissioners. Attempting to unscramble or infer commissioners' true priorities from their stated preferences may be a difficult, if not impossible, task for staff members looking for guidance. As a result, it is not at all clear just how much communication goes on during the budget process.

Finally, it is important to note that the stated (but not felt) priorities of the commissioners are conditioned by and dependent on the underlying planning level. Each commissioner is attempting to raise (or keep) his third-ranked choice above the line while lowering (or keeping) its challenger below the line. This means that the stated priorities of the commissioners will change with changes in the planning level. If only two decision units could be funded, for example, the sophisticated voting strategies may be quite different than when three or four units can receive funding. Sophisticated voting strategies depend crucially on the planning level for overall funding. The sharp separation between "preferences" and "constraints" that was such an attractive feature of current procedures under sincere voting is lost when commissioners vote strategically.

A Closer Approximation

As a final step in the analysis, return to the example used at the beginning of the previous section, above. This example moves the analysis a step closer to the complex realities of the actual procedures. The commissioners' valuations of the decision units are shown in Table 14.3, and the rankings shown in Tables 14.4 and 14.5 are summarized in Table 14.9. This table shows the commissioners' sincere priority rankings, based on the incremental social benefit to cost ratio.[14] The sincere voting strategies involve each commissioner reporting his true priority ranking as shown. These strategies are denoted S_I, S_{II}, and S_{III}. The sincere voting decision results from applying a Borda count to the sincere situation. The FTC's priority ranking, as defined by the Borda count, is shown along with the cost and cumulative cost of each increment. If the overall funding level is $300, then the implied choice of a final budget is (AM, BM, CM). All the minimum levels will be funded with no current levels funded.

Again, it is necessary to examine the commissioners' incentives to adopt sophisticated strategies relative to the sincere situation. In considering sophisticated strategies designed to alter the final budgetary outcomes, the commissioners must consult their rankings of all possible budgets rather than their priority ranking of increments. These rankings are shown in Table 14.6.

As commissioner I's ranking of budgets indicates, he prefers (AC, BC) to (AM, BM, CM), the sincere outcome, but cannot do anything to bring it about. He cannot punish CM, since decision-unit C is already ranked last and the minimum level must be ranked above the current level. He can raise BC's score by 1 point, while lowering AC's by 1, but this would only serve to create a tie with AM and expose him to the possibility of (BC, CM) as an outcome. He

TABLE 14.9
PRIORITY RANKINGS WITH SINCERE VOTING

| | COMMISSIONERS' SINCERE PRIORITY RANKINGS | | | FTC's PRIORITY RANKING UNDER SINCERE VOTING | |
Priority	S_I	S_{II}	S_{III}	Score	Cumulative Amount
1st	AM	CM	CM	BM=15	$100
2d	BM	BM	BM	CM=14	200
3d	AC	CC	CC	AM=10	300
4th	BC	BC	BC	BC= 9	350
5th	CM	AM	AM	CC= 9	400
6th	CC	AC	AC	AC= 6	450

much prefers (AM, BM, CM) to this possibility and, hence, he has no incentive to change his strategy.

As commissioner II's ranking of budgets indicates, he would like to see (BC, CC) as the outcome but he cannot bring this about by changing his strategy. However, he too prefers (BM, CC) to (AM, BM, CM), the sincere outcome. He can improve the outcome then by adopting the strategy S_{II}^*, in which he raises CC by one rank and lowers BM by one rank. This lowers BM's Borda score by 1, affecting nothing, and raises CC's score by 1, causing it to tie with AM. Commissioner II is made better off since he now has a chance to end up with (BM, CC) instead of (AM, BM, CM), depending on how the tie is resolved.

Commissioner III is in a position similar to commissioner II. If he changes his strategy and reports the priority ranking, S_{III}^*, in which he raises CC by one rank and lowers BM by one rank, then he too can create a tie between (BM, CC) and (AM, BM, CM), if commissioners I and II vote sincerely. The dominant strategies for commissioners II and III are to report S_{II}^* and S_{III}^* irrespective of the other's strategy. This creates a new situation, S^*, given by (S_I^*, S_{II}^*, S_{III}^*) and shown in Table 14.10.

As it turns out, these are the sophisticated voting strategies, and S^* is the sophisticated voting situation. None of the commissioners can improve on this outcome by changing their strategies. AM is ranked as high in commissioner I's ranking as it can be, while CC is ranked as low as it can be. The reverse is true for commissioners II and III. The sophisticated voting decision leads to a final budget of (BM, CC).

Several features of this example are worth noting. First, under sophisticated voting the commissioners' priority rankings, the commission's priority

TABLE 14.10
PRIORITY RANKINGS WITH SOPHISTICATED VOTING

	COMMISSIONERS' SOPHISTICATED PRIORITY RANKINGS			FTC's PRIORITY RANKING UNDER SOPHISTICATED VOTING	
Priority	S_I^*	S_{II}^*	S_{III}^*	Score	Cumulative Amount
1st	AM	CM	CM	CM=14	$100
2d	BM	CC	CC	BM=13	200
3d	AC	BM	BM	CC=11	250
4th	BC	BC	BC	AM=10	350
5th	CM	AM	AM	BC= 9	400
6th	CC	AC	AC	AC= 6	450

ranking, and the final budget outcome all differ from what they would be under sincere voting. Unlike in the previous example, where sophisticated voting seemed merely to add "noise" to the budget processing without affecting the final outcome, this example shows the potential for sophisticated voting to affect final commission decisions.

Was the effect for good or evil? In an important sense, the sophisticated decision can be judged an improvement over the sincere decision: (BM, CC) majority dominates (AM, BM, CM). The sophisticated decision is closer to the (feasible) majority alternative (BC, CC), than is the sincere decision. This movement does not go all the way to the majority alternative, however, since there is nothing commissioners II and III can do under current procedures to bring it about. Whether or not this is an unambiguous improvement depends on one's normative view of the Borda count relative to majority rule as was discussed in the previous section.

Second, the commissioners were not able to determine their sophisticated strategies without consulting their preference rankings for *all* possible budgets. However, one of the major advantages of the incremental approach is that it supposedly economizes on scarce decisionmaking resources by not asking the commissioners how they would rank all possible budgets that could be produced from all the decision-unit increments. This calculation, nevertheless, is necessary for sophisticated voting under current procedures. A related point, and one commented on earlier, is that the sophisticated strategies depend crucially on the planning level for the total budget. Strategies and stated priorities will vary as the planning level varies, which robs the procedures of one more of their attractive features.

Finally, the extent of strategic manipulation is restricted by two aspects of the incremental procedures. One is illustrated by this example, the other is not. The requirement that minimum levels for a decision unit be ranked at least as high as current levels and that current levels, in turn, must be ranked at least as high as expanded levels, reduces the scope for rewarding one's preferred increments falling around the planning level and punishing those of other commissioners. The fact that the units are only assigned scores ranging from 1 to 5—instead of, say, 1 to 150 as might be the case under a straight Borda count—also reduces the scope for strategic manipulation for essentially the same reason. If commissioners voted sincerely, though, this coarse scoring method would most likely be a drawback, since it reduces the precision in the commissioners' rankings.

Concluding Remarks

What follows from the above analysis are two pessimistic, yet fundamental, conclusions about the reliability of the budget procedures at the FTC as a means of aggregating the individual priorities of commissioners into a collective decision for the commission.

First, there are many methods by which the diverse and sometimes conflicting values of individual commissioners can be incorporated into the commission's decision. There are familiar majoritarian methods and positional methods, the Borda count being only one of many variants. There are still other methods not considered here. Regrettably, even if commissioners behave in a sincere and truthful fashion, these various methods will not necessarily lead to the same decision for the FTC. Different methods produce different results. For example, a Borda count applied on an incremental basis may result in a different final budget than if it is applied on a total basis to all possible budgets, and both these decisions may differ from the majority alternative that would result from a comparison of all possible budgets. The difficulty here is compounded, since no one method is clearly superior to all others. Each embodies different ethical principles and efficiency considerations.

Second, even if a particular voting procedure has been agreed on as fair and appropriate for the decision at hand, the outcomes that result may fail to be compelling or to have meaning because of the presence of strategic manipulation of the FTC's choice. As the modern literature on collective choice has established, all voting procedures embody some potential for strategic manipulation. Certain procedures, such as binary procedures with informed voters, are less susceptible to manipulation than others, such as plurality voting and the Borda count.[15] In some cases, as was illustrated here, attempts at manipulation may simply cancel one another out with no effect on the final decision, but in others the effect may be detrimental. No general predictions are possible about the efficiency implications of strategic manipulation. Nevertheless, it is clear that the budget procedures used at the FTC are particularly susceptible and conducive to such attempts. Any evaluation of these budgetary procedures must proceed beyond their superficial attractions to address these deeper issues.

[*An Appendix for this chapter appears after the following Notes.*]

NOTES

1. The budget procedures used at the FTC during this period were derived from the zero-base budgeting (ZBB) concept introduced by the OMB during the Carter adminis-tration. The distinguishing feature of FTC procedures, compared to other executive departments and agencies, is that the final priority ranking was based on a formal aggregation of the priority rankings of individual commissioners through a system of point voting. The collective choice aspects of these procedures are the focus of the present paper. For a critical analysis of ZBB in general, see the insightful discussion of Thomas Hammond and John Knott, *A Zero-Based Look at Zero-Base Budget* (New Brunswick, N.J.: Transaction Books, 1980).

2. The actual budgetary choices—decision units and funding increments—for 1983 are shown in the appendix to this chapter. In this case there were 47 decision units and a total of 107 funding increments.

3. This was no small advantage since, as noted above, in the 1983 budget process there were 47 decision units and a total of 107 funding increments. The number of possible budgets that could be constructed from these increments would run into the millions. The most conscientious commissioner (or even his attorney adviser) would have a difficult time providing an ordinal ranking of this many items.

4. For proponents of ZBB the procedures embodied the definition of "rationality": budgeteers were required "to clarify objectives, measure performance, consider alter-natives, rank activities in order of priority, and choose only the most important." See Hammond and Knott, *A Zero-Based Look*, pp. 1–7, for summary of these views.

5. For a clear and interesting analysis of a wide set of voting methods that addresses similar issues to those considered here, see William Riker, *Liberalism Against Populism: A Confrontation Between the Theory of Democracy and the Theory of Social Choice* (San Francisco: W. H. Freeman, 1982), especially chapters 2 and 4. Riker, however, does not consider the incremental procedure that is the focus of the present paper.

6. For an analysis and justification of the Borda count as a method of aggregating preferences, see Duncan Black, "Partial Justification of the Borda Count," *Public Choice* (Winter 1976): 1–15, and H. P. Young, "An Axiomatization of Borda's Rule," *Journal of Economic Theory* 9 (September 1974): 43–52.

7. These procedures are capable of handling substitutability and complementary relationships so long as the commissioners recognize these interrelationships and view

their priority ranking as representing sequential steps in the construction of a final budget. In this case, prior units included in the sequence may affect the valuation of later units. See Hammond and Knott, A Zero-Based Look, pp. 49–51, for a discussion of the problems these interrelationships caused budgeteers at the National Aeronautics and Space Administration, Environmental Protection Agency, and Department of Housing and Urban Development.

8. In fact, all possible budgets could be paired against one another in a simple majority vote and then ranked according to the order in which budgets dominate or can defeat alternative budgets. This majority rule ranking could then be compared to the ranking obtained through the Borda count.

9. For a fuller discussion of the philosophical issues involved here, see Riker, Liberalism Against Populism.

10. For further discussion of this criticism of ZBB see Hammond and Knott, A Zero-Based Look, pp. 53–55.

11. The classic analysis of sincere versus sophisticated voting is Robin Farquharson, Theory of Voting (New Haven, Conn.: Yale University Press, 1969). Recent major contributions to this literature are Richard McKelvey and Richard Niemi, "A Multi-stage Game Representation of Sophisticated Voting for Binary Procedures," Journal of Economic Theory 18 (1978): 1–22; John A. Ferejohn, "Sophisticated Voting with Separable Preferences," Mimeographed, Social Science Working Paper (Pasadena: California Institute of Technology, March 1975); Nicholas Miller, "Logrolling, Vote Trading, and the Paradox of Voting: A Game Theoretical Overview," Public Choice (Summer 1977): 51–75; and Richard Niemi and A. Frank, "Sophisticated Voting Under the Plurality Procedure," in P. Ordeshook and K. Shepsle, eds., Political Equilibrium (Boston: Nijhoff, 1982). For an analysis of sincere and sophisticated behavior in the legislative context, see Arthur Denzau and Robert J. Mackay, "Gatekeeping and Monopoly Power of Committees," American Journal of Political Science 27 (1983): 740–61, and Robert J. Mackay and Carolyn L. Weaver, "The Power to Veto" (Working Paper, Hoover Institution, Stanford University, November 1984).

12. The modern literature on collective choice has established that all (nondictatorial) voting schemes embody some potential for strategic manipulation. On this general result, see Allan Gibbard, "Manipulation of Voting Schemes: A General Result," Econometrica 41 (1973): 587–601, and Mark Satterthwaite, "Strategy Proofness and Arrow's Conditions," Journal of Economic Theory 10 (1976): 187–217. The purpose of this section is not to repeat this general point but rather to examine the likely form and effect of strategic manipulation for the particular voting scheme under consideration.

13. See Niemi and Frank, "Sophisticated Voting."

14. Remember that one procedural constraint was imposed on the commissioners' stated priority rankings: the minimum-level funding for a particular decision unit had to be ranked higher than the current level of the same decision unit. The current level of one decision unit, of course, could be ranked above the minimum level of another decision unit.

15. See William Ludwin, "Strategic Voting and the Borda Method," *Public Choice*, 33 (1978): 85–90, for an analysis of strategic voting under the Borda count. See McKelvey and Niemi, "A Multistage Game," and Ferejohn, "Sophisticated Voting," for analyses of the attractive features of binary procedures with majority rule when voters behave in a sophisticated fashion.

APPENDIX:
ANALYSIS OF COMMISSIONERS' RANKINGS

Decision Unit	Level	Decision Package				Executive Director Priority	Commissioners' Priority				
		Workyears	Cumulative Workyears	$	Cumulative $		Chairman	Dixon	Pertschuk	Bailey	Total
Maintaining Competition											
AA Energy: Petroleum Industry	M	36	36	1,822	1,822	4	3	4	5	4	16
	C	5	41	205	2,027	2	2	2	2	2	8
	E	—									
AB Energy: Non-Petroleum Industry	M	30	30	1,170	1,170	5	5	5	5	5	20
	C	5	35	213	1,383	3	4	3	3	3	13
	E	4	39	168	1,551	1	2	1	2	2	7
BB Foot Industries	M	82	82	2,924	2,924	5	4	4	5	4	17
	C	11	93	395	3,319	3	2	3	3	2	10
	E	9	102	331	3,650	1	1	1	1	1	4
CB Transportation	M	29	29	1,092	1,092	4	4	4	4	4	16
	C	2	31	77	1,169	2	1	2	2	3	8
	E	—	—								
CE Professional Health Services	M	53	53	1,916	1,916	5	5	5	5	5	20
	C	6	59	288	2,204	2	3	2	3	5	13
	E	5	64	225	2,429	1	2	1	2	2	7
DA Industrywide Matters	M	44	44	1,708	1,708	4	4	4	4	3	15
	C	2	46	72	1,780	2	1	2	2	1	6
	E	—	—								
DB Mergers and Joint Ventures	M	87	87	3,330	3,330	5	5	5	5	5	20
	C	10	97	415	3,745	3	3	3	4	5	15
	E	10	107	167	3,912	2	2	2	3	2	9

DC Horizontal Restraints	M	31	31	1,124	1,124	5	5	5	4	5	19
	C	4	35	109	1,233	2	5*	2	2	2	11
	E	4	39	192	1,425	1	2	1	1	2	6
DD Distributional Restraints	M	50	50	1,727	1,727	5	4	5	5	5	19
	C	7	57	234	1,961	3	2	3	2	5	12
	E	6	63	245	2,206	2	1	2	1	3	7
EA Compliance	M	22	22	798	798	5	5	5	5	5	20
	C	2	24	91	889	3	3	3	3	2	11
	E	2	26	76	965	1	1	2	2	1	6
W10 Other Direct Mission Resources	M	25	25	1,280	1,280	4	4	4	4	4	16
	C	—									
	E	—									
Consumer Protection											
Product Reliability and Standards	M	43	43	1,502	1,502	5	5	5	5	5	20
	C	10	53	359	1,861	3	3	3	3	3	12
	E	—									
Marketing Abuses	M	50	50	1,869	1,869	4	4	5	4	5	18
	C	7	57	220	2,089	2	2	3	2	2	9
	E	—									
Professional Services	M	22	22	803	803	5	5	4	4	5	18
	C	—									
	E	—									
Occupational Deregulation	M	28	28	992	992	5	5	4	5	5	19
	C	3	31	114	1,106	2	2	1	1	3	7
	E	—									
Advertising Practices	M	50	50	1,672	1,672	5	5	5	5	5	20
	C	7	57	246	1,918	3	3	3	3	3	12
	E	5	62	198	2,116	2	1	2	1	1	5

ANALYSIS OF COMMISSIONERS' RANKINGS (continued)

Decision Unit	Level	Decision Package Workyears	Cumulative Workyears	$	Cumulative $	Executive Director Priority	Chairman	Dixon	Pertschuk	Bailey	Total
Food and Drug Advertising	M	29	29	1,060	1,060	5	4	5	5	4	18
	C	3	32	122	1,182	2	2	3	3	2	10
	E	—									
Energy	M	30	30	1,068	1,068	5	5	5	5	5	20
	C	4	34	149	1,217	2	2	2	3	3	10
	E	—									
Product Information	M	46	46	1,679	1,679	5	5	5	5	5	20
	C	8	54	356	2,035	3	3	3	3	2	11
	E	—									
All Other Compliance	M	44	44	1,523	1,523	4	4	4	5	4	17
	C	—	—								
	E	3	47	134	1,657	2	1	3	2	1	7
Credit Practices	M	65	65	2,301	2,301	5	4	5	5	5	19
	C	10	75	322	2,623	3	1	3	3	3	10
	E	—									
Substantive Support	M	27	27	1,256	1,256	4	4	4	4	4	16
	C	—									
	E	1	28	191	1,447	1	1	1	1	2	5
Regulatory Analysis	M	16	16	1,292	1,292	4	5	4	5	4	18
	C	2	18	193	1,485	2	2	2	1	1	6
	E	—									
Economic Support	M	14	14	604	604	4	5	4	4	2	15
	C	1	15	22	626	2	2	2	2	1	7
	E	—									

Other Direct Mission Resources	M	28	28	1,489	1,489	4	4	4	4	4	4	16
	C	—										
	E	—										
Economic Activities												
F01 Quarterly Financial Reports	M	38	38	1,092	1,092	4	3	4	4	4	4	15
	C	5	43	157	1,249	2	2	2	2	2	3	9
	E	4	47	100	1,349	1	1	1	1	1	1	4
F02 Economic Policy Analysis	M	21	21	779	779	5	5	4	5	5	4	18
	C	2	23	62	841	3	3	2	2	2	3	10
	E	2	25	86	927	1	2	1	1	1	2	6
F09 Line of Business	M	27	27	808	808	4	4	3	4	3	4	14
	C	3	30	81	889	3	2	2	3	3	3	10
	E	3	33	118	1,007	1	1	1	1	1	1	4
F0M Other Direct Mission Resources	M	17	17	646	646	4	4	4	4	4	4	16
	C	2	19	72	718	1	1	1	1	1	2	5
	E	2	21	58	776	1	1	1	1	1	1	4
Commissioners	M	36	36	1,377	1,377	5	5	5	5	5	5	20
	C	4	40	150	1,527	3	4	3	3	3	4	15
	E	—										
Executive Director	M	13	13	559	559	5	5	5	5	5	3	18
	C	1	14	62	621	3	3	3	3	3	1	10
	E	—										
Office of Policy Planning	M	15	15	591	591	4	5	4	4	4	2	15
	C	1	16	70	661	2	3	1	2	2	1	7
	E	1	17	59	720	1	1	1	1	1	1	4
Office of the General Counsel	M	79	79	2,784	2,784	5	5	5	5	5	5	20
	C	9	88	309	3,093	3	3	4	3	3	3	13
	E	—										

ANALYSIS OF COMMISSIONERS' RANKINGS (*continued*)

| Decision Unit | Level | Decision Package | | | | Executive Director Priority | Commissioners' Priority | | | | |
		Workyears	Cumulative Workyears	$	Cumulative $		Chairman	Dixon	Pertschuk	Bailey	Total
Office of Secretary											
Records Division	M	35	35	820	820	4	4	5	4	4	17
	C	4	39	86	906	3	3	3	3	2	11
	E	—									
Services Division	M	16	16	466	466	4	4	4	4	4	16
	C	2	18	53	519	2	3	2	2	3	10
	E	—									
Information Division	M	26	26	608	608	4	3	4	4	4	15
	C	3	29	69	677	2	2	2	2	3	9
	E	—									
Office of Public Affairs	M	10	10	347	347	5	5	5	5	4	19
	C	1	11	43	390	3	3	3	2	2	10
	E	—									
Administrative Law Judges	M	22	22	847	847	5	4	5	3	4	16
	C	2	24	104	951	3	2	2	2	2	8
	E	2	26	74	1,025	1	1	1	1	1	4
Presiding Officers	M	7	7	270	270	3	2	3	3	3	11
	C	1	8	30	300	1	1	1	1	1	4
	E	—									
Adm. and Management											
Admin. Services	M	46	46	1,094	1,094	4	4	4	4	5	17
	C	5	51	122	1,216	2	2	2	2	3	9
	E	5	56	116	1,332	1	1	1	1	1	4

Budget and Finance	M	25	25	800	800	4	4	5	4	4	17
	C	3	28	89	889	3	3	3	3	2	11
	E	3	31	89	978	1	1	1	1	1	4
Information System	M	22	22	1,275	1,275	4	5	4	4	3	16
	C	2	24	142	1,417	2	3	2	2	1	8
	E	3	27	142	1,559	1	1	1	1	1	4
Personnel	M	28	28	808	808	5	4	5	4	4	17
	C	3	31	90	898	3	3	2	3	2	10
	E	3	34	90	988	1	1	1	1	1	4
Library	M	13	13	536	536	4	4	4	4	5	17
	C	1	14	60	596	2	3	3	2	4	12
	E	1	15	41	637	1	2	1	1	3	7
Procurement and Contracts	M	6	6	181	181	5	5	5	5	5	20
	C	1	7	20	201	3	3	3	5	3	12
	E	1	8	20	221	1	1	1	1	1	4

SOURCE: Federal Trade Commission Budget Documents, 1983.

Chapter 15

Voting Patterns of FTC Commissioners

RONALD S. BOND & JAMES C. MILLER III

THE Federal Trade Commission (FTC) is a collegial decisionmaking body consisting of five commissioners, each appointed to a seven-year term. The terms are staggered, and no more than three commissioners can be from the same political party.

Commissioners carry out their collegial responsibilities in two major ways. First, they vote to establish overall policies for the agency, seen most clearly in the budget priorities mutually determined each year. Second, they vote on a myriad of specific issues, the most important of which deal with authorizing the staff to sue companies for possible law violations, deciding whether such companies are guilty or innocent, and determining an appropriate remedy if they are found guilty.[1] Commissioners are expected to express their independent judgments, and some variety is assured by the limit on the number belonging to one political party and the staggering of terms.

Although commissioners of independent agencies have been known to disagree, the extent of such disagreement (or agreement) has not heretofore been the subject of comprehensive study. Nor have the reasons for such disagreement (or agreement). Although an expansive study of these questions, perhaps involving several agencies, is beyond the scope of the present paper, we can bring to bear some rather interesting data that illuminate the extent of

The views expressed here are those of the authors and do not necessarily reflect those of the Federal Trade Commission, individual commissioners, or other staff.

TABLE 15.1
MEASURES OF AGREEMENT AMONG COMMISSIONERS REGARDING
BUDGET PRIORITIES, FISCAL YEARS 1977 THROUGH 1983

	1977	1978	1979	1980	1981	1982	1983
1. Number of commissioners	5	5	4	5	4	4	5
2. Average correlation between rankings of pairs of commissioners	.666	.847	.845	.819	.831	.741	.613
3. Average correlation between rankings of chairman and other commissioners	.749	.864	.855	.843	.825	.677	.614
4. Average correlation between rankings of commissioners other than chairman	.611	.836	.837	.803	.837	.804	.612
5. Correlation between rankings of executive director and chairman	.977	.938	.979	.959	.884	.882	.829
6. Average correlation between rankings of executive director and commissioners other than chairman	.764	.889	.880	.862	.899	.803	.746

SOURCE: Federal Trade Commission.

disagreement at the FTC in recent years. In addition, the data may be used to determine whether the extent of disagreement (or agreement) is more related to party affiliation or to the president who nominated them.

BUDGET PRIORITIES

Once a year the commission engages in an elaborate process of establishing budgetary priorities to recommend to the Office of Management and Budget (OMB). Each commissioner uses a five-point scale to register the intensity of his or her preference for each item in a large set of alternatives prepared by the staff. Each commissioner has equal numbers of 5's, 4's, 3's, 2's, and 1's to allocate. The commission's major programs are listed, each usually with three funding levels: minimum, current (or base), and expanded.[2] The collection of these specific alternatives are "ranked" according to their cumulative scores. Once ranked, items are accepted into the budget seriatim until the OMB's funding and personnel ceilings have been exhausted.

Prior to the commissioners' assignment of ranks to the various program levels, the agency's executive director assigns ranks that are subject to the same

TABLE 15.2

AVERAGE CORRELATION COEFFICIENTS:

PAIRS OF COMMISSIONERS APPOINTED BY THE

SAME PRESIDENT AND HAVING THE SAME PARTY AFFILIATION

	1977	1978	1979	1980	1981	1982	1983
Appointed by same	.611	.854	.829	.799	.826	.836	.722
president	(6)	(4)	(2)	(4)	(2)	(1)	(2)
Having same party	.740	.885	.857	.818	.835	.755	.608
	(2)	(3)	(3)	(4)	(2)	(3)	(4)
All commissioners	.666	.847	.845	.819	.831	.741	.613
	(10)	(10)	(6)	(10)	(6)	(6)	(10)

NOTE: The numbers in parentheses represent the numbers of pairs of commissioners that constitute the average.

SOURCE: Federal Trade Commission.

constraints as those of the commissioners (though his rankings are not counted in the cumulative scores). Since in reality the executive director serves at the pleasure of the chairman, his rankings can ordinarily be viewed as a signal of the chairman's preferences. In a year when there is minimal disagreement among commissioners, the chairman's rankings may be expected to be similar to those of the executive director. In a year when disagreements are substantial, however, the chairman, like other commissioners, may choose to assign ranks strategically, in an attempt to anticipate and counter the rankings of commissioners whose priorities are thought to be different.[3]

To measure the degree of agreement or disagreement among commissioners, simple correlation coefficients were calculated between all possible pairs of commissioners and the executive director for each year from 1977 through 1983. The individual correlation coefficients are shown in the Appendix of this chapter. Table 15.1 presents selected coefficients and averages for the seven-year period.

The average correlations shown in line 2 of Table 15.1 reveal substantially more disagreement in 1977, 1982, and 1983 than in 1978 through 1981. The years 1977 and 1982 were the first years of newly appointed chairmen under newly elected presidents (Jimmy Carter and Ronald Reagan), whose political parties were different from that of their predecessors. Lines 3 and 4 reveal that the underlying disagreements in 1977 and 1982 were of different sorts, however. In 1977 there was more agreement between Chairman Michael Pertschuk and the other commissioners than among the other commissioners themselves. In 1982 the principal source of disagreement was between Chairman James C. Miller III and the other commissioners.

TABLE 15.3
AVERAGE CORRELATION COEFFICIENTS:
RANKINGS OF PAIRS OF COMMISSIONERS BY
APPOINTING PRESIDENT AND BY PARTY AFFILIATION

	1977	1978	1979	1980	1981	1982	1983
Ford	.611	.841	.796	.833	.851	—	—
	(6)	(3)	(1)	(1)	(1)		
Carter	—	.892	.862	.788	.800	.836	.729
		(1)	(1)	(3)	(1)	(1)	(1)
Reagan						—	.714
							(1)
Republicans	.597	—	—	.762	.749	.755	.698
	(1)			(1)	(1)	(3)	(3)
Democrats	.884	.885	.857	.836	.921	—	.336
	(1)	(3)	(3)	(3)	(1)		(1)
Carter/Ford	.749	.842	.855	.829	.834	.789	.743
	(4)	(6)	(4)	(6)	(4)	(2)	(2)
Reagan/Carter						.609	.473
						(2)	(4)
Reagan/Ford						.814	.654
						(1)	(2)
Republican/Democrat	.607	.857	.836	.820	.829	.727	.617
	(4)	(3)	(3)	(6)	(4)	(3)	(6)
Average	.666	.847	.845	.819	.831	.741	.613
	(10)	(10)	(6)	(10)	(6)	(6)	(10)

NOTE: The numbers in parentheses represent the numbers of pairs of commissioners that constitute the averages.
SOURCE: Federal Trade Commission.

The underlying correlation matrices provide insight into the differences between the periods. In 1977 it was the former chairman, Calvin J. Collier, who disagreed not only with the newly appointed chairman, but also with the other commissioners. When the former chairman resigned and a new commissioner, Robert Pitofsky, was appointed by the newly elected president, agreement increased substantially, as reflected in the 1978 coefficients on lines 2, 3, and 4 of Table 15.1.

In 1982, however, it was the chairman who disagreed with the other commissioners. When a second commissioner, George W. Douglas, was appointed by the newly elected president, disagreement between the chairman and the other commissioners increased even further, as evidenced in the coefficient for 1983 on line 3. Disagreement among the commissioners generally also increased as shown by the coefficients for 1983 on lines 2 and 4. Reference to the underlying, correlation matrix for 1983 reveals that Douglas disagreed with Carter appointees Pertschuk and Patricia Bailey even more than did Miller.

Table 15.2 groups pairs of commissioners into those appointed by the same president and those having the same party affiliation. The table also shows the overall average of all possible pairs of commissioners. It reveals that commissioners having the same party affiliation showed higher levels of agreement than commissioners appointed by the same president for all years except 1982 and 1983. Table 15.3 provides more detail. Commissioners are grouped by the individual appointing presidents and political parties, and average correlation coefficients are calculated both within and across groups. What Table 15.3 appears to show is that notwithstanding the disagreement in 1977 between the former chairman and the commissioners, there was a relatively high level of agreement between commissioners appointed by Presidents Ford and Carter. In all years except 1978, the average correlation among Carter and Ford appointees was higher than the average between all pairs of commissioners. Even in 1978, the average correlation among Carter and Ford appointees was about as high as the average correlation among Ford appointees.

Table 15.3 also reveals that through 1981 there was considerably more agreement among the Democratic commissioners than between the Republican commissioners. In fact, agreement between Republicans and Democrats as measured by the average correlation coefficients in the table was greater through 1981 than agreement between the Republicans themselves. The coefficients for 1983, however, show a distinctly different pattern. Taken together, the coefficients suggest that the priorities of the Reagan appointees have been substantially different from the priorities of the Carter and Ford appointees.

Votes on Law-Enforcement Matters

Although the commission delegates to its staff the authority to make numerous decisions concerning the opening, progress, and termination of law-enforcement matters, it reserves to itself decisions on certain crucial matters. For example, a vote by the commission is required to initiate, complete, or terminate rulemakings and to issue, amend, or rescind complaints, consents, and final orders. The commission may also choose to vote on such matters as the opening and closing of initial and full-phase investigations. However, since the number of "optional" votes may vary from year to year for a variety of reasons, we focus exclusively on commission voting patterns where a vote is actually required: consents, final orders, complaints, and petitions to reopen.[4]

Table 15.4 presents data for 1977 through 1983. Line 7 shows the total number of such events for which votes were recorded, and line 8 shows the percent of these votes that were not unanimous. Lines 1 through 6 show the

TABLE 15.4

NUMBER OF COMMISSION VOTES AND PERCENT OF VOTES WITH DISAGREEMENT

	1977	1978	1979	1980	1981	1982	1983
1. Number of consents and final orders	139.0	90.0	139.0	119.0	79.0	53.0	81.0
2. Percent with disagreement	3.6	4.4	0.7	1.7	5.1	9.4	17.0
3. Number of complaints and amendments	12.0	15.0	9.0	16.0	10.0	6.0	9.0
4. Percent with disagreement	25.0	13.3	11.1	25.0	10.0	0	22.0
5. Number of petitions to reopen	5.0	5.0	4.0	19.0	16.0	25.0	36.0
6. Percent with disagreement	0	0	0	0	6.2	16.0	36.0
7. Total number	156.0	110.0	152.0	154.0	105.0	84.0	126.0
8. Percent with disagreement	5.1	5.5	1.3	3.9	5.7	10.7	23.0

NOTE: Data for 1981 through 1983 were taken directly from the agency's computerized matter tracking system. Since votes were often not entered into the computer system prior to 1981, data for earlier years were derived from a variety of agency records. The data cover 100 percent of the relevant votes for 1981 through 1983; for 1977, 1978, 1979, and 1980 estimated coverage is 85 percent, 82 percent, 91 percent, and 96 percent, respectively. Data are for calendar years.

SOURCE: Federal Trade Commission.

same statistics by type of matter. This table reveals that the percentage of votes involving disagreement was slightly higher in 1982 than in previous years and was dramatically higher in 1983. The data by type of matter, however, suggests that most disagreement focused on petitions to reopen existing orders. Disagreement on consents and final orders showed some increase, but disagreement on complaints and amendments thereto was lower in 1982 than in any of the previous years and was lower in 1983 than in 1977 or 1980.

Table 15.5 focuses on those votes where there was disagreement. The data for 1983, for example, reveal substantial disagreement between Miller and Pertschuk and between Douglas and Pertschuk. They also reveal little disagreement between Miller and Douglas and likewise between Bailey and Pertschuk.

In 1982 Miller and Bailey disagreed every time there was a vote reflecting any disagreement among commissioners. Commissioner Clanton showed relatively little disagreement with either Miller or Pertschuk. In 1981 Clanton showed relatively high disagreement with his colleagues, while Bailey, Pertschuk, and Commissioner Robert Pitofsky agreed on every vote where there was some disagreement.

TABLE 15.5
PERCENT OF VOTES WITH DISAGREEMENT
IN WHICH PAIRS OF COMMISSIONERS DISAGREED: 1981–1983

1981	Clanton	Pertschuk	Dixon	Bailey	Pitofsky
Clanton		60	83	67	67
Pertschuk			40	0	0
Dixon				50	33
Bailey					0
Pitofsky					
1982		Miller	Clanton	Pertschuk	Bailey
Miller			25	38	100
Clanton				22	67
Pertschuk					67
Bailey					
1983		Miller	Clanton	Pertschuk	Bailey	Douglas
Miller			52	93	70	15
Clanton				43	29	45
Pertschuk					26	96
Bailey						65
Douglas						

SOURCE: Federal Trade Commission.

CONCLUSIONS

The data presented here imply that commissioners agree far more than they disagree, but the sources of their disagreements appear to be complex. Democrats appointed by Presidents Ford and Carter appear to have agreed among themselves more than did the Republicans. With the arrival of the Reagan appointees, however, the situation changed. Commissioners appointed by the same president showed more agreement than commissioners having the same party affiliation. Moreover, the extent of disagreement over priorities (where commissioners have considerable latitude) does not appear to be greater than disagreement over legal interpretations (where commissioners are guided by statutory language and court interpretations).

Of course, we have presented data for only one agency and for its most recent history—an especially beleaguered and contentious time at that. Whether or not these conclusions would hold for other independent agencies is uncertain. But since only the subject matter, not the incentives, would be different, we would be surprised if the variance were truly great.

APPENDIX

Following are tables of the correlation coefficients of commissioners' budget rankings for 1977–1983. All information was drawn from the Federal Trade Commission files.

1977

	Pertschuk	Collier	Dole	Clanton	Dixon	Executive Director
Pertschuk	1.000	.418	.831	.862	.884	.977
Collier		1.000	.340	.597	.340	.459
Dole			1.000	.753	.829	.844
Clanton				1.000	.808	.874
Dixon					1.000	.877
Executive Director						1.000

1978

	Pertschuk	Pitofsky	Dole	Clanton	Dixon	Executive Director
Pertschuk	1.000	.892	.831	.863	.893	.938
Pitofsky		1.000	.774	.845	.871	.908
Dole			1.000	.819	.842	.833
Clanton				1.000	.862	.887
Dixon					1.000	.927
Executive Director						1.000

1979

	Pertschuk	Clanton	Dixon	Pitofsky	Executive Director
Pertschuk	1.000	.854	.850	.862	.979
Clanton		1.000	.796	.858	.876
Dixon			1.000	.858	.876
Pitofsky				1.000	.887
Executive Director					1.000

1980

	Pertschuk	Clanton	Bailey	Dixon	Pitofsky	Executive Director
Pertschuk	1.000	.864	.820	.875	.812	.959
Clanton		1.000	.762	.833	.823	.880
Bailey			1.000	.847	.731	.841
Dixon				1.000	.822	.896
Pitofsky					1.000	.833
Executive Director						1.000

1981

	Clanton	Pertschuk	Bailey	Dixon	Executive Director
Clanton	1.000	.874	.749	.851	.884
Pertschuk		1.000	.800	.921	.940
Bailey			1.000	.791	.800
Dixon				1.000	.958
Executive Director					1.000

1982

	Miller	Clanton	Bailey	Pertschuk	Executive Director
Miller	1.000	.814	.632	.586	.882
Clanton		1.000	.818	.759	.936
Bailey			1.000	.836	.759
Pertschuk				1.000	.714
Executive Director					1.000

1983

	Miller	Douglas	Clanton	Bailey	Pertschuk	Executive Director
Miller	1.000	.714	.707	.593	.443	.829
Douglas		1.000	.600	.521	.336	.714
Clanton			1.000	.793	.693	.879
Bailey				1.000	.729	.779
Pertschuk					1.000	.614
Executive Director						1.000

NOTES

1. Commissioners vote on specific proposals, known as "motions." By convention, a simple majority determines the outcome; in case of a tie, the motion fails.

2. The minimum level is usually some 10 percent below the previous year's level. The current level represents the additional resources needed to move from minimum to current, which is usually equal to the previous year's level. The expanded level represents the additional resources needed to raise current to expanded, which is usually 10 percent above the previous year's level.

3. See Robert J. Mackay, "The FTC Budget Process: Zero-Based Budgeting by Committee" (Chapter 14 in this volume).

4. The data exclude the relatively small number of votes on rulemakings.

Conclusion

Chapter 16

Concluding Thoughts on the Politics of Regulation

GORDON TULLOCK

THE activities of government can be roughly divided into collecting taxes, making gifts to people, performing services, and regulating the behavior of citizens and groups. This list is not absolutely comprehensive, since governments also borrow money and perform acts that can by no stretch of the imagination be regarded as services. Nevertheless, it will do for present purposes.

Regulating the behavior of individuals or groups is an ancient activity—the laws against murder are just one example of this. In modern times, however, when we use the word "regulation" we normally mean economic controls. Frequently, as in the case of the Federal Trade Commission (FTC), a regulatory board is involved in such controls. Some of these boards, in essence, operate cartels by preventing prices from falling to the equilibrium level. Others control prices and standards of service in more complex and less easily specified ways. Still others, such as the Environmental Protection Agency, are engaged in a variety of activities to control the behavior of the citizenry for environmental or safety ends.

The FTC is very nearly unique in that it is actually a police organization set up for the ostensible purpose of preventing private citizens and companies from violating the laws against monopolization. When Congress initiated the Sherman Act, the old common-law rule—which said that contracts creating monopolies are not enforceable—was transformed into a statutory rule, and the creation of monopolies was made a crime. Years later, Congress decided to supplement the Department of Justice in its antitrust activities with a separate agency, and so the FTC was created.

It is not at all obvious that the reason Congress took this action was because it thought the Justice Department was failing to suppress monopolies efficiently. The concern may have been that the Justice Department was failing to suppress "cutthroat" competitors who were threatening monopolies.

If we look over the entire spectrum of government activity, we observe immediately that the creation of monopolies is one of the government's major preoccupations. It is traditional to say that the tariff is the "mother of monopolies," and certainly no one who contemplates the U.S. trade-barrier structure would raise any questions about this, except possibly to call attention to the existence of quotas as well. Agriculture has been thoroughly monopolized by the Department of Agriculture, which not only restricts production, thus raising the price of food, but also uses the taxpayers' money to subsidize the farmers in return for their agreeing to reduce production. The Department of Agriculture also exports food abroad, not so much because the government feels sorry for starving foreigners as because this gets rid of an otherwise embarrassing stockpile of food in the United States.

For long periods of time the Civil Aeronautics Board and the Interstate Commerce Commission cartelized their respective industries. The exact beneficiaries of this cartelization varied from time to time and from place to place, but that it was not a procompetitive activity is clear. The government also sponsored the creation of monopolies of labor, ocean shipping, and, oddly enough, oil and gas. There seems to be no doubt that, since 1973, U.S. government policy has provided an important source of support for the Arab states' oil cartel (OPEC) that has taken so much money away from Americans and, for that matter, from other consumers of petroleum products.

In 1973, when OPEC was first established, the price of oil rose rapidly. Those Americans who had the good fortune to own oil wells in areas outside the cartel—especially in the United States—stood to make a large sum of money. The great majority of Americans, however, stood to lose money if the price of oil in the United States were simply permitted to rise (as it was allowed to do, for example, in Germany and England).[1] U.S. consumption would certainly have fallen; it is even possible that the reduction, which would have had to be absorbed entirely by OPEC, might have been enough to break the cartel. Of course, it might not have been enough.

This course of action was not followed. A price control was imposed with the objective of preventing the wealthy people who owned oil wells from making large profits. Only domestic oil could be controlled, of course, and domestic supplies were not enough to fill the U.S. demand at the controlled price. This led not only to the long lines at gas stations,[2] but also to the creation of an allotment plan. The essence of this plan was that owners of U.S.

fuel in the ground were compelled to subsidize the import of Arab fuel, the international price of which was much higher. The net effect of this, according to some rough calculations I made at the time, was that for every three dollars taken away from an American who owned an oil well, two went to the Arabs and one to the American consumer. At the same time, U.S. imports of oil were much higher than they would have been if the plan had not been adopted, and drilling for new wells in the United States was discouraged. It seems quite possible that if this price-control plan had not been implemented, the necessary production cutbacks imposed on OPEC would have been sufficiently large to dissolve the cartel's coherence.[3]

With time, the transfer of profits from Americans to the Arab states became less significant. A group of small U.S. refineries, built especially for the purpose of benefiting from the details of the regulations, gradually transferred into their own pockets a large part of the money that had previously been going to the Arab states. The OPEC cartel might have vanished then were it not for another protective activity on the part of the U.S. government: restrictions on exploration for oil in the United States. Today, drilling for oil is heavily restricted in the onshore part of the national domain or in the continental-shelf and outer-shelf areas. It is impossible to say what would have been found had drilling been made easy and cheap, but it could hardly have led to the production of less oil than the United States now has.[4]

Obviously, in the area of oil and gas, the regulatory rules that I have been describing can only be explained in terms of public ignorance. The principle beneficiaries were the Arab states, and their political influence in the United States has not been great. Losers fall into two categories: the owners of oil wells that were already available in 1973, and the American public. An ill-informed American public, which was seeking short-run gains and was unaware of the long-run losses, succeeded in beating out the oil-well owners.[5]

While all of this may seem to have little to do with the FTC, it indicates the extent to which regulation is apt to be subject to strong political pressures. These pressures are not by any means limited to those of well-organized special interest groups. The FTC is almost unique in that it does not seem to have any overt, well-organized, single interest pressing it. (The Civil Aeronautics Board, for example, is pressured by the airplane companies and, in particular, by the airplane manufacturers, and the Interstate Commerce Commission feels the push of the railroad and trucking industries.) Nevertheless, the FTC does respond to a large number of more minor pressures. As the reader will have noted from the essays above (see, in particular, chapters 2, 6, 8, and 11), companies subject to competition that looks like it might cost them money may well be able to get the FTC to put restrictions on that competition. Moreover, companies that are already in trouble with the FTC may be able to get their congressional representatives to extricate them. In most cases, these actions will involve fairly small-scale economic enterprises that only occasionally have anything to do with the FTC.

One can, I think, see three general groups that have been able to influence the FTC. The first of these is a large collection of small companies. This group believes that the development of modern industry and the tendency to produce large plants has been to its disadvantage, and it wants protection. Badly organized, these small companies may not have obtained any significant protection from the FTC, but there is no doubt that they have had an influence on the agency's behavior. They have had an even greater influence on the FTC's language and on how the agency describes its actions and intent.

The second group, intriguingly enough, is big industry. The big industries are well equipped with Washington lobbyists and frequently find it to their advantage to complain to the FTC—not normally about a small company undercutting their price, but about a small company doing things it thinks the FTC can be convinced are unethical. It has been suggested by a number of people, including some of the authors in the present volume, that much of the FTC's effort to prevent "deceptive advertising" and to control certain aspects of the standards of various commodities has actually been an effort to prevent small businesses from cutting into the profits of large businesses. This criticism may well have a significant impact, but it does not have much effect on what the FTC says. The FTC will never say that it is trying to protect a large company from competition by preventing new entrants in its market from engaging in aggressive advertising. It might, however, say this with respect to a small company, if the aggressive advertiser were a large company.

The third pressure group is a combination of the FTC staff and the FTC bar (for further discussion see also chapter 8). This group has a distinct real interest in elaborating and making regulations more complex and in simply expanding the power and jurisdiction of the FTC. This interest is immediately visible in the civil servants who work at the FTC, but it should be said that some of them, the economists, may have less of a motive than almost anyone else. The economists tend to move from the FTC back to academic life, where knowledge of the details of the FTC's behavior is of no great value. This is not to say it is of zero value, but it is not highly valuable. The economists who stay in the FTC, of course, are different. Other permanent civil servants in the FTC have a motive to expand the FTC and to increase its power.

Lawyers are at least as mobile as the economists, on average, but, unlike the economists, their non-FTC income rises sharply with increased complication of FTC rules and increased FTC power. Drastic simplification of the FTC rules, for example, would be a catastrophe for those lawyers and law firms that practice before it. A simple reduction in FTC activity or jurisdiction would be equally bad. Further, they have a positive and fairly strong incentive to make the FTC's activities too complicated for the casual student. This creates a situation in which their specialized knowledge is of value.

Note in this connection that this knowledge need not be real specialized knowledge. It might simply be a claim to specialized knowledge. Assume that the FTC, after listening to the parties, regularly went off and flipped a coin to make its decisions, but kept this practice a secret. So long as potential clients did not know that this was happening, they could reasonably assume that the FTC's decisionmaking procedures were extremely complex and esoteric and that an expert adviser was needed. Since normally both sides would have expert advisers, one side frequently being a group of employees of the FTC itself, it would follow that one set of expert advisers would be beaten. Thus, the fact that any particular expert adviser hired who loses a case would not prove anything, just as the fact that an expert adviser hired who wins a case would not prove anything. So long as the FTC kept its decisionmaking procedure a secret, an "expert" could continue making large sums of money. An outsider could not tell which of the FTC cases were, in fact, the most difficult to argue. Eventually the market might take care of the situation, but this would take a long time.

In the real world, of course, the FTC does not flip coins, but its decision-making procedures are not well elucidated in its formal reports. Under the circumstances, the highly paid specialized representative can probably offer a better chance of success than the one without that background. Thus, the highly intelligent lawyers who go to work for the FTC can look forward to a period of steadily increasing income provided only that the FTC does not follow a simple and straightforward set of rules in its decisions and, of course, that it continues having a fairly wide scope of activities. Under the circumstances, we would expect that the lawyers would favor both expansion and complication.

Note that I am not arguing that the FTC staff and the specialized FTC bar deliberately go out and attempt to make things complicated; they are far more likely to try simply to work out "good" solutions to problems. They have no motive, however, to seek simple solutions or solutions that reduce the scope of the FTC's activities.

The situation is made more complicated by the fact that, over time, most human beings come to the view that whatever they are doing is a desirable activity. Thus, the personnel at the FTC and the FTC bar are likely to come to the conclusion that their activities are desirable and hence should be expanded. The FTC regulations on the labeling of fur and fur products is a good example.[6] There does not seem to be any particular motive for this activity except that the FTC began doing it some time ago and that it does give some employment, though probably not highly paid, to FTC personnel and the FTC bar. Although this is just an example, it seems likely that the same attitude runs through the whole regulations procedure. (For further discussion of this point, see chapters, 2, 3, 4, and 10.)

Adding to the complexity of the whole process and hence making it more expensive, it turns out there is a random component. Consider the fact that when a new problem comes before the FTC and the commissioners do not fully understand it—either because it is, in fact, quite difficult or because they do not try very hard—they must nevertheless make a decision. Furthermore, once they have made a decision, it will be formally written up by members of the staff who are probably not fully aware of exactly what it was that led the commissioners to make the decision they did. The result will be a change in the FTC regulations, law, or precedents, but a change that is essentially random. It seems likely that a large part of all of the FTC decisions meet this criteria. The commission is called on to make many decisions in cases for which there are simply no strong public policy arguments. Under the circumstances, the commissioners are called on to make decisions and in some cases to write regulations, but there is no particular reason to believe that these regulations are motivated by anything other than the need to decide.

Although the FTC's incentives tend toward larger and more complex rules, this tendency is always subordinated to external political pressures. Congress can, after all, change the FTC's terms of reference any time it wants to. Chairman James C. Miller III had a strong desire to reduce FTC personnel when he came to the agency, yet he was almost completely unable to do so because Congress did not like the idea and passed laws cementing various individuals and offices into his organizational chart. In most of these cases, the special-interest group was, quite literally, the civil servants. They were able to point out to their congressional representatives that they would be fired if their offices were abolished. Normally, they were able to develop some favorable publicity by claiming that whatever it was they were doing was desirable. This was particularly true when what they were doing was investigating potential violations of something as arcane as the antitrust laws. It is always possible to maintain that any company has, somewhere within its jurisdiction, somebody who might conceivably be violating the antitrust laws.

Antitrust activity has the interesting characteristic that the arguments for it are all of a public-interest nature. For example, we would be better off if there were no monopolies except patent monopolies in our society, yet none of us has much to gain from the termination of any given monopoly. Thus we should all be in favor of antitrust legislation and pay relatively little attention to the details because they have little or no effect on us personally. Indeed, it is possible to argue that breaking down private monopolies (as opposed to the government-sponsored monopolies) would not be of any great value to any of us even if all of them were disposed of. Further, the rent-avoidance cost of this activity would be high, although the major costs of establishing monopolies are already sunk. In other words, we are already less wealthy than we would have been had the resources not been invested in seeking that particular monopoly. Abolishing the monopoly does not bring those resources back into existence. This point has been emphasized by Robert Tollison.[7] Indeed, if we abolish a particular monopoly somewhere, this may provide people with incentives for investing resources and trying to recreate it, whereas letting it remain quietly in existence would not lead to this particular resource loss.

This is almost the perfect area for political pressure to be exerted. On one side we have a general public good; on the other side, a number of specific private goods. If it is possible to have an apparatus that is set up nominally to promote the public good, while actually providing private goods to small, well-organized groups under cover of generating that public good, we have a lawyer's paradise. It is unfortunately true that this is the situation at the FTC and, to a lesser but nevertheless genuine extent, at the Department of Justice's Antitrust Division. If I sue you, alleging that you are a monopolist and offering as evidence that you have been undercutting my prices and hence trying to drive me out of business, the average citizen who does not study the matter carefully is apt to assume that I am probably in the right and you are in the wrong. If I allege that you are making false statements in your advertising, this assumption is even more likely, especially if your statement is technical, since it is always possible to misinterpret such a statement. The average citizen who does not know what the statement means specifically anyway may well be taken in by my misinterpretation.

The creation of rules by Congress is also subject to this kind of pressure. The objective of Congressional members is to produce something that has a specific payoff to their constituencies under the cloak of public interest. Unfortunately, the activities of the FTC lend themselves particularly well to this goal. I am not, of course, arguing that the FTC is unusual among government bureaus in this respect, but it is a good example.

Why do we observe governments engaging in this kind of activity? In particular, why does Congress, instead of simply making detailed rules, delegate a good deal of the rulemaking authority to administrative bodies? I can understand the delegation of the actual enforcement of rules, but it seems from a political standpoint that it would be easier to ensure a favorable payoff on a particular set of rules if the politicians themselves made them.

It is not just with the regulatory bodies that this problem arises. The Anglo-Saxon tradition of common law, in which the courts themselves not only enforce the rules but also make a great many of the rules they enforce, is another example of the same problematic system. In both cases, it is generally thought that the legislature (or whatever relevant voting body) can impose any rules it wishes on the courts or the regulatory agencies, but a large part of the detailed working out of the rules is left to them. Since these details normally have a good deal of rent potential, this is surprising. When I was in law school, I was told about the common-law and regulatory bodies. It was only afterwards that I realized their mere existence meant that legislatures were giving up part of the potential rents of their jobs.

It is so much a matter of our present-day consciousness that the courts—not legislatures or rulers—will enforce the law, that we fail to remember that this is essentially a new policy. The Roman Senate directly heard cases and later, as the empire became larger, directly heard appeals. The emperor also directly heard appeals and sometimes directly participated in courts in the first instance. Hearing cases is one of the traditional duties of a king. Why Western culture moved away from this particular activity in the post-Renaissance period is not obvious.

These are puzzles for which I frankly do not have answers. I think we can offer an explanation for the delegation of detailed power on the grounds, quite simply, that the legislature and political officials cannot themselves directly make an immense number of detailed decisions.[8] Making major decisions and then delegating the making of minor decisions subject to considerable supervision by politicians affords the opportunity to maximize effective power. In so doing, political officials run into the usual problems of agency. The courts or the administrative bodies will not carry out the politicians' desires perfectly, but they may nevertheless be better off than if they tried to deal with everything themselves. This is particularly true in the case of regulatory bodies, since their resistance to legislative intervention in individual cases is much less serious than that of the courts.

Thus, the justification for a regulatory board, or for any other lawmaking or government institution, is the generation of a wide range of benefits, which we can call public goods, or the reduction of extreme externalities. In practice there is no doubt that governments do engage in this latter kind of activity, demonstrated by such bodies as police forces, military forces, and a weather bureau. It is equally obvious, however, that a large part of government activity is devoted to generating particular benefits for small groups of people. Although wide spread, this is characteristically carried on with little or no discussion of it. If Richard Posner is right, that one of the effects of the FTC's accurate labeling activities is to make it hard for small companies to compete with big ones, then it is clear that this particular activity (or at least the explanation for it) would have to be kept out of the public eye if the FTC is to continue doing it.[9] In fact, it is so thoroughly unnoticed that, except for the limited number of people who have read Posner's article, not all of whom believe it, almost no one has even suspected that this is the actual motive. It is even likely that the attorneys and other officials enforcing antitrust law or bringing complaints before the FTC—although they are aware of the benefits and injuries to different parties in a particular piece of litigation—do not realize what the general pattern is.

Note, however, that although this is true of regulation, it is also true of a great deal of the law. The farm program is essentially a matter of straightforward legislation and originally involved just exactly this kind of deception— although by now I think the true effects have become pretty well known.

Further, this extreme lack of public information generally requires that the particular activity be undertaken in an inefficient way. If we accept Posner's explanation for the labeling provisions, then the large companies who are protected by it could be protected much more efficiently at a much lower cost by direct taxes or fines imposed on their small competitors. We will never see this because the public would not put up with it. Hence a less efficient method is chosen.

It is unfortunate that the market does not work well when there are large externalities and, unfortunately, there are many areas where the externalities are large. I think we can truthfully say that the government does not work well anywhere but where the externalities are large, and in those cases it may well work better than the market. Thus regulation, whether it constitutes a restriction of the frequency of murders or the FTC's ostensible efforts to control monopolies, is a sensible solution for a number of problems. Unfortunately, it has fairly severe difficulties and these mean that regulation will probably never work well. This is not an argument for refraining from all regulation, but for being realistic in our expectations. We should not expect a great deal of good to come out of a regulatory board. It may be better than no regulatory board, and it will possibly cure some defects of the market, but, at the same time, it will bring with it some of its own defects.

This is simply an argument for not being too optimistic, though we should certainly try to see what we can do about making regulatory agencies more efficient. The attitude of those who turn to regulatory boards because there is a defect in the market and expect them to work perfectly is more likely to lead to boards that behave imperfectly than if they were set up by more cynical people. What is required here is a combination of a reasonable amount of cynicism with respect to the functioning of government agencies and the realization that, in spite of the difficulties, these agencies may be the best solution we have. This requires careful thought and a good deal of further research.

In the particular case of the FTC we are fortunate with regard to research. The FTC research arm has contained a number of people who have been interested in studying government restraints as well as the functioning of bureaucracies. This volume chronicles the bulk of the work by these scholars. As a result, I think we can truthfully say that we know more about the actual functioning of the FTC than about any other part of the federal bureaucracy.

Indeed, we may know more about the functioning of the FTC than about any other bureaucracy in the world.

All of these papers have focused on just one bureaucracy, but there is every reason to believe that we can apply the lessons to many bureaucracies and, in particular, to many regulatory agencies. For example, competition between the FTC and the Department of Justice is demonstrated in chapter 7 as improving the efficiency of both. That competition would improve efficiency is not particularly surprising, but the conventional wisdom is that "duplication" must be avoided. As another example, the army and navy were put into the Department of Defense on these grounds shortly after the end of World War II, and our military machine has never fully recovered. How this became conventional wisdom in a society in which competition is thought to be highly desirable for almost any kind of production is a mystery. The fact that it remains conventional wisdom is well established and the studies in this volume will, I hope, tend to undermine it.

The picture of the FTC given in this book is completely consistent with what we may call the "public-choice approach," whereby a number of individuals attempt to maximize their own well-being, albeit with some concern for the public interest. The problem is designing a set of public institutions so that, assuming the employees will take the public-choice approach, the outcome is truly to the public's advantage. The big problem, of course, is that for most of us individually, rent seeking is apt to pay off more highly than attempting to set up an organization that will serve the public interest. Unfortunately, if we all engage in rent seeking, we will all be worse off than if all of us pursued the public interest. It is the classic "prisoners' dilemma."

In keeping with tradition, I have no definite answers to the problem of the prisoners' dilemma in this case or in others. Nevertheless, in general we are more likely to be effective if we understand the problem than if we do not. Clearly, the research presented in this volume is a major step forward in our understanding.

NOTES

1. The price of oil actually rose more rapidly than the cartel price because of the existence of heavy taxation on oil and petroleum in those countries.

2. To a large extent the gas lines were simply the result of bad organization on the part of the petroleum authorities—they sent the oil to the wrong places.

3. Another problem concerning oil and gas prices was the environmental protection law suits several years earlier that delayed the construction of the Alaskan pipeline. If the pipeline had begun producing at its original target date of 1973, and if the United States had not had price controls, it seems certain that the OPEC cartel would have collapsed.

4. The areas that are open for drilling today have largely been open for over a hundred years, and the prospects of finding more oil in them are not great.

5. Prior to 1973, however, the oil-well owners had been able to use the government to keep the price of oil above the true equilibrium price by import controls.

6. See Richard Posner, *Regulation of Advertising by the FTC* (Washington, D.C.: American Enterprise Institute, 1973).

7. Robert E. McCormick, William F. Shughart II, and Robert D. Tollison, "The Disinterest in Regulation," *American Economic Review* 74 (December 1984): 1075–79.

8. For a discussion of the rationales for delegation, see Richard Posner, "The Behavior of Administrative Agencies," *Journal of Legal Studies* 1 (1972): 323–44.

9. Posner, *Regulation of Advertising.*

Bibliography

Adams, Walter. "Dissolution, Divorcement, and Divestiture: The Pyrrhic Victories of Antitrust." *Indiana Law Journal* 27 (Fall 1951): 1–36.

"After Brief Shutdown, FTC Gets More Funds," *New York Times*, May 2, 1980, p. D1.

American Association of Advertising Agencies. *Advertising Agencies: What They Are, What They Do, and How They Do It*. New York, 1976.

———. "Qualifications for Membership." In *1982/83 Roster and Organization of the 4A's*. New York, 1982.

American Bar Association. *Report of the American Bar Association Commission to Study the Federal Trade Commission*. Chicago, 1969.

Anderson, Gary, and Tollison, Robert. "A Rent-Seeking Explanation of the British Factory Acts." In David C. Colander, ed., *Neoclassical Political Economy*. Cambridge, Mass.: Ballinger, 1984.

Anderson, James E. *Public Policy Making*. New York: Praeger, 1975.

Arams, Bill. "The Networks Censor TV Ads for Taste and Deceptiveness." *Wall Street Journal*, September 30, 1982, p. 33.

Aranson, Peter. "The Uncertain Search for Regulatory Reform." Working Paper no. 79-3. Law and Economics Center, University of Miami, 1979.

Armentano, Dominick T. *Antitrust and Monopoly: Anatomy of a Policy Failure*. New York: John Wiley and Sons, 1982.

Arnold, Thurman W. *The Folklore of Capitalism*. New Haven, Conn.: Yale University Press, 1937.

Asch, Peter, and Seneca, J. J. "Is Collusion Profitable?" *Review of Economics and Statistics* 58 (February 1976): 1–12.

Auerbach, Carl A. "The Federal Trade Commission: Internal Organization and Procedure." *Minnesota Law Review* 48 (1964): 383–522.

Averitt, Neil W. "The Meaning of 'Unfair Methods of Competition' in Section 5 of the Federal Trade Commission Act." *Boston College Law Review* 21 (January 1980): 227–300.

————. "Structural Remedies in Competition Cases Under the Federal Trade Commission Act." *Ohio State Law Journal* 40 (1979): 781–845.

Barke, Richard, and Riker, William H. "A Political Theory of Regulation with Some Observations on Railway Abandonments." *Public Choice* 39 (1982): 73–106.

Baruch, Bernard M. *American Industry in the War.* New York: Prentice-Hall, 1941.

Baum, Daniel J. "Antitrust Functions of the Federal Trade Commission: Area Discrimination and Product Differentiation." *Federal Bar Journal* 24 (Fall 1964): 579–608.

Becker, Gary S. "Crime and Punishment: An Economic Approach." *Journal of Political Economy* 76 (March–April 1968): 169–207.

————. "A Theory of Political Behavior." Working Paper no. 006-1. Center for the Study of the Economy and the State, University of Chicago, 1982.

Bell, Howard H. "Self-Regulation by the Advertising Industry." *California Management Review* 16 (Spring 1974): 58–63.

Bernstein, Marver H. "Independent Regulatory Agencies: A Perspective on Their Reform." *The Annals* 402 (March 1972): 14–26.

————. *Regulating Business by Independent Commission.* Princeton, N.J.: Princeton University Press, 1955.

Bickart, David O. "Civil Penalties Under Section 5(m) of the Federal Trade Commission Act." *University of Chicago Law Review* 44 (Summer 1977): 761–803.

Black, Donald. *The Behavior of Law.* New York: Academic Press, 1976.

Black, Duncan. "Partial Justification of the Borda Count." *Public Choice* (Winter 1976): 1–15.

Blair, John M. "Planning for Competition." *Columbia Law Review* 64 (March 1964): 524–42.

Blaisdell, Thomas C. *The Federal Trade Commission: An Experiment in the Control of Business.* New York: Columbia University Press, 1932.

Blum, John M. *The Republican Roosevelt.* 2d ed. Cambridge, Mass.: Harvard University Press, 1977.

————. *Woodrow Wilson and the Politics of Morality.* Boston: Little, Brown, 1956.

Bork, Robert H. *The Antitrust Paradox.* New York: Basic Books, 1978.

————. "The Legislative Intent and the Policy of the Sherman Act." *Journal of Law and Economics* 9 (1966): 7–48.

Boyle, Stanley E. "Economic Reports and the Federal Trade Commission: 50 Years' Experience." *Federal Bar Journal* 24 (Fall 1964): 489–509.

Brodley, Joseph. "Statement Before the National Commission to Review Antitrust Laws and Procedures." Mimeographed. Washington, D.C., October 26, 1978.

Brozen, Yale. "The Impact of FTC Advertising Policies on Competition." In Divita, ed., *Advertising and the Public Interest.* Washington, D.C.: American Enterprise Institute, 1974.

Buchanan, James M., and Stubblebine, William C. "Externality." *Economica* 29 (1962): 371–84.

Buchanan, James M.; Tollison, Robert D.; and Tullock, Gordon, eds. *Toward a Theory of the Rent-Seeking Society.* College Station: Texas A&M Press, 1980.

Buchanan, James M., and Tullock, Gordon. *The Calculus of Consent.* Ann Arbor: University of Michigan Press, 1962.

Burns, Arthur R. *The Decline of Competition.* New York: McGraw-Hill, 1936.

Calvert, Randall L.; Moran, Mark J.; and Weingast, Barry R. "Congressional Influence over Policymaking: The Case of the FTC." Mimeographed. St. Louis, Mo.: Washington University, November 1984.

Calvert, Randall L., and Weingast, Barry R. "Congress, the Bureaucracy, and Regulatory Reform." Mimeographed. St. Louis, Mo.: Center for the Study of American Business, Washington University, 1980.

Cary, William L. *Politics and Regulatory Agencies.* New York: McGraw-Hill, 1967.

"Caught in a Cross Fire of Praise at the FTC." *New York Times,* March 20, 1977, sec. 3, p. 3.

Clabault, J. M., and Block, M. *Sherman Act Indictments, 1955–1980,* 2 vols. New York: Federal Legal Publications, 1981.

Clark, John D. *The Federal Trust Policy.* Baltimore, Md.: Johns Hopkins University Press, 1931.

Clark, Timothy; Kosters, Marvin H.; and Miller, James C., III, eds. *Reforming Regulation.* Washington, D.C.: American Enterprise Institute, 1980.

Clarkson, Kenneth W., and Muris, Timothy J. "The Federal Trade Commission and Occupational Regulation." In Simon Rottenberg, ed., *Occupational Licensure and Regulation.* Washington, D.C.: American Enterprise Institute, 1981.

———, eds. *The Federal Trade Commission Since 1970: Economic Regulation and Bureaucratic Behavior.* Cambridge, Eng.: Cambridge University Press, 1981.

Coase, Ronald H. "Payola in Radio and Television Broadcasting." *Journal of Law and Economics* 22 (October 1979): 269–328.

Cochran, Thomas C., and Miller, William. *The Age of Enterprise.* New York: Macmillan, 1942; Harper Torchbook, 1961.

Cohen, Dorothy. "The FTC's Advertising Substantiation Program." *Journal of Marketing* 44 (Winter 1980): 26–35.

Cohen, Kalman, and Cyert, Richard M. *Theory of the Firm.* 2d ed. Englewood Cliffs, N.J.: Prentice-Hall, 1975.

Cohen, Stanley E. "Ad Industry Goes only Partway with Miller." *Advertising Age,* November 1, 1982.

———. "FTC Memo Hits Ad Self-Regulation." *Advertising Age,* February 7, 1983.

Commission on Organization of the Executive Branch of the Government (Hoover Commission). *Task Force Report on Regulatory Commissions (Appendix N).* Washington, D.C., 1949.

"Conclusions and Recommendations from Federal Trade Commission Transition Team Report Submitted to President Reagan." *BNA Antitrust and Trade Regulation Reports,* November 29, 1981, sec. G.

Congleton, Roger D. "A Model of Asymmetric Bureaucratic Inertia and Bias." *Public Choice* 39, no. 3 (1982): 421–25.

Congressional Record. 63d Cong., 2d sess., July 13 and 31, September 5, 1914. Vol. 51.

————. 66th Cong., 1st sess., October 20, 1919. Vol. 58.

————. 69th Cong., 1st sess., March 20, 1926. Vol. 67.

————. 93d Cong., 2d sess., October 8, 1974. H.R. Doc. no. 366, vol. 120.

————. 94th Cong., 1st sess., October 8 and 22, 1975. Vol. 121. Natural Gas Legislation.

————. 96th Cong., 1st sess., September 20 and November 14, 1979. Vol. 125.

————. 96th Cong., 2d sess., March 26, May 21, 1980. Vol. 126 (daily edition).

————. 97th Cong., 1st sess., September 21, 1981. Vol. 127.

"Congress Threatens to Extract Some of the FTC's Sharpest Fangs." *National Journal*, March 27, 1982, p. 535.

Cooter, Robert, and Marks, Stephen, with Mnooking, Robert. "Bargaining in the Shadow of the Law: A Testable Model of Strategic Behavior." *Journal of Legal Studies* 11 (1982): 225–53.

Cottle, Rex L.; Macaulay, Hugh H.; and Yandle, Bruce. *Labor and Property Rights in California Agriculture.* College Station: Texas A&M Press, 1982.

Cox, Edward F.; Fellmeth, Robert C.; and Schulz, John E. *The Nader Report on the Federal Trade Commission.* New York: Richard W. Baron, 1969.

Crain, W. Mark, and Tollison, Robert D. "Constitutional Change in an Interest Group Perspective." *Journal of Legal Studies* 8 (January 1979): 165–75.

————. "Legislative Size and Voting Rules," *Journal of Legal Studies* 6 (1977): 235–40.

Cramton, Roger C. "Regulatory Structure and Regulatory Performance: A Critique of the Ash Council Report." *Public Administration Review* (July–August 1972): 284–91.

Croly, Herbert. *The Promise of American Life.* New York: Macmillan, 1909.

Cuff, Robert D. *The War Industries Board: Business-Government Relations During World War I.* Baltimore, Md.: Johns Hopkins University Press, 1973.

Cushman, Robert E. *The Independent Regulatory Commissions.* New York: Oxford University Press, 1941.

Cyert, Richard M. "Oligopoly and the Business Cycle." *Journal of Political Economy* 63 (February 1955): 41–51.

Davidson, Roger H. "Breaking Up Those Cozy Triangles: An Impossible Dream?" In Susan Welch and John G. Peters, eds., *Legislative Reform and Public Policy.* New York: Praeger, 1977.

Davis, G. Cullom. "The Transformation of the Federal Trade Commission, 1914–1929." *Mississippi Valley Historical Review* 49 (December 1962): 437–55.

De Alessi, Louis. "An Economic Analysis of Government Ownership and Regulation." *Public Choice* 19 (1974): 1–42.

"Debate: The Federal Trade Commission Under Attack: Should the Commission's Role Be Changed?" *Antitrust Law Journal* 49 (1982): 1481–97.

Denzau, Arthur, and Mackay, Robert J. "Gatekeeping and Monopoly Power of Committees." *American Journal of Political Science* 27 (1983): 740–61.

Diver, Colin. "The Assessment and Mitigation of Civil Money Penalties by Federal Administrative Agencies." *Columbia Law Review* 79 (December 1979): 1436–1502.

Dixon, Richard G., Jr. "The Independent Commissions and Political Responsibility." *Administrative Law Review* 27, no. 1 (Winter 1975): 1–16.

Dodd, Lawrence C., and Schott, Richard L. *Congress and the Administrative State.* New York: John Wiley and Sons, 1979.

Downs, Anthony. *Inside Bureaucracy.* Boston: Little, Brown, 1967.

Eckbo, B. E. "Horizontal Mergers, Collusion, and Stockholder Wealth." *Journal of Financial Economics* 11 (1983): 241–73.

Eckert, R. D. "On the Incentives of Regulators: The Case of Taxicabs." *Public Choice* 14 (1973): 83–99.

Edwards, Corwin. *The Price Discrimination Law.* Washington, D.C.: Brookings Institution, 1959.

Ehrlich, Issac. "Capital Punishment and Deterrence: Some Further Thoughts and Additional Evidence." *Journal of Political Economy* 85 (August 1977): 741–88.

Ellert, J. C. "Antitrust Law Enforcement and the Behavior of Stock Prices." *Journal of Finance* 715 (1976): 715–23.

Elzinga, Kenneth G. "The Antimerger Law: Pyrrhic Victories?" *Journal of Law and Economics* 12 (1969): 43–78.

———. "Goals of Antitrust." *University of Pennsylvania Law Review* 125 (1977): 1191–1213.

Elzinga, Kenneth G., and Breit, William. *The Antitrust Penalties.* New Haven, Conn.: Yale University Press, 1976.

"The Escalating Struggle Between the FTC and Business—Executives Openly Challenge the Actions and Policies of the Newly Activist Agency." *Business Week,* December 13, 1976, p. 53.

Farquharson, Robin. *Theory of Voting.* New Haven, Conn.: Yale University Press, 1969.

"Federal Trade Commission: '43 Grad Transforms Agency into a 'Growling Watchdog.'" *University of Pennsylvania Law Alumni Journal* (Fall 1971): 9.

Fenno, Richard F. *Congressmen in Committees.* Boston: Little, Brown, 1972.

———. *Home Style.* Boston: Little, Brown, 1978.

———. *Power of the Purse: Appropriations Politics in Congress.* Boston: Little, Brown, 1966.

Ferejohn, John A. *Pork Barrel Politics.* Stanford, Calif.: Stanford University Press, 1974.

———. "Sophisticated Voting with Separable Preferences." Mimeographed. Social Science Working Paper. Pasadena: California Institute of Technology, March 1975.

Ferejohn, John A., and Fiorina, Morris P. "Purposive Models of Politics." *American Economic Review* 65 (1975): 407–14.

Fiorina, Morris P. "Bureaucratic (?) Failures: Causes and Cures." Mimeographed. Publication no. 43. St. Louis: Center for the Study of American Business, Washington University, 1981.

———. *Congress: Keystone of the Washington Establishment.* New Haven, Conn.: Yale University Press, 1977.

———. *Representatives, Roll Calls, and Constituencies.* Lexington, Mass.: Lexington Books, 1974.

Fog, Bjarke. "How Are Cartel Prices Determined?" *Journal of Industrial Economics* 5 (November 1956): 16–23.

Friedman, Alan. "An Analysis of Settlement." *Stanford Law Review* 22 (1969): 67–100.

"FTC Data Indicates Bureau of Competition, Not Antitrust Division, Sights Bigger Targets." BNA *Antitrust and Trade Regulation Reports*, July 3, 1980, p. A7.

"FTC Enforcement Against Municipalities." CCH *Trade Regulation Reports*, September 4, 1984, p. 7.

"FTC Not Needed, Budget Chief Says." *Chicago Tribune*, February 23, 1981, p. A1.

"FTC Temporarily Closed in Budget Dispute." *Washington Post*, May 1, 1980, p. B1.

"FTC to Require Public Proof of Ad Claims." *Wall Street Journal*, June 11, 1971.

Furubotn, Eirik G. "Decisionmaking Under Labor Management: The Commitment Mechanism Revisited." *Zeitschrift für die gesamte Staatswissenschaft* 135 (1979): 216–27.

Furubotn, Eirik, and Pejovich, Svetozar. *The Economics of Property Rights*. Cambridge, Mass.: Ballinger, 1975.

Gellhorn, Ernest. "Regulatory Reform and the Federal Trade Commission's Antitrust Jurisdiction." *Tennessee Law Review* 49 (1982): 471–510.

———. "Two's a Crowd: The FTC's Redundant Antitrust Powers." *Regulation* 5 (November–December 1981): 32–42.

———. "The Wages of Zealotry: The FTC Under Siege." *Regulation* 4 (January–February 1980): 33–40.

Gibbard, Allan. "Manipulation of Voting Schemes: A General Result." *Econometrica* 41 (1973): 587–601.

Goldberg, Milton. "The Consent Decree: Its Formulation and Use." Occasional Paper no. 8. East Lansing: Graduate School of Business, Michigan State University, 1962.

Goldman, Eric F. *Rendezvous with Destiny*. New York: Alfred A. Knopf, 1952.

Goldschmid, Harvey J.; Mann, H. Michael; and Weston, J. Fred, eds. *Industrial Concentration: The New Learning*. Boston: Little, Brown, 1974.

Gordon, Richard L. "Miller Asks for Ad Rule Review." *Advertising Age*, October 25, 1982.

———. "Substantiation Proposals Emerge." *Advertising Age*, July 18, 1983.

Gould, Jay. "The Economics of Legal Conflict." *Journal of Legal Studies* 2 (1973): 279–300.

Handler, Milton. "The Constitutionality of Investigations by the Federal Trade Commission." *Columbia Law Review* 28 (June 1928): 708–33.

———. "Reforming the Antitrust Laws—Dual Enforcement, FTC's Mission." *New York Law Journal* 188 (April 18, 1982): 4.

———. "Unfair Competition and the Federal Trade Commission." *George Washington Law Review* 8 (January–February 1940): 399–426.

Harris, Joseph P. *Congressional Control of Administration*. Washington, D.C.: Brookings Institution, 1964; Anchor Books, 1965.

Harrod, R. F. "Imperfect Competition and the Trade Cycle." *Review of Economics and Statistics* 18 (February 1936): 84–88.

Hawley, Ellis W. "Herbert Hoover, the Commerce Secretariat, and the Vision of an 'Associative State,' 1921–1928." *Journal of American History* 61 (June 1974): 116–40.

———. *The New Deal and the Problem of Monopoly*. Princeton, N.J.: Princeton University Press, 1966.

Hay, G. A., and Kelley, D. "An Empirical Study of Price-Fixing Conspiracies." *Journal of Law and Economics* 17 (April 1974): 13–38.

Healey, John A. "The Federal Trade Commission Advertising Substantiation Program and Changes in the Context of Advertising in Selected Industries." Ph.D. diss., University of California at Los Angeles, 1978.

Heclo, Hugh. "Issue Networks and the Executive Establishment." In Anthony S. King, ed., *The New American Political System.* Washington, D.C.: American Enterprise Institute, 1978.

Henderson, Gerard C. *The Federal Trade Commission: A Study in Administrative Law and Procedure.* New Haven, Conn.: Yale University Press, 1924.

Herring, E. Pendleton. "The Federal Trade Commissioners." *George Washington Law Review* 8 (January–February 1940): 339–64.

———. *Public Administration and the Public Interest.* New York: McGraw-Hill, 1936.

Hershey, Robert D., Jr. "Lobbyists Take Aim at the FTC Antitrust Rules." *New York Times*, September 26, 1982, p. F9.

Hicks, John D. *Republican Ascendency, 1921–1933.* New York: Harper and Row, 1960; Harper Torchbook, 1963.

Hilton, George. "The Consistency of the Interstate Commerce Act." *Journal of Law and Economics* 9 (1966): 87–113.

Himmelberg, Robert F. *The Origins of the National Recovery Administration: Business, Government, and the Trade Association Issue, 1921–1933.* New York: Fordham University Press, 1976.

———. "The War Industries Board and the Antitrust Question in November 1918." *Journal of American History* 52 (June 1965): 59–74.

Hirschleifer, Jack. "Comment." *Journal of Law and Economics* 19 (August 1976): 241–44.

Hofstadter, Richard. *The Age of Reform.* New York: Alfred A. Knopf, 1966.

———. *The Paranoid Style in American Politics and Other Essays.* New York: Alfred A. Knopf, 1966.

Hultgren, Thor, and Peck, Merton R. *Costs, Prices, and Profits: Their Cyclical Relations.* New York: Columbia University Press, 1965.

Jaenicke, Douglas W. "Herbert Croly, Progressive Ideology, and the FTC Act." *Political Science Quarterly* 93 (Fall 1978): 471–93.

Joskow, Paul L. "The Determination of the Allowed Rate of Return in a Formal Regulatory Hearing." *Bell Journal of Economics and Management Science* 3 (1972): 632–44.

———. "Inflation and Environmental Concern: Structural Change in the Process of Public Utility Price Regulation." *Journal of Law and Economics* 17 (1974): 291–327.

Kalt, Joseph P. "Political Economy of Federal Energy Policy." Mimeographed. Cambridge, Mass.: Harvard University, 1979.

Katzmann, Robert A. "Capitol Hill's Current Attack Against the FTC." *Wall Street Journal*, May 7, 1980, p. 26.

———. *Regulatory Bureaucracy: The Federal Trade Commission and Antitrust Policy.* Cambridge, Mass.: MIT Press, 1980.

Kau, James B., and Rubin, Paul H. "Self-Interest, Ideology, and Logrolling in Congressional Voting." *Journal of Law and Economics* 22 (1979): 365–84.

Kaufman, Herbert. "Why Organizations Behave as They Do: An Outline of a Theory." *Administrative Theory* (1961): 37–73.

Kauper, Thomas E. "Competition Policy and the Institutions of Antitrust." *South Dakota Law Review* 23 (Winter 1978): 1–30.

Kaysen, Carl. *United States v. United Shoe Machinery Corporation: An Economic Analysis of an Antitrust Case.* Cambridge, Mass.: Harvard University Press, 1956.

Keller, Morton. "The Pluralist State: American Economic Regulation in Comparative Perspective, 1900–1930." In Thomas K. McCraw, ed., *Regulation in Perspective.* Cambridge, Mass.: Harvard University Press, 1981, pp. 56–94.

Kemp, Kathleen A. "Instability in Budgeting for Federal Regulatory Agencies." *Social Science Quarterly* 63, no. 4 (December 1982): 643–60.

Kittelle, Sumner S., and Mostow, Elmer. "A Review of the Trade Practice Conferences of the Federal Trade Commission." *George Washington Law Review* 8 (January–February 1940): 427–51.

Klein, Benjamin V., and Leffler, Keith B. "The Role of Market Forces in Assuring Contractual Performance." *Journal of Political Economy* 89 (August 1981): 615–41.

Kohlmeier, Louis M., Jr. *The Regulators.* New York: Harper and Row, 1969.

Kolko, Gabriel. *The Triumph of Conservatism: A Reinterpretation of American History, 1900–1916.* New York: The Free Press, 1963.

LaBarbera, Priscilla. "Advertising Self-Regulation: An Evaluation." *MSU Business Topics* (Summer 1980): 55–63.

Lambin, Jean J. *Advertising Competition and Market Conduct in Oligopoly over Time.* New York: American Elsevier, 1976.

Lande, Robert H. "Wealth Transfers as the Original and Primary Concern of Antitrust: The Efficiency Interpretation Challenged." *Hastings Law Journal* 34 (September 1982): 65–151.

Landes, William, and Posner, Richard. "Adjudication as a Private Good." *Journal of Legal Studies* 8 (1979): 235–84.

Landis, James M. *The Administrative Process.* New Haven, Conn.: Yale University Press, 1938.

Latham, Earl. *The Group Basis of Politics.* Ithaca, N.Y.: Cornell University Press, 1952.

———. "The Politics of Basing Point Legislation." *Law and Contemporary Problems* 15 (Spring 1950): 272–310.

Leading National Advertisers, Inc. *LNA Multi-Media Report Class/Brand $.* New York, January–December 1970.

Leuchtenburg, William E. *Franklin D. Roosevelt and the New Deal, 1932–1940.* New York: Harper and Row, 1963.

———. "The Impact of the War on the American Political Economy." In Arthur S. Link, ed., *The Impact of World War I.* New York: Harper and Row, 1969.

———. *The Perils of Prosperity, 1914–32.* Chicago: University of Chicago Press, 1958.

Levine, Michael. "Revisionism Revised? Airline Deregulation and the Public Interest." *Law and Contemporary Problems* 44 (1981): 179–95.

Liebeler, Wesley J. "The Role of the Federal Trade Commission, Proceedings of the

Symposium: Changing Perspectives in Antitrust Litigation." *Southwestern University Law Review* 12 (1980–1981): 166–229.

Lindsay, Cotton M. "A Theory of Government Enterprise." *Journal of Political Economy* 84 (October 1976): 1061–76.

Link, Arthur S. "What Happened to the Progressive Movement in the 1920s?" *American Historical Review* 64 (July 1959): 833–51.

———. *Wilson: The New Freedom.* Princeton, N.J.: Princeton University Press, 1956.

———. *Woodrow Wilson and the Progressive Era, 1910–1917.* New York: Harper and Row, 1954; Harper Torchbook, 1963.

Lippmann, Walter. *Drift and Mastery.* New York: Mitchell, Kennerly, 1914.

"Local Government Damage Immunity." *CCH Trade Regulation Reports*, October 31, 1984, p. 4.

Long, William; Schramm, Richard; and Tollison, Robert. "The Determinants of Antitrust Activity." *Journal of Law and Economics* 16 (1973): 351–64.

Lowi, Theodore J. *The End of Liberalism.* 2d ed. New York: W. W. Norton, 1979.

Ludwin, William. "Strategic Voting and the Borda Method." *Public Choice* 33 (1978): 85–90.

MacChesney, Brunson, and Murphy, Walter D. "Investigatory and Enforcement Powers of the Federal Trade Commission." *George Washington Law Review* 8 (January–February 1940): 581–607.

Machlup, Fritz. *The Political Economy of Monopoly.* Baltimore, Md.: Johns Hopkins University Press, 1952.

MacIntyre, A. Everette, and Dixon, Paul Rand. "The Federal Trade Commission After 50 Years." *Federal Law Journal* 24 (1964): 377–424.

MacIntyre, A. Everette, and Volhard, Joachim J. "The Federal Trade Commission." *Boston College Industrial and Commercial Law Review* 11 (May 1970): 723–83.

Mackay, Robert J., and Weaver, Carolyn L. "Agenda Control by Budget Maximizers in a Multi-Bureau Setting." *Public Choice* 37 (1981): 447–72.

———. "The Power to Veto." Working Paper, Hoover Institution, Stanford University, November 1984.

Magnuson, Warren G., and Carper, Jean C. *The Dark Side of the Marketplace: The Plight of the American Consumer.* Englewood Cliffs, N.J.: Prentice-Hall, 1968.

Maloney, Michael T., and McCormick, Robert E. "A Positive Theory of Environmental Quality Regulation." *Journal of Law and Economics* 25 (April 1982): 99–123.

Maloney, Michael T.; McCormick, Robert E.; and Tollison, Robert D. "Achieving Cartel Profits Through Unionization." *Southern Economic Journal* 46 (October 1979): 628–35.

Marvel, Howard P. "Factory Regulation: A Reinterpretation of Early English Experience." *Journal of Law and Economics* 20 (October 1977): 379–402.

Marx, Karl. *Capital: A Critical Analysis of Capitalist Production.* New York: International Publishers, 1947.

Masson, Robert, and Reynolds, Robert. "Statistical Studies of Antitrust Enforcement: A Critique." Paper delivered before the American Statistical Society, 1977.

Mayhew, David R. *Congress: The Electoral Connection.* New Haven, Conn.: Yale University Press, 1974.

McCarty, Harry C. "Trade Practice Conferences." *Corporate Practice Review* 2 (June 1930): 19–29.

McCloskey, Robert G. *The American Supreme Court.* Chicago: University of Chicago Press, 1960.

McCormick, Robert E., and Tollison, Robert D. *Politicians, Legislators, and the Economy: An Inquiry into the Interest Group Theory of Government.* Boston: Nijhoff, 1981.

McCormick, Robert E.; Shugart, William F., II; and Tollison, Robert D. "The Disinterest in Regulation." *American Economic Review* 74 (December 1984): 1075–79.

McCraw, Thomas K. *Prophets of Regulation.* Cambridge, Mass.: Belknap, 1984.

————. "Regulation in America: A Review Article." *Business History Review* 49 (Summer 1975): 162–83.

McFadden, Daniel. "Conditional Logit Analysis of Qualitative Choice Behavior." In Paul Zarembka, ed., *Frontiers in Econometrics.* New York: Academic Press, 1974.

————. "The Revealed Preferences of a Government Bureaucracy: Theory." *Bell Journal of Economics and Management Science* 6 (Autumn 1975): 401–16.

————. "The Revealed Preferences of a Government Bureaucracy: Empirical Evidence." *Bell Journal of Economics and Management Science* 7 (Spring 1976): 55–72.

McFarland, Carl. *Judicial Control of the Federal Trade Commission and the Interstate Commerce Commission, 1920–1930.* Cambridge, Mass.: Harvard University Press, 1933.

McGrew, T. J. "Antitrust Enforcement Has More Staff Than Policy." *Legal Times of Washington* 4 (October 12, 1981): 11.

McKelvey, Richard. "General Conditions for Global Intransitivities in Formal Voting Models." *Econometrica* 47 (1979): 1085–1111.

McKelvey, Richard, and Niemi, Richard. "A Multistage Game Representation of Sophisticated Voting for Binary Procedures." *Journal of Economic Theory* 18 (1978): 1–22.

Media Records, Inc. *Expenditures of National Advertisers in Newspapers.* New York, 1970.

Meier, Kenneth J. "The Impact of Regulatory Organization Structure: IRCs or RAs?" *Southern Review of Public Administration* (1980): 427–43.

Meredith Associates. "Report to the Chairman, Federal Trade Commission: Attorney and Attorney Manager Recruitment, Selection, and Retention." Mimeographed. July 1976.

Migué, Jean-Luc, and Bélanger, Gérard. "Toward a General Theory of Managerial Discretion." *Public Choice* 17 (1974): 27–43.

Miller, Nicholas. "Logrolling, Vote Trading, and the Paradox of Voting: A Game Theoretical Overview." *Public Choice* (Summer 1977): 51–75.

Monsen, R. Joseph, and Downs, Anthony. "Large Managerial Firms." *Journal of Political Economy* 73 (1965): 221–36.

Montague, Gilbert H. "The Commission's Jurisdiction over Practices in Restraint of Trade: A Large-Scale Method of Mass Enforcement of the Antitrust Laws." *George Washington Law Review* 8 (January–February 1940): 365–98.

Monsarrat, John. *The Case of the Full Service Agency.* New York: American Association of Advertising Agencies, 1971.

Moore, Thomas G. "The Applied Theory of Regulation: Political Economy at the Interstate Commerce Commission, a Comment on the Alexis Paper." *Public Choice* 39 (1982): 29–32.

Moore, Thomas Lane, III. "The Establishment of a 'New Freedom' Policy: The Federal Trade Commission, 1912–1918." Ph.D. diss., University of Alabama, 1980.

Mowry, George E. *The Era of Theodore Roosevelt.* New York: Harper and Row, 1958; Harper Torchbook, 1962.

Muris, Timothy J. "The Efficiency Defense Under Section 7 of the Clayton Act." *Case Western Reserve Law Journal* 30 (1980): 381–432.

———. "Rules Without Reason: The Case of the FTC." *Regulation* 5 (September–October 1982): 20–26.

Nadel, Mark V. *The Politics of Consumer Protection.* Indianapolis, In.: Bobbs, Merrill, 1971.

"Nader's Bid to Require Proof of Ad Claims to Be Studied by FTC." *Wall Street Journal,* December 14, 1970.

Nagle, Thomas T. "Do Advertising-Profitability Studies Really Show That Advertising Creates a Barrier to Entry?" *Journal of Law and Economics* 24 (October 1981): 333–49.

National Advertising Review Board. *Advertising Self-Regulation and Its Interaction with Consumers.* New York: A. B. Primer, n.d.

———. "Self-Regulation of National Advertising." NAD Case Report. New York, July 15, 1983.

National Commission to Review the Antitrust Laws and Procedures. *Report to the President.* Washington, D.C.: GPO, January 22, 1979.

Neale, A. D., and Goyder, D. G. *The Antitrust Laws of the U.S.A.,* 3d ed. London: Cambridge University Press, 1980.

Nelson, Philip. "Advertising as Information. *Journal of Political Economy* 82 (July–August 1974): 729–54.

———. "Information and Consumer Behavior." *Journal of Political Economy* 78 (March–April 1970): 311–29.

Nicosia, Francesco U. *Advertising Management and Society.* New York: McGraw-Hill, 1974.

Niemi, Richard, and Frank, A. "Sophisticated Voting Under the Plurality Procedure." In P. Ordeshook and K. Shepsle, eds., *Political Equilibrium.* Boston: Nijhoff, 1982.

Niskanen, William A. *Bureaucracy and Representative Government.* Chicago: Aldine-Atherton, 1971.

———. "Bureaucrats and Politicians." *Journal of Law and Economics* 18 (December 1975): 617–43.

———. "Nonmarket Decision Making: The Peculiar Economics of Bureaucracy." *American Economic Review* 58 (May 1968): 293–305.

Noll, Roger G. "Governmental Administrative Behavior: A Multidisciplinary Survey." Mimeographed. Working Paper. Pasadena: California Institute of Technology, 1976.

———. *Reforming Regulation: An Evaluation of the Ash Council Proposals.* Washington, D.C.: Brookings Institution, 1971.

Noll, Roger G., and Owen, Bruce M., eds. *The Political Economy of Deregulation.* Washington, D.C.: American Enterprise Institute, 1983.

O'Conner, Kevin. "The Divestiture Remedy in Sherman Act Section 2 Cases." *Harvard Journal of Legislation* 13 (1976): 698–775.

Olson, Mancur. *The Logic of Collective Action: Public Goods and the Theory of Groups.* Cambridge, Mass.: Harvard University Press, 1965.

Orzechowski, William. "Economic Models of Bureaucracy: Survey, Extensions, and Evidence." In Thomas E. Borcherding, ed., *Budgets and Bureaucrats: The Sources of Government Growth.* Durham, N.C.: Duke University Press, 1977.

Oster, Sharon. "The Strategic Use of Regulatory Investment by Industry Sub-Groups." *Economic Inquiry* 20 (October 1982): 604–17.

Palmer, John. "Some Economic Conditions Conducive to Collusion." *Journal of Economic Issues* 6 (June 1972): 29–38.

Pashigian, B. Peter. "A Theory of Prevention and Legal Defense with an Application to the Legal Costs of Companies." *Journal of Law and Economics* 25 (October 1982): 247–70.

Pattanaik, P. "Threats, Counter-Threats, and Strategic Voting." *Econometrica* 44 (1976): 91–103.

Paul, Arnold M. *Conservative Crisis and the Rule of Law.* Ithaca, N.Y.: Cornell University Press, 1960.

Peles, Yoram. "Rates of Amortization of Advertising Expenditures." *Journal of Political Economy* 79 (1971): 1032–58.

Peltzman, Sam. "Constituent Interest and Congressional Voting." Mimeographed. Chicago: Graduate School of Business, University of Chicago, 1982.

———. "The Effects of FTC Advertising Regulation." *Journal of Law and Economics* 24 (December 1981): 403–48.

———. "Toward a More General Theory of Regulation." *Journal of Law and Economics* 19 (August 1976): 211–48.

Pertschuk, Michael. "A Law to Call Your Own." Mimeographed. Prepared for the Commission on the Operation of the Senate. Washington, D.C., 1975.

———. *Revolt Against Regulation: The Rise and Pause of the Consumer Movement.* Berkeley: University of California Press, 1982.

Pfunder, Malcolm R.; Plaine, Daniel; and Whittemore, David. "Compliance with Divestiture Orders Under Section 7 of the Clayton Act: An Analysis of the Relief Obtained." *Antitrust Bulletin* 17 (1972): 19–180.

"Pfizer's Advertising of Sunburn Reliever Is Challenged by FTC." *Wall Street Journal,* April 14, 1970.

Pitofsky, Robert. "Beyond Nader: Consumer Protection and the Regulation of Advertising." *Harvard Law Review* 90 (1977): 661–701.

———. "The FTC Ad Substantiation Program." *Georgetown Law Journal* 61 (July 1973): 1427–52.

Plott, Charles R. "Axiomatic Social Choice Theory." *American Journal of Political Science* 20 (1976): 511–95.

Plott, Charles R., and Levine, Michael E. "A Model of Agenda Influence on Committee Decisions." *American Economic Review* 68 (1977): 146–60.

Poole, Keith T. "Dimensions of Interest Group Evaluation of the U.S. Senate, 1969–1978." *American Journal of Political Science* 25 (1981): 49–67.

Posner, Richard A. *Antitrust Law: An Economic Perspective.* Chicago: University of Chicago Press, 1976.

————. "The Behavior of Administrative Agencies." *Journal of Legal Studies* 1 (1972): 305–47.

————. "The Federal Trade Commission." *University of Chicago Law Review* 37 (1969): 47–89.

————. *Regulation of Advertising by the FTC.* Washington, D.C.: American Enterprise Institute, 1973.

————. *The Robinson-Patman Act: Federal Regulation of Price Differences.* Washington, D.C.: American Enterprise Institute, 1976.

————. "A Statistical Study of Antitrust Law Enforcement." *Journal of Law and Economics* 13 (October 1970): 365–419.

President and Fellows of Harvard College. "A Failing Agency: The Federal Trade Commission." Mimeographed. Working Paper no. C-14-76-119. Cambridge, Mass.: Kennedy School of Government, Harvard University, 1976.

President's Advisory Council on Executive Organization. *A New Regulatory Framework: Report on Selected Independent Regulatory Agencies.* Washington, D.C.: Government Printing Office, 1971.

Price, David E. *The Commerce Committees: A Study of the House and Senate Commerce Committees.* New York: Grossman, 1975.

Priest, George, and Klein, Benjamin. "The Selection of Disputes for Litigation." *Journal of Legal Studies* 13 (1984): 1–76.

"Proposed Budget Cuts Fuel Debate over FTC's Role." *Legal Times of Washington* 3 (February 23, 1981): 1.

Redford, Emmette S. "Regulation Revisited." *Administrative Law Review* 28 no. 3 (Summer 1976): 543–68.

Reich, Robert. "Consumer Protection and the First Amendment: A Dilemma for the FTC." *Minnesota Law Review* 61 (1977): 705–41.

Reissman, Leonard. "A Study of Role Conceptions in Bureaucracy." *Social Forces* 27 (March 1949): 305–10.

"Report of the ABA Commission to Study the FTC." *BNA Antitrust and Trade Regulation Reports.* Special Supplement no. 427, September 15, 1979, pp. 115–18.

Riker, William. *Liberalism Against Populism: A Confrontation Between the Theory of Democracy and the Theory of Social Choice.* San Francisco: W. H. Freeman, 1982.

Ripley, Randall B., and Franklin, Grace A. *Congress, the Bureaucracy, and Public Policy.* 2d ed. Homewood, Ill.: Dorsey Press, 1980.

Rogowsky, Robert A. "The Department of Justice Merger Guidelines: A Study in the Application of the Rule." *Research in Law and Economics* 6 (1984): 135–66.

————. "The Economic Effectiveness of Section 7 Relief." *Antitrust Bulletin* 31 (Spring 1986): 187–233.

————. "An Economic Study of Antimerger Remedies." Ph.D. diss., University of Virginia, May 1982.

Roll, D. L. "Dual Enforcement of the Antitrust Laws by the Department of Justice and the FTC: The Liaison Procedure." *The Business Lawyer* 31 (July 1975): 2075–85.

Romer, Thomas, and Rosenthal, Howard. "Political Resource Allocation, Controlled Agendas, and the Status Quo." *Public Choice* 33 (1978): 27–43.

Roosevelt, Theodore. *The Foes of Our Own Household.* New York: George H. Doran, 1917.

———. "The Trusts, the People, and the Square Deal." *Outlook*, November 18, 1911, pp. 649–56.

Ross, Tom. "Winners and Losers Under the Robinson-Patman Act." *Journal of Law and Economics* 27 (October 1984): 243–72.

"'Round and 'Round on RPM." *Regulation* (January–February 1984): 19–32.

Rourke, Francis E. *Bureaucracy, Politics, and Public Policy.* 2d ed. Boston: Little, Brown, 1976.

———. *Bureaucratic Power in National Politics.* 2d ed. Boston: Little, Brown, 1972.

Rublee, George S. "The Original Plan and Early History of the Federal Trade Commission." *Proceedings of the Academy of Political Science* 11 (January 1926): 666–72.

Salop, Steven C., and Scheffman, David T. "Raising Rivals' Costs." *American Economic Review* 73 (May 1983): 267–71.

Salop, Steven C.; Scheffman, David T.; and Schwartz, Warren. "Raising Rivals' Costs in a Rent-Seeking Society." In *The Political Economy of Regulation.* Washington, D.C.: Federal Trade Commission, 1985.

Satterthwaite, Mark. "Strategy Proofness and Arrow's Conditions." *Journal of Economic Theory* 10 (1976): 187–217.

Scherer, F. M. *Industrial Market Structure and Economic Performance.* 2d ed. Chicago: Rand McNally, 1980.

Schlesinger, Arthur M., Jr. *The Coming of the New Deal.* Boston: Houghton Mifflin, 1958.

———. *The Crisis of the Old Order, 1919–1933.* Boston: Houghton Mifflin, 1957.

Schwert, G. William. "Measuring the Effects of Regulation: Evidence from the Capital Markets." *Journal of Law and Economics* 24 (April 1981): 121–58.

Shepsle, Kenneth A. *The Giant Jigsaw Puzzle: Democratic Committee Assignments in the Modern House.* Chicago: University of Chicago Press, 1978.

———. "James Q. Wilson's 'The Politics of Regulation': A Review Essay." *Journal of Political Economy* 90 (February 1982): 216–21.

Shepsle, Kenneth A., and Weingast, Barry R. "Structure and Strategy: The Two Faces of Agenda Power." Paper presented at the annual American Political Science Association meetings. New York, 1981.

———. "Structure Induced Equilibrium and Legislative Choice." *Public Choice* 37 (1981): 503–19.

Siegfried, John. "The Determinants of Antitrust Activity." *Journal of Law and Economics* 18 (1975): 559–81.

Singer, James. "The Federal Trade Commission—Business's Government Enemy No. 1." *National Journal*, October 13, 1979, pp. 1676–80.

Sloan, J. B. "Antitrust: Shared Information Between the FTC and the Department of Justice." *Brigham Young University Law Review* 4 (1979): 883–912.

Stevens, W. H. S. "The Federal Trade Commission's Contribution to Industrial and Economic Analysis: The Work of the Economic Division." *George Washington Law Review* 8 (January–February 1940): 545–80.

Stigler, George J. *The Citizen and the State.* Chicago: University of Chicago Press, 1975.

———. "The Economic Effects of the Antitrust Laws." *Journal of Law and Economics* 9 (October 1966): 225–58.

———. "Monopoly and Oligopoly by Merger." *American Economic Review* 40 (May 1950): 23–34.

———. "The Optimum Enforcement of Laws." *Journal of Political Economy* 78 (May–June 1970): 526–36.

———. "The Process of Economic Regulation." *Antitrust Bulletin* 17 (1972): 207–35.

———. "The Theory of Economic Regulation." *Bell Journal of Economics and Management Science* 2 (Spring 1971): 3–21.

———. "A Theory of Oligopoly." *Journal of Political Economy* 72 (February 1964): 44–62.

Stillman, R. "Examining Antitrust Policy Toward Horizontal Mergers." *Journal of Financial Economics* 11 (1983): 225–40.

Stone, Alan. *Economic Regulation and the Public Interest: The Federal Trade Commission in Theory and Practice.* Ithaca, N.Y.: Cornell University Press, 1977.

Telser, Lester G. "A Theory of Self-Enforcing Agreements." *Journal of Business* 53 (January 1980): 27–44.

Thompson, Huston. "Highlights in the Evolution of the Federal Trade Commission." *George Washington University Law Review* 8 (January–February 1940): 260–75.

Thorelli, Hans. *The Federal Antitrust Policy.* Baltimore, Md.: Johns Hopkins University Press, 1954.

Tollison, Robert D., ed. *The Political Economy of Antitrust: Principal Paper by William Baxter.* Lexington, Mass.: Lexington Books, 1980.

Tullock, Gordon. "A (Partial) Rehabilitation of the Public Interest Theory." *Public Choice* 42 (1984): 89–99.

Twiss, Benjamin R. *Lawyers and the Constitution.* Princeton, N.J.: Princeton University Press, 1942.

U.S. Bureau of the Budget. *Federal Trade Commission Study 4 (No. CF-60-124).* 1960.

U.S. Commission on Organization of the Executive Branch of the Government. *The Independent Regulatory Commission.* Princeton, N.J.: Princeton University Press, 1955.

U.S. Congress. House. Committee on Appropriations. *Agriculture—Environmental and Consumer Protection Appropriations for 1974. Hearings Before the Subcommittee on Agriculture—Environmental and Consumer Protection of the House Committee on Appropriations.* 93d Cong., 1st sess., 1973.

———. *Agriculture—Environmental and Consumer Protection Appropriations for 1973. Hearings Before a Subcommittee of the House Committee on Appropriations.* 92d Cong., 2d sess., 1972.

———. *Departments of State, Justice, and Commerce, the Judiciary, and Related Agencies Appropriations for 1981. Hearings Before the Subcommittee on the Departments of State,*

Justice, and Commerce, the Judiciary, and Related Agencies of the House Committee on Appropriations. 96th Cong., 2d sess., 1980.

————. *Hearings Before the Subcommittee on the Departments of State, Justice, and Commerce, the Judiciary, and Related Agencies of the House Committee on Appropriations.* 97th Cong., 2d sess., 1982, p. 242.

————. *Hearings Before a Subcommittee of the House Committee on Appropriations.* 97th Cong., 1st sess., 1981, p. 695.

————. *Hearings Before a Subcommittee of the House Committee on Appropriations.* 98th Cong., 1st sess., 1983, p. 155.

————. *Independent Offices Appropriation Bill for 1937. Hearings Before the Subcommittee of the House Committee on Appropriations.* 74th Cong., 2d sess., 1936.

U.S. Congress. House. Committee on Energy and Commerce. *Federal Trade Commission Reauthorization, 1983. Hearings Before the Subcommittee on Commerce, Transportation, and Tourism of the House Committee on Energy and Commerce.* 98th Cong., 1st sess., 1983.

U.S. Congress. House. Committee on Government Operations. *Impact of OMB-Proposed Budget Cuts for the Federal Trade Commission. Hearings Before a Subcommittee of the House Committee on Government Operations.* 97th Cong., 1st sess., 1981.

————. *Oversight of Federal Trade Commission Law Enforcement: Fiscal Years 1982 and 1983. Hearings Before the Commerce, Consumer, and Monetary Affairs Subcommittee of the House Committee on Government Operations.* 98th Cong., 1st sess., 1983.

U.S. Congress. House. Committee on Interstate and Foreign Commerce. *Federal Trade Commission Practices and Procedures. Hearings Before the Special Subcommittee on Investigations of the House Committee on Interstate and Foreign Commerce.* 93d Cong., 2d sess., 1974.

————. *H. R. Rep. No. 533.* 63d Cong., 2d sess., 1914.

————. *Hearings Before the Special Subcommittee on Small Business and the Robinson-Patman Act.* 91st Cong., 1st sess., 1969.

————. *Regulatory Reform, Volume IV. Hearings Before the Subcommittee on Oversight and Investigations of the House Committee on Interstate and Foreign Commerce.* 94th Cong., 2d sess., 1976.

U.S. Congress. House. Committee on Interstate and Foreign Commerce. Subcommittee on Oversight and Investigations. *Report on Federal Regulation and Regulatory Reform.* 94th Cong., 2d sess., 1976.

U.S. Congress. House. Committee on the Judiciary. *Investigation of Conglomerate Corporations. Hearings Before the Antitrust Subcommittee of the House Committee on the Judiciary.* 91st Cong., 2d sess., 1970.

U.S. Congress. House. Select Committee on Small Business. *Staff Report on Statistics on Federal Antitrust Activities.* 84th Cong., 1st sess., 1956.

U.S. Congress. House. Staff of the Subcommittee on Monopoly of the House Committee on Small Business. *Report on the United States Versus Economic Concentration and Monopoly.* 79th Cong., 2d sess., 1946. Committee Print.

U.S. Congress. Senate. Committee on Appropriations. *Agriculture—Environmental and Consumer Protection Appropriations for Fiscal Year 1973. Hearings Before a Subcommittee of the Senate Committee on Appropriations.* 92d Cong., 2d sess., 1972.

———. *Agriculture—Environmental and Consumer Protection Appropriations for Fiscal Year 1972. Hearings Before a Subcommittee of the Senate Committee on Appropriations,* 92d Cong., 1st sess., 1971.

———. *Departments of State, Justice, and Commerce, the Judiciary, and Related Agencies Appropriations for 1980. Hearings Before a Subcommittee of the Senate Committee on Appropriations.* 96th Cong., 1st sess., 1979, pt. 2.

———. *Departments of State, Justice, and Commerce, the Judiciary, and Related Agencies Appropriations for 1983. Hearings Before a Subcommittee of the Senate Committee on Appropriations.* 97th Cong., 2d sess., 1982, p. 887.

———. *Independent Offices and Department of Housing and Urban Development Appropriations for Fiscal Year 1971. Hearings Before a Subcommittee of the Senate Committee on Appropriations.* 91st Cong., 2d sess., 1970.

U.S. Congress. Senate. Committee on Commerce. *Appointments to the Regulatory Agencies: The Federal Communications Commission and the Federal Trade Commission (1949–1974).* Report prepared by James M. Graham and Victor H. Kramer. 94th Cong., 2d sess., 1976. Committee Print.

———. *Nomination of Caspar W. Weinberger to Be Chairman of the Federal Trade Commission. Hearings Before the Senate Committee on Commerce.* 91st Cong., 1st sess., 1970.

———. *Nomination of Lewis A. Engman, to Be a Commissioner of the Federal Trade Commission. Hearings Before the Senate Committee on Commerce.* 93d Cong., 1st sess., 1973.

———. *Nomination of Miles W. Kirkpatrick to Be Chairman of the Federal Trade Commission. Hearings Before the Senate Committee on Commerce.* 91st Cong., 2d sess., 1970.

U.S. Congress. Senate. Committee on Commerce, Science, and Transportation. *Federal Trade Commission—Divestiture. Hearings Before the Subcommittee for Consumers of the Senate Committee on Commerce, Science, and Transportation.* 96th Cong., 1st sess., 1979.

U.S. Congress. Senate. Committee on Governmental Affairs. *Study on Federal Regulation: Regulatory Organization.* 95th Cong., 1st sess., 1977. Vol. V.

U.S. Congress. Senate. Committee on Interstate Commerce. *S. Rep. No. 597.* 63d Cong., 2d sess., 1914.

U.S. Congress. Senate. Committee on the Judiciary. *Federal Trade Commission Procedures. Hearings Before the Subcommittee on Administrative Practice and Procedures of the Senate Committee on the Judiciary.* 91st Cong., 1st sess., 1969.

———. *Oversight of Antitrust Enforcement. Hearings Before the Subcommittee on Antitrust and Monopoly of the Senate Committee on the Judiciary.* 95th Cong., 1st sess., 1977.

———. *Report on Regulatory Agencies to the President-Elect.* Report prepared by James M. Landis. 86th Cong., 2d sess., 1960.

———. *S. Rep. No. 1005.* 94th Cong., 2d sess., 1976, pt. 1.

———. *S.2387 and Related Bills. Hearings Before the Subcommittee on Antitrust and Monopoly of the Senate Committee on the Judiciary.* 94th Cong., 1st sess., 1975.

U.S. Department of Commerce. Bureau of the Census. *Historical Statistics of the United*

States, Colonial Times to 1970. 2 vols. Washington, D.C.: Government Printing Office, 1975.

U.S. Department of Justice. Report on the Robinson-Patman Act. Washington, D.C.: Government Printing Office, 1977.

U.S. Department of Justice, Antitrust Division. "Merger Guidelines." Washington, D.C., May 30, 1968.

U.S. Federal Trade Commission. Annual Report. Washington, D.C., 1925, 1927, 1928, 1929, 1939, 1979.

————. Civil Penalties: Policy Review Session. Washington, D.C., July 1982.

————. Federal Trade Commission Decisions. Vols. 77–93. Washington, D.C.: GPO, 1970–1979.

————. Food Investigation: Report of the Federal Trade Commission on the Meatpacking Industry. Summary and Part I (Extent and Growth of the Five Packers in Meat and Other Industries). Washington, D.C., 1919.

————. Summary Report on Holding and Operating Companies of Electric and Gas Utilities. 74th Cong., 2d sess., 1935. S. Doc. no. 92, pt. 73-A.

————. Trade Practice Submittals 1919 to 1923. Washington, D.C., 1923.

U.S. General Accounting Office. Closer Controls and Better Data Could Improve Antitrust Enforcement." Washington, D.C., 1980.

U.S. Office of Management and Budget. Additional Details on Budget Savings. Washington, D.C., April 1981.

U.S. Office of the President. Economic Report of the President. Washington, D.C.: Government Printing Office, 1982.

Vaill, E. E. "The Federal Trade Commission: Should It Continue as Both Prosecutor and Judge in Antitrust Proceedings?" Southwestern University Law Review 10 (1978): 763–94.

Van Hise, Charles R. Concentration and Control: A Solution of the Trust Problem in the United States. New York: Macmillan, 1912.

Vilkin, R. "FTC Massacre Received Minimal OMB Attention." Legal Times of Washington 3 (February 23, 1981): 7.

Voight, Fritz. "German Experience with Cartels and Their Control During Pre-War and Post-War Periods." In J. P. Miller, ed., Competition, Cartels, and Their Control. Amsterdam: North Holland, 1962, pp. 169–213.

von Mises, Ludwig. Bureaucracy. New Haven, Conn.: Yale University Press, 1944.

Wagner, Susan. The Federal Trade Commission. New York: Praeger, 1971.

Watkins, Myron L. "An Appraisal of the Work of the Federal Trade Commission." Columbia Law Review 32 (February 1932): 272–89.

Watkiss, David K. "Statement Before the National Commission to Review Antitrust Laws and Procedures." Mimeographed. Washington, D.C., September 12, 1978.

Weaver, Suzanne. Decision to Prosecute: Organization and Public Policy in the Antitrust Division. Cambridge, Mass.: MIT Press, 1977.

Weibe, Robert H. Businessmen and Reform: A Study of the Progressive Movement. Cambridge, Mass.: Harvard University Press, 1962.

Weidenbaum, Murray, et al. "On Saving the Kingdom—Advice for the President-Elect from Eight Regulatory Experts." Regulation 4 (November–December 1980): 14–35.

Weingast, Barry R. "The Congressional-Bureaucratic System: A Principal-Agent Perspective." *Public Choice* 44 (1984): 147–91.

———. "Regulation, Reregulation, and Deregulation: The Political Foundations of Agency-Clientele Relations." *Law and Contemporary Problems* 44 (1981): 147–77.

Weingast, Barry R., and Moran, Mark J. "The Myth of the Runaway Bureaucracy—The Case of the FTC." *Regulation* 6 (May–June 1982): 33–38.

Wier, P. "The Cost of Antimerger Lawsuits." *Journal of Financial Economics* 11 (1983): 207–24.

Wilcox, Clair. *Public Policies Toward Business.* Chicago: Richard D. Irwin, 1955.

Wildavsky, Aaron. *The Politics of the Budgetary Process.* 1st ed. Boston: Little, Brown, 1964.

"Will ANA Heed Call of FTC's Muris?" *Advertising Age*, November 15, 1982, p. 3.

Williamson, Oliver E. *The Economics of Discretionary Behavior: Managerial Objectives and the Theory of the Firm.* Englewood Cliffs, N.J.: Prentice-Hall, 1964.

———. *Markets and Hierarchies.* New York: The Free Press, 1975.

———. "Wage Rates as a Barrier to Entry: The Pennington Case in Perspective." *Quarterly Journal of Economics*, 82 (February 1968): 85–116.

Wilson, James Q. "The Rise of the Bureaucratic State." *The Public Interest* 41 (1975): 77–103.

———, ed. *The Politics of Regulation.* New York: Basic Books, 1980.

Wilson, Woodrow. *The New Freedom.* New York: Doubleday, Page, 1913.

Wines, Michael. "Doctors, Dairymen Join in Effort to Clip the Talons of the FTC." *National Journal*, September 18, 1982, pp. 1589–93.

Winter, Ralph. *The Consumer Advocate Versus the Consumer.* Washington, D.C.: American Enterprise Institute, 1972.

Yandle, Bruce. "Care Labeling: Does Any One Care?" *Review of Industrial Management and Textile Science* 20 (Spring 1981): 21–28.

———. "Models of Political Economy of Regulation." Paper presented at the Southern Natural Resources Committee meeting, Charleston, S.C., September 1984.

Young, H. P. "An Axiomatization of Borda's Rule." *Journal of Economic Theory* 9 (September 1974): 43–52.